REVIVAL

REVIVAL

D. Martyn Lloyd-Jones

Marshall Pickering

Pickering and Inglis
Marshall Pickering
3 Beggarwood Lane, Basingstoke, Hants RG23 7LP, UK

Copyright © 1986 Bethan Lloyd-Jones
First published in 1986 by Pickering and Inglis Ltd
Part of the Marshall Pickering Holdings Group
A subsidiary of the Zondervan Corporation

British Library CIP Data
Lloyd-Jones, D. Martyn
Revival.
1. Church renewal – Great Britain
I. Title
262'.0017 BV600

ISBN 0–7208–0652–6
Text Set in Linotron Times by Input Typesetting Ltd, London
SW19 8DR
Printed in Great Britain by Guernsey Press Ltd., Guernsey C.I.

Contents

Chapter 1

Mark 9.28–29

And when he was come into the house, his disciples asked him privately, Why could not we cast him out? And he said unto them, This kind can come forth by nothing but by prayer and fasting (Mark 9.28–29).

I am calling your attention to these two verses, and to the second in particular, in order that we may consider together the great subject of revival, and of the need, the urgent need, of a revival in the Church of God at the present time for I am persuaded that this is a very urgent matter. In a sense, of course, all preaching should promote revival, and it is only as we, as Christian people, understand the doctrines of the Christian faith that we can ever hope truly to see the need of revival, and therefore to pray for it. But it does seem to me that there are certain considerations which call for a special and an unusually direct and explicit dealing with this subject at the present time.

The first of these considerations is the appalling need. But I have a subsidiary reason also for calling attention to this matter and that is that it happens to be the year 1959, a year in which many will be calling to mind and celebrating the great revival, the great religious awakening, the unusual outpouring and manifestation of the Spirit of God, that took place one hundred years ago, in 1859. In that year there was a revival, first in the United States of America, and afterwards in Northern Ireland, in Wales and parts of Scotland, and even in certain parts of England, and this year there are many who will be calling this to mind and commemorating that great and signal movement of the Spirit of God. I believe it is right that we should participate in this, and understand why it is being done, and why the Church of God should be very concerned about it at this present juncture. This is obviously a matter for the whole Church and not merely for certain of her leaders. The history of revivals brings that out very clearly for God often acts in a most unusual manner, and produces

7

revival and promotes it and keeps it going, not necessarily through ministers but perhaps through people who may have regarded themselves as very humble and unimportant members of the Christian Church.

The Church is so constituted that every member matters, and matters in a very vital sense. So I also call attention to this whole subject, partly because, I sense that there is a curious tendency, today, for members of the Christian Church to feel and to think that they themselves can do very little, and so they tend to look to others to do all that is needed for them. This, of course, is something which is characteristic of the whole of life today. For instance, men and women no longer take exercise in sport as they used to. Instead, people tend to sit in crowds and just watch other people play. There was a time when people provided their own pleasure but now the radio and television provide their entertainment and pleasure for them. And I fear that the tendency is even manifesting itself in the Christian Church. More and more we see evidence that people are just sitting back in crowds while one or two people are expected to be doing everything. Now that, of course, is a complete denial of the New Testament doctrine of the Church as the Body of Christ, where every single member has responsibility, and has a function, and matters, and matters in a most vital sense. You can read the Apostle's great expositions of that doctrine, for example in 1 Corinthians 12, where you find that he says that our less comely parts are as important as the more comely parts, that every part of the body is to function and is to be ready for the Master's use, and always to be usable.

That is why I believe that this is a matter which really deserves the most urgent attention of every one of us. Indeed, I do not hesitate to go so far as to say that unless we, as individual Christians, are feeling a grave concern about the state of the Church and the world today, then we are very poor Christians indeed. If we are people who come to the Christian Church merely in order to get some personal help, and no more, then we are the veriest babes in Christ. If we have grown at all, then we must have a concern about the situation, a concern about the state of society, a concern about the state of the Church and a concern about the armour of almighty God. It is, I repeat, a matter that should come home to every one of us.

So let us start considering this incident in Mark 9, and especially these two verses at the end of the account, which constitute a

kind of epilogue to the story. In the earlier verses we are told
how our Lord had taken Peter and James and John and had gone
up into 'an high mountain apart' with them. And on that Mount
of Transfiguration they had witnessed the amazing event that took
place there. But then they were coming down from the mountain,
and they found a crowd of people surrounding the remaining
disciples, with much argument and disputation. They could not
understand what it was all about, when suddenly a man stepped
forward and spoke, 'In a sense,' he said, 'I am responsible for
this. I have a son here, a poor boy who has been subject to fits,
to attacks of convulsions from his childhood,' (it does not matter
what it was exactly) 'and,' he continued, 'I brought this boy along
in order that you might heal him. I came to your disciples and
they could do nothing. They tried, but they failed.'

Our Lord, you remember, put a few questions to the man, and
elicited certain information, and then quite simply proceeded to
exorcise the devil out of this boy, and the boy was healed and
restored in a moment.

Having done that, our Lord went into the house, and the
disciples went with him. And when they got into the house, the
disciples turned to our Lord, and said, 'Why could not we cast
him out?' It is very easy to understand their feelings. They had
tried their utmost, but they had failed. They had succeeded in
many other cases. Here they had failed altogether. And yet in a
moment and with extreme ease our Lord just spoke a word and
the boy was healed. 'Why could not we cast him out?' they said
and our Lord answered and said, 'This kind can come forth by
nothing but by prayer and fasting.'

Now I want to take this story and use it as a very perfect
representation of the present position. Here, in this boy, I see the
modern world, and in the disciples I see the Church of God,
almost at this present hour. Is it not obvious to all of us, that the
Church is patently failing, that she does not count even as much
as she did in the memory of many of us today? Certainly she does
not count as she did seventy, eighty or a hundred years ago. The
whole situation speaks eloquently to that. And here is the Church,
certainly trying, like the disciples, doing her utmost, perhaps in a
sense more active than she has ever been, and yet obviously failing
to deal with the situation. And so we can understand the feelings
of the disciples only too easily, conscious of failure, aware of
certain things that have happened which indicate that there is a
possibility of success, and yet not achieving success. And the
question therefore that we ask, or certainly should ask, and ask

9

urgently, is 'Why cannot we cast him out? What is the matter? What is the cause of the failure? What is the explanation of the situation which confronts us?'

Here, in this story, our Lord seems to me to be dealing with that very question. And the principles that he laid down on that occasion are as vital and as important today as they were when he uttered them on that famous occasion. Fortunately for us, they divide themselves up very simply into three main headings. Why could not we cast him out? The first answer is 'this kind'. There we have a significant statement. Why could not we cast him out? 'Oh,' says our Lord, 'this kind can come forth by nothing but by prayer and fasting.' He is telling them, in other words, that the first thing they have to learn is to differentiate between case and case. Clearly what was at the back of the disciples' question was this: our Lord had sent them out to preach and to cast out devils, and they had gone out, and they had preached and had cast out many devils. Indeed, we read in Luke 10 that on one occasion they had been so successful and had come back with so much elation, that they were very guilty of pride. Our Lord had to rebuke them, saying, 'Rejoice not, that the spirits are subject unto you; but rather rejoice, because your names are written in heaven' (Luke 10.20). They were full of jubilation, of excitement. They said that the very devils had been made subject to them, and they had seen Satan, as it were, fall before them.

So, on this occasion, when this man brought his boy to them, they approached the problem with great confidence and assurance. They had no doubt that they were going to succeed. And yet in spite of all their efforts the boy was no better at all, he was as desperate as he was when the father first brought him to them. So naturally they were in trouble, and our Lord helped them just at that point. He said, 'this kind': there is a difference between 'this kind' and the kind with which you have been dealing hitherto, and with which you have been so successful.

This is a principle that one cannot but notice in reading through the New Testament. In an ultimate sense, of course, the problem is always the same. This, like the others, was a case of devil possession. Ah yes, but there is a difference, as it were, between devil and devil. In that evil kingdom there are gradations, there is a kind of hierarchy. You remember how the Apostle Paul puts it in Ephesians 6: 'For we wrestle not against flesh and blood . . .' – against what then? ' . . . principalities, against powers, against the rulers of the darkness of this world, against spiritual wickedness in high places.' There is a gradation, and at the head of all is Satan himself, 'prince of the power of the air, the spirit that now worketh in the children of disobedience' (Eph. 2.2). There he is, with all his mighty power. But under him are these various other spirits and powers and forces, which vary much in strength and power. Therefore, the disciples could very easily deal with the lesser ones and master them, and exorcise them. But here, says our Lord, is a spirit of greater power. He is not like those other feebler spirits that you have been able to master. This kind is altogether different, and therefore constitutes a much greater problem.

It is important for us to grasp this self-same principle, for it is still as true today as it was then. The first thing, therefore, that we must consider is this whole problem of diagnosis. 'This kind'. The problem with the disciples was that they had rushed into an attempted treatment before they had understood the nature of the problem. And here is the lesson that the Church so badly needs to learn at this present time. We are all such activists; we are all so busy. We are practical people, we say. We are not interested in doctrine and we must be doing something, so we rush off to our activities. And perhaps that is the main cause of our failure. We have not stopped to consider 'this kind'. We may not be as aware as we should be of the real essence of the problem which is confronting us. But it is a universal rule and principle that it is sheer madness and waste of energy to attempt any kind of treatment until we have first established an accurate diagnosis. Of course, it is a great relief to be doing things. I am always reminded of the people who during the last war used to confess that what they really could not stand was just to be sitting in an air raid shelter. They felt that the strain was intolerable and they were going mad! But if they could only get up and walk about somewhere, or if they had something to do, they all immediately felt better. It is a great relief to have something to do. But it is not always very intelligent just to be doing something. There is this danger, of rushing into activity before we fully realise the nature of the problem by which we are confronted.

So, as we look at the expression, 'this kind', I wonder whether as Christian people we are aware of the real depth of the problem which confronts us, in a spiritual sense, at this present time. I ask that question because it seems to me to be so clear, from the activities of many, that they have not even begun to understand it. They are carrying on with certain methods which were once successful, and they pin their faith to them, and they do not realise that they are not only not successful, but that they cannot be, because of the nature of the problem that is confronting them. It is not enough that we should be aware of some general kind of need, because that is always there. When this man brought his boy to the disciples, there was an obvious need, but that had been true in the other cases in which they had been successful. The need is common to all, so that the mere fact that we are aware of it says nothing. The problem for us is the precise nature of this need, what is its exact character? And it is there that we have to think and to realise that we need a little subtlety and understanding in our approach, in order to make our diagnosis.

Let me give you an illustration to explain what I mean. Imagine that you are walking along a country road, and as you walk along you suddenly see a man lying on the side of the road. He does not make any move when you come along, so obviously he has not heard you, and you come to the conclusion that this man is in a state of unconsciousness. Very well, so far so good, everybody is agreed about that. Yes, but the really important question is why that man is lying in that state of unconsciousness. Because there are many possible reasons for this. One reason may be that the man has been taking a very long walk, and he has suddenly felt so tired that he cannot proceed any further. So he had just taken a rest and fallen asleep, and he is sleeping so soundly that he did not hear you as you walked along.

But there are other possible explanations. The man may be in that condition because he has suddenly become ill. He may have had a haemorrhage into his brain which has rendered him unconscious. Or, again, he may be in that unconscious condition because he has been taking some drug. He may have taken too much alcohol or some other drug. He is poisoned. I need not go into any other possibilities. My point is that if you want to help this man it is not enough just to say that he is unconscious. You must discover exactly the cause of his unconsciousness. Even if it is the case that the man is just asleep, well, it may be raining and he may be in danger of getting wet and getting a chill. And so, if you want to help him, all you have to do is to shake him and to shout at him and he will wake up. And when you tell him, that he is endangering his health by lying there and sleeping in the rain, he will be grateful to you, and you will have solved the problem without doing anything further. But if the man has a drug in his system, if he is under the influence of some poison, then your shouting and your shaking will not help him. If this is true, then the situation is more serious, and if you really are going to do anything of value to help the man, you must take measures which will get rid of the poison in his system, and administer certain antidotes, and proceed to deal with him according to the particular necessity. Or if he is suffering from some disease then again, the treatment will be quite different.

There, I think, we see in a picture the importance of establishing a clear diagnosis. Oh yes, everybody is aware that there is a need, but the question is what is the need? This is the thing which demands our most urgent attention at this present time, and it seems to me that until the Christian Church, until Christian people as individuals in the Church, are aware of the nature of the problem, we cannot begin to deal with it as we should. And here I see a very great difference between today and two hundred years ago, or indeed even one hundred years ago. The difficulty in those earlier times was that men and women were in a state of apathy. They were more or less asleep. Going back, certainly two hundred years, there was no general denial of Christian truth. It was just that people did not trouble to practise it. They more or less assumed it. And in a sense, all you had to do then was to awaken them and to rouse them, and to disturb them out of their lethargy. That was also the position a hundred years ago and at the end of the Victorian era. All you needed at that time was an occasional campaign just to rouse people and to awaken them. And that seemed to be sufficient.

But the question is whether that is still the position. Are we right if we diagnose that to be the state of affairs at the present time? What is 'this kind'? What is the problem that is confronting us? I feel increasingly, that as we examine this truly, we shall see that the kind of problem facing us is altogether deeper and more desperate than that which has confronted the Christian Church for many a long century. For the problem for us is not apathy, it is not a mere lack of concern and lack of interest. It is something much more profound. It seems to me to be a complete unawareness, even a denial of the spiritual altogether. It is not just apathy, it is not that people really have at the back of their minds what is right and true, but are not doing anything about it. No, the whole notion of the spiritual has gone. The very belief in God has virtually gone. We need not at this point seek the causes of this, but the fact is that because of some supposed scientific knowledge, the average man today thinks that all this belief about God and religion and salvation, and all that belongs to the realm of the Church, is something that should be entirely dismissed and forgotten. He believes that it has been an incubus on human nature all through the centuries, that it has been something that

13

has been preventing the development and the forward march of the human race, and that it should be got rid of. The modern man is impatient with it all. He dislikes it and he dismisses it *in toto*.

Now surely, this is something which we should recognise. It is very difficult for us, because we are Christian people, and because we are interested in these things, to realise the mentality and the attitude of those who do not belong to the Christian Church, but that I would suggest to you is what they are thinking. Not only that, the authority of the Bible is no longer recognised. In past times people did recognise the Bible to be the word of God. They did not practise it or listen to it, but if you asked them what they thought of it, they would admit that, yes it was the good old book, God's book, and, yes, they felt that they were sinners. But that is no longer the case. It is regarded as an ordinary book, to be treated like any other book. It is just literature, which is to be criticised, analysed and subjected to our knowledge, historical, scientific and everything else, just a book amongst books. No longer is it acknowledged as the divine, inspired word of God.

Take the essential truths about our Lord and Saviour Jesus Christ. These are no longer believed as they once were. He is regarded as just a man amongst men, a great man, of course, but nothing more than that. His deity is denied, his virgin birth is denied and his atoning death is denied. He is just a social reformer, just a political agitator, merely someone who laid down certain ethical views with respect to life, which we would do well to practise. Let me give you an illustration of this. A man like Bertrand Russell, for instance, has said that the Christian Church should be telling the nations and the governments what they ought to do, and not to do, about bombs, and yet he himself writes a book saying Why I am not a Christian. You see, that is the kind of thing we find today. All that is really of value to us about the Lord is denied, and he is reduced to the position of a mere human teacher or of some kind of great example.

And then, over and above all that, we are confronted by the way in which people live. It is no longer merely a question of immorality. This has become an amoral or a non-moral society. The very category of morality is not recognised at all, and men and women are virtually in the position of saying 'evil be thou my good'. Surely, we all see this if we read our newspapers with intelligent eyes. We find a defence, as it were, of immorality, a justification of it in terms of medicine, or a man's constitution, or in terms of a denunciation of the taboos of the past. And things which should never be mentioned are even allowed to be presented on the stage, as long as they do not violate certain canons of decency. Now, surely, it is time that we who are Christian people, had a living understanding of the position which confronts us, that is, the state of society. Our terminology no longer means anything to the masses of the people. They are in a position of plenty, plenty of money, able to get everything they want, and they are unconcerned about spiritual things: no interest in the soul, no interest in the higher things of life, just eating and drinking and enjoying themselves. They have got what they want and all they are anxious to do is to hold on to it.

There, then, as I see it, is something of 'this kind' – the problem with which you and I are confronted. Now it is essential that we understand this because in the second place our Lord goes on to say that 'this kind can come forth by nothing but . . .' There are certain things which are quite useless, when they are applied to 'this kind'. In other words, what our Lord was saying to the disciples can be put like this. He said, in effect, 'You have failed in this particular case because the power that you had and which was sufficient and adequate for the other cases, is inadequate and of no value here. It just leaves you utterly helpless and hopeless and it leaves the boy in his diseased and powerless condition.'

And surely this is the second step which we need to take at the present time. Is it not becoming obvious at last that so many of the things in which we have trusted and to which we have pinned out faith, are proving to be of no avail? Now, do not misunderstand me. I am not saying that there is anything wrong in these things in and of themselves. The power that the disciples had was a good power, and it was able to do good work in casting out the feeble devils, but it was of no value in the case of that boy. That is the argument, so all the things that I am going to mention are quite all right as far as they go. I am not saying that they are wrong, what I am saying is that they are not enough, and until you and I come to see that, and until we see the greater need, we will just continue as we are in our utter ineffectiveness, in spite of all our efforts, organisings and endeavours.

What are some of these things that are proving to be useless? Let me just indicate some of them to you, because these are the things on which the Christian Church is still relying. These are the things to which Christian people are still pinning their faith. Let me begin with apologetics – the belief that what we really have to do is to make the Christian faith acceptable to and commendable to the men and women of today. To this end books

15

are written, lectures are delivered, and sermons are preached, in an attempt to produce and present the Christian faith in a philosophical manner to the modern man. And so you take the books which deal with the philosophy of religion, you take the great works of past philosophers, the great Greek philosophers and others, and you say that Christianity fits into this, that it is rational and so on, and so you show the utter reasonableness of the Christian faith. That is apologetics, presenting itself in the form of philosophy.

In particular, at the present time, we are interested in doing this in terms of science, reconciling science with religion. We argue that the people of today, are scientifically minded, that they have this scientific outlook, and that, of course, they cannot believe the gospel and the Scriptures, because they seem to them to dispute the scientific facts, especially as far as miracles and such things are concerned. The Church, therefore, argues that what is necessary is to reconcile science and religion, and so we clutch at any scientist who even remotely hints that in some vague way he believes in God. What excitement there was when a recent Reith lecturer, a scientist, even seemed to indicate that he believed that after all there may be a God who may have created at the beginning. And we find this wonderful! You see the pathetic state we have got into, that we should become excited when a man like that, great scientist though he may be, seems even to allow the possibility that there is a God and there is a Creator. And we are so pleased about it, and we all mention it to one another, and say that this is marvellous! It shows, you see, that we are pinning our faith to this kind of thing. What we really ought to say is, 'Does he really? How kind of him! How nice of him!' And then perhaps we should pause for a moment and say, 'Why has it taken him all these years to come even to that nebulous conclusion?' But it is indicative of our whole attitude that we should clutch at these men, whoever they are, and however vague their statements. It shows that ultimately we really believe that the way to deal with the modern situation is through our apologetics. Ah, we want to show that, after all, the Bible does not deny science. Science is the authority and the Bible has got to be fitted in. And we think that by that kind of effort and endeavour we are going to deal with the present situation.

Then again it is done in terms of archaeology. Do not misunderstand me, archaeology is very valuable – thank God for everything that it produces which does confirm the biblical history – but if we are going to depend upon archaeology, well then, God help

16

us all. There are different schools amongst the archaeologists, and they have their different interpretations. But there seems to be this tendency to clutch at every straw, feeling that this is what is going to prove that the Bible is true. And in the same way we clutch at well-known men. What excitement there was when the late Professor Joad wrote a book in which he acknowledged that the war had driven him to believe in evil and to believe in God! But, why all this excitement? It indicates our pathetic faith and belief in these methods which are nothing but apologetics.

It was exactly the same way at the beginning of the eighteenth century, when people were pinning their faith on Bishop Butler and his great analogy of religion, and the Boyle lectures, and so on. These, they taught us, are the things that are going to show the truth of Christianity, but they did not do that. 'This kind' can come forth by nothing along that line.

Then let us come to methods. How tragic it is to see the way in which men are pinning their faith upon particular methods. One of these is the excitement about new translations of the Bible. This is based on the belief that the man of today, who is not a Christian, is outside the Church because he cannot understand the Authorised Version. These technical terms, this Elizabethan language, justification, sanctification: this means nothing to the modern man. What he wants, you see, is a Bible in modern language, in modern slang, in the modern idiom, and then men will read it. Then they will say, 'This is Christianity,' and they will embrace it. And so we are having fresh translations, one after another. Everybody buys them because all we need is the Bible in modern up-to-date language. Is this not tragic? Is that what is keeping people from Christ? Do you think that people two hundred years ago knew anthing more about justification and sanctification than they do today? Were those the common terms of a thousand years ago? Is that the difficulty? No, it is the heart of man, it is the evil that is in him. It is not a question of language, it is not a question of terminology, yet we pin our faith to this. Do not misunderstand me, there may be some value in modern translation, though nothing like as much as people think. You have got to go a long way to improve on this Authorised Version, and we need to be careful with the modern translations, they may mislead theologically. But, whatever their value, that is not going to solve the problem.

What else is there? Oh, the belief in the radio and the television. We must make use of these media, we say. Everybody is listening. Take the gospel to their homes. Give them these short snappy messages, that is the way to do it. So we pin our faith on it. Then there is advertising. Big business succeeds because it advertises, so we must advertise the Church, and set up our publicity agencies in the Church. In this way we will tell the people what the Church is and what she is doing, in the belief that if we only tell them the truth, they will jump at it and want it and take it, as they do the various commodities that are advertised in these ways. And people seem to believe this. They think that 'this kind' can come forth by such methods as this. What we need, they say, is new magazines, new literature, new tracts, and off we go and distribute all these. We write articles in a semi-popular form – now people will get the message, we say.

And then of course, there is popular evangelism, in which all this is put to practice. Everything that can appeal to the modern man, the last word in presentation is used, in the belief that when it is done, and you do it with a modern technique, then you will get hold of the modern man. But I think that the time has now come to ask this simple question: what are the results? Is the modern problem being touched at all? Of course these various methods, the apologetics and the others may indeed lead to individual conversions. We are all aware of that. Almost any method you like to employ will do that. Of course there are individual conversions, but my question is this – what of the situation, what of the bulk of men and women, what of the working classes of this country, are they being touched at all, are they being affected at all? Is anybody being affected, except those who are already in the Church or on the fringe of the Church? What of the spiritual and religious condition of the country? What of the whole state of society? Is this being touched at all by all our activities?

Well, my answer would be that it all seems to put us into the position of the disciples who had tried to cast the devil out of the boy, these men who had been so successful in many another case, but who could not touch this case at all. And our Lord gives them the explanation, 'this kind' can come forth by nothing like this. By what, then? 'This kind can come forth by nothing but by prayer, and fasting.' You failed there, he said in effect to these disciples, because you did not have sufficient power. You were using the power that you have, and you were very confident in it. You did it with great assurance, you were masters of the occasion, you thought you were going to succeed at once, but you did not. It is time you paused for a moment and began to think. It was your ignorance of these gradations in power amongst evil spirits that led to your failure, and to your crestfallen condition at this moment. You have not sufficient power. I did what you could not do because I have power, because I am filled with the power that God gives me by the Holy Spirit, for he gives not the Spirit by measure unto me. You will never be able to deal with 'this kind' unless you have applied to God for the power which he alone can give you. You must become aware of your need, of your impotence, of your helplessness. You must realise that you are confronted by something that is too deep for your methods to get rid of, or to deal with, and you need something that can go down beneath that evil power, and shatter it, and there is only one thing that can do that, and that is the power of God.

And we, too, must become aware of that, we have got to feel it until we become desperate. We must ask ourselves how we can succeed if we do not have this authority, this commission, this might and strength and power. We must become utterly and absolutely convinced of our need. We must cease to have so much confidence in ourselves, and in all our methods and organisations, and in all our slickness. We have got to realise that we must be filled with God's Spirit. And we must be equally certain that God can fill us with his Spirit. We have got to realise that however great 'this kind' is, the power of God is infinitely greater, that what we need is not more knowledge, more understanding, more apologetics, more reconciliation of philosophy and science and religion, and all modern techniques – no, we need a power that can enter into the souls of men and break them and smash them and humble them and then make them anew. And that is the power of the living God. And we must be confident that God has this power as much today as he had one hundred years ago, and two hundred years ago, and so we must begin to seek the power and to pray for it. We must begin to plead and yearn for it. 'This kind' needs prayer.

Now, this is but the introduction to the theme that we are going to consider, but it leads me to ask this question: are you really concerned about the present position? Are you desperately concerned about it? Are you praying about it? Do you ever pray for the power of God in the Church today? Or are you just content to read the weekly newspapers which tell us about all these various efforts and to say, 'It is all right, the word is going on.' 'This kind cometh not forth but by prayer and fasting.' This word fasting is not in all the ancient manuscripts, but it implies not only literal, physical fasting, but concentration. The value of fasting is that it enables you to give your undivided attention to a subject. So what our Lord said to the disciples is this: you will never deal with this sort of problem until you have been praying, concentrating in prayer, waiting upon God, until he has filled you with the power. When you know you have got it, then you go out with authority. That is the way, and that is the only way. Surely no one should need to be convinced, today, that nothing short of a mighty outpouring of the Spirit of God is adequate to deal with our situation in this mid-twentieth century? Are you really still trusting to these other things? Here is the vital question. Have you seen the desperate need of prayer, the prayer of the whole Church? I shall see no hope until individual members of the Church are praying for revival, perhaps meeting in one another's homes, meeting in groups amongst friends, meeting together in churches, meeting anywhere you like, and praying with urgency and concentration for a shedding forth of the power of God, such as he shed forth one hundred and two hundred years ago, and in every other period of revival, and of reawakening. There is no hope until we do. But the moment we do, hope enters. Oh, when God manifests his power, it happens as it happened in the case of this poor boy. With apparent ease, in an effortless manner, the devil is exorcised, and the boy healed and restored to his father. When God arises, his enemies are scattered, that is the story of all the great revivals of history. But we shall not be interested in revival until we realise the need of 'this kind', the futility of all our own efforts and endeavours and the utter absolute need of prayer, and seeking the power of God alone.

Chapter 2

Genesis 26.17–18

And Isaac departed thence, and pitched his tent in the valley of Gerar, and dwelt there. And Isaac digged the wells of water, which they had digged in the days of Abraham his father; for the Philistines had stopped them after the death of Abraham: and he called their names after the names by which his father had called them (Gen. 26. 17–18).

This incident in the life of Isaac has much to teach us in our consideration of the whole question of revival. The picture, is one of Isaac in trouble, in a difficulty. If you read the context, you will find that he had been living in another part of the country, and God had blessed him in a very striking manner. So much so that Isaac had become the object of envy of those who were living round and about him, and they had forced him to move. 'Abimelech said unto Isaac, Go from us; for thou art much mightier than we . . .' (26.16). And so Isaac was compelled to move with his family and all his servants, possessions and belongings. Then he came to this valley of Gerar and decided that he would dwell there. Of course, the moment he arrived he was confronted by an urgent and a very desperate need – and that was the need of water. I do want to emphasise that, because the need, in other words, was the need for something that is absolutely essential to life, in addition to being essential to well-being. He was not merely confronted by the problem of seeking some beauty spot where he might pitch his tent, or erect some kind of dwelling place for himself. He was not looking for entertainment, or for luxuries, he was not looking for any kind of accessory to life. The whole point of the story is that he was looking for something that is an absolute essential, and without which life cannot be maintained at all.

I emphasise that because as I have already indicated, the first thing we must realise about the situation we are in today is its desperate character. It is urgent. In other words, the trouble, as

21

I see it, with the Church today is that she does not realise, as she should, that her primary need, and her urgent need at the moment, is the need of life itself. The problem confronting us is not a problem of methods, or of organisation, or of making a slight adjustment here and there, or improving things a little bit, or keeping them up-to-date, or anything like that. It seems to me that we are really down to this basic issue. The problem of society today is not a superficial problem, it is a very radical one. The whole outlook upon life is involved. And serious observers, as you know, are appalled as they contemplate what is really taking place. A well known medical authority, charged with being behind the times and old-fashioned, said recently that he almost wished that he were dead as he contemplated certain things that are taking place. So appalled was the man at the whole trend of life and of living that he was even capable of expressing himself in such sentiments. Now that is the situation, and it is the situation confronting the Church. There is no doubt that we have been living on the capital of the past – as you go round this country and look at the congregations, you will see that very quickly. You can carry on for a certain length of time on tradition, and by custom, and habit, but the point is bound to come when you cease to have any capital left and then you realise that you are facing something absolutely ultimate, something which is fundamental. And that, as I say, is the whole situation today of the Christian Church. We really are in the position of this man Isaac. And the problem confronting us is the need of life itself, the need of that fundamental power and vigour in every activity of the Church which really can make an impact upon the world, and do something vital and drastic with regard to the whole trend of affairs at the present time; the need of life, the need of power, the need of the Spirit himself.

There are times in the Church when what is needed is some sort of line or adjustment here or there, but that is not the trouble today. This is not a minor matter, it is not a third-rate or a fourth-rate matter that is in the balance at the moment. It is the whole life of the Church. It is the whole question of a spiritual outlook upon life, over and against everything that is represented by the world.

Now, the great lesson taught us here is this. What did Isaac do when he was face to face with this particular need? Here is our message. And you notice, first of all, what he did *not* do. It is so significant, and so important for us to understand this. He has been driven out; he has been forced to move. He has a family, possessions, servants and animals, and if they do not find water soon, then life itself will come to an end. They will perish. What then, face to face with this urgent need, does he do? Well, you notice that he does not send for the prospectors, he does not send for the water diviners, or for men who are experts in seeking and discovering fresh supplies of water. No, the whole message is that 'Isaac digged again the wells of water which they had digged in the days of Abraham, his father'. Here again, is a message, that surely is sorely needed. Because when one looks at the Church in general the whole outlook today seems to be the very reverse of that of Isaac.

The kind of thing you read constantly in the books and the religious journals is this. What we need, they say, is a message for this atomic age, or a message for this second Elizabethan period. And, therefore, we must all be engaging in a quest for truth, a search for the message that is needed. So we call in the prospectors, we look to the scientists, we look to philosophy, and then psychology has its contribution to make. We call for the latest knowledge and learning, we want the very last advance in science and in culture in every shape and form. The whole idea is that the world is in a very serious predicament and therefore it behoves all men of understanding to come together and pool their resources, call a congress of world faiths, bring in everybody who believes in any religion and worships any sort of god. At the present time, the thing that is most obvious about the life of the Church in general is the multiplicity of consciences, and there they are, trying to find the formula. Trying to discover some word, trying to discover some message. 'It's this atomic age we're in,' they say, 'we must have a message for it.' And so on. Instead of doing what Isaac did, we are calling in the prospectors, the water-diviners, trying to see if we can discover a source or supply of water somewhere that will enable us to continue.

No, the emphasis in these verses is, I repeat, that Isaac did nothing of the kind. But what he did was this: 'Isaac digged again the wells of water which they had digged in the days of Abraham, his father.' Why did he do this? Well, I think that the wisdom of this is perfectly clear, and quite obvious. Isaac realised that his situation was such that it was no time for experimentation. The position was so urgent that if they did not have water and that very quickly, they would all perish. And in such a position, he argued like this: 'There is no need for us to prospect and send for the water-diviners. My father, Abraham, was once in this area, and if there was one thing that characterised Abraham above

23

everything else it was that he was an expert on this very question of finding water and sinking wells.' If you read the story of Abraham in the early chapters of Genesis, you will find exactly what I mean by that statement. Isaac knew that Abraham had found water wherever he went; he always succeeded and he dug his wells, and he had an abundance of water. So Isaac said 'My immediate business is to make certain that we have got a supply. Then having got a supply, and being sure of it, if we like we can prospect, we may try to seek for a further supply, we may experiment.' But the man who experiments in the midst of a crisis is a fool. The first thing to do is to make certain that you have a guaranteed supply, that you have that vital source which will enable you to live and to continue, and then perhaps allow you to do these various other things. That, it seems to me, was clearly the reasoning of Isaac. He said, 'Ah, my father was here. Now then, where did he sink these wells? You can go there with confidence for you will find water there.' So back he went to the wells of water which they had dug in the days of Abraham, his father.

This then brings us inevitably to our theme. I would like to lay it down as a principle that there is great value in the reading of Church history and a study of the past, and nothing, surely, is more important for us at this present time than to read the history of the past and to discover its message. I suggest that we should do so for the very reasons which impelled Isaac to dig again the wells which they had dug in the days of Abraham, his father. It is very foolish to ignore the past. The man who does ignore it, and assumes that our problems are quite new, and that therefore the past has nothing at all to teach us, is a man who is not only grossly ignorant of the Scriptures, he is equally ignorant of some of the greatest lessons even on secular history. Yet, I think you will agree, that is the mentality that is governing the outlook of the vast majority at the present time. The basic assumption is that our problems are new, that they are quite unique, and that the Church and the world have never been confronted by such problems before.

Now, there is one very interesting thing about the year 1959. It is, as I have been saying, the centenary of that mighty outpouring of the Spirit of God which was experienced in the United States, and in Northern Ireland, and Wales, and Scotland, and in even parts of England, but it is also the centenary of something else, and that is the publication of the famous book by Charles Darwin called *The Origin of Species*. And there is no doubt but that it is Darwin's book that is governing the outlook of the vast majority today, not only in the world, but also, alas, in the Church.

The Darwinian philosophy, of course, in its essence is just this question of evolution, which is said to affect the whole of life. Darwin himself was not much concerned about that, but his co-tutors, people like Huxley, and still more, perhaps, the philosopher Spencer, took hold of this principle. They said in effect, 'This is working in the whole of life, this progress, this development, this advancement. Everything is going upwards, moving forwards, and therefore, at any given point you are, of necessity, in a superior position to that which went before.' Now, the Church has taken hold of this idea, and therefore she tends to argue that our position in the twentieth century is essentially different from any position that has ever been known before. So in view of this, we must ignore the past, we can forget it, it cannot possibly help us. It was not confronted by our problems and difficulties, it has not our knowledge, and so on and so forth. So the whole outlook and mentality today is one which is opposed to going back, to 'digging again the wells which they had digged in the days of Abraham. . . .'

Now, this is, of all the fallacies, the most fatal. And for these reasons. God is still the same. God is the same today as he was a hundred years ago. Indeed, God is the same as he was a thousand years ago, and two thousand years ago, and away back six thousand years ago in the time of Abraham. God is from everlasting to everlasting. He does not change at all. But not only is that true, it is equally true that man is still the same. If it could be established that God is somehow different and that man is somehow different, I would be ready to listen to this argument, that assumes that our problems are unique, and that therefore we must not look back. But man is still precisely the same as he always has been.

It is to me almost incredible and incomprehensible that anybody who has ever read the Bible at all, or even indeed human history, could possibly dispute this, even for a second. What superficial thinkers we are. We are assuming that because man can travel in an aeroplane, and split the atom, he is somehow different from his forefathers who could not do these things. But man himself has not changed. Man himself, you discover by looking into how he thinks, what he is really interested in, how he acts. And man today is, primarily and fundamentally, interested in the very things that interested him four thousand years ago, in the time of

Abraham. If we just read the newspapers we see that the major interests of Man are still, eating, drinking, making war, sex and pleasures of various kinds. They are all here in the Old Testament, and man is still doing the same things. Look at the major social problems confronting us today, and you will find all of them in the Bible: theft, robbery, violence, jealousy, envy, infidelity, divorce, separation, perversions, all these things, are in the Bible. These are the problems of man today, as they have always been.

So we are not confronted by a new problem. Abraham had the problem of finding water, Isaac had precisely the same problem. All the differences are on the surface, they are irrelevant, and they are immaterial. God remains the same, man remains the same, yes, and the New Testament reminds us that the solution to the problem remains the same: 'Jesus Christ the same yesterday, today and for ever' (Heb. 13.8). So there is nothing, it seems to me, that is quite so hopeless as this tacit assumption of the modern man, in his overweening conceit and pride, that he is something different, and that his problems are quite new, and entirely and essentially different from those confronting all his forefathers. No, listen to the wisdom of Isaac, see the urgency of the position and remember that Abraham was a man who knew what he was doing. The history of the past has a great deal to tell us.

What, then, does it tell us? The first principle is this. If you look back across the history of the Christian Church, you immediately find that the story of the Church has not been a straight line, a level record of achievement. The history of the Church has been a history of ups and downs. It is there to be seen on the very surface. When you read the history of the past you find that there have been periods in the history of the Church when she has been full of life, and vigour, and power. The statistics prove that people crowded to the house of God, whole numbers of people who were anxious and eager to belong to the Christian Church. Then the Church was filled with life, and she had great power; the Gospel was preached with authority, large numbers of people were converted regularly, day by day, and week by week. Christian people delighted in prayer. You did not have to whip them up to prayer meetings, you could not keep them away. They did not want to go home, they would stay all night praying. The whole Church was alive and full of power, and of vigour, and of might. And men and women were able to tell of rich experiences of the grace of God, visitations of his Spirit, a knowledge of the love of God that thrilled them, and moved them, and made them feel that it was more precious than the whole world. And, as a consequence of all that, the whole life of the country was affected and changed.

I could give you endless examples of this, but let me take one only, which is perhaps the most notable of all, and that is the evangelical awakening of two hundred years ago. Many secular historians are ready to agree that it was the evangelical awakening in the time of Whitefield and the Wesleys that probably saved this country from an experience such as they had in France in the French Revolution. The Church was so filled with life and with power that the whole of society was affected. Furthermore, the influence of that evangelical awakening upon the life of the last century is again something that is admitted freely by those who are aware of the facts. And, indeed, the same thing happened a hundred years ago in the revival to which I have been referring. And so it has happened in every revival.

Now that is what you find when you go back into history. The Church has not always been as she is now. You read of these tremendous periods of life and vigour and of power. Ah, yes, but what you also notice – and this is why it is so encouraging to look back – is that these glorious periods of revival and of re-awakening have often followed periods of great drought, great deadness, apathy and lifelessness in the history of the Church. In every case, as you find these great peaks, you will find the troughs. You will see that the Church has many times been as she is today, counting so little in the life of the world and of society; so lacking in life, and vigour, and power, and witness, and all that accompanies it. You will find that that has happened many and many a time before. There has been the same desperate, urgent need as confronts us today. And then, after that, has come this mighty uplift, this outpouring of the Spirit of God. So there we have one good reason for going back into the history of the past, instead of just looking at our own problems and saying, 'Now then, what can we do about improving the technique and improving our methods in this respect or that?' We must go back and learn this lesson of history, the existence of these awful troughs and the only way in which the Church can be lifted out of them.

My second principle is this – and any reading of Church history, even that which is cursory and superficial, will, I think, bring out this principle abundantly clearly – that every time you get one of these great, and glorious, and mighty periods, you will find that in every instance it seems to be a returning to something that had obtained before. Indeed, I will go further – you will find that every one of them seems to be a returning to what you can read in the book of the Acts of the Apostles. Every time the Church is thus revived, she seems to be doing what Isaac did; she is going back to something that had happened before, rediscovering it, and finding the ancient supply. There is nothing I know of that is more striking in the history of the Church than just that principle. Read the story of the great revivals with which God has visited the Church throughout the centuries, and you will find that it always seems to be almost precisely the same thing.

Then, try it another way. Having tried it like this historically, try it geographically. Read the stories of revivals in England, Great Britain, America, Africa, China, Manchuria, Korea, India, it does not matter where you go, turn to any part of the world you may like to choose. It does not matter where you are, nor when, you will find every time that what has happened, and what is happening, seems to be an exact repetition of what has always happened at such times, and on such occasions. Now this is surely something that we cannot afford to ignore. In our desperate need at the present time, in this urgent need of life and power, this water without which we can achieve nothing, and cannot even exist, here is a great record and testimony that comes to us from the past. God has dealt with such occasions in ages past, and he is still the same. There is a supply available, if only we will go to it and go for it. That is the message.

That, then, brings me to my next principle. Isaac, in his wisdom, decided to go back. He was going to make certain of a supply. So he commanded his men to go to those old wells which had been dug by Abraham, his father. And when they went back to the old wells, they found that the Philistines had stopped them after the death of Abraham. We are told exactly the same thing in verse 15: 'For all the wells which his father's servants had digged in the days of Abraham his father, the Philistines had stopped them, and filled them with earth.' In other words, they went back to the old wells, yes, but though the water was still there, they could not see it. The water was not available, and they could not use it.

Now, here is a wonderful picture, is it not? There, down in the depths, is that old pristine supply of water, and here are men in a desperate need. They say, 'Now, the water is there. But the problem is how can we get hold of it? What has happened here? What has gone wrong? Why are we not seeing water? Why can we not put in our vessels and draw water?' And the answer is that the Philistines had stopped the wells. They had filled them up with earth and with rubbish and refuse, so that although the water was there it was not available, and it was not visible. If there is one thing I want to stress, and to impress more than anything else, it is this principle. My dear friends, there is only one explanation for the state of the Christian Church today. It is the work of the Philistines. The water is there, so why do we not see it? Why are we not able to drink of it? The Philistines have been here, and they have filled the wells with the earth and the rubbish and the refuse.

That is the immediate matter confronting us and the one thing that tempts me at times to be impatient is that the Church does not seem to see this, or to realise it, and is not ready to face it. And what makes me even more impatient is that so many evangelical people are not ready to face this either. 'I am not a controversalist,' says a man. 'I like to preach a positive gospel. We must be kind and loving. We must not be critical in these times, the problem is so urgent. We must all stand together. If a man calls himself a Christian, let us all get under the same umbrella.'

Now, I maintain that as long as you indulge in that kind of thinking and mentality, the problem will go from bad to worse. *The* cause of the problem is the work of the Philistines and it is nothing but that.

Let me emphasise this, therefore, by putting it like this. The problem confronting the Church today is not the new circumstances in which we find ourselves. That is what we are always being told, is it not? until we are all, I hope, sick and tired of it. The radio, the television, the motor car, and all the things that are being offered to the modern man, these, we are told, are the problem. The Church has never had such a battle to fight in her life as she has now against all these things that draw people away. We think we are such experts on these things, do we not? And they are all completely irrelevant, every one of them. Let me tell you why. In different forms those things have always been there. Now that is where it is so important to read history. Before that evangelical awakening of two hundred years ago the churches were as empty as they are today, perhaps even more so, and they could not get the people to come to listen to the preaching of the gospel. Why? Because they were interested in other things. 'But,' says someone, 'they had not got televisions!' I know. But they greatly enjoyed cock fighting and card playing; they greatly enjoyed gambling and they greatly enjoyed drinking. The world has never been at a loss to find an excuse not to go to Church to listen to the preaching of the gospel. The thinking of today is so monstrously superficial. Because there is a change in the form of the pleasure, we think that the whole situation is new, and we talk about this problem of the twentieth century, and all the things that are against us. Hell and the Devil have always been against us. The world has always hated the message, and people of the world have never been short of an excuse to avoid it. There is nothing in that argument at all.

'Ah, but wait a minute,' says someone. 'What about the new knowledge? Perhaps you are right in what you say about the sins of two hundred years ago, and four thousand years ago, but, my dear sir, what about the new knowledge? Here is our problem, here is this peculiar something that applies only to the twentieth century. An act was passed in 1870 giving popular education, and if you ignore that, you are going to fly in the face of fact. Everybody is educated now, and everybody has got learning, so they listen to these great men about science and about the atom. Man is cultured today and so sophisticated and there is this tremendous advance in knowledge all along the line. Are you asking us to believe that the problem and the position are still exactly the same?'

Yes, I am, and for the good reason that all this, agreed, tremendous advance in scientific knowledge has nothing whatsoever to do with this problem. *Nothing whatsoever*. If you could show me how this new knowledge in any way makes any difference to God, I would be ready to listen. But it does not. He is the God who made the earth. Man is only just beginning to discover what God did, and what God has done, and what God is still doing. So, you see, it makes no difference to God at all. Where is there any glimpse, or glimmer of modern knowledge, that in any way touches or affects this problem of God and man – and of man's soul in its relation to God? And the Lord Jesus Christ, who he is and what he has done? What has any of this knowledge to do with that? It has nothing at all.

But further than that, I can remind you of this. We talk about our modern knowledge, as if it had changed the whole situation. If you read the history of the Church two hundred and fifty years ago you find that that was the period of deism, the period before the great evangelical awakening of that time when, as I have reminded you, people did not go to places of worship. Why? Because of their knowledge. They said exactly the same thing. There had been a great scientific awakening in the middle of the seventeenth century. Isaac Newton and others had lived then. Harvey had discovered the circulation of the blood. The Royal

Society had been founded, you remember, in the early days of Charles II. The whole world had become scientific and rationalistic. Read the story of the fight the Church had with rationalism. At the end of the seventeenth and the beginning of the eighteenth century you will find that people then were saying exactly what they are saying now. It was this new knowledge, this new understanding. All the physics, and astronomy, and all these things had been brought into being. There, they said was the problem. The fact of the matter is that the Church has always had to meet the self-same argument. And it is as irrelevant and as futile today as it has always been in the previous centuries.

Then let me mention one other argument that is being brought forward by the Church. As well as our peculiar circumstances, and this new knowledge, there is also the divided Church. Oh, this, we are told, is *the* thing. 'Of course,' they say, 'you are perfectly right when you emphasise that the position is desperate and that unless something happens soon, indeed, the whole future of the Church is involved. But,' they continue, 'there is only one cause and explanation of it all – the divided Church.'

So the thing that is being emphasised above everything else, is the need for Church unity. We must come together. We must all be one in a great organisation, then we will be able to confront the problem. They say that you will never get blessing while the Church is divided. You cannot evangelise while the Church is divided. Those are their statements.

What is the answer to that? Again, it is all in Church history. You see, they do not read it. And if they do read it, they forget it. They are so blinded by their prejudice, that they deny blatant facts. The first of these is that in the past, even when the Church has been acutely divided, more so than she is today, God has sent revival. Great blessing has been experienced. There were endless divisions in the Church a hundred years ago, in America and in Northern Ireland. They were divided up into the same denominations as today, and even more so. Yet, though that was the fact, God sent his blessing and poured out his Spirit. It is a lie to say that the division of the Church is the one cause of the lack of blessing. It is not that. Because history shows very plainly that God sends this blessing even when the Church is divided, and that the coming of the revival has two main effects. One, that it blesses practically all the denominations, irrespective of their divisions, and for the time being brings them together in a marvellous unity. There has never been anything that has so promoted spiritual unity as revival.

31

But a revival also, invariably, has another effect, and that is that it creates a new and fresh division. And it does so because those who have experienced the blessing and the power of God are naturally one and they come together. But there are others who dislike it all, and who criticise it, and condemn it all, and who are outside it all, and the division comes in. John Wesley never wanted to leave the Church of England, but Methodism had to come out, and was driven out. The division was caused by the revival. It has happened every time. Take the Protestant Reformation. Luther did not set out to divide the Church of Rome, but the blessing of the revival divided the Church of Rome into Protestantism and Roman Catholicism. You always get this. It is pure history. And yet we are told that the one obstacle to revival is the divided Church. It is just unutterable rubbish, it is the rubbish of the Philistines. This is the thing, amongst others, that is standing between us and the water, and the supply that we are so sorely in need of. So we must dismiss all these things, and realise that these are not the hindrances, these are not the problem. The problem, as Isaac found, is that this nefarious work of the Philistines has been blocking the wells, concealing water, standing between the people and the blessing of God.

Next, clearly, we must go on to consider what this work of the Philistines is. We must be honest and blunt. We have got to be plain and clear, and we must have the courage of conviction. We need the witness and the testimony of the Spirit as we do so. Let us pray for it, that God will give us honest minds to face the facts as they are, that we may see the real cause of trouble. So that, having seen it, we shall be able to emulate the example of Isaac, and clear out the rubbish of the Philistines, to come once again across the ancient supply of the water of God, the power of the Spirit. And enter with all God's people into a period of unusual blessing, and a mighty outpouring of his Holy Spirit.

Chapter 3

Genesis 26.17–18

And Isaac departed thence, and pitched his tent in the valley of Gerar, and dwelt there. And Isaac digged again the wells of water, which they had digged in the days of Abraham his father; for the Philistines had stopped them after the death of Abraham: and he called their names after the names by which his father had called them (Gen. 26. 17–18).

As we continue with our consideration of the activity of the Philistines, I want to show you again that the history of the Church herself establishes this principle that I laid down in the last chapter. Church history demonstrates, beyond any doubt whatsoever, that the trouble has always been due to the fact that the Philistines have blocked the wells and have thrown in material that lies between the people in their need, and the supply of water that is there down at the bottom.

Let me give you the evidence. I think I can summarise the history of the Christian Church in this respect, in this way. The concealing, and the neglect of certain truths, and certain aspects of Christian truth, has always been the chief characteristic of every period of declension in the long history of the Church. That is my first point. If you read the history of the Church, and look at these periods of declension, when the Church was moribund and did not seem to count at all, you will find that without a single exception the thing that has most characterised the life of the Church at such a time has been either a denial, or else a concealing, or else a neglect of certain vital truths which are essential to the whole Christian position.

I could illustrate this at great length. Let me just give you the most notable examples. Take, for instance, the Dark Ages, followed by that period leading up to the Protestant Reformation of the sixteenth century. What was the great characteristic of the Church then? It was this precise thing; the vital truths of salvation could not be seen, they were entirely hidden, cluttered up, covered over, by all that mass of teaching which characterised the Roman Catholic Church of that time. These people had no spiritual life, they were kept in darkness, and in ignorance, they did not know the great truths of the gospel and of salvation. Why not? Because they were covered over by these other things.

But then, come forward to the eighteenth century. Before the great evangelical awakening of the eighteenth century, that revival which, particularly in this country, we associate with the names of Whitfield and the Wesleys, you will find exactly the same thing. Before that great revival the condition of the Church was again just as I am describing it to you. It was moribund; it was useless; the vast majority of people did not attend a place of worship, and there was little evidence at all of any vital Christianity. What was it due to? Well, the whole state of the Church at that time was again a repetition, more or less, of that which obtained before the Reformation, in a slightly different form, of course. What was it? It was that the great cardinal doctrines of the Christian faith were not being preached. They were not believed. The controlling climate was what was called deism. That system of truth which, more or less, cut off God from an active interest in his own universe. Deism and rationalism were in control. There were certain men who were disturbed about this. There was the great Bishop Butler, who wrote his famous analogy of religion. He wrote that book in order to try to counter the deadness of deism and of rationalism. But that, you see, was the state of the Church. The living water of salvation was hidden, cluttered up, by all this rationalism and philosophy.

And again, in a most interesting way, when you come to read the history preceeding the outbreak of the great rivival of 1859, particularly in Ireland, you will find exactly the same thing. The period before the revival was, again, characterised by this same deadness, a terrible deadness, and it took a particular form. Years before that revival (I am thinking particularly of the twenties and the thirties) the Presbyterian Church in Northern Ireland had gone astray in its doctrines. It had espoused a doctrine which is called Arianism, and Arianism denies the eternity and the Godhead of the Lord Jesus Christ. Arius taught that the Lord Jesus Christ was a created being, that he was not co-equal and co-eternal with the Father. It denied him his Godhead. Now that was the cause of the state of the Church, its utter deadness and uselessness. And it was only when that was corrected and swept aside, and the Church came back to the true doctrine, that the revival broke forth amongst the people. There, then, is my first piece of evidence. The concealing, and the neglect of certain vital truths have always been the chief characteristic of the life of the Church in every period of deadness and of declension.

Secondly, no revival has ever been known in the history of churches which deny or ignore certain essential truths. I regard that as an astoundingly important point. You have never heard of a revival in churches, so-called, which deny the cardinal, and fundamental, articles of our Christian faith. For instance, you have never heard of a revival amongst the Unitarians, and you have never heard of it because there has never been one. That is a sheer fact of history, and surely it behoves us to face that fact.

Thirdly, you will find very clearly in the history of the Church that such churches have always opposed, and have always persecuted, those who have been in the midst of revival. This again is history and not my opinion. A hundred years ago, when this great revival broke out, the Unitarians opposed it in the United States, in Northern Ireland, everywhere. They always oppose revival. They are bound to be consistent with themselves. They are rationalists, and they hate it. You will also read in the history of Northern Ireland, for instance, that a hundred years ago the Roman Catholic church of that time was actually putting on sale the so-called holy water, and urging people to sprinkle it upon themselves, and even to drink it, in order to avoid, and to evade, this thing which was being called revival. I refer to these things, not because it gives me any pleasure to do so, but for one reason only, that if we really are concerned about revival we have got to discover the things that hinder revival. And it is the concealing of vital truths and doctrines, that has always done this.

My last principle under this heading is that without a single exception it is the rediscovery of these cardinal doctrines that has led ultimately to revival. There is always a preliminary to revival. It appears to come suddenly, and in a sense it does. But if you look carefully into the history, you will always find that there was something going on quietly, there was a preliminary, a preparation unobserved by people. And the preparation, invariably, has been a rediscovery of these grand, and glorious, central truths. Take, for instance, the history of the Protestant Reformation. It was only after Martin Luther had suddenly seen the grand truth of justification by faith only that the Protestant revival came. It was getting back to that truth, in the epistles to the Galatians and the Romans, that prepared the way for the outpouring of the Spirit. It happened in this country and in every country where the Reformation spread. It was the same in the seventeenth century. Not to the same degree perhaps, but it was the emphasis on these truths that led to the great blessing that was experienced in the Puritan era.

And then everybody, surely, must know that that was what happened in the eighteenth century. There you had that deadness. Bishop Butler wrote his book, *The Analogy of Religion* and the 'Boyle lectures' were started in an attempt to counter this rationalism, but it availed nothing. Then suddenly the revival seemed to come. Whitefield, the Wesleys, and others like them appeared. Yes, but how did revival come through these men? Well, the story is well known. What really made it possible for John Wesley to have the experience he had in Aldersgate Street, when his heart was 'strangely warmed' by the Holy Spirit, was something that happened three months earlier. He had the experience in Aldersgate Street on May 24th 1738, yes, but in March 1738 his eyes were opened to the truth of justification by faith only. The famous conversation, on the journey between London and Oxford, between Peter Bülow and Wesley, was all about justification by faith only. It was only after he had seen that, and it had gripped him, that the Holy Spirit came upon him, and began to use him.

And this is not only true of Wesley, the same thing had already happened, in a sense, to Whitefield. And, certainly, if you turn to Wales you find precisely the same thing. At that time, the greatest preacher there was a man called Daniel Rowland, and Bishop Ryle ventures to say that he was possibly the greatest preacher since the apostles. Now his story was exactly like the others. He was a curate, he was a preacher, but his ministry was useless and dead, and nothing happened.

Then one day, he went and listened to a preacher called Griffith Jones, and he was convinced and convicted of the truth of justification by faith only. And it was only a few months after seeing that truth, and realising it, though he had not yet felt its power, that suddenly one day, as he was taking a communion service, the Holy Spirit came upon him, and filled him, and a great revival broke out in Wales in the eighteenth century. Now, this is always the case. And, as I have already reminded you, it was the same a hundred years ago, particularly in Northern Ireland. It was as they got rid of this Arianism, and saw the importance of the full truth concerning the person of our Lord and Saviour Jesus Christ, that the mighty blessing came.

So I am urging that there are certain truths which are absolutely essential to revival. And while these truths are denied, or are neglected, or ignored, we have no right to expect the blessing of revival. The Philistines keep on coming, and they throw in their earth, and their rubbish, and the water of life is hidden out of sight. Now, I confess freely, that if I consulted my own inclinations, I would not be referring to these things. I know that I am again exposing myself to the charge of censoriousness, and criticsm of others, and of separatism, and of individualism, and non-co-operation, but after all if a man allows his own feelings, and his own reputation, to affect his declaration of the truth he believes, he has no business to speak at all. It is no pleasant task for me to have to have to refer to these things. I do so only because I have this profound conviction, on the basis of Scripture (supported fully, as I have been showing you, by the history of the Christian Church) that while these truths are neglected, denied, or even ignored, you cannot have revival. We must start with this work of the Philistines. It is no use saying, 'Let's pray for revival.' There is something we have to do before that. The work of the Philistines must be cleared out. That is what Isaac did. 'He digged again the wells that they had digged in the days of Abraham, his father.' They cleared out the rubbish, and the refuse, and the earth, and there was the water as before. Every revival shows clearly that that preliminary work has always been done.

There are therefore, certain things which I must put before you, certain truths which must be believed. Revival cannot happen while these truths are denied, and so we must look at them, and we must take them in the right order.

What then, are the truths that are denied and concealed by the nefarious work of the Philistines? Here is the first. The truth concerning the sovereign, transcendent, living God who acts, and who intervenes, and erupts into the history of the Church, and of individuals. I must start with that. It is the foundation of all doctrines. Consider, for instance, what the Apostle Paul wrote to Timothy. Things were difficult. Timothy was troubled, he was losing hope, he was wondering what the future was going to hold. Paul was aged and facing death, and there was Timothy, frightened and alarmed. Paul writes to him, and says, 'What are you saying is very true, I know about these people who are denying the truths and so on.' And then he says to him, 'Nevertheless the foundation of God standeth sure'. (2 Tim. 2.19). The basis of everything is the sovereign, transcendent, living God, who in his eternal, glorious freedom, acts, intervenes, and interferes with the life of the whole Church and of individuals. And if there is anything that is more obvious than anything else in the life of

37

the Church today, it is the failure to start with, and to believe, that truth.

What do we have today? We have the god of the philosophers, and the god of the philosophers is not the sovereign, transcendent, living God, he is an abstraction. They talk about the 'uncaused cause'. What a way to speak of God! God is not an abstraction. God is not a philosophic concept. God is, and he alone is. He is life, and the author of all life and being. And they argue about him with their pipes in their mouths, and talk about him as if he is a term that they can handle and bandy about. You will never have revival in such conditions. God, I say, is not an abstraction, someone to be argued with, and fitted into our schemes. Philosophy has always been the curse in the life of the Church, and it is the curse today.

Another way in which this glorious truth about God is being concealed is by what people call ' the philosophy of immanence'. God in everything. Not God transcendent, but God immanent. They say that God is in everything, he is in the whole of nature. It is not exactly a pantheism, but it comes very near to it. But the argument is that because God is in everything, you do not expect him to act from the outside. God is everywhere, in everything, everything is sacred, and they dislike the distinction between the sacred and the secular. That is another way of denying his sovereignty and his eternal transcendence.

And then there is this other belief which I have referred to as deism. It is very common today, though it is not often given that name now. It was called that two hundred years ago, but it should be given the name today as well. It is a belief about God which believes in him as the Creator only. It says that God having created the world, has no further interest in it. Deism admits a kind of divine providence, but only in the realm of things material, not at all in the realm of the moral, and not at all in the realm of the spiritual. God is, as it were, shut out of his own universe. He made it like a great watchmaker making a watch, and having done so he just allows it to go on, on its own. We need not stay with this, but I do ask you to examine even your own thoughts, and to realise the thoughts that are controlling so many in the Christian Church today. Their ideas of God that he is a God who does not intervene. He is a God who does not act, a God whom they are always having to approach: they are always moving while he remains away in some distant eternity, absolutely impassive and immovable. He is this remote God. And they consequently do

38

not believe in revival, because that means essentially God acting, God coming in, God breaking in.

So if we have the god of the philosophers, or the god of the deists and the rationalists, we shall never experience revival. Indeed prayer almost becomes a waste of time and quite ridiculous. And how often that is precisely many people's attitude to prayer. It is something formal and mechanical – you either read your prayers, or you muddle them up. There is no living contact, nothing is expected, God is banished into his own eternity, and man occupies the centre of the stage. It is his thoughts about God that matter, not God's thoughts about him. What is your belief in God? Do you believe in the sovereign, transcendent, everlasting God of the universe, who is active still? Our Lord said 'My Father worketh hitherto, and I work'. (John 5. 17) Not your immanentist, nor some transcendence that almost banishes him out of the universe, but both God above, and yet with us, active and interfering, a God that visits his people. How can we pray to him, unless we are clear and correct in our ideas of the sovereign, living God? The work of the Philistines, you see, has been to obscure that, and that work must be got rid of before we can get back again to the water.

The second truth which has been hidden follows from the first. It involves the authority of this book, the authority of the Bible. The work of the Philistines is invariably this – we must consider it generally because there are groups and divisions even amongst the Philistines – they deny revelation. Of course, if their view of God is what I have been describing, you cannot have revelation. They do not believe in inspiration. They do not really believe that God has revealed the truth concerning himself, in propositions, and in statements, as they are recorded in the Bible. What then, is their position? How do they arrive at truth? Their answer is that they arrive at truth by searching for it, by their reasoning, by their understanding and by their speculation.

Now, this can be put very simply. The whole emphasis today is upon man's search for God, as if God had never revealed himself at all. But the whole case of the Bible is that God is searching for man, and that he has revealed himself to man, because man by searching cannot find God. That is its fundamental proposition. And that is what is being denied. Everything today is being governed and controlled by the philosophers and the thinkers, by what they think about God, and they defy God, and they make God after their own image, and he is not God, he is a lie.

Now my argument is that as long as this is the case, we have no right to talk about revival, or to expect it, still less to hope for it. What is our final authority in all these matters? What do I know about God, and the possibility of blessing, apart from what I have in the Bible? And do I claim that my mind and reason can select what is right in it and what is wrong, and that I need only hold on to what I happen to agree with? That makes me the authority, not this book. That makes my reason the standard, not God's revelation.

If you read the history of all the revivals of the past, you will find that they have been periods when men and women have believed this book to be the word of God. They have believed it literally, they have regarded it as the revelation of God, and the truth concerning him, and man's relationship to him, and all that is involved. And they have believed that this book has been written by men who have been divinely inspired. They have submitted themselves to it, they have not stood above it as judges, and as those who can decide what is right and what is wrong. But the Philistines have been terribly active during the last hundred and fifty years. And conditions are as they are today because people have no authority at all. They have denied the authority of the Scripture, they have set up their own opinions, philosophy, science, learning – all these things. The supernatural element is discounted, miracles are disbelieved, science is supposed to be incompatible with them. All these things have been covered over. Any direct activity on the part of God is suspect because it does not fit into the systems of the philosophers. These are urgent matters, I plead with you, read the history of the past, and I think you will discover that there has never been a revival when men have put their ideas and opinions before the authority of the word of God.

The third great cardinal article of belief which has been ignored is man in sin and under the wrath of God. Here is a doctrine that the natural man abominates. He feels that it is insulting to him. He has always been like that. Go back again and read the histories, and you will find in all those periods of deadness and of declension that people did not believe in sin in that way. They did not believe in the wrath of God. And I suppose there are no two things in connection with the Christian faith that are so abominated today, as the doctrine of sin, and the doctrine of the wrath of God. People are attempting to explain away sin in terms of psychology. They say it is insulting to mankind, and as for this idea of the wrath of God – 'Why,' they say, 'it is not God at all.

That is the tribal God of the Old Testament.' One prominent preacher said not so long ago that he did not believe in 'the God of the Old Testament that sat on the top of Mount Siniai, shouting out his wrath and his condemnation'. He said he believed in the God of Jesus. They say that the idea of the wrath of God is incompatible with the doctrine of God as love.

Now I am calling such statements the work of the Philistines because the mere history of every revival brings this out immediately. Men and women in the midst of revival are, at first, conscious of two things above everything else. One is their own unutterable sinfulness. When you have a revival you see men and women groaning, agonising under the conviction of sin. They are so conscious of their unworthiness, and their vileness, that they feel that they cannot live. They do not know what to do with themselves. They cannot sleep. They are in an agony of soul. If you read the history, you will see that that is the thing which stands out. The fact that is taught in the Bible is that the human heart is 'deceitful above all things, and desperately wicked: who can know it?'(Jer. 17. 9).

'In me,' says the Apostle Paul, '(that is, in my flesh,) dwelleth no good thing. . . . O wretched man that I am!'(Rom. 6.18,24). And in revival men and women feel as Paul did. They see their own sinfulness, they are horrified and cry out for deliverance.

But then that confronts them with the wrath of a holy God, and that is the cause of their most intense agony. They know they are deserving of this wrath, and that God, to be God, must hate sin with all the intensity of his divine nature and being. And they know he does so, he has told us so in his word. It is in the Old Testament and in the New. The Jesus whom people put up against the Old Testament, he taught about the wrath of God. He spoke about hell, he spoke about the place where 'their worm dieth not, and the fire is not quenched'. (Mark 9. 44) It is he who uttered these thoughts. It is everywhere in the New Testament as well as in the Old. And I know of nothing that is so terrifying in the whole of the Bible, as that statement there in the last book, in Revelation 6, which tells us of those men and women who at the end, when they see him, will call to the mountains, and the rocks to fall upon them and to hide them – from what? From the wrath of the Lamb, the Lamb of God, the incarnation of his love. It is his wrath that is the most terrifying thing of all. That is what happens in every period of revival and of re-awakening. Men quake in the presence of the living, and the holy, God. And as they see their own unworthiness, they do not know what to do,

41

nor where to turn. And they are in agony, perhaps for days and days.

That is what you get in revival, and yet, is not this the very truth that is being denied and abominated at the present time? Is this not the thing above all things on which the Philistines have cast their earth, and their refuse? Oh, I am not just contending for doctrine, God forbid that I should do so, and I am not anxious to strive, yet I would make this point urgently because of my profound conviction that until men and women in the Christian Church (I am not thinking of those who are outside) are humbled, and abased, and fall to the earth before this holy, and righteous, yes, to use the term of Jonathan Edwards, angry God, I see no hope of revival. It is our arrogance, it is our pride, it is our tendency to set ourselves up and to define God after our own image, instead of falling and prostrating ourselves before him, it is that, which stands between us and these mighty blessings.

Furthermore, if we have not this foundation, there is no point in proceeding. You see, it is not enough to say you believe in the Lord Jesus Christ. We shall be considering the doctrine of his person and his work, but you cannot believe in him truly unless you start with that sovereign, transcendent, holy God, who is and who acts. If you do not submit yourself entirely to the revelation that he has given, and if you are not aware of the plague of your own heart, and the foulness of the nature that you have inherited originally from Adam; if you do not see your hopelessness, and your utter despair, before this holy, righteous God, who hates sin with the whole of his being, you have no right to talk about revival, or to pray for it. What revival reveals above everything else is the sovereignty of God, and the iniquity, the helplessness, the hopelessness, of man in sin.

May God give us grace to meditate on these things. How do you think of God? How do you approach God? What is your attitude in his presence? Let us start with ourselves. This is personal, it is for everyone of us. In revival God takes hold of unknown men that nobody ever heard of, insignificant, so-called, members of the Church. And it is through such people that he has often done his mightiest works. Who knows it may be someone whose name has never been heard, who may be the very instrument of God in the revival for which we long? Therefore, I appeal to you, consider these things. Are you clear about them? Is there any evidence of the work of the Philistines in your life and in your heart? If there is, clear it out. Come back to the foundations.

Chapter 4

Genesis 26.17–18

And Isaac departed thence, and pitched his tent in the valley of Gerar, and dwelt there. And Isaac digged again the wells of water, which they had digged in the days of Abraham his father; for the Philistines had stopped them after the death of Abraham: and he called their names after the names by which his father had called them (Gen. 26.17–18).

We have been considering how the immediate task of the Church, if she is genuinely and truly concerned about revival, is to get rid of this rubbish and earth which the Philistines poured into the wells, and which have choked the supply of water. The way to revival is not just to say, 'Let's pray about it.' Of course, we must pray, and I hope to emphasise that, and to emphasise it strongly. But what I am saying is that there is something we must do before we pray. There are certain preliminary conditions attached to prayer. To go on our knees and to utter words is not of necessity prayer. The Bible from beginning to end makes it perfectly plain and clear that God can only be approached in certain ways, and on certain conditions. And if we do not observe those conditions, we are not praying, and there will be no value in our exercises. Let me put it like this. The need, we say, is the need of an outpouring of the Spirit of God. But clearly, by definition, the Spirit of God can only be outpoured on, and can only honour, his own truth. The Holy Spirit cannot honour a lie. He cannot honour a negation of the truth. The Spirit who is poured out in revival is the same as the one who led these people to write the books of the Bible. It is he who has given the truth, and safe-guarded its writing in an infallible manner. This is the truth of the Spirit. So, if we want the blessing of the Holy Spirit, clearly, we must make sure that our position conforms to his truth. And we have no right to ask for his blessing, unless we observe the conditions that he himself has laid down.

And that is why I say that the first task is to get rid of the rubbish of the Philistines. It is a painful process. I admit freely that I would prefer not to have to do this. It would be much simpler to say, 'Let us pray,' and organise prayer meetings. But if we believe the Bible at all, we cannot do that. It is a contradiction in terms. We must follow the biblical order. We have been considering that the first things we must get rid of are doubting or denying vital doctrines of the faith. Now, you notice my emphasis here. I say that the first work of the Philistines is that they deny, or cast doubt upon, or neglect, or ignore, certain vital and essential doctrines. I am not concerned about any other doctrines. There are doctrines and doctrines. There are doctrines that are absolutely essential to the Christian position. There are others which we believe to be right, but which we cannot say are essential. And I am concerned only about those bare essentials. This is no time for refinements, it is a time for being concerned about fundamentals. So, we have been considering some of these doctrines. We have looked at the doctrines of the transcendence and the sovereignty of God, and the authority of the Bible and the doctrine of man in sin and under the wrath of God. But that brings us on to another of the most essential doctrines. And that of course is the person of the Lord Jesus Christ. He is central, he is crucial. You read your Bible and you find that he he is everywhere. He is in the Old Testament. It is all looking forward to him; it is a book of promises concerning him and his coming, and what he is going to do when he comes. A man who does not find the Lord Jesus Christ in the Old Testament is spiritually blind. And the New Testament, of course, is nothing but an exposition and a delineation of him. The Gospels and the book of Acts are all about this blessed person. He is at the centre. In the last analysis the Bible is a book about him, because it is in, and through, him that God visits and redeems his people, and provides this great salvation.

And then, take the work of the Holy Spirit. We realise the need of the power of the Spirit and we know that the Church should be praying for a visitation of the Spirit. But the supreme work of the Holy Spirit, as our Lord himself has told us, is to glorify the Lord Jesus Christ. He said 'But the Comforter, which is the Holy Ghost, whom the Father will send in my name, he shall teach you all things and bring all things to your remembrance, whatsoever I have said unto you' (John 14.26). 'He shall not speak of himself' (John 16.13) No, 'He shall glorify me.' (John 16.14). So the supreme work of the Holy Spirit is to focus attention on, and to point to, the Lord Jesus Christ.

And then, if you turn to the historical evidence and read the accounts of all the revivals that have ever been known in the long history of the Church, you will find invariably that the very centre of the life of the Church, at that time, has been the Lord Jesus Christ, himself. Or consider the great hymns which were written, and which became so popular, two hundred years ago. There are so many of them, written by Charles Wesley, Philip Doddridge, Isaac Watts, William Williams, and by many others. What is the great theme of these hymns? It is the Lord Jesus Christ. There is nothing more typical of the eighteenth century revival and awakening than such words as, 'Jesus, lover of my soul, let me to thy bosom fly . . .'. Into the midst of all the deism and the philosophical preaching, that had characterised the end of the seventeenth and the beginning of the eighteenth century, came this warm, devotional, vital, spiritual, preaching about the Lord Jesus Christ, and people's personal knowledge of him. Those hymns are full of it. And you will find that it is exactly the same in every other period of revival. All is concentrated on him. The favourite hymns that were sung a hundred years ago, in all the countries that were visited by revival, were just these hymns about the person of our Lord and Saviour Jesus Christ. And it has been the same in every revival experience everywhere in this present century.

Is it not clear, then, for all these reasons, that if the Lord Jesus Christ is not crucial, central, vital, and occupying the very centre of our meditation and our living, our thinking, and our praying, that we really have no right to look for revival? And yet, what is the position? If you go and talk to many people, even in the Church, about religion, you will find that they will talk to you at great length, without ever mentioning the Lord Jesus Christ. I an never tired of putting it like this, because it is something that I am so familiar with in my experience as a pastor. People come and talk to me about these things, and I put my question to them. I say 'If you are unhappy about yourself this is the way to decide. What if you had to die tonight, how would you feel?'

'Oh,' they say, 'I believe in God.'

'All right,' I reply, 'what will you say when you stand in the presence of God? What are you relying on?'

'Well,' they say, 'I have always tried to live a good life, I have done my best, I have tried to do good, I have tried to avoid sin.'

'Yes,' I say, 'that's very good. But nevertheless you have sinned, haven't you?'

'Oh yes, I have sinned.'

'So,' I ask, 'what do you do about your sin? What will you say to God, in the presence of God, about your sin?'

'Well,' they say, 'I believe God is a God of love.'

'And how does that help you?'

'Well,' they say, 'I believe that if I acknowledge my sin to God and then ask him to forgive me, he does forgive me, and I am relying upon that.'

So I press them, and I go on with my questions and cross-examination. And they continue to give the same sort of answer.

The point I am making is that they do not even mention the name of the Lord Jesus Christ. They believe in forgiveness, and they see their need of it, and they want it, but they seem to think that they can get forgiveness from God apart from the Lord Jesus Christ. They do not really see the meaning of the communion bread and wine, his death, his blood shedding. They do not seem to understand that. They seem to think that they can go to God directly without the Lord Jesus Christ at all. There is a great deal of so-called Christianity which is quite Christ-less. He does not seem to come in to their thoughts. He does not seem to be absolutely vital, so that if you blotted him out of history, these people would be in exactly the same position. They seem to be living very much on the level of the Old Testament saints, and not even that at times, because those saints were looking forward to the coming of the Messiah, whereas these people do not seem to see any need for him at all.

Clearly, then, this is the work of the Philistines. Anything that in any way conceals the Lord Jesus Christ, anything that in any way takes him out of the centre and puts him anywhere else, is the work of the Philistines. And oh, how busy and active the Philistines have been during this present century in particular. There are certain things, my dear friends, about which there should be no discussion at all. And the first is his unique deity; his eternity. Read those descriptions given of him by the Apostle Paul in Colossians chapter 1. He is before all; it is by him that all things consist; he is eternal, co-equal with the Father. There must be no discussion about this. There is no time to waste in arguing with people who deny the unique deity of the Lord Jesus Christ, his eternity, his equality with God, his incarnation, and the blessed truth of the two natures in his one person. Go back to every period of revival, and there is no dispute about this. This is the thing in which they glory, this is the thing which makes their very life, and to me these things are absolute essentials. I just do not understand the man who can say he believes in him and yet not believe in the virgin birth, or his miracles, and not believe in his literal, physical resurrection.

The Apostle Paul does not argue about this. He says, 'If Christ be not risen, then,' he says, 'is our preaching vain, and your faith is also vain. . . . ye are yet in your sins' (1 Cor. 15. 14, 17). Now that is the literal resurrection that Paul is talking about in 1 Corinthians 15. He is not talking about the persistence of the Spirit of Christ. He is not merely arguing that although dead he is still able to help us. No, he is talking about the literal, physical resurrection. And he says, 'If this is not true, then all I have preached is wrong.' Yet, there are people calling themselves Christians, and Christian preachers today, who deny the physical resurrection of our Lord, and say it does not matter. I say that, as long as you are in that position, you have no right to pray for revival, nor to expect it. Because the Holy Ghost is one of the witnesses of the resurrection. Do you remember how the Apostle Peter puts it? He says, 'And we are his witnesses of these things; and so is also the Holy Ghost, whom God hath given to them that obey him' (Acts 5. 32). The Holy Ghost is a witness to these things, witness to his incarnation, witness to his ministry, his teaching, his miracles, witness to his death, witness to his glorious, literal, physical, resurrection, witness to his ascension: 'We are his witnesses . . . so is also the Holy Ghost.' How then can you ask the Holy Ghost to bless you and come down in power, when you deny the very thing that he is given to witness, the very person whom he is sent to glorify?

So, then, what is the use of saying, 'Let us pray', if we are not clear about these things? You will never get at that water in the wells until you have cleared out the rubbish of the Philistines. Revival, above everything else, is a glorification of the Lord Jesus Christ, the Son of God. It is the restoration of him to the centre of the life of the Church. You find this warm devotion, personal devotion, to him. It leads to our hymns, our anthems of praise: Christ the centre of the life of the Church. Do you not see the necessity for getting rid of this work of the Philistines? There is no value in so-called Christianity which does not exalt him, and live for him, and live to testify to him.

But that in turn leads me on to his work; his person first, yes, but now his work. What do I mean by his work? Well, I want to emphasise particularly his atonement, his death upon the cross, his broken body and his shed blood. Again I am quoting to you pure fact which you can check for yourselves. You will find that in every period of revival, without exception, there has been a

47

tremendous emphasis upon the blood of Christ. The hymns that have been sung most of all in periods of revival, have been the hymns about the blood. I could quote them to you in several languages. There is nothing more characteristic than this. We find that the Apostle has put it again for us in Colossians 1: 'Having made peace . . .' – how did he make peace? ' . . . through the blood of his cross' (v.20).

Of course, I know perfectly well when I say a thing like that I am saying something that is unusual and highly unpopular at the present time. There are Christian preachers who think they are being clever in pouring ridicule upon this theology of blood. They dismiss it with scorn. 'The Old Testament religion,' they say, 'wallowing in blood. The blood of bulls and of goats, and all this materialising and talking about the blood of Christ.' Of course they say that. And that is why the Church is as she is. But in periods of revival, she glories in the cross, she makes her boast in the blood. Because as the author of the epistle to the Hebrews puts it, there is only one way in which we can enter with boldness into the holiest of all, and that is by the blood of Jesus (see Heb. 10. 19). This is the thing that the Holy Ghost honours. This is the thing to which he bears witness, that the Son of God came into this world and was made a little lower than the angels. What for? For the suffering of death, that he might taste death for every man.

The very nerve, and centre, and heart, of the Christian gospel is this, 'Whom God hath set forth to be a propitiation through faith in his blood' (Rom. 3. 25). 'That he might be just, and the justifier of him which believeth in Jesus' (Rom. 3: 26). 'In whom we have redemption through his blood, the forgiveness of sin' (Eph. 1. 7). 'Without shedding of blood, is no remission [of sin]. (Heb. 9. 22). The very heart of our gospel is that God 'hath made him to be sin for us, who knew no sin; that we might be made the righteousness of God in him'. (2 Cor. 5. 21) Listen to what the greatest preacher the Church has ever known liked to say about himself: 'But God forbid that I should glory, save in the cross of our Lord Jesus Christ, by whom the world is crucified unto me, and I unto the world' (Gal. 6. 14). That is the thing in which he makes his boast and his glory. Then again, he says to the Corinthians, 'I determined not to know anything among you, save Jesus Christ, and him crucified' (1 Cor. 2. 2).

And yet, men say that his death on the cross was but an accident, or just the death of a pacifist, or something like that. They do not see its centrality; they do not see that it was by dying there that he achieved our salvation; that it was because God had laid on him the iniquity of us all, that we are forgiven and are free. 'Ah,' they say, 'it is mechanical, it is almost merchandised. You are making of this thing something which is almost material. It is just a great display of the love of God.' But it is not. The cross is the point at which the holy, everlasting, and eternally just, and righteous God is making a way of salvation, by visiting the punishment of our sins upon his only begotten, dearly beloved, Son. I see no hope for revival while men and women are denying the blood of the cross, and are pouring scorn upon that in which we should make our boast.

> When I survey the wondrous cross
> On which the Prince of glory died,
> My richest gain I count but loss,
> And pour contempt on all my pride.
> *Isaac Watts*

They have thrown the refuse, and the earth, and all the rubbish, upon this blessed fact of the death and the blood, and the cross. And it is not surprising that the Church is as she is. It is not surprising that the world is as it is, when our central message is being hidden. What have we? There is no hope, I say, until we get rid of this work of the Philistines. Clear out the rubbish that is concealing the most precious truth of all.

And that in turn, brings me to the next doctrine, which is the person, and the work, of the Holy Spirit. Here, in many ways, is the most practical of all the doctrines that I have been dealing with. And, here alas, I shall feel compelled to say things which do not only apply to the people who hitherto have been chiefly in our minds, those who deny the authority of the Scripture, and those who dismiss the doctrine of sin and of atonement. Here, alas, we shall have to say things of which it seems to me, many evangelicals are equally guilty. I say this, therefore, with profound regret. But if we are concerned about revival it must be said. The Philistines have always been concerned about concealing the person and the work of the Holy Spirit, or, if you like, they have been guilty in various ways of quenching the Spirit. How do they do this? Well, here are some of the ways. One is to forget him and to ignore him altogether. And there are many people who do that. Of course, if you ask them, they say that they believe in him, but in practice they forget him altogether.

I do not stop with that. There are others who, while they do not forget him, regard him only as an influence; they do not believe in Him as a person. 'Oh,' they say 'there is an influence of God's Spirit.' But they do not talk about the person of the Holy Spirit, and that must grieve him terribly. Our Lord talks about sending *him*. He says, 'I will pray the Father and he will give you another Comforter'; 'I will not leave you comfortless'; 'He will guide you into all truth.' Jesus talks about him. Yes, we are Trinitarians, we believe in God, the Father, the Son, *and* Holy Spirit. And how can we expect him to visit us and to bless us if we talk about 'it'? Would you like to be talked about as 'it'? Would you like to be thought of as just an agency or power? Of course you would not. There is nothing more insulting to a person than to cast doubt in any way upon the personality. And that is what men and women are doing with the Holy Spirit, they are talking about 'it', an influence. No, he is a blessed person.

Or let me put it to you like this. He is not given the place that is indicated in our Lord's teaching in chapters 14 to 16 of John's Gospel. Read those chapters again. Not only does the Lord speak about the Holy Spirit as 'he', as a blessed person, but he describes the functions of the Holy Spirit. He tells us what the Holy Spirit is going to do, how he is standing at our side, how he speaks to us, how he prompts us, how he brings us back to the truth and makes truth known to us, how he enlightens us and gives us understanding, how he can convict the world of sin and righteousness and of judgment. The ministry of the Holy Spirit. There are those who have suggested that the book we call the book of the Acts of the Apostles should be called the book of the Acts of the Holy Spirit, and there is a great deal of truth in that.

But we must move on to what is, of course, the most crucial point of all in connection with the doctrine of the person and the work of the Holy Spirit in this matter. And that is the question of outpourings of the Holy Spirit, or, if you prefer, baptisms of the Holy Spirit. This is obviously the crucial point with regard to this whole question of revival, because I take it that by definition what a revival means is an outpouring of the Spirit of God; the Spirit of God coming in power upon a person or a number of persons at the same time. Read the stories of revival and that is what you will find. But now, the work of the Philistines, of course, is to deny and to dispute it. And it is being done by many people in many ways. Some people dispute it by just dismissing it as hysteria. 'Ah,' they say, 'what you call revivals are nothing but mass hysteria. Simple people getting worked up. You see,' they say, 'that is why you get accounts now of revival sometimes in the

Belgian Congo, or perhaps in certain islands off the north west of Scotland. You do not get them in a country like this. It is simple people, mass hysteria.' You are familiar with that teaching, I take it. That is purely the work of the Philistines. And there are people who call themselves Christians who do not hesitate to say that the so-called great revivals of history are nothing but evidences of mass hysteria. Is there anything that can be more grieving to the Spirit than that? They say, 'You know, we should not expect that kind of thing in a country like this with educated, sophisticated people. You only get that amongst primitive people.' I know of nothing which comes nearer to blasphemy against the Holy Ghost than that. And may I solemnly warn you that our Lord, himself, taught that whosoever shall speak a word against the Son of Man, that is to say against himself, shall be forgiven. But whoever blasphemes, he says, against the Holy Ghost, shall not be forgiven, neither in this world, nor in the world to come. Let us be careful, my beloved friends, lest we become guilty of this terrible blasphemy of attributing the work of the Holy Spirit of God to something psychological, to some hysterical manifestation. Let us be careful as we speak about these things.

But, then, there are others, who, while not dismissing it as hysteria, seem to me to be equally guilty of quenching the Spirit, because they argue like this. They say, 'Baptism of the Holy Spirit is something which is non-experimental. The baptism of the Holy Spirit is that which happens to every man when he is born again, when he is regenerated. So we are all baptised with the Spirit, we have all received this baptism.' Now, remember, they are talking about the thing which is described in the second chapter of Acts. And they say, 'Yes, that was the baptism of the Holy Spirit. But we all get that now, and it is unconscious, we are not aware of it, it happens to us the moment we believe and we are regenerated. It is just that act of God which incorporates us into the Body of Christ. That's the baptism of the Spirit. So it is no use your praying for some other baptism of the Spirit, or asking God to pour out his Spirit upon the Church, or to baptise the Church afresh with his Holy Spirit, a baptism of power. This is non-experimental, and as it has happened to all of us, we must not ask for it.'

Or, the argument is put another way. It is taught that what happened on the day of Pentecost happened once and for ever, that it cannot be repeated, and therefore that it is wrong for us to pray that the Holy Spirit should be poured forth. They say, 'God, on the day of Pentecost, did pour forth his Spirit upon the

Church. And the Holy Spirit has been in the Church ever since. So,' they teach, 'it is actually wrong to pray for an outpouring of God's Spirit.' It is not surprising that, as that kind of preaching has gained currency, people have stopped praying for revival, and the Church is as she is today.

Then there are others, it seems to me, who are guilty of the same thing in this way. They speak only of being filled with the Spirit. They say, 'That is the thing you should concentrate on. Surely all that is demanded of Christian people, and of Church members, is that they should go on being filled with the Spirit, and as long as they are filled with the Spirit, what more is necessary?' They say, 'There is no need to pray for these baptisms or visitations that you are talking about. Why not simply tell the people to go on being filled with the Spirit?' And so, you see, we have arrived at a position where all that is necessary is that we should evangelise on the one hand, and then we should teach the converts about the importance of going on being filled with the Spirit. And as long as we do these two things, nothing more is necessary. And I am suggesting, and very seriously too, that that is the main reason why people have not been praying for revival. They do not see the necessity for it. They never think in terms of the Spirit suddenly coming down upon the Church, for instance as he did not only on the day of Pentecost, but on the next day, also. You will find it recorded in Acts chapter 4. There were the church members all together, they were praying to God, and we are told that suddenly while they were praying the Holy Ghost came down upon them, and the walls of the building in which they were met, were shaken. As it happened, there was a further baptism, an outpouring of the Spirit, on Cornelius and his household, and this happened too, in other places. But all that is left out, it is forgotten. You see, the belief now is that you do not need that sort of thing. Evangelise and then give this other teaching about being filled with the Spirit, and there is no room left for an outpouring of the Spirit, it is not expected, and it does not happen.

Then, there is a pathetic group of people, and, in a way, these are the most pathetic of all, who say not only that you should not pray for a visitation of the Spirit like this, you should not pray for revival at all. Their argument runs like this: 'We are,' they say, 'living in the last days. The advent of Christ is at the door. The Holy Spirit has been withdrawn, and if God is withdrawing the Holy Spirit what right have you to pray for a coming, and an outpouring of the Spirit? Prophecy should make it perfectly plain to you that there never can be another revival, because Christ is coming, and coming so quickly there is not time for revival. So you should not even be praying for it.'

Now I say that that is the most pathetic objection of all, because that whole argument is based upon an attempt to interpret one chapter only in the Scriptures: 2 Thessalonians 2. It is based on the assumption that what they believe and teach is the only possible explanation of that chapter. And on the most doubtful exposition conceivable of an exceedingly difficult and doubtful passage, such people say positively, and imagine that they are being very scriptural in saying it, that, therefore, you definitely should not pray for revival. They have fixed the times and the seasons, you see. But the Scriptures tell us not to be concerned about times and seasons. The Scriptures tell us that even the Lord Jesus Christ Himself did not know the day of his second coming, that only God knew. But these people have arrived at it, and they are so certain of it that they say that we must not pray for revival because the Holy Spirit is being withdrawn. Such persons, it seems to me, are guilty of this terrible sin of quenching the Spirit, and are partly responsible, therefore, for the spiritual drought, and the whole condition of the Christian Church at the present time.

In other words, I would put it to you that what so many are disputing and denying and ignoring, is what I would call the immediate and direct action of the Holy Spirit. They say that the Spirit only works through the word, and that we must not expect anything from the Spirit apart from that which comes immediately through the word. And so, it seems to me, they are quenching the Spirit, because I read in Acts 13 that the Holy Ghost said unto the church at Antioch, 'Separate me Barnabas and Saul. . . .' And I read in chapter 15 that the council in Jerusalem said, 'It seemed good to the Holy Ghost, and to us. . . .' I read in chapter 16 that Paul was anxious to preach the gospel in Asia but the Spirit 'suffered him not'. He wanted to preach in Bithynia, and the Holy Spirit restrained him and stopped him. The living, powerful, activity of the Spirit; the Spirit coming directly, as it were, and controlling, and leading, and guiding, and giving orders, and indicating what was to be done; the Spirit descending upon them; that is what you always have in revival. But that is the thing that seems to have gone entirely out of the minds of men and women.

As I close this chapter, let me put this fact to you again. To me it is very striking and significant. Check what I am going to say for yourselves. Look at many books which have been written in this present century on the doctrine of the Holy Spirit and try and find for me a paragraph, or a section, or a chapter, on revival. Now, here are books, you see, written on the person and the work of the Holy Spirit, and they do not mention revival. They do not mention a visitation of God's Spirit, an outpouring of God's Spirit, they do not even mention it. I could give you the authors. Not a word about revival. Why not? There is no doubt that it is because of the teaching I have been describing: they do not believe in revival any more. All you have got to do is to go on being filled with the Spirit, and you exhort the whole church to do that. There is no thought in their minds of the Spirit suddenly coming upon people, in the way that he always does in revival, and doing his wonderful works. Now if you go back and read books which were written on the person and the work of the Holy Spirit, say, round about 1860, by Smeaton, for example, and others, there you will find sections on religious awakenings, religious revivals. They deal with it specifically. In the past they always did, but during the last seventy to eighty years, this whole notion of a visitation, a baptism of God's Spirit upon the Church, has gone.

Even Evangelical writers do not mention revival. They do not even think of it. And surely this is to quench the Holy Spirit of God because the Holy Spirit not only has what we may call his ordinary work, he has his extraordinary work, and that is revival. Of course, we must evangelise, of course we must preach about being filled with the Spirit, yes, but over and above that we must cry unto God to pour out his Spirit upon the whole Church. And that is revival, the descent, the outpouring of the Spirit over and above his usual, ordinary work; this amazing, unusual, extraordinary thing, which God in his sovereignity and infinite grace has done to the Church from time to time during the long centuries of her history.

Examine again your doctrine of the Holy Spirit, and in the name of God, be careful lest, in your neat and trimmed doctrine, you are excluding and putting out this most remarkable thing which God does periodically through the Holy Spirit, in sending him upon us, in visiting, in baptising us, in reviving the whole Church in a miraculous and astonishing manner.

Chapter 5

Genesis 26.17–18

And Isaac departed thence, and pitched his tent in the valley of Gerar, and dwelt there. And Isaac digged again the wells of water, which they had digged in the days of Abraham his father; for the Philistines had stopped them after the death of Abraham: and he called their names after the names by which his father had called them (Gen. 26.17–18).

As we return to this passage and read of Isaac's need to clear his father's wells of the rubble of the Philistines, I have no hesitation in asserting that the main cause of the state of the Christian Church today, and the whole state of the world, in consequence, is the terrible apostasy that has increasingly characterised the Church for the last hundred years. And, therefore, we have started with this: We have to get rid of this rubbish. And so, we have been considering what these vital doctrines are, the neglect of which, or the misunderstanding of which, or the denial of which is ever a mark of the Philistines. We have dealt with several great doctrines and now there are other doctrines, two especially, that I must just note. Obviously the doctrine of justification by faith only is absolutely essential. There has never been a revival but that this has always come back into great prominence. This doctrine means the end of all thinking about ourselves and our goodness, and our good deeds, and our morality, and all our works. Look at the histories of revivals, and you will find men and women feeling desperate. They know that all their goodness is but filthy rags, and that all their righteousness is of no value at all. And there they are, feeling that they can do nothing, and crying out to God for mercy and for compassion. Justification by faith. God's act. 'If God does not do it to us,' they say, 'then we are lost.' And so they wait in utter helplessness before him. They pay no attention, and attach no significance to all their own past religiosity, and all their faithfulness in church attendance, and many, many other things. They see it is all no good, even their religion is of no value, there is nothing that is of value. God must justify the ungodly. And that is the great message that comes out, therefore, in every period of revival.

And, of course, it is important for this reason: holding to this doctrine, people are always very conscious, at such times, of the immediate possibility of salvation. That, as you know, is a striking feature of all revivals. In the words of Goldsmith, 'The fools that came to scoff remained to pray'. Men who came in out of sheer curiosity were suddenly laid hold of by the Spirit, and there and then the great transaction was done, and they left as new people. Now, if we do not hold the doctrine of justification by faith, we cannot possibly believe in such immediate work, and such immediate results. And in the Church there is still a good deal unconsciously, of holding on to works, and of regarding this whole matter of salvation as something that results from what we do – as if we could make ourselves Christian people!

So, it is essential that we should be clear about this great doctrine. It was the thing that revolutionised the life of Martin Luther, and ushered in the Protestant Reformation, the thing that was again rediscovered in the eighteenth century by Whitefield and the two Wesleys, and by Rowland and Harris in Wales, and by all these men who were so used of God. It was the realisation of justification by faith that really led to the outpouring of the Spirit. It has always been the case. And so we cannot afford to neglect, or to ignore this crucial doctrine.

Then, the other is, of course, the doctrine of regeneration. I suppose this was, in particular, the great doctrine of two hundred years ago. Again, it emphasises the absolute necessity of the work of the Holy Spirit. It reminds us that nothing will suffice except a man be born again, that he be given a new nature. That there is no value in any decision on the part of man unless it is indicative of his change of nature. This is a point that I could easily elaborate. We do know psychologically that it is possible to make people take decisions, and to persuade them to almost anything you like. The cults can do that, the false religions can do that. That is why they are thriving so much at the present time. New religious movements that are far removed from orthodoxy can get their results and they are increasing. You are familiar with them – these various people who come round to your doors. These movements are succeeding, and they have mass meetings, and large numbers of decisions. We know that by bringing pressures to bear upon the mind these things can be done. So, therefore, the fact that a man decides to be religious and to change his life in certain ways, does not prove at all that he is a Christian.

What makes us Christians? The work of regeneration; the Holy Spirit of God doing a work down in the very depths of the personality, and putting there a new principle of life, something absolutely new, so that there is the 'new man'. Now that, always, is a doctrine that comes out in every period of revival and of re-awakening. And that is how you get, invariably at such times, these remarkable and dramatic changes. Men who had been utterly hopeless, and who had been abandoned even by their dearest relatives and friends; men who had even abandoned themselves, feeling that nothing could be done for them, feeling utterly hopeless, feeling rejected of all people and of God: suddenly this work takes place, and they find themselves new creatures with an entirely new outlook on living, and anxious to live a new kind of life. Regeneration. It stands out in the story and in the history of every revival that has ever taken place in the long history of the Christian Church. In other words, everything about a revival emphasises the activity of this sovereign God. He is intervening. He is working. He is doing things. And this is shown very plainly by the results and the effects of the work of regeneration.

There, then, are some of the main, and what I would call the essential, crucial doctrines. These are doctrines about which there must never be any dispute at all. I feel we have all wasted too much time in arguing with people about these doctrines. They are the bare essentials, and without them we have no right at all to pray for, or to expect, the influence and the demonstration of the Holy Spirit of God.

So orthodoxy, defined in those terms, is an absolute essential and to deny them is error and heresy, the work of the Philistines, that ever blights the work of the Church and produces these appalling periods of spiritual drought, such as that in which you and I are living at the present time. We must start, therefore, with the absolute necessity of orthodoxy in those vital respects.

Then, having said that, I come on to a second group of considerations which are particularly applicable to those of us who claim to be evangelical. It is very difficult to make hard and fast distinctions in these matters. There are some things, perhaps, that I would include under this next heading that some of you would prefer to put under the heading that is to follow. However, the classification is not vital, and yet it is good that we should classify as far as we can. So my next heading is *defective orthodoxy*. The first was orthodoxy, and we were mainly concerned there with people who are not orthodox. I move on now to consider the case of those who are orthodox, but whose orthodoxy is defective in certain respects. And to me, this is again of very vital importance, because, alas, we are well aware of the fact that there are many individuals and many churches who are orthodox but who seem very lifeless. Why is it that the Spirit of God does not descend upon every evangelical church? What is the matter? There must be something wrong. I want to suggest, therefore, some of the things which constitute defective, or, if you like, eccentric orthodoxy.

The first and foremost trouble under this heading is to be concerned about *the person, rather than* with *the person himself*. The trouble with the people who were not orthodox was that they were wrong in their doctrines about God and about the Lord Jesus Christ and about the Holy Spirit. But now I am indicating that there is a terrible danger of our putting the doctrines, the true doctrines, about the persons into the place of the persons. And that is absolutely fatal. But it is a very familiar snare, which traps evangelical people, and orthodox people. You can be orthodox but dead. Why? Well, because you are stopping at the doctrines, you are stopping at the definitions, and failing to realise that the whole purpose of doctrine is not to be an end in itself, but to lead us to a knowledge of the person and to an understanding of the person, and to a fellowship with the person.

The New Testament itself deals with this at great length in many places. And the history of the Church certainly brings it out very clearly. There are, indeed, churches today, and denominations, that are perfectly orthodox yet are quite dead. They do not seem to be used at all in the salvation of souls, nor really in giving their people assurance of salvation. Why? It is because they remain only on the level of doctrine – this intellectual concern and this intellectual correctness. It is a terrible thing to substitute even true doctrines for a living realisation of the person.

And this applies also to preaching. Of course a preaching which is non-doctrinal is in the end quite useless. Yes; but let us remember there is a difference between preaching about doctrines and preaching doctrinally. By that I mean that you can preach doctrines in a purely intellectual and mechanical manner. You start with your doctrine, you expound it, and you end with it, and you have preached about the doctrine. That is not the business of preaching. The business of preaching is to preach doctrinally about God, about the Lord Jesus Christ, and about the Holy Spirit and their work for us in our salvation. You see, there are constantly snares in this Chritian life. We have that powerful adversary, the Devil, who is ever trying to ruin everything that God does, and to rule over us, so we have to be careful. We must not spend our time merely with the definitions and the statements, and stop at them, thus failing to arrive at a knowledge of the persons, and failing truly to receive and to live the full Christian life. Dead orthodoxy, in practice, is as bad as heterodoxy, because it is quite useless.

The next thing I would emphasise is, again under this heading of defective orthodoxy, still taking it mainly from the standpoint of the doctrines themselves. It is *a lack of balance, a lack of true scriptural proportion in the understanding of the doctrines, and the presentation of the doctrines that are absolutely essential to salvation*. If we lack a balance in the scriptural proportion of doctrines we shall find ourselves becoming dry and arid and useless. As the Apostle Paul puts is, Knowledge puffeth up, but charity edifieth – builds up (1 Cor. 8.1). And there is nothing in which this is more likely to take place than in a lack of balance with respect to doctrines – in an excessive emphasis on certain aspects of truth, so that they monopolise the whole of our attention.

This is not just my opinion. Read the history of the Church and you will find that invariably this error has led to that result. Read the New Testament, was that not the trouble with which the Apostle deals in Romans 14? There were certain people who were saying that nothing mattered but this question of eating meats. They were talking about it day and night, whenever you met them they brought it into the conversation. This was the thing. They were dividing the church and they were condemning one another. But look here, says Paul, that is not the Kingdom of God! 'The kingdom of God is not meat and drink; but righteousness, and peace, and joy in the Holy Ghost (Rom. 14.15).

Here then, is something of which we must always be aware. This is the subtle temptation that the Devil always brings to those who are alive and alert spiritually, and rightly concerned about doctrine. I have no hesitation in asserting that there are large numbers of people who have been so over-concerned with the question of prophecy that they themselves have become dry and useless. And there are churches of which that is true. The whole of their time is spent upon prophecy. Whenever you meet them the first thing they talk about is 'Have you seen this item in the news? Don't you see that that is a fulfilment . . . ?' And the whole time they are occupied with times and seasons. Prophecy absorbs the whole of their attention. They very rarely talk to you about the Lord Jesus Christ. They rarely tell you about experiences they have had with him. They do not give you the impression that they are holy, sanctified people. No, they are just experts on times and seasons.

I remember a man I once encountered as I was travelling to preach somewhere. I was sitting in the compartment of a train when in came this man carrying a copy of *The Times* and a Bible. I diagnosed exactly, and immediately, what he was, and what he was going to do. And I proved to be right. Oh yes, he was interested only in prophecy; he had got it all worked out, and *The Times* was just the proof of what the Scripture said. The whole attention is absorbed in prophecy even, as we have seen in the case of some people, to the extent that they say that a revival is impossible. They do not know that people said such things centuries ago, that men have always been saying that the Lord is at hand, and that therefore you do not pray for revival because he is coming. And so they quench the Spirit, and revival does not come.

But that is only one illustration. Is it not true that there are some people who really do seem to exalt baptism, and particular modes of baptism, to the supreme position? Are there not others who seem to think that speaking with tongues is the one thing that matters? Their whole doctrine of the Holy Spirit is really a question of speaking with tongues. They are always talking about it, this is the test, and other people are excluded, if they have not spoken in tongues. With others it is a question of church order. There are those who still teach that episcopacy is absolutely essential to the Church. There are those who would almost say the same thing about presbytery. And so, in a time of drought like this, when God's name is being violated and ignored by others, in this awful period in which we live, there are people who occupy the whole of their time with church government, or forms of service, and other such matters.

Now these are all ways of quenching the Spirit. You must not exalt to the primary and the central position matters which belong to the periphery. I ask you, therefore, to examine yourself with regard to your interest in doctrine. Do your doctrines conceal the Persons? Are you maintaining a balance and a right and a due proportion? What is the first thing you talk about when you meet people? Do you give them the impression that you are a man who has one idea and lives for one doctrine only, or do you give the impression that you know God and the Lord Jesus Christ, and are having business and transactions with them? Do you give an impression that there is love in your heart, the love of God that is drawing people to him, and making them anxious to know him even as you know him? Oh, there is nothing so tragic as this foolish lack of balance. The history of the Church, the history of revivals, shows so clearly that when people go off at tangents, as it were, and are monopolised by one thing, the Spirit is always quenched and the work is always hindered. Let us pray for balance. Let us pray for sanity. We have not received 'the spirit of fear; but of power, and of love, and of a sound mind'. (2 Tim. 1.7) Discipline, balance, order. Let us, therefore, examine ourselves as we look at these things.

Then the next matter is, in many ways, a still more important one – *a defective doctrine of the Church*. I have an uncomfortable feeling that this, perhaps, has been the particular trouble with those who are orthodox and evangelical. There are big public meetings and gatherings instead of a meeting together of the saints; movements, rather than the gathered saints. The whole idea of the Church as we find her in the New Testament, seems to be going out. And we all think now in terms of general meetings and gatherings, especially if they are very big ones. And we come together from all parts, and we travel in our buses, and our coaches on Saturday or any other night, it does not matter when it is. We are no longer preparing for the gathering of the church on Sunday.

I suggest that you consider this matter very seriously and carefully. I think that if you study the history you will find that as the tendency to think in terms of big meetings and movements, rather than in terms of the local church has increased, so the frequency of revivals has decreased. Now that is an historical statement. You will find that same emphasis on meetings, and gatherings, outside the realm of the Church. 'Let's have a neutral hall,' they say as if there were something wrong in the church. 'Ah, but,' they say, 'the man in the street won't come into the church.' Well, that is possibly true up to a point, but let me remind you that if you get a revival in your church the man in the street, and all his friends, will come crowding in. He always has done so. The man in the street has always been outside, how has he come in in the past? He has come in because he has suddenly heard that something strange and wonderful is happening in that church. He responds as the church did in Jerusalem on the day of Pentecost. The Holy Spirit came upon the apostles and the news went abroad that these people were speaking in strange languages. And they

61

said, 'What is this?' So they went along, to see, out of curiosity. 'These men are full of new wine,' they said. You see, they were attracted, the news went abroad.

That is how it has happened in the past. The man in the street is only attracted finally by power. And, indeed, the question arises whether the man in the street *is* attracted even by our organised mass meetings. Is it not rather that you find evangelical people travelling from all parts of the country, and that what you have is just a great evangelical mass meeting, and the man in the street is still outside? Therefore, let us look into this. The unit through which God has always worked has been the Church. You read the history and the story of revivals. Read the story of 1859 in Ulster, and you will find that it started in a little gathering where the saints came together. That idea seems to have gone. But the Church, you know, consists of the gathered saints, God's people coming together because they are God's people, and because, therefore, they want to pray to God together. Let us get rid of this notion of the neutral, so-called, mass meeting, and let us realise that God's unit is the Church, the gathering of his saints, his people. It is to them he comes. He says, 'Where two or three are gathered together in my name, there am I.' We say, 'Ah, but you must have two or three thousand at least.' No, no! 'Two or three gathered together in my name, there am I.' Why do we allow the ideas of big business to govern our thinking and our strategy, rather than the teaching of the New Testament itself, as exemplified in the long history of the Church?

There, then, are what I would call the main troubles with defective orthodoxy, as regards doctrine itself. But now I come to the realm of practice. Unfortunately, I have to go through these things in detail because I am convinced that these are the things that are keeping God's people from even thinking about revival. They get so excited about these other things that they never think about the whole situation, and the need for revival. So when we consider practice, we find that it is an extension of what I have just been saying. Take the increase in the element of entertainment in connection with religious work. Have you observed it? They now talk about the programme, not the order of service. And have you noticed the items in the programme? I must confess that increasingly, as I look at, and read about the programmes of certain meetings, I am reminded more of a variety performance than of anything else. And you will notice, if you keep your eye on the advertisements, that they are even using the terms. They say 'presented by' or 'sponsored by', or 'featuring' so and so. I have seen numerous advertisements like this – gatherings announced at such and such a place, and then 'featuring . . .'. We know where this terminology has come from, do we not? It is not from the Church of God – this whole idea of entertainment, with films and so on being used. We need to go back and read our history, we do not find this kind of thing in revival, it is the very opposite. This is the flesh, this is man, this is carnal. And, with regret, I feel I must add, so is the place that is given to singing these days.

I am no opponent of singing, we are to sing God's praises in psalms and hymns and spiritual songs. Yes, but again there is a sense of proportion even here. Have you not noticed how singing is becoming more and more prominent? People, Christian people, meet together to sing only. 'Oh,' they say, 'we do get a word in.' But the singing is the big thing. At a time like this, at an appalling time like this, with crime and violence, and sin, and perversions, God's name desecrated and the sanctities being spat upon, the whole state of the world surely says that this is not a time for singing, this is a time for preaching. I am reminded of the words of Wordsworth about Milton, 'Plain living, and high thinking are no more.' It is almost true of us to say plain speaking and high thinking are no more. We are just singing. We are wafting ourselves into some happy atmosphere. We sing together. My dear friends, this is no time for singing. 'How shall we sing the Lord's song in a strange land?' (Ps. 137.4). How can we take down our harps when Zion is as she is?

This is no time for singing, it is a time for thinking, for preaching, for conviction. It is a time for proclaiming the message of God and his wrath upon evil, and all our foolish aberrations. The time for singing will come later. Let the great revival come, let the windows of heaven be opened, let us see men and women by the thousands brought into the Kingdom of God, and then it will be time to sing. Let us beware of this subtle temptation to entertain the people, thinking that thereby we can attract them and save them, thinking that thereby we can keep ourselves happy. I know that this tendency is not as great in this country as it is in certain other countries. In some countries it is indeed appalling and alarming. I have even taken part myself in a religious conference – regarded as the greatest evangelical conference in the United States of America – where at the commencement of every service, which was meant to be biblical, and teaching, and uplifting, there was forty minutes of singing of various types and kinds. Xylophone solos, organ solos, people singing, all forty minutes of it. There was a short prayer, no Scripture reading at all, and then a brief time for the message. It is not like that in times of revival, believe me. And it will not be like that again when God graciously has mercy upon us, and looks upon us, and visits us. I ask you solemnly, is this a time for entertainment? Is it not a time, rather, for fasting, for sackcloth and ashes, for waiting upon God in an agony of soul? You cannot mix singing with that, these things do not go together.

And then let me mention another thing, which again in a sense, is a continuation of this same matter. Do you think that evangelism is the main thing at the present time? Or is it rather the life of the Church? Can we act on the assumption that all is well with the Church and, therefore, try to bring in people from the outside? I just ask you again to read the history, and you will find that revival always starts by something being done in the *Church*. It starts in the Church. You cannot revive something that is not there, you can only revive life which is drooping and languishing. And the order historically has been this: that something has happened to one man or a group of people in a church, and then, as a result of that, and the outpouring of God, mighty evangelism takes place. You start with a church, then it spreads outwards. But it seems to me that today we are ignoring the Church altogether, and that all the energy, and the money, and the enthusiam, is entirely in evangelism, and the Church remains where she was, unless, indeed, she is even getting worse. It is because her life is not being fed, and because she is being stimulated externally and on the surface all the time, and not being deepened, and not being made more spiritual. Read again the history, and you will find that the Church, the local unit, the gathering of God's saints, is always the place of the beginning. And it is only as you have a truly revived Church that mighty evangelism can take place. That is the story of revivals.

And that brings me to another heading under this general heading of defective orthodoxy. And now I refer, not so much to doctrine directly, nor even to practice directly, I am now thinking about the spirit. The spirit. It is a terrible thing, but you and I can be absolutely right and orthodox in doctrine and yet wrong in spirit. What are the manifestations of the wrong spirit? First and foremost, pride, pride of life. Is there anything more terrible than to be snobbish, to give great prominence to pride of position and pride of birth? Have these things any place in the Church of God? Read the second chapter of James' epistle, where he reprimands the early Christians severely for treating the man with the golden ring on his finger in a different manner from the way in which they treat the man in rags. Pride. Pride of life. There is nothing more opposed to the spirit of the lowly and the meek Jesus of Nazareth than that. God have mercy upon us.

But it does not stop merely at pride of life. Pride of knowledge is equally bad. 'Ah, yes, I'm the Christian that reads a lot. I am the man who knows the doctrine. I am the man who has read all the works of all the Puritans. That other person over there, he knows nothing about it.' Pride of knowledge. 'I am the great theologian. I am unlike that publican over there who has not got the brains, nor the understanding, to grasp these things.' Pride of knowledge, what an ugly thing this is also. 'Knowledge puffeth up'– of course it does. May God preserve us from it. If we are proud, in this sense, even as in the other, we have no right to expect dealings from the Spirit of God.

And pride of understanding. 'I have got it all. It is all plain to me, cut and dried. That other person knows nothing.' All right, I know that I need to speak on both sides. The other person very often almost boasts of his lack of understanding. When I say a thing like that, I always think of a man whom I once met. I was due to preach for a weekend in a certain town and he met me at the station, and then, before I had had time to say almost anything to him, he said, 'Well, of course, I am not one of the great people in this church, I am just, you know, a very ordinary, humble man. I am not a great theologian, I am not a great speaker. I do not take part in the prayer meeting, but you know I am just the man who carries the visiting preacher's bag.' 'Oh, what a wonderful man I am!' I thought. To be proud of your ignorance is as bad as to be proud of your knowledge and understanding. Any form of pride is hateful and offensive in the sight of God.

Other troubles in this matter of spirit, are these. Censoriousness. We are to speak the truth in love. We are to be guided by 1 Corinthians 13. We are all terrible sinners, are we not? We are all very guilty in this respect. We are censorious. There is all the difference in the world between a man carrying out the apostolic injunction to rebuke as well as to exhort, and that man being censorious. We must not be censorious.

Neither, to go on to another trouble, must we ever be contentious. Contentiousness is fatal. The history of revivals proves this very clearly. Even when you have had a revival, if the spirit of contention comes in, if men begin to divide on doctrines that are not absolutely essential to salvation, the Spirit is quenched. You find it in the eighteenth century, in the disputing between Wesley

65

and Whitefield, and their various followers. The work was arrested for a while. You had it in Wales. There was a dispute between Daniel Rowland and Howell Harris which went on from 1751 to 1763 and it was an arid and a barren period. Then they came together once more, and the Spirit came down again. Contentiousness is of the Devil.

Let us, then, be careful. We are told in the epistle of Jude to contend earnestly for the faith, and we must do this. If we do not we are sinning. We are set for the defence, as well as the propagation, of the gospel. And we must defend it, and contend for these doctrines that I have been enumerating, even unto blood if necessary. But that is not to be contentious. What is fatal is to be contentious, to develop a party spirit, to put up labels, and to be more concerned about the label than about the Lord Jesus Christ himself. That is contentiousness, like the man who always brings the same matter up the moment you meet him. It does not matter what you say about the glory of God and Christ's blood, he will say, 'Ah, but you have not emphasised this,' – something that he is particularly interested in, and which is not absolutely essential to salvation. Contentiousness.

We must always be careful about these things. It is because we are concerned about the truth that the Devil, in order to wreck it all, will press us beyond measure, and bring us into this position where we are quenching the Spirit. I could add pettiness and quarrelling, self-importance. You know the Christian Church is riddled with this sort of thing. And how can you expect the blessing of God upon it? I know churches, little churches, struggling to keep going, but the whole situation is ruined by pettiness, smallness, jealousy and envy, and self-importance. Then I can add to that triviality and busyness, instead of holiness and being concerned to be ready to be used of God. There is nothing that is so characteristic of every period of revival than a great and a profound seriousness.

Do not take my word for these things, read them for yourselves. Read again how, when the saintly Robert Murray McCheyne walked into his pulpit at Dundee, before he had opened his mouth, people would begin to weep and were broken down. Why? Well, there was a solemnity about the man. He had come from the presence of God. He did not trip into his pulpit lightly and crack a joke or two to put everybody at ease and to prepare the atmosphere. No, there was a radiance of God about him. There was a terrible seriousness. And if we believe in a holy God, and in the wrath of God upon sin, if we believe that without the gospel men and women are going to hell, how can we trifle, how can we be flippant and jocular? No, there is nothing that is so characteristic of revival as a great, and a deep, and a profound seriousness with respect to the things of God.

And lastly, we can be perfectly orthodox and yet our orthodoxy can be useless if we are failing in our lives, if we are disobedient to God's holy laws, if we are guilty of sin, and continuing in known sin. If we put our own desires before him, well, we have no right to expect revival, however orthodox and correct we may be in all our doctrines and in all our understanding. You will invariably find that when revival comes men and women are profoundly, and deeply, convicted of sin. They feel that even God cannot forgive them. They have been in the Church, yes, but they have been living a life of sin, and they have known it and they have done nothing about it. When revival comes they are put into hell, as it were, and they are horrified and alarmed. They may feel so terrible about it that they stand up and confess it. That may or may not happen, but they are certainly convicted. And so sin in any shape or form is ever one of the major hindrances to a visitation of the Spirit of God.

I have been dealing with what I have called defective or eccentric orthodoxy. May God give us grace to ponder these things, to meditate upon them, to consider them in the light of Scripture, and in the light of the history of revivals, and to apply the truth to ourselves.

Chapter 6

Genesis 26.17–18

And Isaac departed thence, and pitched his tent in the valley of Gerar, and dwelt there. And Isaac digged again the wells of water, which they had digged in the days of Abraham his father; for the Philistines had stopped them after the death of Abraham: and he called their names after the names by which his father had called them (Gen. 26.17–18).

We come now to another step in this matter of hindrances to revival, a step which, alas, again we have of necessity, to consider. I cannot think of a better description of this than the term 'dead' orthodoxy, and I suppose that the history of the Church throughout the centuries indicates quite clearly that this, of all dangers, is perhaps the greatest danger. Certainly it is the greatest danger confronting many of us at the present time. It is the greatest danger confronting the individual who is evangelical in his outlook, as it is indeed the greatest danger confronting any individual church or groups of churches, that can be described as evangelical. It is an appalling thought but it is nevertheless true, that there is such a thing as dead orthodoxy.

Let us then analyse what we mean by this, an analysis which is indeed painful, and yet is essential. What are the manifestations of this condition? First of all I would suggest that we look at it more or less in general, as an attitude, as a general condition. And I think that the word that sums up this condition most perfectly is the word contentment. I hesitate to use the word smugness, but perhaps we could put the two together and say a smug contentment. Now, by that expression I mean something like this: it is the condition of people who believe the truth, and know that they believe the truth. There is no question about that. You question them, you catechise them, and you will find that they are correct and orthodox. There is no fault to be found with their creed, or with their belief. But there is this element of contentment about it because they not only believe these things

68

but are satisfied with themselves – self-satisfied. They are the people who believe the truth, over and against the others who do not believe the truth, and who are not orthodox, the liberals, the people who used to be called modernists. Now of course, it is right to be orthodox, and the unorthodox are wrong, but the way in which we look at ourselves can be so terribly sad. It can ruin even the correctness of our belief if this element of smugness comes in, this feeling of contentment, and of satisfaction. As Job could not help saying to those friends who came to comfort him, 'No doubt but ye are the people' (Job 12.2). Now, it is the attitude that we see so perfectly illustrated there in those friends of Job. Oh, all they said was right, but it was of no use to poor Job, indeed, it was making his condition worse. And what he objected to in them was this very smug contentment which I am trying to describe.

And, still another way in which this attitude manifests itself is that the main concern is, of course, defensive. Seeing that we are right, as we certainly are, the only thing we have to do, is to defend our position. So you will find that an individual, or a church, that is guilty of this state, spends most of the time purely on the defensive. What is called apologetics becomes very prominent. It becomes the main interest. The books which are published and which are read by such people are almost invariably apologetic. Defending the position, you see. Now, I believe that this is a very serious and important matter, and if I were asked to give an opinion on the state of evangelicalism, for about the last eighty years, I would say that this has been its greatest characteristic. It has withdrawn itself, as it were, and has erected some kind of iron curtain, or protective mechanism, and most of the energy has been given to defence, to apologetics. And it is so pathetic to notice the way in which almost anything is clutched at and used. If any sort of man who is prominent in society, even hints vaguely that he believes the Christian faith, he is taken hold of at once – he becomes the great Christian – and rumours circulate as to profound spiritual experiences in the royal family and others. We are always defending our position. And great is the interest, the excitement, the energy given to that. It is a defensive and a negative attitude, and it is a part of this dead orthodoxy which is content simply with maintaining its own position.

There is another term that is used in the Scripture to define this. And that is the condition of being 'at ease in Zion' – you remember that expression in the book of the prophet Amos chapter 6 verse 1? This is the description, it seems to me, of people who are anxious to have sufficient religion to make them feel safe, but who require nothing beyond that. They are out for safety and they want some kind of security. There is always, after all, that great fact of death in the distance, and what lies beyond. And there are many people who become interested in religion for this reason only. They are not interested in the thing itself, they have no real positive desire after God, but they have got this very definite negative interest in safety. These are the people whom we may describe as being interested in religion only as a kind of parachute. You never know when it may be needed, accidents may take place. So it is very good to have this mechanism at hand. Ah, but you must not spend the whole of your life thinking about it. You must not be too serious, you must not be too concerned about this, though it is good to have it. So while you give the main part of your life, and your interest to things that belong to this world, you just make this provision in case of need. Just enough religion to make you feel safe, but no more than that.

Then, of course, this leads, in turn, to something else. And I think you will recognise the description as I go along. Such people are always very fond of what you may describe as 'general messages'. They do not want anything too particular, they want a little general uplift. They want something that, in general, is going to help them. So what they like is something that is interesting. They are interested in general ideas. Religion, they feel, does provide a good outlook on life. True – but you do not want too much of it, so you confine yourself to general ideas and thoughts. You say, 'How interesting. How uplifting.' And then, of course, they like quotations from literature. 'How beautiful, and how wonderful it is.' Now I am trying to give you a description of what I would call late Victorian and Edwardian religion, speaking very generally. And, alas, it has persisted: 'We have got our religion; we feel it is all right.'

So then, what do we do when we come to go into God's house? Well, we do not preach on the great doctrines of salvation. 'No,' they say, 'we are interested in character studies – tremendously interesting. We take these Bible characters and we go through them leisurely. And how entertaining it is! It is almost as good as a novel. Nothing to disturb us, of course. We are looking on at men like Abraham or Isaac. It is interesting to see these characters, and their differences and so on.' You look up literature of the end of the last century and the beginning of this, and you will find that there were endless books published just along this line.

Character study, studies in this and that, which are typical of this leisurely approach to the Bible. And it is all so general and so remote, all so interesting, so far removed from us and our problems. That is the kind of thing that has been so common.

But next to this I must put, of necessity, a dislike of being searched and of being disturbed. The teaching must always be general, I say. It must always be remote. It must always be far away from us somewhere. It must never come too near to us. I have often quoted that statement of Lord Melbourne, Queen Victoria's first Prime Minister, who expressed all this so perfectly when he said, 'You know things have come to a pretty pass if religion is going to start being personal.' That is it. Religion is all right, it is something general, it is something there in the background which I am going to turn to and make use of when I need it, but it must not disturb me. Oh, this is all in the Old Testament. The people cried out to the prophets and said, 'Speak unto us smooth things'.

Read the Old Testament, and you will find that the false prophets were always much more popular than the true prophets. Poor Jeremiah, how he suffered at their hands. He was not the only one. Why were the false prophets so popular? Well, is it not obvious, their message was this: they said, 'Peace, peace,' when there was no peace. The charge brought against them was that 'They have healed also the hurt of the daughter of my people slightly, saying Peace, peace; when there is no peace' (Jer. 6.14) – these preachers and prophets who gave people the impression that all was well with them, that they were God's people, that they had nothing to worry about. But the true prophet came, and he searched, and he probed, and he condemned, and he rebuked. And they said, 'Who is this fellow?' If I may say so in passing, the thing that has given me greatest pleasure, and greatest encouragement of all the things I have ever been told that people say about my ministry, is this. It was said by a lady, who remonstrated, and said, 'This man preaches to us as if we were sinners!' Quite so. You see, you must not be searched, you must not be examined, you are all right. Of course, denounce those sinners who are outside, or those liberals, but, why, we are the people who are orthodox! We do not need that, we need instruction. We want these general lectures, these addresses, these character studies. How interesting, how nice. But we must not be disturbed. There is nothing wrong with us. And so such people, as you see everywhere in the Bible and in the history of the Church, have always disliked anything that searches them, or makes them feel uncomfortable, or probes them.

And, therefore, I bring it finally to this point. There is nothing vital in the religion and in the worship of such people. They expect nothing, and they get nothing, and nothing happens to them. They go to God's house, not with the idea of meeting with God, not with the idea of waiting upon him, it never crosses their minds, or enters into their hearts that something may happen in a service. No, we always do this on Sunday morning. It is our custom. It is our habit. It is a right thing to do. But the idea that God may suddenly visit his people, and descend upon them, the whole thrill of being in the presence of God, and sensing his nearness, and his power, never even enters their imaginations. The whole thing is formal, it is this smug contentment. I heard a man once describe such people in this way: he said, 'They give me the impression that as they go to their churches, they are really just paying a morning call on the Almighty.' It is the right, and the correct thing to do. And they believe in doing it. Ah, yes, but there is no conception that God may suddenly meet with them, and that something tremendous may happen. We must examine ourselves. Do we go to God's house expecting something to happen? Or do we go just to listen to a sermon, and to sing our hymns, and to meet with one another? How often does this vital idea enter into our minds that we are in the presence of the living God, that the Holy Spirit is in the Church, that we may feel the touch of his power? How much do we think in terms of coming together to meet with God, and to worship him, and to stand before him, and to listen to him? Is there not this appalling danger that we are just content because we have correct beliefs? And we have lost the life, the vital thing, the power, the thing that really makes worship worship, which is in Spirit and truth.

Well, there are some of the manifestations of this dead ortho-doxy, which I have summed up under a general heading of a state of contentment, a smug contentment.

But let us look at it from a slightly different angle. The second characteristic of this dead orthodoxy – and it follows, of course, directly from the first – is a dislike of enthusiasm. Now, this is a most important subject. If you like it in more biblical terms, I could put it like this: it is to be guilty of quenching the Spirit. Dislike of enthusiasm is to quench the Spirit. Those who are familiar with the history of the Church, and in particular with the history of revivals, will know that this charge of enthusiasm is the one that has always been brought against people who have been most active in a period of revival. Some of you may have seen and read the book written by Ronald Knox, called *Enthusiasm*. The whole thesis of that book is that you have periods of enthusiasm, which he regards as aberrations! With his cold intellectual detachment he does not like enthusiasm.

Now, as I say, it has been a common accusation throughout history. Read, for instance, the stories of the men of the eighteenth century. A charge that George Whitefield constantly had to answer and rebuff at the hand of bishops was this charge of enthusiasm. They said, 'Look here, we're not objecting so much to your doctrine, it is the way you are preaching it, it is the way you are doing it.' John Wesley was constantly charged in the same way, even by his own mother, Susannah Wesley. Why could he not preach like everybody else? What was he so excited about? Why all this disturbance? Susannah Wesley was a very godly woman, but she could not understand this son of hers, who suddenly had become an enthusiast. One of the things that comes out very clearly as you read the literature of that eighteenth century in terms of the Christian Church, is that this charge was constantly brought forward.

So, then, we must look at this subject, because clearly this opposition to what is called enthusiasm, can be one of the greatest hindrances of all to revival. And it is the particular danger of people who are in a state of dead orthodoxy. I admit freely that it is an extremely difficult subject. There are certain lines that are very, very difficult to draw. And yet we must of necessity do this. The Bible compels us, and so does the history of the Church. And, fortunately for us, it is a subject that is dealt with in the Scriptures so we are not left without some guidance in forming our opinions. Read 1 Corinthians 14 for yourselves because that is the very subject with which the Apostle was dealing there. And the moment you get a revival, then this becomes the important chapter, and you have to go to it at once, because life has come in and you have got the problems of exuberance, or excessive manifestations of uncontrolled life and living.

So, as we look at the state and the condition of the Church today we must take hold of this teaching to see where we stand. Now as I understand the matter, there are two great principles laid down in the New Testament for our help and guidance. The line is rather difficult to draw, but it is here. The first principle is that everything must be done decently and in order (1 Cor. 14.40). But there is another statement: 'Quench not the Spirit' (1 Thess. 5.19). So we must now look at these two positions, so clearly found in the New Testament, and see what it is that characterises each one of them.

First, then, 'Let everything be done decently and in order.' That is written to people who were guilty of certain things and one of those things was confusion. There was a great deal of confusion in the church of Corinth, and it arose from the fact that sometimes they were all speaking together. They had got excited about this question of speaking in tongues, they were not looking at it in a scriptural manner, and they were all speaking at the same time. And they were prophesying, two or three talking at the same time. And the Apostle said that this was quite wrong: 'God is not the author of confusion, but of peace' (1 Cor. 14.33). He says if strangers should come in, and see you all like this, they would come to one conclusion only. You remember how he puts it: 'Will they not say that ye are mad?' (14.23). That is no testimony for the gospel. If all are speaking at the same time, and people do not know how to listen in a controlled manner, 'Why,' says the Apostle in effect, This is sheer confusion, and the whole gospel is brought into disrepute. Look out upon nature and creation, and what you see above everything else is order. God is not the author of confusion, but of peace.'

And yet, there are genuine Christian people, who no doubt have had a very real experience and an experience of the power of the Spirit, who almost seem to have got into the condition in which they regard confusion as the hallmark of Christianity, and feel that unless they are all shouting together at the same time, the Spirit is not present. But it is sheer confusion. So they need to read 1 Corinthians 14, and to observe how the Apostle tells them that they must speak one at a time. And if the first man realises that another brother has something to say, he must stop and give the second brother the opportunity.

'But, ah,' these people will always reply, 'we cannot help ourselves. It is the Spirit that is in us. We cannot control ourselves.' And then the Apostle utters this profound word to them. He says, ' . . . the spirits of the prophets are subject to the prophets' (14.32). So if a man ever tells us that he is so filled with the Spirit that he cannot contain himself, but must always be shouting, we say, 'The spirits of the prophets are subject to the prophets.' And as long as a man can control himself, he must do so, and he must make an effort to do so. There must be no confusion. Confusion always brings the gospel into disrepute.

Then I must mention a second element which comes with the first one, and that is excitement, or a false sense of joy. Now that can be purely of the flesh. There are many things that can excite people. Listen to a broadcast of a football match, and there you will hear it; excitement, animal excitement. The shouting, until they lose their very voices in their shouts. It is entirely of the flesh. Now that can come into the realm of worship and of religion. And again there are some people who seem to think that this is necessary, and they deliberately work it up, try to produce it. They get people into an excited state in which they do not know what they are doing, imagining that they are very happy, but it is of the flesh. It is a false joy. And so the Apostle gave that injunction to the members of the church at Corinth, that they must do these things properly. One has a psalm, another a spiritual song, and another a word of prophecy. 'Let everything be done decently and in order.' says the great Apostle.

And then the third element is emotionalism. You notice I am not saying emotion, I am saying emotionalism. And there is all the difference in the world between those two things. Emotionalism is a state and a condition in which the emotions have run riot. The emotions are in control. They are in a kind of ecstasy. And if emotionalism is bad, how much worse is a deliberate attempt to produce it. So any effort which deliberately tries to work up the emotions, whether by singing, or incantation, or anything else, or, as you get it in primitive people, in various dances and things like that, all this, of course, is just condemned by the New Testament. The mere playing on the emotions is never right. It is something which is condemned right through the Bible. The emotions are to be approached through the understanding, through the mind, by truth. And any direct assault upon the emotions is, of necessity, false and is inevitably bound to produce trouble. So emotionalism, and especially any artificially produced emotionalism, is undoubtedly a great hindrance to revival, because it brings it all into disrepute.

The history of revivals is most interesting on this very subject. Is is often the first thing that is said against a revival: 'This is sheer emotionalism. Look at the confusion, this is just animal excitement, people are beside themselves, this is mass hysteria.' These are the charges that always have been brought and always will be brought. And that is why the New Testament tells us to prove all things, and to hold fast only to that which is good. I am again quoting from 1 Thessalonians 5:21. The same problem was to be found in the church at Thessalonica. Here were people who had been filled with the Spirit, and these things tended to manifest themselves. I hope later to deal with the reasons why that tends to happen. I am merely noting it as a fact at the moment. So the Apostle says, 'Look here, prove all things, test the spirits', try them, make sure that this is the Holy Spirit, and that it is not merely the flesh, or the Devil working at the flesh to counterfeit the true, and thereby to bring the whole thing to disrepute in the eyes of the people. There, in general, it seems to me, is the interpretation of the injunction, 'Let everything be done decently and in order.' It is an apostolic injunction, and we must hold on to it come what may. But we must also hold on to the next.

'Quench not the Spirit.' What does this mean? Now some people in the Church are very clear about that first one, that everything be done decently and in order. Why, they are experts on it. The trouble is that they are so clear on that that they are guilty of quenching the Spirit. In their reaction from the false they have gone to another position which is equally false. What do I mean? Well, take that fear of confusion, for instance. That is no danger as far as these people are concerned, is it? Their position is that everything is perfectly controlled, everything is nice, orderly, correct, formal, and above all respectable. If you take certain churches and consider them in the light of the New Testament epistles, you will see the difference. They do not need whole tracts of the New Testament because their churches are in this formal, dead, and utterly respectable position. It is very interesting to observe certain things from the historical standpoint. You will always observe that when forms of service become formal, the Spirit is less in evidence, and you move further away from the New Testament. The very characteristic of the New Testament Church was this sponteneity, this life, this living quality, this vivacity. But, as you fall away from the Spirit and his influence, everything becomes formal. So you have forms of service. You will find that the Church in every period of declension becomes much more formal in her services, she adopts forms of service and she tends to turn to liturgy, and to ritual. All this is a part of formal religion.

But, on the other hand, every time you get a revival you find all that kind of thing stopping. You come back to the simplicity of the New Testament. The contrast, if I may put it without being at all offensive, is between a cathedral service and a service with the Lord Jesus Christ sitting in a boat by the lakeside, or these people meeting in one another's houses in Corinth, Thessalonica, Rome, and everywhere else. That is the contrast. No pomp, no ceremony, no ritual, no processions, no vestments, no dressing up. No, but a freedom of the Spirit and things happening. And the people singing out of their hearts. That is what you get in every period of awakening and of revival. When the Church is not in revival there is an emphasis upon choirs, and not merely choirs, but paid choirs, and paid quartets and soloists in the choirs. And the congregation just sits, or stands and listens, and the choir even does the singing for them. This is quenching the Spirit. There is no need to say to such people, 'Let everything be done decently and in order.' That is their one concern.

Furthermore, have you not noticed the appalling tendency in the life of the Church today to have programmes? Everything is mapped out. I know that up to a point these things have to be done, but surely we are in danger of quenching the Spirit. Every item is put down, and the time is put by it. A man starts at this point, he ends at another. My friends in the ministry tell me that they find this more and more as they go round preaching in different churches from Sunday to Sunday. I am now repeatedly told that even in evangelical churches the visiting minister is handed an order of service paper, and it is literally put down before him. Eleven o'clock – Scripture sentences, and then on through the list with everything timed up to twelve noon – Benediction. To me, this is very serious. I know that there is no merit in long sermons as such. There is no point in length for the sake of length, but that is not the question. The question is, are we giving the Holy Spirit an opportunity? Are we so tied by our programmes that he is excluded? Why this formality? Why this tying down of everything? What if the Spirit should suddenly come? I do commend this matter to you very seriously.

For what it is worth, if it is of any interest to anybody, this is my main reason for not preaching on the radio. I once asked one of the religious directors, 'What would happen to your programmes if the Holy Spirit suddenly took over?' And he was honest enough to admit that really that question had never entered their minds. Of course not. They are tied to their programmes. I can understand it in an official matter like that where you must have exact timing. What I am concerned about is that that element should come into the Christian Church. It is coming into this country. You have had it for years in the United States of America, everything to the minute, the technique, all produced to order. As I have said before, it does indeed remind one of some kind of performance, put forward with slickness and everything to the second, always at the same point. I ask, in the name of God, where is there room for the freedom of the Spirit? No, in this way we are controlling our religion instead of being controlled by

77

it. And believe me, when a revival comes we shall experience what has always been experienced, we shall be taken out of time, we shall forget time. We may start our service at the usual time, but God alone knows when it will end. The freedom of the Spirit! In being afraid of confusion, we can go to the other extreme of quenching the Holy Spirit of God.

And then, take this question of the fear of artificial excitement and false joy. Again we can be so afraid of these things, that we can become guilty of quenching the Spirit. Let me put this in terms of an incident which happened in my own experience. During my holidays, a few years ago, I went to a church service in a certain place on a Sunday morning. Good congregation, devout people, absolutely orthodox, with a man of God preaching. His text was, 'the rainbow in the cloud'. Glorious, 'the rainbow in the cloud'. But that poor man was so afraid of a false joy that the whole of his sermon was given to the false joy, and the dangers of a false peace. I am not criticising my brother, we are all fallible. But you see, the effect it left upon me was that there was nothing there but the cloud, and we could not see the rainbow. He was so afraid of the false that he quenched the true. We are people of extremes, and we swing the pendulum violently. And there are churches that are orthodox, but absolutely dead, because they are so afraid of false excitement, and the excesses of certain spiritual movements, that they quench and hinder the Spirit and deny the true.

My last point is that in our fear of emotionalism, some of us may be in grave danger of banishing emotions altogether. Oh, there may be plenty of sentiment, but I am not talking about sentiment. Sentiment is weak and flabby. Sentiment is that which a hard man puts on to persuade himself that he still has some feeling within him. No, we do not want sentiment, sickly, maudlin sentiment, we want emotion, that God-given quality. When did you last weep because of your distance from God? Some of us have forgotten how to weep, my friends. When did we last weep for joy, out of sheer joy and the sense of the glory of God? Many of us are afraid of emotions. Our whole training and upbringing, the whole attitude to life, is one that curbs the emotions. We feel that it is not quite respectable, it is not nice. We are steeling our emotions, curbing this God-given thing. It is true of many branches of life today. That, perhaps, is why you no longer have many great preachers. Eloquence is distrusted. Everything is just conversation, and casual, and you must not have fervour, and you must not be moved, and you must not allow anybody to move you, and nobody must be moved at all. Everything must be a quiet statement. You must even talk about the cross of Christ quietly. You must speak about the glory of the Lord, and being filled with the Spirit, quietly, with an absence of emotion. Some people are so afraid of emotionalism that there is an absence of a true, and a healthy, and a God-given emotion amongst them.

What is it all due to? I believe it is due to a pseudo-intellectualism, a false sense of what is respectable and I am profoundly convinced that this may be one of the greatest hindrances to revival. You see, we pride ourselves on our learning. In effect, we think, 'Of course, our forefathers had revivals because they lacked our control, and our discipline, they were not educated as we are. They were crude and primitive. And so you can still get revivals amongst such people, but not amongst us. We are intellectual.' God have mercy upon us. One of the greatest intellects that this world has ever known was the Apostle Paul. But look at him as he is moved by a grand sweep of emotion. He starts off on a point, but suddenly he names Christ, and he is lost. He forgets what he is saying, and he burst out into his magnificent eloquence. And then he comes back to his point again. Disorder, if you like, inconsistencies, anacolutha, use your terms. Yes, but it is the glory of the man; this giant intellect, who could be moved by the truth, moved to tears. I read of George Whitefield, preaching, and as he was preaching about the glories of grace and of salvation, the tears were pouring down his cheeks, and those who listened to him were weeping too. It is true of all these men, yet we may be so hard and so intellectual and so controlled. This is not a plea for emotionalism, which I have denounced, it is a plea for emotion. God save us from being so afraid of the false that we quench the Spirit of God, and become so respectable, and so pseudo-intellectual that the Spirit of God is kept back, and we go on in our dryness and aridity, and in our comparative futility, and helplessness, and uselessness. Oh, let us consider these two great propositions of the New Testament. 'Let everything be done decently and in order', certainly, but in the name of God, quench not the Spirit, despise not prophesyings, and let us come to God's house in freedom, ever expecting the power to descend upon us, and to have an experience of God and of Christ that will melt us, and move us, and break us, and make us forget ourselves. Let us approximate a little more closely to the Church as she is depicted in the pages of the New Testament. 'Quench not the Spirit.' Despise not prophesyings, but at the same time prove all things, and hold fast to that which is good.

Chapter 7

Genesis 26.17–18

And Isaac departed thence, and pitched his tent in the valley of Gerar, and dwelt there. And Isaac digged again the wells of water, which they had digged in the days of Abraham his father; for the Philistines had stopped them after the death of Abraham: and he called their names after the names by which his father had called them (Gen. 26.17–18).

We remain still with the account of Isaac and the wells because we have found this old story to be a very true picture of our search for the living water of revival. As a result of the work of the Philistines, the wells are choked, and we have dealt with much of the rubbish – a lack of orthodoxy, defective orthodoxy and now, let me remind you, we are examining the problem of dead orthodoxy.

So, then, what are the other manifestations of this condition? Well, one is a failure to apply the truth. It is one thing to believe the truth, it is a very different thing to apply it. We did listen, and apply the truth, initially, otherwise we would not be Christians at all. But it is possible for us, once we have done the initial thing, to go on, content with just listening to, or reading the truth, and never applying it to ourselves, or examining ourselves in the light of it. Is this not one of the most alarming possibilities in the Christian life? We may go regularly to our church, Sunday by Sunday. We may read the Bible, and we may read books which help us to understand the Bible. And ever and again we are disturbed, we feel a sense of conviction, we feel the rightness of what is put before us and we are aware of an inadequacy within ourselves, but unfortunately we do nothing about it. The feeling comes and then it goes. As the prophet Hosea puts it, 'Your goodness is as a morning cloud, and as the early dew it goeth away' (Hos. 6.4) – it appears, it vanishes. This is, it seems to me, one of the most terrible dangers in connection with the Christian life as a whole; that we are content with a surface disturbance, but never really face it, never really get down to the situation, and to the problem. We never proceed to consider this disturbance, and to say, 'Well now, what is this, and what can I do about it?'

I believe, too, this is one of the greatest dangers afflicting all congregations. We may feel something during the service, and we may say, 'I am going to deal with that.' But then, going out of the service we start talking to people, and we talk about other things, what we felt in the meeting is gone, and it never comes back. In this way we spend our lives, aware of superficial temporary disturbances, which never lead to anything at all. I must not stay with this. But it does seem to me that that was the essential trouble with the Children of Israel, as we find their condition depicted in the writings of the prophets of the Old Testament. They would feel slight disturbances, and the false prophets would heal them too quickly – and we are all false prophets with respect to ourselves. That is one manifestation of this failure to apply the truth.

But I would put it in another way. Is there not a general tendency to neglect altogether the art of meditation, the art of real thinking? As one reads the story of the Church, and especially as one reads the story of the Church in better periods, when God's people and God's cause counted mightily in this land, as one reads about the Church in general, and the individual biographies of Christian people, one cannot but be struck by the extraordinary contrast beween them and ourselves. Meditation played such a big part in their lives. They would spend hours thinking, meditating, ruminating, if you like, upon the word. But this is something that has almost disappeared. And our excuse, of course, is that we are all too busy. And we *are* too busy. Our whole lives are cluttered up with things that finally will not matter at all. Our programmes are so full. 'We haven't got time,' we say. And you can be so busy in the work even of the Christian Church that you are doing great harm to your soul. You can become superficial and dry, and eventually useless. No, meditation is absolutely essential. There is a line in a well-known hymn which puts it perfectly: 'Take time to be holy. . . .' And you have got to take time to be holy. But we today are rushing hither and thither, full of activities, and our Christian spiritual life is so superficial. Of course on paper it may look very wonderful. And the religious journals will report it. They are only interested in activities, because it is what they call news. Somebody is doing something, that is news. Meditation is something that you can not put into your news columns, it is too deep, it is not sufficiently spectacular. But the way to test the Christian life is by depth, by true understanding, which is only obtained by meditation, and by thought. And this is a part of the discipline of the Christian life. And you will find that it is invariably present in time of true revival.

Then let us go on to consider another matter, which follows from that. Meditation always leads to true self-examination. But today self-examination is not popular. There are those who would even teach that self-examination is wrong. 'No,' they say, 'you must not do that, you must always be looking to the Lord.' And they say that in a wrong way. Of course, our whole life ultimately is a life of looking to the Lord, but not at the expense of self-examination. The Scriptures exhort us to examine ourselves, to test ourselves, to prove our own selves. And, I must say that once more, the literature of the past brings this out so clearly. Read the life of any man who has ever been used of God in a signal manner in connection with revival, and you will always find that he was a man who had examined himself, and had become alarmed about himself. It has always been the thing that has led him to God and to prayer – his astonishment at himself. But if we do not examine ourselves we will never truly pray, and our lives will be lived entirely on the surface. Now, how little we hear about self-examination! Oh, we believe in having a quiet time, a short reading of Scripture, a hurried prayer, and we have done everything. But where is self-examination? How much talk is there about mortification of the flesh – mortification of our members that are on the earth? These are the apostolic injunctions: 'Mortify therefore your members which are upon the earth' (Col.3.5). 'If ye through the Spirit do mortify the deeds of the body . . .' (Rom.8.13). These are Paul's instructions, but we never hear about these things. It is because we have a false notion concerning sanctification, and, again, we say, 'We are looking to the Lord.' And thus our life is lived entirely on the surface. It is not only lacking in depth, it is lacking in a true, and a vital holiness. These are but aspects of this failure to apply the truth.

But to balance the truth and to put it fairly I must go on to say that while it is probably true of the majority that they do not believe in self-examination at all, and do not do it, there are some who are guilty of a faulty self-examination. And this can be equally bad. There are those who are guilty of a dead orthodoxy, because of a misapplied self-examination. There is a wrong way of examining ourselves, as well as a right way. The right way, of course, is the one that is indicated in the Scriptures, and that always leads to a good result; the wrong way leads to morbidity and to a false introspection. This is a very subtle matter, but there are many good people, today, in the Christian Church, who are absolutely orthodox, who do take time, and are concerned about self-examination, yes, but they are utterly paralysed, and they are quite useless, because, in a sense, they do nothing else. They simply spend the whole of their time in examining themselves. They look inwards, and they dwell upon their own unworthiness, and they are so conscious of all their sins, and their unworthiness, that they never do anything. Their whole time is taken up about their condition. Indeed, they are so busy examining themselves, and they are so depressed as a result of doing it, that they have no time to pray for revival or for anything else. They are always praying about their own souls, and their own personal condition.

Now, obviously this is quite wrong, and it is quite as bad as the superficial kind of life that never examines itself at all. So we can lay down as a principle that the Christian should never be spiritually depressed and miserable, never. A miserable Christian is a contradiction in terms. The Christian has no right to be depressed in this way. So why are people so often in this condition? It seems to me that the answer is that they are not examining themselves in the light of the Scriptures. For if you follow the scriptural method you will do something like this: you will allow the truth to search you; you will apply it to yourself; you will preach to yourself; you will talk to yourself; you will meditate about these things. You will bring yourself under conviction, and you will not let yourself escape. But you do not stop at that. Having thus found your true condition, you will allow the Scriptures to lead you to the Lord Jesus Christ, and to the cleansing of his blood. In other words, any Christian who is depressed and morbid, and introspective is really failing to apply the doctrine of justification by faith only. If you stop in your sins, if you stop in the dust and the ashes and in the sackcloth, I say, you are not scriptural. You must go on from that and look to him, and apply again the truth to yourself. You must be certain that you end in a condition of thanksgiving and praise, with a realisation that your sins are covered and blotted out, and that you are renewed, and that you are able to go forward.

You see how subtle all this is. But is it not true at the present time? There are many who are not praying for revival because they are living such a superficial life. They do not even see the need of revival. They are busy, and active, and they are rushing here and there. There is no time to think about revival. All is well, they say. Look at it – at the appearance, on the surface. They are not aware of their real condition, as I am going to show you. But then there are these others who are so morbidly self-centred and turned in upon themselves that really they have no time to think of anybody else. In this way, you see, the absence of self-examination, or a faulty self-examination, can both lead to this condition of dead orthodoxy.

But let us turn to something else which is more positive, and which I do want to emphasise chiefly at this point. I would put it thus as a heading. Dead orthodoxy is commonly guilty of a failure to realise the glorious possibilities of the Christian life, and it therefore leads to a consequent failure to realise our own poverty. I am talking about the failure to realise the possibilities of the Christian life in this present world. I mean the kind of thing that the Apostle Paul writes about towards the end of Ephesians 3. I urge you to read some of these great verses. The Apostle says that he is praying for the Ephesians. They have believed the gospel for some time; they have been sealed by the Spirit.

They are fine Christian people, but he is praying this for them:

That he would grant you, according to the riches of his glory, to be strengthened with might by his Spirit in the inner man; that Christ may dwell in your hearts by faith; that ye, being rooted and grounded in love, may be able to comprehend with all saints what is the breadth, and length, and depth, and height; and to know the love of Christ, which passeth knowledge, that ye might be filled with all the fulness of God.' (Eph.3.16–19).

That is what I mean.

I mean also what Paul had in mind in Philippians 3. Here is his position. He says his concern is that he may:

Be found in him, not having mine own righteousness, which is of the law, but that which is through the faith of Christ, the righteousness which is of God by faith: that I may know him [says this man who knew him so well] and the power of his resurrection, and the fellowship of his sufferings, being made conformable unto his death (Phil.3.9–10).

There are what you may call the heights and depths of this Christian life – the possibilities open to the Christian in this present world. And you find that, not only in the Scriptures, but, let me repeat, as you read the biographies of the saints, as you read the stories of what happens to people in a time of revival, you find yourself reading of people who have realised these possibilities. They have come into an intimate knowledge of God, and of the Lord Jesus Christ. They know what it is to be visited by them, they know what it is to be raptured by their presence. There is a story of an old Puritan who had an experience once when he was walking over a mountainside. It was a barren road, and he sat down by a well to drink a little water with the bread that he carried in his pocket as his meal. And there, suddenly, the Lord Jesus Christ came to him, and gave him manifestations of himself. And this man said that he learnt more during that one brief experience than he had learned in fifty years of reading, and studying, and of meditation. That is always a possibility.

You find it again as you read the history of revival. You hear of people talking about these communications, and about their dealings with God and with the Lord Jesus Christ, the realisations of his presence, the manifestations of his love; of being almost overwhelmed by a sense of the nearness of the Lord Jesus Christ, of being filled with a sense of God's glory and of his love. You will find this in the lives of people like Jonathan Edwards and, as I constantly point out, of Christians of all shades of theological opinion. You find it in Whitefield, in Wesley; you find it in the lives of men like Finney or Moody and in the lives of many saints.

Are we experiencing these things ourselves? Do we realise that these are possibilities? Revival, as we shall see more and more, is God making himself manifest in this living way. But this is possible apart from revival. This can happen to the individual. Why do we not know these things? Why are we not thirsting, and longing, and yearning, for them? I think I can give a partial explanation. It is because we are so like the people in the church at Laodicea. This is what is said to them, you remember, by the risen Lord, 'Because thou sayest, I am rich, and increased with goods, and have need of nothing; and knowest not that thou art wretched, and miserable, and poor, and blind, and naked' (Rev.3.17). And, you know, that is the condition of the Church today. I am speaking even of many evangelical people, and evangelical churches. We are poor, and naked, and wretched, and miserable, and blind, and we do not know it. We say in effect, 'We are the evangelical people, we are all right.' But are we all right? It does not help to examine ourselves in the light of those who are obviously wrong, that is a very simple thing to do, and it may persuade us that we are 'all right'. Like the Laodiceans, we have got everything. But what have we really got? No, I fear that the trouble with us is that we are blind to our true spiritual state and condition. Alas, we will persist in examining ourselves in the light of activities. And if we are busy, we imagine all is well. But, my dear friend, the test of a Christian is not his busyness and his activity, it is his knowledge of God, it is his knowledge of the Lord Jesus Christ. It is not difficult to be busy, but when you try to realise his presence, you will soon discover that you have got to give time to this.

Or, if I may put it another way, I believe it is partly due to the fact that in a sense we are much too concerned with ourselves rather than being concerned with him. There is a teaching which has been very popular for a number of years and which is put perfectly in the title of a famous book, *The Christian's Secret of a Happy Life**. That is the controlling outlook. What must I do to be happy? Oh, but that is not the question. It should be the 'Christian's Secret of a Life with God', the Christian secret of the knowledge of God. What I should aim at is not simply that I be delivered from certain sins that worry me. Of course they should be got rid of, but the thing to be concerned about is not even that. It is, 'That I may know him, and the power of his resurrection, and the fellowship of his sufferings . . .' (Phil.3.10). Yes, says Paul, 'Not as though I had already attained . . .' (v.12). *Paul* saying that? He is dissatisfied, because, you see, his standard was not his happiness, but the possibilities of knowing the Lord, and the power of his resurrection, and the fellowship of his sufferings. We are too subjective, self-centred, concerned just about ourselves, wanting to get rid of our little problems. You may feel that you are free from problems, but the question I would ask you is this – to what extent do you know him? Do you know much about the breadth, and the length, and the depth, and the height of his love? Is it your greatest desire to know the love of Christ, which passeth knowledge, and to be filled with all the fulness of God? When did you last test yourself by that standard? That is the question. If we are not testing ourselves by these standards, though we may be orthodox, we are dead.

And another element, it seems to me, in this, is that in a most extraordinary way we seem to be excluding experience altogether. The slogan is, 'Take it by faith.' Of course, that is essential in your conversion – justification by faith only. And it is right to say to someone at that point, 'Believe this word. Risk your all upon it. Trust yourself to it.' That is a correct initial statement to make,

*By Mrs Pearsall Smith.

86

but you must not stop at that. You then say to him, 'Now, that is all you do at this moment. But if you do that you will be given an experience, an assurance, and you will know for certain.' But so often that second step is left out today, and many people teach that experiences do not matter. 'Do not worry about your feelings,' we are told, right through the whole of the Christian life. From beginning to end it is, 'Take it by faith, do not worry about your experiences.' They say it almost in a patronising way. 'There are some people,' they add, 'who talk about great experiences, but that is not great faith. You know real faith is a man who believes, though he has felt nothing.'

Well, as I say, that is all right at a preliminary stage, but if you have never felt anything, if you have never had any experience, I say it is not faith, it is mere intellectual assent, and intellectual belief. Because the whole of the Bible teaches experiences of God. And we are meant to experience God. We are meant to *know* him, not simply to believe, and to go on 'holding to our beliefs,' and 'taking it by faith'. That is only the first step, and it is to be followed by a realisation, by an understanding. And I feel that it is this error at this point that accounts for so much of dead orthodoxy, and is such a grievous hindrance to revival.

Let me sum it up like this: I am not interested in experiences as such. I am not saying that men and women should simply seek experiences. No, what I am saying is, seek God, seek to know God, seek to know his love, seek to be filled with this knowledge, and all the fulness of God. No, not the experience itself, but to experience him, and to know him. These men of the Bible knew him. They spoke to him. They realised his presence. So have all the others whose lives I have been quoting to you. But this seems to have vanished out of our whole conception and I suggest that this may be because we have become so afraid of false experiences that we are shutting out experience altogether. We are so afraid of certain excesses that we are guilty even of quenching the Spirit. This is a painful matter – I am saying it to myself as well – but the trouble with all of us is that we are much too healthy. Humility is not frequently observed today. A bouncing superficial self-confidence is the order of the day, not meekness, humility, mourning for sins and a consciousness of unworthiness and imperfection. No, we are resting on our oars. We are satisfied.

Oh, how unlike the Apostle Paul we are. You remember what he says: 'Forgetting the things which are behind. . . .' They are wonderful things. Go over his story again, remind yourself of it. But what does he say? 'Forgetting those things which are behind, and reaching forth unto those things which are before, I press toward the mark for the prize of the high calling of God in Christ Jesus'. (Phil.3. 13–14). He is pressing forward. I know very few Christian people who give me the impression of pressing forward. Sitting back is more usual today. I do not see people straining at the leash, longing for more, desiring, seeking, working for more, praying for more. 'I press toward the mark . . .' says Paul. Christian people do not seem to be living like this. Rather, it seems to me, that instead of pressing forward toward the mark, they are simply turning round and round in a circle. I do not see much evidence of advance and of growth. People are saved, they are given things to do, they are taken here and there, and they go on like that for the rest of their lives. Very busy, very active, some of them, so much so that they have nervous breakdowns, they become tired, overworked people. What is the matter with them? They are going round and round in a circle, they are not pressing on toward the mark. There is no growth, there is no development. And you may spend fifty years of a very busy life in preaching the gospel, or in organising this or that, and you may know God no better at the end of the fifty years than you did at the beginning.

And this is wrong. We are meant to grow in grace, and in the knowledge of the Lord. We are meant to be pressing forward toward the mark, forgetting the past, desiring what he is holding it out before us: 'That I may know him, and the power of his resurrection, and the fellowship of his sufferings.' It is a terrible thing, but the trouble with us is that our lives are not centred on him. They are not dominated by him. We say, 'Ah, yes, we are working for him.' And then we leave him alone, and we go on and on in our little activities. We ask his blessing on what we are doing, but oh how often do we seek him, himself! God, and the Lord Jesus Christ and the presence of the Spirit in our lives, that is true Christianity. It is men who have sought that who have always been used of God in revival. Read their stories. You need not take my word for it. These are always the preliminaries to revival. These people who have been greatly used have felt that they are like the Laodiceans, they say, 'We have got nothing. Oh, how naked we are.' And they have gone to him, and they have sought him.

Another manifestation of a dead orthodoxy, and one which follows from the others, is a lack of true concern for the glory of God. Is that true of us, I wonder? Have we a true concern for the glory of God in this godless age? I am not asking whether you are irritated by the sin of the age. That is not my question. It is a simple thing to be irritated and to be annoyed by the blasphemy and the sin and the vice, the lewdness, and the perversions, and all that we see in our streets, and in the newspapers. It is an easy thing to be annoyed and to be irritated. But you need not be a Christian to be irritated. The Pharisees were annoyed in that way. What is the test of a Christian? It is the presence of a grief and a sorrow in the heart, because of the way in which men are not glorifying God. Read the Psalmist, go back to your Old Testament, look at the Psalmist breaking his heart, as he sees men ignoring God, uttering their blasphemies about him, desecrating his sanctities. It broke the Psalmists' hearts. They were grieved in Spirit, they could not sleep, it was a burden and a concern to them.

Does this modern generation affect us like that? Do we know a grief because of the state of God's cause? Are we concerned about his glory, and his honour amongst the people? To what extent do we feel a longing and a desire for the manifestation of God in his glory? How often do we say to ourselves, 'Oh, that he would arise, and scatter his ememies?' (see Ps.68.1). How often are we aware of such feelings within us? Or are we simply thinking of it in terms of our activities, and the success of our church, or some organisation we may happen to be interested in? Is it God-centred, is it a grief for God's sake, is it a desire that he may manifest his glory again? That is what always appears in times of revival. Not that the Church may be benefited, not even that the people may come crowding into the Church. No, the primary thing is that God and his glory may be made known. That is the primary concern.

And then that, in turn, leads to the next thing, which is a corresponding lack of true concern for the souls of those that are outside. 'Ah, but,' you say, 'I am very interested in mission work. And I am very active in connection with such things.' That is not what I am asking you. I am not asking you whether you are doing the done thing in the Christian life, namely to support missionary activities at home and abroad. I am asking whether you really have got a grief in your heart, and in your mind, because of the state of the unbeliever? Do we know much about what the fathers used to call a burden for souls? Does the thing press upon us? Now, Christian people, it should, if we really believe what we claim to believe. If we really believe that those people are dishonouring God, and that they are going to hell, it should be a burden to us, but it is not, again, because we are so busy, because we do not stop to think and to work it out; because we do not analyse it; because of our inadequate notion of God and his glory, and of the real state of these people. Is there not an absence of this godly concern, this burden for the souls of the lost?

I think that I could prove this to you, if necessary. I have been told by many pastors, in all parts of this country, that they have experiences like this. They say, 'We have got plenty of people in our churches who will attend as often and as regularly as you like, particularly if there are big mass meetings, but who simply will not come to the weekly prayer meeting.' Now that is the thing we have to explain. If they had a real burden and concern for souls, they would be there praying regularly, in the unspectacular little prayer meeting. That is the test. The man who is really feeling the burden is a man who is being pressed by it, and pressed to his knees, and pressed into the presence of God. His supreme activity is prayer. He does other things, of course, but the big thing, the vital thing to him is prayer. For he realises that this is a province that God alone can deal with. He knows the burden. And a man who is burdened is a man who prays.

A lack of burden for the souls of the lost, then leads to a lack of really urgent prayer. It leads to a lack of prayer that is really hopeful and expectant. There is praying and praying. And true prayer is only possible when men and women have a God-consciousness, when they know what it is to realise the presence of the holy God, when they begin to have a zeal for his holy name and for his cause, and a compassion for souls, and a feeling of the pressure of the burden of their condition on their spirits. It is then, and then only, that we truly pray. Oh, we can be whipped up to pray, but that is not prayer. We can organise this thing, but that is not prayer. People are always ready to be organised, because it is so much easier to do things we are commanded to do and told how to do, than really to be alone, as it were, with just God and ourselves facing this matter, and going on doing so. That is the way to prayer. It is the only way to prayer. It seems to me that the diagnosis of the condition, therefore is that today our essential trouble is that we are content with a very superficial and preliminary knowledge of God, his being, and his cause. And content with that, we spend our lives in busy activism, instead of pausing to realise the possibilities, instead of realising our own failure, and realising that we are not attracting anybody to Christ, and that they probably see nothing in us that makes them desire to come to him. The inevitable and constant preliminary to revival has always been a thirst for God, a thirst, a living thirst for a knowledge of the living God, and a longing and a burning desire to see him acting, manifesting himself and his power, rising, and scattering his enemies.

God grant that we all may face these questions and continue to face them. To what extent do we know God? To what extent can we say honestly that we are forgetting the things that are behind and that we are pressing forward toward the mark; that our supreme desire is to know him, and the power of his resurrection, and the fellowship of his sufferings, being made conformable unto his death? 'If by any means I might attain unto the resurrection from among the dead' – to what extent do we know the fulness of God, and this love of Christ which passes knowledge? To what extent are we experiencing these things? Are they living realities to us? The thirst for God, and the longing for the exhibition of his glory are the essential preliminaries to revival.

Chapter 8

Joshua 4.21–24

And he spake unto the children of Israel, saying, When your children shall ask their fathers in time to come, saying, What mean these stones? Then ye shall let your children know, saying, Israel came over this Jordan on dry land. For the Lord your God dried up the waters of Jordan from before you, until ye were passed over, as the Lord your God did to the Red sea, which he dried up from before us, until we were gone over: That all the people of the earth might know the hand of the Lord, that it is mighty: that ye might fear the Lord your God for ever (Josh.4.21–24).

We have up to this point, been considering the hindrances and the obstacles to revival, because obviously that is where we must of necessity begin. But that is not sufficient. Though we start there and realise that there are certain conditions and certain rules that must always be observed it is not enough that we stop there. We must go beyond that point, because if we do not we shall end in discouragement. Having examined ourselves, having seen the situation as it is, we see that the problem is surely and certainly one with which no human power is adequate to deal. It is because so many fail to see this that they are still bustling and busying with their various activities and organisations. There is no hope until we come to the end of that. The situation is such that man is impotent to deal with it. And that is why I say that we should rejoice in the fact that we can go on together now to look at this whole subject positively and a little more directly.

I would remind you again that this very question of the need of revival is of vital importance to the Christian Church, and the minds and prayers of Christian people throughout the world should be channelled and directed into the matter of this urgent need. I am going to quote some words by Albert Barnes, a famous expositor in the last century, because they seem to me to put this thing so perfectly. He wrote like this:

That day which shall convince the great body of professing Chri-
stians of the reality and desirableness of revivals will constitute a
new era in the history of religion and will precede manifestations
of power like that of Pentecost.

I am certain that that is absolutely right! The greatest problem
confronting us in the Church today is that the vast majority of
professing Christians are not convinced of the 'reality and the
desirableness of revivals'. As I have pointed out, this is a subject
that has scarcely been mentioned. Men and women have been so
busy in other directions that they have not even thought of it, still
less prayed urgently for it. And yet, as Albert Barnes says, it is
surely most important that we should do so and therefore,
anything that is going to help us to do it is of the greatest value,
and one of the best aids that I know of in this respect is to consider
the story of the great revivals of the past.

That is why, in this centenary year, we are reminding ourselves
of what happened in 1859, that wonderful year in the history of
God's people.

But let us be clear about this. We are not interested in all this
merely from the historical standpoint. Our interest must never be
merely an antiquarian interest. There is no point in reading about
revivals just for the sake of reading the history in the stories. No,
our motive and our interest must be to read and to study and to
consider what has happened in the past, in order that we may
discover the great principles that underly this matter, in order, in
other words, that we may discover what it is that we should be
seeking and praying for in our own day and generation. It should
be a utilitarian, rather than an antiquarian interest and motive,
that should govern us. In other words, I suggest that we should
make use of everything that we can find which tells us about a
hundred years ago, in exactly the same way as God intended the
Children of Israel to use the twelve stones that he commanded
them to take out of the middle of the river of Jordan and to set
up at Gilgal.

Now I am calling your attention to this interesting incident
because it does seem to me to be speaking very directly to us at
this present hour. Here God did something unusual, something
strange, something marvellous and miraculous. He had delivered
the Children of Israel first of all from their enemies, the Egyptians
– he divided the Red Sea and they went through on dry land.
And here they were, they had been in the wilderness for forty
years, and there, on the other side of the river of Jordan, lay the

promised land of Canaan, the place they were looking for, and longing for, the land of blessing, the land flowing with milk and honey. What a contrast to the wilderness!

Yes, but the question was how could they go through the river? And the answer was that God divided the waters of Jordan, and they went through – again on dry ground. And God, you remember, gave this commandment to Joshua, and Joshua in turn gave it to the people. Take out, he said, twelve stones from the very spot where the priests stood as they held the Ark. Take out twelve stones and then set them up there in Gilgal. And why? Well, the reason is given here in our text.

Now it seems to me that our remembering of the 1859 revival is comparable to these twelve stones that are there at Gilgal. Our position is this, and my whole business, as we study this subject, is, in a sense, just to create in you this very question, 'What mean these stones?' What is all this that you are talking about? What are these books and pamphlets? What are these meetings? What is this thing? We know nothing about it. As the Jewish Children in their day were going to ask, 'What mean these stones?', so I trust that the main outcome of our study will be to lead the men and women of our day to ask, 'What is this and what is its relevance to us?'

So let us continue with our consideration of these verses. The thing that strikes us at once, of course, is that it is most extraordinary that this kind of thing should be necessary. Would you not have thought that with an event like this in their history, there would be no need to remind any generation of the Children of Israel of this? They are so remarkable, these two incidents, the crossing of the Red Sea and the River Jordan, they are such outstanding events that you would have thought that there would never be any need to remind people in some visible, external, objective way of such things. Yet God gave the commandment because he knows human nature so well, and what he knows about us is that it is simply astonishing to notice how easily we can forget. Even a memorable event like this could soon be forgotten, could be blotted right out of the minds and the consciousness of subsequent generations of the Children of Israel. So, 'Put up the stones,' says God, so that they will be a reminder, the people will be arrested, they will say, 'What are these stones about? What does this mean?', and then the answer will be given to them.

Now this is one of the first things we all have to realise about ourselves, this tendency to forget. Yes, to forget even the greatest and the most wonderful things. It is true in every realm. I suppose that, in the last analysis, one of the most devasting effects of sin is the way in which it puts a paralysis upon the mind and even the upon the memory. This is not confined to religion, it is true in every realm. How soon are great men forgotten! Men who dominated the scene in their day and generation mean nothing at all to subsequent generations who, if they suddenly see a monument, say, 'Who was he? What did he do?' Though these men did such outstanding things in their time and their contemparies thought that they would never be forgotten, time passes and other generations come; they are soon forgotten. 'A generation arose that knew not Joseph.'

There is nothing more transient than reputation, in that sense. But it is not only true of great men, it is true of great events. Some of the most outstanding events of history are soon forgotten. A generation arises that forgets all about the sacrifices of its forefathers, who may have fought even unto death for some great principle or for some great liberty. Generations arise that know nothing about it and are really not interested in it at all. They take all the fruits and all the benefits, and they never trouble even to ask, 'How is it that these things have ever come to us?' Now, that is human nature, is it not? What is the cause of this and, particularly, what is the cause of this in the realm of religion? Why does it become possible that generations will arise that will even forget a thing like this so that God has to give his commandment about these stones? Let me briefly suggest some answers to this.

Perhaps the main causes are absorption with ourselves, and with our own particular age and generation, and particularly our absorption with our own activities. We are so self-centred, so busy doing what we are doing. We seem to be unaware of the fact that people lived in this world in past ages and centuries, before we ever came here. There is a morbid self-centredness and self-concentration. People's lives are bound entirely by their own circle, and how infrequently do they look out from inside it. Curtains of various descriptions are not new. There have always been Iron and Bamboo and other curtains. It is amazing to observe how small life can be. We live this circumscribed little existence, with our little activities, and we never look out beyond, and we are aware of nothing else. And, of course, added to that, there is a feeling, which is particularly characteristic of today, that the past cannot possibly help us, because of all our advances and all our wonderful knowledge, and our techniques and our astounding abilities. We are the masters. What has the past got to say to us? There is a great deal of that feeling, and it has been true, of course, of every generation before us, and it will be true of the generations to follow us. They will look back at us, if they do at all, and will just dismiss us. We are mere tyros in these matters.

But, in the last analysis, I believe that the explanation is – I repeat – this subjectivism of ours. And this subjectivism vitiates even our reading and our studying of the Bible. We are all so morbidly concerned about ourselves and our own problems that we even to go to the Bible as a book which is going to help us with our problems. We want some help, we want this and that and we go to the Bible, as if it were some sort of dispensary to deal with the so called 'mumps and measles of our souls'. Our very *approach* to the Bible is so subjective instead of being objective. How often, I wonder, do we go to the Bible saying to ourselves, 'I am going to read the Bible because I want to see what God has done; I am going read my Bible in order that I can look at God acting and intervening in history'? But, the Bible is not just a book that answers my little questions and tells me various things that I may want to know; the Bible is the record of the activity of God, the manifestations of God, God's mighty acts and deeds. I am going to look on. I am going to stand back and I am going to see what God, the Lord has done, 'that all the people of the earth might know the hand of the Lord, that it is mighty' (Josh.4.24). The acts of God. But I am afraid we do not read the Bible like that any longer, do we? We want just a little word to help us. We want a nice little thought to start the day. We just want something before we offer up our brief and hurried prayer before we rush off. Beautiful thoughts. Do not misunderstand me. I am going to say a thing that can be grievously misunderstood. I verily believe that the main trouble of most evangelical people today is that they read their Bibles too devotionally, which means, I say, subjectively. And this mighty panorama of the acts of the living God is something that we seem to be unaware of and the result is that we need to be reminded of what God has done. It is all here for us, but we pass by, we do not notice, so we must put up some stones, some memorial, something to arrest attention.

This is a principle which you find in many places in the Bible. Look at the communion service, for example. The principle is exactly the same. We are so dull and so stupid as the result of sin, that we might even forget this, the death of the Son of God for us and his agony and his shame and all that he endured on the cross. And his eternal love for us, we would even forget that. So the Lord himself ordained and commanded that we should meet together and break bread and drink wine: 'This do in remembrance of me.' It is the setting up of the stones in Gilgal once more. We are such, and we suffer so much from this fell spiritual lethargy, that we need objective memorials, we constantly need tangible reminders, something outside ourselves that will lead us to ask, 'What does this table mean?' 'What mean these stones?' God condescends to our weakness, and our lethargy and our stupidity by providing us with external memorials of his almighty acts and deeds. And so it is that I, for one, thank God for 1959. Simply because it happens to be a hundred years away from 1859. You notice that I am holding on to this point and I am doing so for this reason. This is our eighth consideration of this question of revival and if I have not hitherto succeeded in rousing you to ask – 'What means it?' – if there has not arisen in you this new interest and curiosity, it has all been in vain. It is not enough just to study all this and to be aware of *something*. Are we really becoming concerned as to what it all is? What does all this record mean? And I hope to show that the real and complete answer is given in these verses at the end of Joshua 4. It is all here. God, you see, has given his own explanation, and I have nothing to do but to hold it before you.

First and foremost, it means that we are reminded of *facts*. 'What mean these stones?' Subsequent generations are going to ask that question. They will be going along casually, perhaps out on a walk or on a journey, and suddenly they will see these twelve stones and they will say, 'What is the meaning of this?'

And the reply, said Joshua, will be, 'These stones are here as a memorial to something that once happened.'

History, not theories; not ideas, but facts. What is the meaning of the bread and wine? Oh, the fact – that he was crucified under Pontius Pilate. Our whole position depends upon facts. I wish that I could stop here and deal only with this because we are living in an age when there is a most subtle theological teaching which would have us believe that you can dispense with the facts and hold on to the teaching. It is a lie! 'What mean these stones?' Facts! Crossing the Red Sea, crossing Jordan, in this miraculous manner. Facts, facts of God.

And it is exactly the same with what we are celebrating this year. It is a simple actual fact of history that something amazing and wonderful happened a hundred years ago. Something literally took place in 1859 which was so much fact that it even began to be

97

reported in the newspapers. And they very rarely report anything unless it is political. The only sermons they are interested in are sermons that introduce politics in some shape or form. They are not interested in spiritual matters, but they were actually reporting what happened in 1859. It became front page news. That was phenomenal! Facts. Acts. Something that belongs solidly to the realm of history.

But, as the explanation here tells us, this is not something utterly unique which only happens once. Did you notice, 'Then ye shall let your children know saying, Israel came over this Jordan on dry land. For the Lord your God dried up the waters of Jordan from before you until ye were passed over, as the Lord your God did to the Red sea, which he dried up from before us, until we were gone over'? I want to emphasise that point. What happened in 1859 is only one in a great series. It is but one example, but one illustration of something that has been happening periodically in the history of the Christian Church right through the running centuries. It is one example of what we call 'revival', a 'revival' of religion, and it is only one example. There have been many others.

Let me just give you a few illustrations in passing. Long before even the Protestant Reformation, there was quite a religious revival in this country associated with the name of John Wycliffe and the Lollards. That was a revival, as definitely as what happened in 1859. Then, of course, the same thing happened on the continent of Europe with that great man John Huss. There in Moravia, what is now called Czechoslovakia, there was a real revival, associated with his name, and God used him as an instrument and as a channel. It was an amazing movement of the Spirit of God. They had it amongst the Waldensians in Northern Italy. It was a real revival. It happened with that great man called John Tauler,* who was actually a priest and a preacher in the Roman Catholic Church. The Spirit of God came upon him and it lead to a revival in his area. It was the same thing exactly.

Then, of course, there was the Protestant Reformation. Let us never forget that this was a revival as well as a reformation. We must not think of that as being merely a theological movement. It was that, but in addition there was a revival, the Spirit of God was shed abroad and people were listening to preaching. Preaching and the reading of the Bible were of supreme importance. That is a religious awakening. And that is what we mean

*John Tauler, 1300–1361.

98

by revival. You find it in the seventeenth century, and you have it, in an amazing manner, two hundred years ago, in the great Evangelical awakening associated with the names of Whitefield and the Wesleys and many, many others. You find it again at the close of the eighteenth and the beginning of the nineteenth century. And then there was this notable, remarkable event which took place from 1857 to 1859 in America, Northern Ireland, Wales, Scotland, Sweden and in other parts of the world.

This, then, is only one in a series of events that have been happening throughout the long history of the Christian Church. And you will find, as you read the stories of every one of them, that they share certain things in common. They have the same general characteristics. God moved at Jordan, said Joshua, exactly as he did before, at the Red Sea. Certain general characteristics are common to all these experiences, in spite of time, in spite of country, in spite of civilisation, in spite of everything else.

So, then, what was it that happened a hundred years ago? What was this event that falls into this series? What is revival? We can define it, as a period of unusual blessing and activity in the life of the Christian Church. Primarily, of course, and by definition, a revival is something that happens first in the Church and amongst Christian people, amongst believers. That, I repeat, is true by definition. It is *revival;* something is revived and when you say that, you mean that there is something present that has got life. But the life was beginning to wane, to droop, and had become almost moribund, and some people said, 'That is dead, that is finished,' because they could not see much sign of life and activity. Revival means awakening, stimulating the life, bringing it to the surface again. It happens primarily in the Church of God, and amongst believing people and it is only secondly something that affects those that are outside also. Now this is a most important point, because this definition helps us to differentiate, once and for all, between a revival and an evangelistic campaign. To confuse these two things leads to much harm. There is nothing which is quite so foolish as people announcing that they are going to hold a revival. They mean an evangelistic campaign. Alas, this confusion was really introduced by Finney and it has persisted ever since. But it is a gross misunderstanding, it is a confusion of purpose. Let me show you the difference.

An evangelistic campaign is the Church deciding to do something with respect to those who are outside. A revival is not the Church deciding to do something and doing it. It is something that is *done to* the Church, something that happens to the Church.

The two things are essentially different. You can have a great evangelistic campaign, but it may leave your church exactly where it was, if indeed it is not worse. I add that because I am being told constantly that the churches are suffering from what is called a 'post evangelistic campaign exhaustion', that as the result of campaigns, the prayer meetings and the regular meetings of the church are not so well attended. And the same is true of various other organisations, which promote such activities. Evangelistic campaigns, then, have reference mainly to those who are outside, but the whole essence of a revival is that it is something that happens to the Church, to the people inside. And they are affected and moved and tremendous things happen.

So then, what is it that happens? What is this? What mean these stones? What happened a hundred years ago in these various countries? The best way of answering that question is to say that it is in a sense a repetition of the day of Pentecost. It is something happening to the Church, that inevitably and almost instinctively makes one look back and think again of what happened on the day of Pentecost as recorded in Acts 2. Let me give you some of the general characteristics.

The essence of a revival is that the Holy Spirit comes down upon a number of people together, upon a whole church, upon a number of churches, districts, or perhaps a whole country. That is what is meant by revival. It is, if you like, a visitation of the Holy Spirit, or another term that has often been used is this – an outpouring of the Holy Spirit. And the terms are interesting because you see what the people are conscious of is that it is as if something has suddenly come down upon them. The Spirit of God has descended into their midst, God has come down and is amongst them. A baptism, an outpouring, a visitation. And the effect of that is that they immediately become aware of his presence and of his power in a manner that they have never known before. I am talking about Christian people, about church members gathered together as they have done so many times before. Suddenly they are aware of his presence, they are aware of the majesty and the awe of God. The Holy Spirit literally seems to be presiding over the meeting and taking charge of it, and manifesting his power and guiding them, and leading them, and directing them. That is the essence of revival.

And what does that mean? Well, there are general characteristics which you will find in every revival that you can ever read about. The immediate effect is that the people present begin to have an awareness of spiritual things and clear views of them such as they have never had before. Now again I am talking about believers, members of the Christian Church when they suddenly become conscious of this presence and of this power, and the first effect, is that spiritual things become realities. They have heard all these things before, they may have heard them a thousand times and indeed many thousand times, but what they testify is this: 'You know, the whole thing suddenly became clear to me. I was suddenly illuminated, things that I was so familiar with stood out in letters of gold, as it were. I understood. I saw it all in a way that I had never done in the whole of my life.' That is what they say. The Holy Spirit enlightens the mind and the understanding. They begin not only to see these things clearly but to feel their power.

What are these things of which they become so aware? First and foremost, the glory and the holiness of God. Have you ever noticed, as you read your Bibles, the effect on these people as they suddenly realised the presence of God? Like Job, they put their hands on their mouths or like Isaiah they say, 'Woe is unto me! for I am undone; because I am a man of unclean lips.' What is the matter then? Oh, they have just had a realisation of the holiness and of the majesty and the glory of God. That always happens in a revival. It does not always happen in evangelistic campaigns, does it? There can be a lot of laughing and lightness, and obvious organisation in evangelistic campaigns. Never in a revival, but rather awe, this reverence, this holy fear, the consciousness of God in his majesty, his glory, his holiness, his utter purity.

And that, as we have seen, leads inevitably to a deep and a terrible sense of sin, and an aweful feeling of guilt. It leads men and women to feel that they are vile and unclean and utterly unworthy and, above all, it leads them to realise their utter helplessness face to face with such a God. Or, like the publican depicted by our Lord in the parable, they are so conscious of all this that they cannot show their faces. They are far back near the door somewhere, beating their breasts and saying, 'God have mercy, on me, a sinner.' The holiness of God, their own utter sinfulness and wretchedness, their own unworthiness; they realise they have never done anything good at all. Before, they thought they had done a great deal, now they see that it is nothing – useless. Like Paul they begin to talk about it as dung and filthy rags. In their utter helplessness and hopelessness they prostrate themselves and cast themselves upon the love and mercy and compassion of God.

101

It always happens in the Bible. Read the accounts for your-selves. Whichever one you may read, you will always find it. This is the convicting work of the Spirit who takes charge of the situation. And people may be held in that state and position for some time. Sometimes they have been in that state not only for hours but for days and weeks, and months, and they become almost desperate. Then they are given a clear view of the love of God and of the Lord Jesus Christ and especially of his death upon the cross. At last they see it. Oh, they had always believed it theoretically and they had stayed to a communion service, but they had never felt anything, it had never truly become real for them. They had believed it, yes, they were honestly trusting to it, but they had never felt its power, they had never known what it was to be melted by it, to be broken by it. They had never known what it was to weep with a sense of unworthiness and then of love and joy as they realised that 'God so loved the world, that he gave his only begotten Son, that whosoever believeth in him should not perish, but have everlasting life.' Suddenly it all becomes real to them and they are given to know that the Son of God has loved *them* and has given himself for *them*. It becomes an individual and a personal matter: 'He died for *me*, even *my* sins are forgiven', and peace comes into their hearts; joy enters into them and they are lost in love and in a sense of praise of God the Father, God the Son and God the Holy Spirit.

And this now becomes for them the one thing that absorbs them. If they meet anyone they talk about it at once, everybody is talking about it, it is the main topic of conversation, it is the thing that absorbs all their interest. They desire to be together now and to talk about these things and so they get together, and they hold meetings. They meet every night and they begin to talk about these things. They begin to praise God, and to sing hymns to his glory. And then they begin to pray, and there they are, hour after hour, night after night, longing to finish work so they they might get together with other people who have experienced this movement of the Spirit of God. And that, of course, in turn leads them to have a great concern about others who are outside and who do not know these things.

I am giving you a synopsis of what you read in the books. They begin to get a concern for the members of their own family, husband, wife, father, mother, children, brother, sister, who do not know that they are outside. They tell them about it, they feel they must. There is a constraint that is driving them. They talk about it to people, to friends and to everybody, and they begin to pray for them. Prayer is always a great feature of every revival, great prayer meetings, intercession hour after hour. They pray for these people by name and they plead, and they will not let God go, as it were. They are intent on this with a strange urgency.

And then, after a while, hearing of all this and seeing the change in those whom they have known for so long, these others who are outside begin to join the meetings and to say, 'What is this?' So they come in, and they go through the same experience. And so it happens and thousands upon thousands are converted. Indeed, the whole neighbourhood seems to be full of the Holy Spirit. He seems to be everywhere. People are not only converted in meetings, some are converted as they are walking to the meetings, before they have even got there. Some are converted at their work, in a coal-mine, on top of a mountain. Some are awakened in the middle of the night. They went to bed feeling as usual, but they are awakened with an awe-ful sense of sin and they have to get up and pray and plead with God to have mercy. Nobody has spoken to them at that moment – it is the Spirit of God that is acting. He is dominating the whole area. He is filling the lives of all the people.

That is what happens in revival and thus you get this curious, strange mixture, as it were, of great conviction of sin and great joy, a great sense of the terror of the Lord, and great thanksgiving and praise. Always in a revival there is what somebody once called a divine disorder. Some are groaning and agonising under conviction, others praising God for the great salvation. And all this leads to crowded and prolonged meetings. Time seems to be forgotten. People seem to have entered into eternity. A meeting may start at six thirty in the evening, and it may not end until daybreak the next morning with nobody aware of the passing of the hours. They did not have to provide coffee once or twice halfway through. When the Holy Ghost organises things, time, the body and the needs of the flesh are all forgotten.

A revival, then, really means days of heaven upon earth. Let me give you one of the greatest definitions ever written of what is true of a town when there is such a revival or a visitation of the Spirit of God. It was written by the great and saintly Jonathan Edwards about the little town of Northampton in Massachusetts in 1735.

This work soon made a glorious alteration in the town. So that in the Spring and Summer following it seemed, that is to say the town, seemed to be full of the presence of God. It never was so full of love nor so full of joy and yet so full of distress as it was then. There were remarkable tokens of God's presence in almost every house. It was a time of joy in families on account of salvation being brought to them. Parents rejoicing over their children as newborn, husbands over their wives and wives over their husbands. The doings of God were then seen in His sanctuary. God's day was a delight and His tabernacles were amiable. Our public assemblies were then beautiful. The congregation was alive in God's service. Everyone earnestly intent on the public worship. Every hearer eager to drink in the words of the minister as they came from his mouth. The assembly in general were from time to time in tears while the Word was preached. Some weeping with sorrow and distress, others with joy and love, others with pity and concern for the souls of their neighbours.

Jonathan Edwards: *Works*, London 1840, Vol I, p.348.

There, then, I have given you a rough outline of what happens in revival. 'What mean these stones?' Well, that is exactly what happened a hundred years ago in all those different countries. It was the work of God – these visitations of the Spirit of God. Do you know about these things? Are you interested? Are you concerned? Are you moved? Do you not begin to see that if only this happened today, it would solve our problems? This is God visiting his people. Days of heaven on earth, the presidency of the Holy Spirit in the Church, life abundant given to God's people without measure. I trust that we have already seen and felt something that creates within us not only the desire to say, 'What is that fervour? Oh that we might know it. Oh, that it might happen to us', but also that we might feel it to such an extent that we begin to plead with God to have pity and to have mercy and to visit us in that way with his great salvation.

Chapter 9

Joshua 4.21–24

And he spake unto the children of Israel, saying, When your children shall ask their fathers in time to come, saying, What mean these stones? Then ye shall let your children know, saying, Israel came over this Jordan on dry land. For the Lord your God dried up the waters of Jordan from before you, until ye were passed over, as the Lord your God did to the Red sea, which he dried up from before us, until we were gone over: That all the people of the earth might know the hand of the Lord, that it is mighty: that ye might fear the Lord your God for ever. (Josh. 4.21–24).

We have seen some of the general characteristics of revival – a sense of the majesty of God, of personal sinfulness, of the wonder of salvation through Jesus Christ and a desire that others might know it. And we have seen, too, that in a time of revival people are aware of the presidency of the Holy Spirit over everything and the life of the whole community.

Now we must proceed to emphasise certain special points about revival which seem to me to be of very great signigicance. Firstly, it is characteristic of revival that people of all classes are affected by it, people of all ages, people of all temperaments, people of all intellectual types. That is a point that is well worthy of elaboration, though we shall not do so here, but I emphasise it for this reason. Here is one of the final answers to those who would dismiss evangelical conversion in terms of psychology. It is not confined to special types, to the so-called 'religious type'. One of the most striking things in the story of revivals is the fact that you get a cross section of every conceivable type and group in society, irrespective of class, age, temperament and everything else: a most astonishing feature, but one which is found with strange regularity in all the stories.

And then another characteristic is that a revival is something that comes, lasts for a while, and then passes. This is most interesting because it emphasises that revival is a definite action of God. It comes suddenly or gradually, works to some great climax and then it ends perhaps suddenly, perhaps gradually. There is something discreet about it. Sometimes you can give the very date of its beginning and the date at which it ended, and that, as I say, is significant because it establishes once more that revival is the work of God and that it is not something which belongs to the realms of mere psychological experience. With the latter, as long as you have the stimulus and the factors, you continue to get results, but in revival that is not the case.

That leads us to the next point, which is that the results of revival are abiding. There are exceptions. There are some who fall back. But the great feature of revival is that the men and the women who are converted by this power that has entered into the life of the Church, continue. It is not that they come forward as the result of an appeal and you imagine that great things are happening, until you find afterwards that only ten per cent of them hold, which is the figure that is expected, I am told, by most evangelists. That is not the case in revival. In a revival it is an exceptional thing for people not to grow. They abide and they continue.

You will find that the literature bears this out. I have been reminding myself of it again. I have been reading a description given by a number of ministers a hundred years ago, and every one of them volunteers this self same point, namely, that the people were standing and were holding. It was not something that only lasted an evening. Of course they did not test their meetings, they did not call people to come forward. There again is an interesting point of difference between an evangelistic campaign and a revival. In an evangelistic campaign you have to plead with people to come forward, in a revival you do not – they come without your asking. That was put very well by a man who was in the revival that happened in the Congo in recent years. He wrote a little book about his experiences in which he brings it out very eloquently. I quote:

> There I had been preaching for twenty years in that area and pleading with people to decide for Christ at the end of the meet-ings, trying to persuade them to come forward and I was not succeeding. But then this came, this happened and now there was no need to ask them to come forward.

The difficulty was in a sense to deal with the numbers who came.

106

They would even come forward while he was still preaching, he could not stop them. That is something that you get in a revival. And the results are abiding.

There are certain concrete facts that can be given. Let me give you some figures. I have hesitated to do so because figures have, by now, become rather unrealistic in this age which attaches such significance to them. People do not wait to see whether they are true, they are so anxious to proclaim them immediately. Nevertheless, the figures are interesting. I am not emphasising that a given number came forward at the end of a meeting, I am going to give you figures of people who joined the Christian Church, and who continued to be active and zealous members.

It is said that from 1730 to 1745 in the United States, when the great awakening took place under Jonathan Edwards and the Tennants and others, that some 50,000 people joined the Christian churches. From 1857 to 1859 in the great revival that swept the United States, it is computed that half a million people joined the Christian Church. Notice my emphasis – *joined the Christian Church*. They were not admitted immediately. They were tested and examined; they were instructed as catechumens and they were trained. I am not talking about decisions. We have become so accustomed to that, but they did not do that sort of thing in those days. Let us get that right out of our minds. I am referring to people who, having given such clear evidence of their conversion and their regeneration, were admitted into the full membership of the Christian Church. Half a million a hundred years ago in the United States. 100,000 in Ulster alone joined the churches during that time and 50,000 in Wales. And when you remember the population figures you see the significance of these striking facts.

It must also be emphasised that a great zeal for God and for holiness invariably becomes manifest in the members of the church and in these converts. The meetings are crowded. The people are anxious to work. Every enterprise and connection with the church is given a mighty stimulus. You can read, for instance, Edwin Orr's book on the 'Second Evangelical Awakening' which will give you striking facts in that respect. It will show you the number of things that came out of that revival of a hundred years ago. It was not some passing emotion, but something so deep and so profound that people were consumed with a zeal for God and for his name and for his cause. And furthermore, not only did the existing churches become too small, they had to build large numbers of new ones. You see, when there is a revival, it starts as I have shown, in the Church, and the Church is built up, whereas so often when you have evangelistic campaigns, the churches are left exactly where they were.

The numbers of men called to the ministry also increased enormously. This is something, too, that always happens in a period of revival. And then, speaking still more generally, in a time of revival you will find that the moral tone and the moral level, not only of the Church but of the world outside the Church, is visibly affected and raised. You can read statistics provided by the public authorities with respect to prosecutions in police courts and other courts for drunkenness and various other things and the figures are simply staggering. And it can also be seen how practices, evil practices that had characterised the life of a district or a town, suddenly disappear. There is a famous instance of this. There was a great preacher in North Wales about 150 years ago by the name of John Elias. He preached one sermon at a famous fair, a fair that was well known for its debauchery and vice and its sin and wrongdoing. That man by preaching one sermon put an end to that fair once and for ever. He killed it and it was never revived.

That is the kind of thing that you find occurring in a time of revival. But you can have great evangelistic campaigns and you might think from the reports you read that the whole country had become religious. Then you are given the figures for vice and crime and you see that they are not affected at all. That is never true in a revival. Even people who are not converted are influenced and affected. A sobriety enters into the life of the whole community and the general effects of revival will last for quite a number of years after the revival is over.

Now, up until this point we have been looking at the phenomenon of revival in general. But I do want to refer briefly to particular variations, which take place in different revivals, in different places and at different times. While they all share certain general characteristics, you do find these most interesting and, to me, fascinating variations. There are differences, for instance, in the way in which a revival starts; as I have said, it may be sudden or it may be gradual. A revival may come quite unexpectedly, or it may be the case that a number of people have been burdened and have been concerned and have been praying, perhaps over months or even years. Sometimes it is just a handful of people who have been concerned and burdened, and God answers. Have you read these stories? I do plead with you to do so. Read the facts and you will see some of these points illustrated.

Again revival may come in different types of meetings. Sometimes a revival breaks out in a prayer meeting, not some great crowded meeting, but perhaps a little prayer meeting with just a few people. In Northern Ireland it was really three men who met together regularly to pray, just three men. Sometimes it has only been two. It does not matter. In New York a hundred years ago it was one man who prayed alone for some time in that famous midday prayer meeting. So it may come in a prayer meeting or it may happen in a preaching service. It may even happen when an evangelist is holding a series of regular meetings. He may have planned an evangelistic campaign, but suddenly it becomes a revival, something quite different. There is no limit to the ways in which it may start. Jonathan Edwards tells us that he has no doubt at all but that the sudden tragic death of a person in that town of Northampton, in which he ministered, was probably the thing that really proved to be *the* factor that God used. A calamity, some strange happening, something that alarms people or astonishes them, something that makes them realise the fleeting character of life in this world, these are the things that God has often used.

So it may happen with a very small number or it may happen in a great crowd. God is not confined to numbers or to anything else. The Bible is full of examples of that. God's greatest acts have been done with small numbers, with 'remnants'. But it can equally happen with a great crowd. And that is why people who try to lay down rules and regulations – thinking that because it happened once in this way, it is going to happen again in the same way – are showing a complete misunderstanding of the laws of the spiritual realm. There are endless variations in the way in which it begins.

And then consider the variations in the type of man that God uses in revival. This is another most fascinating theme. Sometimes God has used very great men, men like Jonathan Edwards, one of the greatest philosophers of all time, possibly the greatest philosopher that the United States has ever produced. Everybody is agreed about his importance, even men who are not primarily interested in religion. That is why they are still reprinting his works. And he was the man whom God used above all others two hundred years ago in the New England states. Whitefield, too, by any assessment, was a great man, and a great orator. John Wesley by any showing was an outstanding man, a genius of an organiser, and a most able intellectual. Now all these men of the eighteenth century were undoubtedly men of remarkable ability, and they were the men God used to bring this great revival among the masses of the common people.

But here is the interesting thing. God does not always use men like that. He does sometimes, and that seems to be the general rule, because Luther, again, was naturally great, so was Calvin, and so were John Knox, and others. But, you see, he does not always use men of that calibre. When you come to a hundred years ago you find something very different. You find God now using simple, ignorant, unknown, most ordinary men. You find that in the United States and you find it in Ulster. How many of you have ever heard of the name of James McQuilkin? Well he was the man who was used in Northern Ireland a hundred years ago. James McQuilkin was a most ordinary man, but God laid hold of him and began to use him. It was exactly the same in Wales and the name of the man most used there was David Morgan. He was actually a minister of the gospel, but a very ordinary, unknown minister, a man of no gifts whatsoever. But God took hold of that man and used him and made him like a lion for nearly two years. Is this not something worthy of our careful contemplation? Should we not reflect upon it? God takes hold of the weak things of the world and confounds the things that are mighty. It is a part of the principle. It may be a great man, it may be a very little man. It does not matter.

Then think of the area in which a revival takes place and the spread of the revival. It may be very local and it may remain so. But it may involve the whole district. It may involve the whole country, or, as we saw a hundred and two hundred years ago, several countries at the same time. All these facts are full of significance, especially when you think of the attacks of the psychologists who think they can explain away religious phenomena in terms of psychology. I am hoping to deal with that later.

But let us turn now to a vexed question, the question of the so-called 'phenomena' that are sometimes in evidence during a revival. Again, there is great variation here. Sometimes a revival may be powerful and yet more or less quiet. There may be a very deep and a very profound emotion. Large numbers are converted, but quietly. But is is not always like that. Indeed, it comes nearer to being the rule in revival that certain phenomena begin to manifest themselves – phenomena such as these: men and women are not only convicted of sin, but they are convicted by an agony with respect to sin. It is not merely that they see that they are sinners and that they must believe in the Saviour, it comes to them with such overwhelming force that they become even physically ill. They are in a literal agony of soul. You remember the story of John Bunyan do you not? He tells in *Grace Abounding* how he had such an agony of conviction for nearly eighteen months that on one occasion he even felt envious of geese that were grazing in the field. He wished that he had not been born a man at all. This agony, this terrible conviction – you may get that in revival. People are in an agony of soul and groaning. They may cry and sob and agonise audibly. But it does not always even stop at that. Sometimes people are so convicted and feel the power of the Spirit to such an extent that they faint and fall to the ground. Sometimes there are even convulsions, physical convulsions. And sometimes people seem to fall into a state of unconsciousness, into a kind of trance, and may remain like that for hours.

Now all I am anxious to do at this point is to remind you of the facts. They are variable. They may be present, they may not be, but generally in revival you do get something along these lines. We must deal with this point later, because it becomes the focal point of the criticism that is generally levelled against the whole notion of revival.

So then, 'What mean these stones?' What are they telling us? Well, I have been answering that question. It is the kind of thing that happened in 1859. It is the kind of thing that always happens in revival. There are general features, and there are variable features. It is clear, therefore, that what we have to consider is this outstanding event which takes place from time to time in the history of the Christian Church.

But let me take it a step further. If those are the facts, what is the real character or nature of the facts? We must go back to our text. Here are people one day walking past Gilgal and they see these stones set up and they say, 'What mean these stones?' and this is the answer that they are to be given: 'The Lord your God dried up the waters of Jordan from before you, until ye were passed over, as the Lord your God did to the Red sea, which he dried up from before us, until we were gone over.' The children of Israel are to tell the enquirers that these are set up 'that all the people of the earth might know the hand of the Lord, that is mighty'.

These stones remind us of facts, miraculous facts. And if that were true of those stones it is equally true of every revival that has ever taken place. A revival is a miracle. It is a miraculous, exceptional phenomenon. It is the hand of the Lord, and it is mighty. A revival, in other words, is something that can only be explained as the direct action and intervention of God. It was God alone who could divide the Red Sea. It was God alone who could divide the waters of the river of Jordan. These were miracles. Hence the reminder of God's unique action of the mighty acts of God. And revivals belong to that category. Let me examine this. These events belong to the order of things that men cannot produce. Men can produce evangelistic campaigns, but they cannot and never have produced a revival. Oh, they have tried to do so many times, and they are still trying. Alas, Finney has led the whole Church astray at this point by teaching that if you only do certain things you can have a revival whenever you want it. The answer is an eternal No! And that is not my opinion. This is a question of fact. Have we not all known and watched and seen men who have been trying to produce revivals. They have introduced all Finney's methods, they have read his book, they know it by heart and they have tried to do what he teaches, they have tried to make people confess their sins, they have tried to make them conform, they have done everything that Finney said should be done, expecting revival as a result. They have done it all and they have brought great pressure to bear, but there has been no revival. A revival, by definition, is the mighty act of God and it is a sovereign act of God. It is as independent as that. Man can do nothing. God, and God alone, does it. 'Set up these stones.' Why? Well, it is to say that it is the hand of the Lord and it is mighty; it is the sovereign act of God, apart from men. And all the details I have just been giving you, fit into this and illustrate it.

But not only can men not produce a revival, they cannot even explain it, and that again is most important. I would lay this down as a part of the definition. If you can explain what is happening in a church, apart from this sovereign act of God, it is not revival. If you can possibly explain it otherwise, it is not revival. You see that is true of miracles. If you can explain a miracle it is no longer a miracle. That is why it is rather pathetic to see people becoming excited when a man publishes a book with a title *The Bible is True*. The writer is going to prove to us that the miracles of the Old Testament have happened. And what does he proceed to say? Well, he says that this sort of thing happens quite naturally and quite often. There is one illustration which I will mention in order to show my point. You remember when Moses struck the rock and water came gushing out? 'Ah,' says this man, 'we are now in a very happy position, we can really believe this.' On what grounds? During the last war, he continues, a number of soldiers in charge of a sergeant were doing a bit of work in a given place and the men were not doing the work to the satisfaction of the sergeant. So he said, 'Let me have that pick,' and he just took hold of it and accidently just happened to remove a bit of shale from the side of the hedge and water began to trickle out. We can believe, therefore, that when Moses struck the rock the water gushed out. And so we can believe in miracles. Is it not rather pathetic? If you can explain a thing it is not a miracle. A miracle is the direct, sovereign, immediate, supernatural, action of God and it cannot be explained. And that is the essential truth about a revival. You can not explain it.

There are no methods in a revival. If methods are used, you can understand the result, can you not? If you do certain things, you will get certain results. The advertisers know all about that. If you use your methods correctly, you will get your results all right. People are very gullible, you can make them do almost anything you like. And we are living in a age of propaganda, an age which is suggestible. But no methods at all are used in revival. None. Read for yourself. No great crowds, no band, no choir, nothing whatsoever. No preliminary advertising. None of these things at all. And yet the thing happens. You cannot explain it in terms of the methods used, because there are none.

And then, look again at the men who were used. How often has it been the case in revival that you have had the same kind of thing that is described in Acts 4? This was the problem for the religious authorities in Jerusalem. Here was a man who was known to everybody, who used to sit every day at the Beautiful Gate of the Temple asking alms of the people – a man of forty years of age who had never walked at all. But suddenly this man was seen walking and leaping and running into the Temple and praising God, so that everybody knew it. And who had done this? Men called Peter and John. Who were they? This was the problem – ignorant and unlearned men! And yet, the authorities said in effect, 'We cannot deny that a notable miracle has happened and everybody knows it. But here is the enigma. Ignorant and unlearned men are responsible for this – fishermen. Is it possible? Can they have done it? They have no learning, they have no training, they have nothing, and yet it has happened. What can we do?' Men, you see, cannot understand it, they cannot explain it. The results are not commensurate with the powers implied. The answer is that it is God who is using these men.

Now, I have reminded you that it was like that in 1858 and 1859, and, too, in 1904 and 1905, the last major revival in the

British Isles. The man that God used then was a man whose name was Evan Roberts and he was a very ordinary man. But he was the man that God used and you cannot explain that revival in terms of the man. That explanation is totally inadequate. And then take another argument. Look at the change in the man. Look at these apostles of whom we have been reading. Look at them before Pentecost, weak, helpless. Look at them after Pentecost, filled with a blazing power. See the courage with which Peter, who denied his Lord, is now fearlessly facing the hostile crowd and the authorities that have power to put him to death. Look at John Wesley, before May 24th, 1738, a complete failure in the ministry. But look at him afterwards. The same man with the same abilities, the same powers, the same everything, how do you explain the change? You cannot explain it in terms of Wesley. What is it? Oh, it is the Spirit of God that has come upon them. It is a miracle.

And so it was a hundred years ago in Northern Ireland and in Wales. I have mentioned a man called David Morgan, a very ordinary Minister, just carrying on, as it were. Nobody had heard of him. He did nothing at all that was worthy of note. Suddenly this power came upon him and for two years, as I have said, he preached like a lion. Then the power was withdrawn and he reverted to David Morgan again. The same man, you see. You cannot explain it in terms of men. There is only one explanation – 'the hand of the Lord, that it is mighty'. It can take the things that are not, and confound the things that are, and ridicule them.

Consider the places where revival happens. Sometimes it starts in a big city, but sometimes it starts in a village or hamlet. I emphasise this point because it is to me the most glorious of all. You see, when man does something, he likes to do it in big cities, does he not? He does it in a big way and he feels that this is essential to success. But as we consider the revivals of 1857–59 may I use the expression 'the divine humour'? Where did they break out then? It was not in the capital city of Belfast in Northern Ireland, it was in a village you have never heard of called Connor. That is how God does things. When he sent his Son into this world he was not born in Jerusalem but in Bethlehem, the very least of the cities of Judah. Thus God, that we might give the honour and the glory to himself, makes it impossible that we can explain it in terms of men. It is in the Bethlehems, the Connors, the little villages that people have never heard of, that the mighty thing often happens. And it was exactly the same thing two hundred years ago. It was in that little town of Northampton in

New England that the revival broke out. It was in a little hamlet called Trevecca in Wales that Howell Harris was suddenly laid hold of, and in another similar small village that Daniel Rowland was apprehended by God – places you have never heard of, that is how God does it.

And this is the wonderful thing – the next revival may break out in a little hamlet that you and I have never heard of. We people in these big cities of ours may be passed by and God may bring us to nought and do this mighty thing in some unknown little place with a small group of people. That can happen in revival. It can happen anywhere. Thank God! That is what makes life so romantic and so hopeful at the same time. There is no limit. And why is this? To show again that it is the sovereign work of God. You cannot explain it.

Neither, in the third place, can men control it. There is a sudden beginning. There is a sudden ending. You get variations during the revival and men seem to be utterly helpless. While it is perfectly true to say that we can quench the Spirit and be a hindrance, it is never true to say that if we observe all the rules and the conditions that we can produce revival. No. God keeps it in his own hands, beginning, course and end. In everything, we are dependent upon the Holy Spirit and his power.

But, lastly, think of its overwhelming character. 'What mean these stones?' These stones are there to tell us of 'the hand of the Lord, that it is mighty'. A revival is something which, when it happens, leads people to say, as the townspeople said in Jerusalem on the day of Pentecost, 'What is this? What is it?' It is something that comes like a tornado. It is almost like an overflowing tide, it is like a flood. Astounding things happen, and of such a magnitude that men are left amazed, astonished. Let me give you but one illustration which is one of the most lyrical and one of the most wonderful. There was a preacher in Scotland three hundred years ago of the name of John Livingstone of Kilsyth. There was a marvellous day in the life of John Livingstone. He tells us himself in his autobiography that he was a very ordinary preacher. And yet, writing at the end of his life, he looks back and he says, 'You know, there was a day, I shall never forget it, in June 1630. . . .' He was at a communion service at a place called Shotts. Have you ever read of the revival at the Kirk of Shotts? Read it, my friends, this is what happened. They had had their services; they had gone on over the weekend. John Livingstone and a number of others had been spending Sunday night after the services in prayer, and in conferences, as they called them, talking to one another about these things, and Monday morning came and John Livingstone had been asked to preach. He was out in the fields meditating, and suddenly he felt that he could not preach, that the thing was beyond him and that he was inadequate. And he felt like running away. But suddenly the voice of God seemed to speak to him, not in audible language, but in his spirit, telling him not to do that and that God did not work in that way, and it made him feel that he must go back. He preached, he tells us, on Ezekiel 36. And he said, 'I had preached for about an hour and a half. Then,' he said, 'I began to apply my message,' and as he was beginning to apply it, suddenly the Spirit of God came upon him and he went on for another hour in this application. And as he did so, people were literally falling to the ground, and in that one service five hundred people were converted.

Oh, modern people, I have to say this – unfortunately he did not test the meeting. I am not saying that five hundred came forward at the end, they did not do that sort of thing. Five hundred were convicted, some falling to the ground, having to be carried out. Others went out groaning in agony and were in this agony for days. But as the result of that one sermon, five hundred people were added to the churches – truly, permanently, soundly converted. That is the kind of thing that happens in a revival. And poor John Livingstone says that that kind of thing only happened to him on one other occasion. In a long life just these two days, but what days! Not John Livingstone, but 'the hand of the Lord', working in and through John Livingstone. A story, too, is told of a man preaching in a little town called Llanidloes, in Wales, who preached one sermon, and during the next six months a thousand people were added to the churches in the district round about that little town.

What is this? This is 'the hand of the Lord, that is mighty'. At Pentecost you had miracles, speaking with tongues and many other things. They are variable, they do not always happen. But mighty things happen. Miraculous things happen, things that are beyond the explanation and the wit of men. And indeed, if you consult the men whom God has used on such occasions, they will all tell you the same thing. They suddenly, like John Livingstone, became conscious of a power coming upon them. Not themselves. Taken up, taken out of themselves. Given liberty. Given authority. Given fearlessness. Speaking as men of God with the boldness of the original apostles. They knew when the power came, they knew when the power went. You will read it in the journals of Whitefield and of Wesley and all the rest. This is the hand of the Lord. This is the demonstration of the Spirit and of power. It was because he knew so much about this that the Apostle Paul says 'For the weapons of our warfare are not carnal, but mighty through God to the pulling down of strong holds; casting down imaginations, and every high thing that exalteth itself against the knowledge of God, and bringing into captivity every thought to the obedience of Christ' (2 Cor. 10.4–5). That is it.

Or, finally, look at it as it is described in Acts 2. Here are the apostles meeting together for prayer in the upper room. They had been doing it for ten days. Suddenly there came a sound from heaven, as of a rushing, mighty wind, and it filled all the house where they were sitting. That is it. Not always the sound, but always the consciousness of the mighty wind of God. The Spirit of God descends upon preacher, prayers, praying people, those meeting in conference. The sound of a rushing mighty wind. The hand of the Lord, that it is mighty! Do we know anything about that my friends? Do you believe this? Do we believe the facts? Do we believe the explanation? Do we who claim to believe in God and in the Lord Jesus Christ still believe in miracles? In the possibility of miracles? Do we believe in God coming in and doing things that we not only cannot do, but cannot even understand, nor control, nor explain. Yea, I ask you, do you long to know such things? To see such things happening again today? Are you praying for such a visitation? For believe me, when God hears our prayers and does this thing again, it will be such a phenomenon that not only will the Church be astounded and amazed, but even those who are outside will be compelled to listen and to pay attention, in a way that they are not doing at the present time, and in a way that men left to themselves can never persuade them to do.

That is the meaning of the stones. That is why I am calling your attention to revival. This is what God can do. This is what God has done. Let us together decide to beseech him, to plead with him to do this again. Not that we may have the experience or the excitement, but that his mighty hand may be known and his great name may be glorified and magnified among the people.

Chapter 10

Joshua 4.21–24

And he spake unto the children of Israel, saying, When your children shall ask their fathers in time to come, saying, What mean these stones? Then ye shall let your children know, saying, Israel came over this Jordan on dry land. For the Lord your God dried up the waters of Jordan from before you, until ye were passed over, as the Lord your God did to the Red sea, which he dried up from before us, until we were gone over: That all the people of the earth might know the hand of the Lord, that it is mighty: that ye might fear the Lord your God for ever (Josh. 4.21–24).

We have, you remember, been looking at the story in the Book of Joshua because it is a perfect illustration of why it is important for us to have monuments and reminders of the great things which God has done. We have seen that the principles on which God acts never vary. We are called upon to consider historical facts, significant and miraculous facts, and now we must move on to another aspect of this great subject of revival. What is the object and the purpose of it all? Here is this miraculous thing that happened. But why, why did it happen? Or, if I may put my question in a different way, and ask with reverence, why does God do this from time to time? For we have been reminding ourselves that what happened one hundred years ago is but one in a series of similar events. From time to time in the long history of the Church there have been these visitations, these outpourings of God's Spirit. Nothing is clearer in the history of the Church than that. Indeed, that does seem to be the history of the Church. There was a great outpouring of the Spirit on the day of Pentecost. That visitation persisted for some time, but then it began to wane and finally vanished. The Church got into a powerless condition, so much so that some people thought the end had come. Then suddenly God poured out his Spirit again and the Church was raised up to the heights once more. For a time that persisted, but then it, too, gradually passed. So the history of the Church is a sort of graph of ups and downs. That has been happening throughout the running centuries.

Now, the question we are concerned with at this point is – why does God do this from time to time? And the answer is given us very perfectly in these verses that we are looking at now. The first reason given in verse 24 is this – 'that [in order that] all people of the earth might know the hand of the Lord, that it is mighty'. This then is the first reason that is given. God does this thing from time to time, God sends revival, blessing, upon the Church, in order that he may do something with respect to those who are outside him. He is doing something that is going to arrest the attention of all the people of the earth. Here, we must always realise, is the chief reason for ever considering this matter at all. This is my main reason for calling attention to this whole subject of revival and for urging everybody to pray for revival, to look for it and to long for it. This is the reason – the glory of God. You see, Israel alone represented God and his glory. All the other nations of the world were pagan, they had their various gods and they did not believe in nor worship the God of Israel. But God had chosen Israel. He had made a nation for himself in order that through them, and by means of them, he might manifest his own glory and that they might bear this testimony to all the nations of the world. That was the real function of the Children of Israel, and the other nations were watching them and were ready always to scoff at them and to ridicule them. Whenever the nation of Israel was defeated, or seemed to be helpless, or was in any trouble, the other nations would always say, 'Where is their God, the God of whom they have spoken so much and of whom they have boasted so much, where is he? Where is his power?'

And so, the first reason for this miraculous act is – that all these peoples and nations 'may know the hand of the Lord, that it is mighty'. God is vindicating himself, he is asserting his own glory and his own power. He is doing this in order that those on the outside, who scoff and speak in derision, may see something that will pull them up and arrest them and astound them. Now, we must never lose sight of this. It is the main reason for being concerned about revival. We should not seek revival in order that we may have experiences. I have described experiences that do take place in revival, but we do not seek revival primarily for their sake. There are people who do. There are people who always rush to meetings where any kind of experience is promised and they go the rounds from one meeting to another, people who are just itching and thirsting to have experiences, always thinking of themselves. But that is not the way in which it is put here, for the primary thing is the glory of God, the power, and the name of God, and the honour of God. So let us be perfectly clear about that.

There are people who are ready to jump at anything that will solve their problem or the problem of the Church. Some years ago the main sections of the Christian Church were not interested at all in evangelism. They despised it and dismissed it with derision. But today every section of the Church is talking a great deal about evangelism. And the reason is that they are seeing the churches becoming empty, so they will take up anything that may help them to solve the problem of church attendance or even church finance. And they would undoubtedly do likewise with respect to revival, but that is a terrible thing to do. No, our overriding, controlling reason for having any interest at all in these matters should be the glory of God. Does it grieve you, my friends, that the name of God is being taken in vain and desecrated? Does it grieve you that we are living in a godless age – an age when men have sufficient arrogance to speak in public and in private with sarcasm of the record of God's mighty deeds and actions?

But, we are living in such an age and the main reason we should be praying about revival is that we are anxious to see God's name vindicated and his glory manifested. We should be anxious to see something happening that will arrest the nations, all the peoples, and cause them to stop and to think again. So here is the first thing. You will find it constantly in the Scriptures. It is in many ways one of the leading themes, if not *the* leading theme, in the book of the Psalms. Read the Psalms and see those men praying for a visitation of God's Spirit. Every time it is in order that the heathen who are scoffing may be silenced. The Psalmist cries out to God that he should do something that will silence them. This is the end to which they are always looking, that God will do something and speak in such a way, that will call everybody to 'Be still and know that I am God' (Ps. 46.10). That is the great theme of Psalm 46. The nations and their princes are all being addressed; these people who are arguing against God and querying whether there is such a God. 'And listen' says the Psalmist, 'here is the God who makes wars to cease; this is the God who arises and vindicates himself.' Then, having displayed his case, he says, 'Be still,' give up, give in, admit, 'that I am God.'

120

Now, that is the thing of which we are reminded here. God himself told Joshua to tell the people his primary reason for setting up this memorial – that he might thus manifest his glory and silence the people who are outside. And that is what revival has invariably achieved. It has caused those who are outside the Church and those who are inimical to Christianity to pay attention. For it is indeed a phenomenon. It is, as we have agreed, something miraculous. It is something that astounds them and causes them, of necessity, to stop, and to look, and to consider. Of course, their reason for stopping and considering may not be a good one, it may be sheer curiosity, but whatever it is, it does not matter, for it does make them stop and think. We have a classic example of this, of course, in Acts 2. It is the account of what happened on the day of Pentecost, when the Holy Spirit was poured out and we read that the people of Jerusalem and all the strangers who were gathered there, were arrested, and they said, 'What is this?'. A phenomenon. Something was happening, and they were forced to pay attention and Peter had to get up and give his explanation, you remember. That is always what a revival does, and I maintain that there is nothing short of a revival that will have that effect. We have tried nearly everything else, but it does not succeed. The masses of the people even if they show a temporary interest, show no more than that. No, men can never do anything that will have this effect. This is always the action of God. If I may put it bluntly and clearly, what is needed is not a stunt but the action of God that will stun people. That is the difference. Man can produce stunts. And he is very clever at doing that. He can think of something fresh and new, and he will advertise it, but the people know the whole time that it is man's doing. 'It's a stunt,' they say. Now, stunts will never lead to this desired position. But when God arises and God acts, then something is happening that will force men's attention. They cannot understand it. Here psychologists are left without any explanation. They can explain stunts without difficulty but they cannot explain this. That is the difference between man organising something, and God manifesting the right hand of his power and showing that it is mighty.

Now surely this is the crying need of the hour. We are aware of the position of the vast majority of the people of this country; church attendance constitutes but five per cent of the population. And though we may preach, and fast, and sweat, and pray, and do all we can, all our efforts seem to lead to nothing. What is needed is some mighty demonstration of the power of God, some

121

enactment of the Almighty, that will compel people to pay attention, and to look, and to listen. And the history of all the revivals of the past indicates so clearly that that is invariably the effect of revival, without any exception at all. That is why I am calling attention to revival. That is why I am urging you to pray for this. When God acts, he can do more in a minute than man with his organising can do in fifty years. Let us realise this tremendous possibility, therefore, and plead to God to make known his power and to manifest his glory in the midst of a crooked and perverse generation of people – people that even blaspheme his holy name and deny his very existence. For God's sake, for the glory of his name, let us intercede and pray for a visitation of God's Spirit.

There, then, is the first great reason 'that all the people of the earth might know the hand of the Lord, that it is mighty'. The second reason is 'that ye might fear the Lord your God for ever.' That is what I have been emphasising, that revival is of great value to the Church, as well as all it does for the world. That *you* might know, that *you* might fear the Lord your God for ever. So, what does it do for the Church? Let me enumerate some of the things that are taught here quite plainly.

The first thing it does is to give the Church an unusual consciousness of the presence of the power of God. 'That ye [the Children of Israel] might fear the Lord for ever.' Now, in the tenth verse of the previous chapter, it is put much more explicitly and powerfully – 'And Joshua said, Hereby ye shall know that the living God is among you.' That is it. This is going to happen, said Joshua to the people, in order that you may know that the living God is among you. When you read this story of the Children of Israel, you will see very clearly that they needed to be reminded of that. Though they were God's people, though he had done so many things for them and to them, though he had brought them out of Egypt, though he had brought them through the Red Sea, though he had led them in the wilderness where their feet did not swell and where they never lacked food because he fed them with manna, the bread from heaven, yet they were constantly fearful and grumbling, looking at the other nations and peoples and their gods, hesitant and doubtful. They behaved in a manner which makes us feel that they were a people who did not realise their relationship to God. And God did this thing at the river of Jordan in order that they might know that the living God was among them.

Now, this is the supreme need of the Church today. In one way, the main trouble with the Christian Church as she is at this moment, the main trouble with every one of us in our daily life and living, is that we fail to realise that the living God is among us. What is the Church? It is this institution, this body in which God dwells. He has promised that. 'I will be in you. I will dwell in you. I will walk among you.' That is what he says. That is what he said to these Children of Israel (see, for example, Exod. 29.45–46). That is what is transferred in exactly the same way to the Christian Church. The Christian Church is not a human organisation and institution. She is as the Apostle Paul puts it at the end of Ephesians 2, a great building in which God dwells, an habitation of God.

This is an argument that is worked out in many places in the New Testament epistles. But the Church does not seem to realise that today. People will persist in regarding the Christian Church as just an institution, one institution among others, just a human organisation. But that is not the Church, the Church is this body in which God himself dwells. And what he does in revival is to remind us of that. When God acts in revival everybody present feels and knows that God is there. Of course, we believe this. We believe this by faith. Yes, but we should *know* it. We should have a realisation of it. We should be conscious of his nearness. And that is what revival does for us. 'I am going to do this thing,' says God, 'then all of you will realise that I am among you, I am acting in your midst. I, the living God, have come down amongst you. I am in you. You are my people and I dwell in you and I walk in you.' That is what the Church needs to realise today.

But, of course, it is the very thing she does not realise. It is the thing we are always forgetting. But though I put that first, we must remember that God, at the same time, reminds us that the whole power that should be manifest in the Church is his power, that everything which the Church does should be a manifestation of the power of God. What is the gospel? Well, you remember the answer of the Apostle Paul, 'It is the power of God unto salvation to every one that believeth'. (Rom. 1.16). How easy it is to forget that. How easy to preach it as a system, to preach it as a collection of ideas, or just to preach it as a truth. Ah, but you can do that without power. There are people, says the Apostle Paul, who 'have a form of godliness, but deny the power thereof' (2 Tim. 3.5). Christianity is primarily a life. It is a power. It is a manifestation of energy. And as we realise that the living God is among us, we shall realise more and more this tremendous power.

That in turn will lead us to realise that the one thing that matters is that we should be rightly related to God, and always reliant on his power. The Apostle's great claim, you remember, in writing to the Corinthians is this – that when he came to them he did not preach to them with wisdom of men, it was not with 'enticing words of man's wisdom' (1 Cor. 2.1–4). He could have done that. He was a very able man and one who was learned and very well read. But though he was going to a seat of learning – there was a university in Corinth – and he knew the mentality of the Greeks, he did not approach them along that line at all. He tells them later that he became a fool for Christ's sake and many of them despised him because of that. But, says the Apostle, I did not come in that way. In what way, then? Oh, he says, 'in demonstration of the Spirit and of power: that your faith should not stand in the wisdom of men, but in the power of God' (1 Cor. 2.5).

We all need to be reminded of this. Let me make a confession for all preachers. The outstanding temptation – the besetting sin – of every preacher, myself included, is that after you have prepared your sermons you feel that all is well. You have your two sermons ready for Sunday. Well, that is all right. You have your notes, and you can speak, and you can deliver your message. But that is not preaching! That can be utterly useless. Oh, it may be entertaining, there may be a certain amount of intellectual stimulus and profit in it, but that is not preaching. Preaching is in demonstration of the Spirit and of power. And a man has to realise, after he has prepared his sermons, that however perfectly he may have done so, that it is all waste and useless unless the power of the Spirit comes upon it and upon him. He must pray for that.

Yes, but not only he. Those who listen must also pray for that. How many people pray before they go to a service that the Spirit of God might come upon the preacher and use him and his message? The hearers, as well as the preacher must pray for that, otherwise they are looking to him and to his message. No, all together must look to God and realise their utter dependence upon the power that he alone can give. And whenever there is a revival and God's power is manifested, you need not urge people to pray, they do. They want to see more and more of it. Revival, then, encourages us to pray, and that is why it is good for us to read these accounts and look back on what God has done, that we may realise that the living God is among us. And we must pray to him to manifest this power.

Negatively, it means that it delivers us from any and every form of self-reliance, which is the curse of the Church. There is no difficulty at all in explaining the state of the Christian Church today, it is so perfectly simple. I will tell you why the Church is as she is today, it is self-reliance in the following forms.

First, reliance upon scholarship and learning. It came in about the middle of the last century. 'Ah,' people began to say, 'we are now becoming more educated and we have advanced. Of course we do not want the sort of thing they had in past centuries under Whitefield and Wesley and so on. We now want learned sermons.' And so they began to have them. And great attention was paid to form and to style and to diction. Sermons were published and it was obvious as the man was writing them that he had his eye on publication rather than on the service in which he was going to preach his sermon. Everything became learned and scholarly and philosophical and great sermons were delivered. And it is one of the main causes and explanations of the state of the Church today. Reliance upon human learning and knowledge and wisdom.

Then, secondly, of course, the reliance upon organising. In the last hundred years the Church has multiplied her organisations and institutions in a way that she has never done before in all her long history. There have never been so many sub-sections of the Christian Church as during the present century. Every thing is being organised; age groups, everything else. And there are head offices which send you the literature telling you how to do whatever your interest may be, how to handle children, how to handle young people, advice on this and that. All perfectly organised and yet look at the state of the Church. They are relying on the organisation.

Others rely on their own activities. As long as they are busy they think tremendous things are happening. And, of course, if you organise and if you are active, it will be reported in the papers – they must have something to report. And people say, 'Tremendous things are happening. Look at it.' But what is happening? Look at the Church, that is the answer. No, my dear friends, we need to learn once more the difference between bustle and busyness and 'the hand of the Lord, that it is mighty'.

But when God acts and when people realise that the living God is amongst them, they are humbled, they are abased. Men do not count any longer. And the reports are not about what men have done but about what God has done and what happens to men as the result of God's action. A revival always humbles men, abases them, casts them to the floor, makes them feel they can do nothing, fills them with a sense of reverence and of godly fear. Oh, how absent that is amongst us. How *men* are standing forward. But when revival comes, men push back, they are humbled to the ground and the glory is given to God, because it is God's power that is in evidence.

Then my next point, of course, follows by a logical necessity. When all this happens the fear of men is taken away from us in every form. In Joshua 3.10 we read: 'And Joshua said, Hereby ye shall know that the living God is among you, and that he will without fail drive out from before you the Canaanites, and the Hittites, and the Hivites, and the Perizzites, and the Girgashites, and the Amorites, and the Jebusites.'

The Children of Israel were about to enter the promised land and they had been hearing about all these tribes. The spies had been sent forward and they came back and said, 'You know, there are giants in that land and when we looked at them we felt that we were as grasshoppers.' And they were trembling, they were afraid of these great powers that they had got to meet when they entered the promised land. Here is the answer: when you know that the living God is amongst you, what are the Hittites, who are the Girgashites and the Jebusites, what are the whole lot of them put together? They become as nothing. The fear of men is taken away immediately when we realise that the living God is among us. And if ever the Church needed this it is now. The Church is so afraid. She is afraid of organised sin, and her argument is, 'We must be doing something because look at the world. It is attracting the young people, it gives them a happy pleasant Saturday night, entertains them, teaches them how to sing and do this and that. Well now, we must do the same thing. Bring in your pop group, or whatever it is, into your Sunday night service. That is what they like, you see.' The world is doing it and the young people say, 'I like it' and because the Church is so afraid that they are going to lose their young people they feel they must do the same. Oh, what a tragedy, what a departure from God's way.

The Church has been afraid of the young people for a long time and that is why she has multiplied these institutions to try to attract them. And she is afraid, too, of the lure of the modern world. People say, 'What can we do? We are up against the television nowadays. There was not television two hundred years ago. They had no radio, they had no cinema. *There* is our problem. We must do something,' they say. They are afraid of these organisations and powers. And, too, they are terrified of learning and of knowledge. 'Look,' they say, 'at what these experts are saying in the various radio and television programmes and our people hear these things. Is it intellectually respectable to be a Christian? Can you really talk about miracles still? And about dividing the Red Sea and Jordan? Surely people will not believe all that!' So we trim and modify our gospel, because we are afraid of learning and of knowledge and of science. That is what the Church has been doing for a hundred years and that is why she is as she is today. Then people say that Communism is spreading, and if it seems to succeed through using various methods, then we should use them too. They say that we must also make our literature more effective. All right, go on doing these things, but if you rely upon them you are already defeated.

There is no need to be afraid of any of these powers, they have always been there. There is nothing new about all this. The Christian Church has always had to fight the world and the flesh and the devil. She had to fight the Roman Empire at the beginning. She had to fight the malignity of the Jews. She has always had these enemies who are out to exterminate her. And the Church has often quaked and feared, but never when there has been revival, because then they know that the living God is among them 'and he will without fail drive out from before you the Canaanites, and the Hittites, and the Hivites, and the Perizzites, and the Girgashites, and the Amorites, and the Jebusites'. He names them one by one, you see, as I have been trying to do. What have we to fear from of all these things when the living God comes amongst us? Oh, for a touch of his power. Oh, that the Church might realise that this is the answer and then our fear of all our enemies and opponents would vanish like the morning mist. 'Fear Him, ye saints, and you will then have nothing else to fear.' That is how the writer of the hymn puts it and how right he is. Revival does that for us.

And so, to sum it up, it makes us look, and keeps us looking, to him, and dependent upon him. Our supreme need, and our only need, is to know God, the living God, and the power of his might. We need nothing else. It is just that, the power of the living God, to know that the living God is among us and that nothing else matters. So we wait upon him. We look to him. We cry out to him, as Moses did when he was standing before the Red Sea, not knowing what to do, and while the people were grumbling and complaining. God answered Moses and said, 'Wherefore criest thou unto me? Speak unto the children of Israel, that they go forward' (Exod. 14.15). And on they went.

Stand then in His great might,
With all His strength endued;
And take, to arm you for the fight,
The panoply of God.
Charles Wesley

That is what we need, my friends. And that is why I am urging
you to pray for revival. We must look to him. God does this in
order to give us encouragement. To show us that he is among us.
And the reminder of what happened one hundred years ago
should lead us to turn back to him. I say, forget everything else.
Forget *every*thing else. We need to realise the presence of the
living God amongst us. Let everything else be silent. This is no
time for minor differences. We all need to know the touch of the
power of the living God. And let us continue and wait until we
know it.

And thenn, of course, God does this in order to deliver us from
our enemies; enemies without, enemies within. Yes God did all
these things to bring his people out of Egypt, out of the wilderness,
into the blessed land of Canaan. He does it, I say, in order to
lead us to the land of blessing – Canaan, a land flowing with milk
and honey. What does this mean in the Church? It means that
there has never been a revival but that it has led to praise and to
thanksgiving, to enjoyment of the riches of God's grace. The great
characteristic of revival is ultimately praise, adoration, worship,
full enjoyment, full, unmixeed annd evermore.

But, in conclusion, let me just direct your attention to one other
thing. We have considered this great fact of what happens in
revival. We have considered the nature of the fact, the miraculous,
the almighty power of God. WWe have asked the question, 'Why
does God do this?' I want to ask a last question, 'When does God
do this?' You want to know that, I hope. If you are longing and
yearning, I am sure that you are asking the question, 'Oh, when
is God going to do this? We have been praying, many of us for
years. Nothing seems to happen. When does God send revival?'
Well, the answer is here in this story of Joshua and it is confirmed
by the history of the Church.

There seem to me to be two main factors here. The first is this.
God always seems to do this after a period of great trial and
great discouragement. The text, we have seen, reminds us of two
occasions: The crossing of the Red Sea and the crossing of the
river of Jordan. When does he do this marvellous thing? Oh, he
does it then, after you have been in Egypt for a while, in the

bondage, in the captivity, in the cruelty of Egypt, with the task-masters and the lashes of their whips, trying to make bricks without sufficient straw. Bondage, aridity, cruelty, persecution and trial. He does it after Egypt. He does it also after a period in the wilderness. Here are the Children of Israel right before Jordan. Yes, but they had just been forty years in the wilderness, without a home, in the howling, barren wilderness with its storms and its trials, its testings, and its provings – all that had happened to them there. Read the story. And what a sad story it is. Yes, they had had a wilderness experience.

And on top of that they had had another calamity, which, to many of them must have seemed to be the end of all things: Moses, their great leader, had died. He had gone up on to a mountain and he had never come back again. The man who had come to them originally with a message from God and had addressed them in their utter serfdom when they were broken-hearted. The man who had led them through so much. He had gone. And a man called Joshua was left to lead them. Who was he and what was he? The position, you see, seemed to be utterly discouraging. Forty years in the wilderness and without a leader.

Ah, thank God for this. It is after such experiences that God sends revival. After Egypt, after the wilderness experience. God knows the Christian Church has been in this wilderness many a long year. If you read the history of the Church before about 1830 or 1840, you will find that in many countries there used to be regular revivals of religion almost every ten years or so. It has not been like that. There has only been one major revival since 1859. Oh, we have passed through a barren period, with that devastating higher criticism and the evil that it has done, in pulpits, in pews, everywhere. People have lost their belief in this living God and in the atonement and in reconciliation and have turned to wisdom, philosophy and learning. We have passed through one of the most barren periods in the long history of the Church. We have been like the prodigal son in that far country, spending our time in the fields with the swine and living on nothing but husks. Yes, we have been in bondage, we have been in fear, we have suffered persecution and derision and it is still going on. We are still in the wilderness. Do not believe anything that suggests that we are out of it, we are not. The Church is in the wilderness. But thank God it is always after such a period that God acts and does his mighty deeds and shows forth his glory.

The second factor in this story is also most important. It is not only after Egypt, or after the wilderness that God acts. The real moment, the moment of crisis, is when you are right up against the Red Sea, when you are actually on the border of Jordan. It is then he does it. You see, we can be forty years in the wilderness, but the mere fact of being in the wilderness does not produce it. No, it is not only in the wilderness, but when we have actually arrived at this critical position. If I may use modern terminology, God always seems to do this, when we are right up against it and so much against it that we are hopeless and helpless. You remember the picture at the Red Sea? The Children of Israel had been commanded to go on. Where were they to go? Well, they were taken to a point at which on the one side was Pi-hahiroth and on the other side Baal-zephon, two mountains, one on each side of them. Behind them were Pharaoh and his hosts and the chariots, the army of Egypt. And there were the defenceless Children of Israel with nothing to defend them at all – mountain here, mountain there, the enemy behind, and in front the Red Sea. It was a situation of complete and entire hopelessness and despair, with the people grumbling and complaining, asking Moses what it all meant, and Moses had nothing to do but to fall before God. And then the answer came and the Red Sea was divided.

It was exactly the same here at Jordan. We are even given this interesting detail that the river of Jordan was badly flooded for long months at that time of the year. They could not possibly cross it. There they were, facing a flood. How could they get through? It was then that God arose and manifested the right hand of his power and gave a display of his glory. I just put this to you in the form of a challenge. Read the histories and accounts of every revival that has ever taken place and you will invariably find this, that the one man or the group, the little group of people, who have been used in this way by God to send revival, have always known a state of utter desperation and final despair. Every single one of them. Read the journals of Whitefield and Wesley. Read the life history of all these men. They have always come to this place where they have realised their utter and absolute impotence. Their final paralysis. There is the Red Sea. Here is the enemy. There are the mountains. They are shut in, they are shut down, they are crushed to their knees. it is always the prerequisite. It is always the moment at which God acts.

And that is what, I confess, troubles me and discourages me today. The Christian Church is still so healthy, so confident in herself, so sure that she only needs to organise yet another effort, some further activity. She has not come up to the Red Sea. She has never been to Pi-hahiroth and Baal-zephon. She does not know that experience and until she does I cannot see that we have much reason for anticipating a revival of religion and an outpouring of the Spirit of God. It may be, you see, that things infinitely worse than what we have already known will yet have to happen to us. You would have thought that two world wars would have done it, but they have not. You would have thought that the present position would have been enough, but it is not. God have mercy upon us. Until, I say, we arrive there at Pi-hahiroth, Baal-zephon, Migdal, with the enemy, the Red Sea, the utter hopelessness, Jordan in flood, the utter impossibility, and the final despair. May God bring us to that realisation. May he so reveal his own glory and holiness to us. May he reveal unto us our utter impotence and hopelessness. May we see these things in such a way that we shall cease from men and look only unto the living God. And then there is no question but that he will hear us and he will manifest his glory and his power.

Chapter 11

Acts 2.12–13

And they were all amazed, and were in doubt, saying one to another, What meaneth this? Others mocking said, These men are full of new wine (Acts 2.12–13).

In our consideration of revival up to this point, we have looked at it as we see it described in the Scriptures. We have looked at its character in general and we have considered its object and its purpose. We have seen clearly that this is a great and a striking phenomenon, which is primarily designed to revive the Church, and secondarily, to call the attention of the world outside, that men and women may be led and brought to salvation. It is a kind of sign that God gives in this way in order to confirm his work in the Church, and to establish his people, and build them up and encourage them, and at the same time, as I say, it overflows in mighty blessing to those who are without.

Now then, having described it in that way, and having seen its leading features, and characteristics, and especially having considered its object and its purpose, it seems to me that the next logical step is to ask this question: what effect, then, does it have, especially upon those who are without? It is meant to let all the nations of the world know that 'the hand of the Lord, that it is mighty', as we saw it there in the book of Joshua. But the question arises at once, does it have that effect? Are all convinced by it? And it is in order that we may consider that question that we will consider this famous, and well-known section in the second chapter of the book of the Acts of the Apostles. Here an answer is given to that question, which is of very great value to us, and should be of urgent concern to all who are looking for, and longing for, revival. Here, at any rate, is a possible reaction. And we find it not only here, but elsewhere in the Bible. As we read the history of the Church and of revival throughout the centuries, we find that this kind of thing is constantly repeated. We read, 'They were all amazed, and were in doubt, saying one to another, 'What meaneth this?' What is this? You remember how the Holy Spirit was poured out upon the disciples and others with them, 120 people, there in the upper room. And as the result of this mighty outpouring of the Spirit that came upon them, they began to speak in other tongues, and undoubtedly there were many other similar phenomena as well. All this was noised abroad, and the people gathered together from everywhere, and observing, and hearing this, they said, 'What meaneth this?' They were amazed, some doubted, and others mocking said, 'These men are full of new wine': they are drunk. Now, there you see, is a reaction on the part of certain people on this mighty phenomenon which takes place when God pours forth his Spirit.

This is a reaction which is due, as we are told here so plainly in the context, to certain phenomena that may sometimes accompany revivals. There is no doubt at all but that it was the speaking in tongues and the other phenomena which accompanied the outpouring of the Spirit on the day of Pentecost, that led to this reaction. That was the thing that attracted and caused some people to doubt, and to be amazed, and some to mock, and to say that this was just due to the fact that these men were full of new wine. Well now, in the history of revivals you will find, with practically no exception, the same kind of reaction. There are people who disapprove of the whole notion of revival. There are people like that within the Christian Church, as well as people who are outside. So, it seems to me, that it is very important that we should deal with this question of the phenomena.

Now these can be subdivided into various groups. First, there are the tendencies, undoubtedly in most revivals, to an emotional element. I do not think there has ever been a revival without that being present. Some people have been moved very deeply and profoundly, and, sometimes, others behave in a very excitable manner during a period of revival. That is a fact that I am putting before you. I shall deal with possible explanations of this, but at this point I am simply collecting the facts. But there are other phenomena also. And it is these others that have generally been the subject of most criticisms. When I say phenomena, I mean things that happen over and above the fact that large numbers of people are awakened and converted, and large numbers of members of the Church are roused, and quickened. The phenomena I am referring to are in addition to that. And this question of the additional phenomena is a very important, and indeed, a very fascinating one.

Let me make this clear. These phenomena do not always manifest themselves in a revival. Take, for instance, a very interesting fact about the revival of a hundred years ago. I have reminded you repeatedly that this revival was experienced in the United States of America, in Northern Ireland, in Wales, in Scotland, and to some extent in other countries. Now, it is interesting to observe that these additional phenomena which we are going to consider were very little in evidence in the United States, or in Wales, and they were almost non-existent in Scotland, but they were very marked and very striking in Northern Ireland. Now that in itself is an interesting fact, before we go any further, because it establishes the point that these phenomena are not essential to revival. We must keep that in our minds. You can have a revival without these phenomena, and yet it is true to say, that, on the whole, they do tend to be present when there is a revival, though the extent of their presence may vary tremendously from district to district and from country to country.

What, then, are these phenomena to which I am referring? It seems to me that the best way to classify them is to put them under two headings. First of all, there are certain physical phenomena. Under the influence of this mighty power, people may literally fall to the ground under conviction of sin, or even faint, and remain in a state of unconsciousness, perhaps for a considerable time. Now in the revival in 1859 in Northern Ireland, they referred to this as being 'struck', because it was exactly as if a person had been literally struck or hit upon the head, with the result that they fell to the ground in a state of complete unconsciousness. This has frequently happened in revivals in other places, and in different centuries. Then there are people who seem to go into trances. They may be seated or they may be standing, and they are looking into the distance, obviously seeing something, and yet they are completely unconscious, and unaware of their surroundings. They do not seem to be able to hear anything, nor to see anything that may be happening round and about them. They are evidently seeing something with a spiritual eye, which is not visible to others, and a state of trance is the only way in which we can describe it. So there are some of the physical phenomena. There are others, but there is no purpose in my giving a full, or a detailed list. There is a whole group of phenomena which belong, thus, to the realm of the physical, and which have often been regarded as such and have even been treated medically as purely physical phenomena. And, as I say, such things were a very prominent feature of the revival in Northern Ireland in 1859.

But then, in addition to these physical phenomena, there are also certain mental phenomena – things which do not so much attack the body, as clearly affect the mind. Sometimes, for example, the most extraordinary gift of speech is given to people during revival. People who, if they did ever take part in prayer in the church, were very halting and very hesitant, suddenly begin to pray with an amazing eloquence, with extraordinary richness of language that they were never capable of before. There are many instances of this. I once met a man who well remembered the revival of 1904 and 1905 in Wales, and he told me what happened to his own minister. They had had this man as minister in their church for a number of years, he was an able man who always preached what they would call a good and a sound sermon, but he was always halting, and hesitant. He coughed a lot, and was a poor speaker in every respect, apart from his subject matter. Now this man attended a Presbytery meeting one day, something which he had done on similar occasions many many times. At this particular Presbytery numbers of other ministers were giving reports of the events which had been taking place in their churches during the revival. This man listened, and he came back to his own church completely transformed as a preacher. He went into his pulpit the next Sunday, and they really could scarcely believe that he was the same man. All the hesitation had gone, all the impediment had disappeared. He spoke with freedom, with authority, and with a power such as they had never known from him before.

Now his was no isolated case, that kind of thing, that gift of speech is sometimes given in prayer, or in conversation, or in description. Not only that, there is very often a gift of prophecy given. I mean by that, literally an ability to foretell the future. We must face these things because, it does seem to me, that we are in grave danger, with all our learning and knowledge, of quenching the Spirit. I am putting facts before you. You will find this phenomenon of prophecy, this ability to foretell the future, frequently present. It takes many forms. I knew a man whose minister had had this gift, again in the revival of 1904 and 1905. It disappeared completely afterwards, but while the revival lasted he was told beforehand of something that was going to happen in his Church, not once, but morning by morning. He would be awakened out of his sleep at half past two in the morning, and given direct and exact information of something that was going to happen during that day, and it did happen. That is another part of this mental phenomenon.

Again, you find knowledge given to people, which is quite inexplicable. There were cases in Northern Ireland, for instance, of people who could not read and could not write, people who had never been able to read the Bible. But suddenly although they still could not read, they were given an ability to find places in the Bible and to make known the contents. There are endless illustrations along this particular line. Abilities have been given – the gift of discrimination, the gift of understanding, the gift of planning. Here, in this realm of the mental, quite astonishing powers have certainly been given to people for a temporary period.

There then, are the main phenomena to which I am directing your attention, the physical and the mental. These things occur or may occur, during a period of revival. And here is the question that confronts us. What is this? How do you explain it? Now that is why I am putting it in the context of Acts 2. The promised thing happened, the Holy Spirit was poured out, and the results followed, and here were these people at Jerusalem gathering together and asking what all this meant. And some said, 'Why are you asking that question? The thing is perfectly obvious. These men are full of new wine, they are drunk.' And people have continued to adopt that attitude throughout the centuries. Various explanations were put forward a hundred years ago, as they have always been, in every period of revival, and they are still being produced today. And that is why I am calling attention to all this. There are people, who dismiss, and denounce, the whole notion of revival because of these phenomena, and therefore when they are exhorted to pray for revival they say, 'Most certainly not. We do not want that sort of thing. We are not interested in that kind of experience.' And, thus, without realising it, they are often guilty of quenching the Spirit.

So, let us look at some of the explanations that are put forward, and especially today. And may I add that I am particularly concerned about this, because, as you know, there is great interest in this matter at the present time, and I know of nothing that is such a complete answer to some of these modern psychologists who would explain conversion, and everything else, along these physical lines. Let me show you what I mean. There are some who would suggest that all of this is just some form of what is now called 'brainwashing'. They compare it with a technique which is being employed at the present time by the Communists, or they compare it with what was so obviously applied by a man like Hitler in pre-war Germany, and during the War in that country.

'What is this?' people ask, and add, 'The answer is quite obvious. What is happening here is that the minds of these people are being bombarded. They are gradually been worn down. They are brought together in crowds, or they are dealt with, and kept in cells, and they are given insufficient sleep, and insufficient food. Everything is done to break down these people, and their resistance. They speak at them, they shout at them, and they bombard their minds. And then when they have brought them to the point of collapse, they do it still more and with a greater intensity of pressure, and the people do collapse. And then, in the state of collapse, it is the simplest thing in the world to indoctrinate them. You can insinuate your own teaching into their minds, and they will believe it and accept it, they will become devotees of it, and they will go out and try to convert others in turn.'

Well now, what about this explanation? Let us be clear about this. That kind of thing, of course, can be done, and is being done. There is no question at all that that is precisely what Hitler did. There is no doubt at all that that is exactly what other regimes are doing at the present time. By means of a given technique, they can thus break down the resistance of people's minds and insinuate their own doctrines into them. And now, the suggestion that is put forward, is that what happens during these periods of revival is exactly the same thing.

How then do we deal with this? Let me make one thing quite plain and clear. I am concerned to deal only with revival. I am not concerned with evangelistic campaigns. It is very important that we should draw that distinction. And for this reason, that in evangelistic campaigns techniques are used, and used deliberately; but not in revival. Now, I do want to underline and emphasise that difference. I am concerned only about revival, where no techniques are used at all. My argument has reference to nothing but that. I am not concerned at this moment, to deal with what happens in big campaigns.

So, I put it like this. This suggestion, with regard to brainwashing, to give it its general term, completely fails in the matter of revival because it completely fails to explain the beginning of revival. Take, for instance, what happened in Northern Ireland. There it happened in the case of one man, to start with. It was exactly the same in the United States, it all started in just one man. There was no bombardment of the mind of this man, none at all. No technique was employed, it was just one man, who himself became convicted of sin and was converted, and then began to feel an impulse that he should tell others about it. There

137

were no large crowds. There were no special techniques, none whatsoever. That is the amazing thing about the story, that it was just one man, and then two others joining him, praying together for months. Just three men in a prayer meeting. And on and on it went for months, and slowly others began to come in. Now this suggestion, this attempted explanation of the bombardment of the mind fails completely to account for the beginning and the origin of a revival.

Another thing it fails to explain is that it should happen in several countries at exactly the same time. That was not only true a hundred years ago, it was true two hundred years ago. When that great revival occurred under Jonathan Edwards in the New England states, it happened in England also, in Wales, in Scotland, and in other countries. It does not explain that at all. Why should all these things happen at the same time in different places, where there was no contact and no knowledge whatsoever of what was happening? The fact is left without an explanation.

And here is another argument. Many and many a time have men tried to produce a revival. They have read the accounts of revival and then they say, 'Ah now, we see that this is how it happened, that one man began to pray and others joined him. Or perhaps a group began to pray right through a night and then a revival broke out. Now,' they continue, 'we must do this.' So they have copied the very things that have been done during a revival. They have repeated them down to the smallest detail. Again, they may have read Finney's book on revival, his lectures on this subject, and they have put into practice everything that Finney tells them to do. Finney promises that if they do them they will get revival so they have done it all, but there has not been a revival. They have done their utmost with all their techniques and methods, but there has been no revival. They may have had a number of individual conversions, but there has been no revival. And so we see that this explanation of brainwashing completely fails at that point also.

And lastly, it fails altogether to explain these interesting and curious mental phenomena to which I have been directing our attention. It just does not begin to explain them at all. It does explain how you can indoctrinate a man. It does explain how you can bring a man to a decision. It does explain how you can influence the minds of men. Ah, yes, but we are concerned with these inexplicable mental phenomena, these astounding prophecies, this amazing ability that is given and these other wonders.

And this proffered explanation does not even begin to explain such phenomena which you get in connection with revivals.

The second explanation that is commonly put forward is that this is nothing but a case of mass hysteria, 'What's happening here, of course' they say, 'is that these people have just become hysterical. You know what it is for a person to be hysterical? Well, sometimes that becomes a sort of epidemic and large numbers of people become hysterical at the same time.' What of this explanation? First and foremost, I must say, once more, that it completely fails to explain the origin and the beginning. There was no evidence of hysteria at all in that first man, and the first group of men, in Northern Ireland, none whatsoever. There were no phenomena at all there; the same in America and in Wales. Why should this suddenly begin? There is no explanation. Why should it spread? Again, there is no explanation. And may I put before you, as a second answer to this charge, a series of points that were put forward by a doctor Carson, who lived in Northern Ireland a hundred years ago. He was obviously a very wise and careful Christian physician, who was in the midst of all the phenomena, and who carefully collected them, and analysed them, and brought his mind to bear upon them. Now, he pointed out that there were five points which seemed to him to be more than adequate and I entirely agree with him, to exclude this diagnosis of hysteria. And here they are. They are partly medical, but I think you should be interested in them.

Firstly, it is almost an invariable symptom of hysteria that people are conscious of a ball in the throat. They feel they are choking, that there is a lump there and they are going to choke. It is almost invariable in hysteria. There was no evidence of that at all in Northern Ireland a hundred years ago.

Secondly, it is a characteristic of hysteria that people laugh and cry almost at the same time, or change quickly from one to the other. Uncontrollable laughter, then uncontrollable weeping. Sometimes they are almost mixed together, or they may follow in quick succession. There was none of that at all in Dr Carson's experience.

Thirdly, in hysteria you almost invariably have convulsive movements of the limbs, the extremities. He did not see a single case of convulsive movements during the revival.

Fourthly, it is just a strict medical fact, that hysteria is almost entirely confined to the female sex. All the medical authorities you may like to consult will agree with that. Whereas, of course, in Northern Ireland, and in other places where these phenomena appeared, they were found with equal frequency amongst men.

Fifthly, he makes this very good point that even in women hysteria generally occurs in a certain type of woman, whose health is weak and frail. Hysteria is practically confined to such women, and is not true of all women. And once more, the answer is that in Northern Ireland it affected all kinds of women, men, youths – strong, sturdy people.

All this, these five points of Dr Carson's are enough it seems to me to exlude for ever the notion of mass hysteria. But in addition to this medical evidence, I would add as my third point that the character of the men who have observed these phenomena would, I would have thought, have been sufficient to exclude the diagnosis of hysteria. If ever there was a cool, rational, intellectual man, it was the great Jonathan Edwards. He observed these phenomena two hundred years ago, and he believed that they were of God. Jonathan Edwards was not the type of man who was likely to be deluded by hysteria, exactly the opposite. The same is true of others, like Archibald Alexander, who have given their accounts of them. And the same was true of men like Dr Carson and others in 1859. Not only the people to whom and in whom the phenomena happened, but the people who described them and accounted for them, are enough to put that out.

And lastly, my fourth argument is this: the results that followed. Hysteria is utterly useless, it is enervating. There is something almost disgusting about it. It is a waste of energy and it leads to no purposeful or beneficial result at all. It is something of which one should feel ashamed, in every respect, and that includes its results. Whereas I have already reminded you of the amazing and astounding results that have invariably followed in the case of revival.

The third explanation of the phenomena in revival is the psychic explanation. That first one, it seems to me, has no case for it at all, and it is the same with hysteria. But the psychic explanation I would regard as being much more serious, yet modern psychologists hardly ever mention it. It is interesting, in and of itself, how superficial is their attempt at diagnosis. By psychic I mean things like telepathy. I mean strange phenomena which we do not understand but which we know to be true: thought transference, mind transference. I am thinking of things like mesmerism, and hypnotism. These are phenomena which we cannot dispute, but which we find very difficult to explain. The ability of mind to influence mind – there are people who are born with a gift of being able to read other people's minds. Take, for instance, a man like the late Professor Gilbert Murray who was a typical intellectual, not a Christian, but a typical classical humanist. Now Professor Gilbert Murray had the power to read other people's minds. He was often tested. He would be in one room and the other people would be in another and he could tell them what they were thinking. I am sure you have read about this sort of thing, these extra-sensory phenomena, as they are called. There are these experiments with time, and phenomena in the realm of the psychic, which cannot be explained. Now, there are some who would say that this is entirely what happens at a time of revival. But here my answer would be to question them. Why should this suddenly start in people who had given no evidence of having these powers before? Why should it start suddenly? Why should it be so common? Why should it happen to masses of people at the same time? Why should it start suddenly, as it always does in a revival? And, again, they must face the fact of the spiritual results that invariably follow a period of revival.

The fourth explanation that is put forward is that all this is the work of the Devil. That is what the Roman Catholics said about the revival in Northern Ireland a hundred years ago. That is what the Unitarians said. That is what many people in the Church who were virtually nothing but Unitarians said also. And that is what so many people say. They say this is all the work of the Devil. But there are insuperable difficulties for this theory. And here are some of them. Why should the Devil suddenly start doing this kind of thing? What conceivable object can there be in his doing it? Here is the Church in a period of dryness, and of drought, and of aridity, why should the Devil suddenly do something which calls attention to religion and to the Lord Jesus Christ? Let me put that strongly, by putting it in a second way. The very results of revival, I would have thought, completely exclude the possibility of this being the action of the Devil. The main result of revival, as I have constantly reminded you, is that thousands of people are converted to the Lord Jesus Christ and become true believers. The Churches become too small and you have to build larger ones. Men and women crowd in and offer themselves to the ministry, and the gospel spreads in a most astounding manner. Is the Devil likely to do something that leads to that? But listen to our Lord's own answer to the particular charge in Luke 11, verses 15 to 18. Our Lord, one afternoon, cast out a dumb devil:

*And he was casting out a devil, and it was dumb. And it came
to pass, when the devil was gone out, the dumb spake; and the
people wondered. But some of them said, He casteth out devils
through Beelzebub the chief of the devils. And others, tempting
him, sought of him a sign from heaven. But he, knowing their
thoughts, said unto them, Every kingdom divided against itself
is brought to desolation; and a house divided against a house
falleth. If Satan also be divided against himself, how shall his
kingdom stand? because ye say that I cast out devils through
Beelzebub (Luke 11. 14–18).*

And that is the final answer. If this is the work of the Devil, well
then the Devil is an unutterable fool. He is dividing his own
kingdom; he is increasing the kingdom of God and of Christ; he
is bringing people to salvation; he is working against himself. But
the Devil is not a fool. He has amazing wisdom and subtlety and
ability. There is nothing which is so ridiculous as this suggestion
that this is the work of the Devil. And John, in his first epistle,
chapter 4, verses 2 and 3, says, 'Hereby know ye the Spirit of
God:' – if you are in any doubt about which spirit it is – 'Every
spirit that confesseth that Jesus Christ is come in the flesh is of
God: and every spirit that confesseth not that Jesus Christ is come
in the flesh is not of God: and this is that spirit of antichrist,
whereof ye have heard that it should come.' A spirit that leads
men and women to confess that Jesus is the Christ cannot be the
spirit of the Devil, it is the Spirit of the living God.

There, then, we have glanced hurriedly at these false
explanations. What is the true explanation? It is all before us, is
it not?

*And they were all amazed, and were in doubt, saying one to
another, 'What meaneth this?' Others mocking said, 'These men
are full of new wine.' But Peter, standing up with the eleven,
lifted up his voice, and said unto them, 'Ye men of Judaea, and
all ye that dwell at Jerusalem, be this known unto you, and
hearken to my words.*

Then he brings out the negative. *For these are not drunken, as ye
suppose, seeing it is but the third hour of the day. (Acts 2.12–15)*
He deals first with the false explanations and he ridicules them.
He shows how utterly impossible they are. And then he proceeds
to the true explanation – 'But this is that which was spoken by
the prophet Joel.' And he goes on to quote the prophecy of Joel.

142

What, then, is the true explanation? The first thing we must do is remember that even saintly ministers of God have disagreed amongst themselves about the explanation of the phenomena. The Revd. J. H. Moore, the man in whose parish the revival began in Northern Ireland a hundred years ago, disliked the phenomena, and he discouraged them, and there were practically none of them in that parish of Connor. But there were others who did not take the same view. And there have always been differences of opinion. Jonathan Edwards defended them. He believed that in the main they were of the Spirit of God. There was a man called John Berridge, who preached in East Anglia two hundred years ago, who even encouraged them. He believed they were a remarkable sign of the Spirit of God. Wesley and Whitefield, on the other hand, were unhappy and uncertain about them. I say this so that we may see that this is not a simple matter, and that it behoves us all to approach it with caution and, above all, with reverence and with godly fear, lest we may make foolish statements which we will regret later, and become guilty of quenching the Spirit.

How do we approach it? Well, let us approach it from the Scripture because, of course, the Scripture has much to tell us about this. Let us look first at the Old Testament, and read there about the prophets. How did these men receive their messages, and how did they deliver them? The records tell us that they were in the Spirit, or a spirit came upon them. They were in a state of ecstasy. They were sometimes in a state of trance, they were in an exalted mood. Read the stories about King Saul, for instance, how the gift came upon him, and the people asked a question which became a common saying, 'Is Saul also amongst the prophets?' (1 Sam. 10.11). A spirit of prophecy. It is perfectly clear there. Indeed, there is another fact which is generally put in connection with this, that sometimes this spirit could be encouraged by the playing of music. How have you accounted for this prophecy? Peter tells us, 'No prophecy of the scripture is of any private interpretation . . . , but holy men of God spake as they were moved [carried along by] the Holy Ghost' (2 Pet. 1.20–21). How did the prophecy come? How did this divine afflatus come to the man? Be careful, my friends, lest with your intellectualism you dismiss the prophets and the whole phenomenon of prophecy as we have it in the Old Testament. They were certainly laid hold of. They knew something about an ecstatic condition.

But that is the Old Testament, let us now come to the New and look at what happened there. See in Acts 2 what happened to the disciples themselves, these apostles and the other people.

143

Something so extraordinary happened, that to certain people standing there they appeared to be drunk. They said, 'This is nothing but drunkenness, this is sheer madness.' And this charge of madness has often been brought forward. But then consider the apostle's explanation of these remarkable phenomena. He says, 'This is that which was spoken by the prophet Joel.' This is what Joel said was going to happen. 'It shall come to pass in the last days, saith God, I will pour out of my Spirit upon all flesh.' The Spirit had been given before, but he had not been poured out before. A man here, and another man there – then, 'I will pour out.' It will be something overwhelming, it will be something en masse, as it were. 'I will pour out of my Spirit upon all flesh: and your sons and your daughters shall prophesy, and your young men shall see visions, and your old men shall dream dreams: and on my servants and on my handmaidens I will pour out in those days of my Spirit; and they shall prophesy.' And it happened to the mill girls in Northern Ireland. Poor girls who had been brought up in poverty and penury, who were ignorant and who had had practically no education, they suddenly began to prophesy. They displayed amazing knowledge and were able to speak in an unusual manner. Does it not rather look as if the prophet Joel had anticipated this, and prophesied that it was going to happen? Young men, young women, visions, dreams, prophecies, old men dreaming dreams: 'That is what is happening,' said Peter. 'This is the pouring out of the Spirit of God.' And the results are exactly as they were prophesied.

But there are other facts. We read in Acts 10. 10–12 that the Apostle Peter was upon a certain housetop and that he was in a trance, and that in this trance he had a vision of a sheet sent down from heaven full of various beasts. Again, we read in Acts 16 about the Apostle Paul, that he wanted to go and preach in Asia, but the Spirit prohibited him. He then wanted to go to Bithynia, but the Spirit would not let him. And then he had a vision in the night of the man of Macedonia, with his cry for help. We also read in Acts 22 that he says, 'I was in a trance.' Let us be careful lest, with our scientific friends, we be found to deny the Scriptures. When the Spirit comes upon a man he may be in a trance. Then you have only to read 1 Corinthians chapters 12 to 14 to see that there were all kinds of phenomena in the church of Corinth, and the Apostle had to instruct them and to guide them and restrain them and to tell them that everything must be done decently and in order. There, then, is the testimony of the Scripture.

What then is our attempt at an explanation and what are our

conclusions? Let me put them in a series of propositions to you. Does it not seem clear and obvious that in this way God is calling attention to himself and his own work by unusual phenomena? There is nothing that attracts such attention as this kind of thing, and it is used of God in the extension of his kingdom to attract, to call the attention of people. I am sure there is that element. But secondly, we must never forget that the Holy Spirit affects the whole person. Other influences do, too, any powerful stimulus affects the whole person. Have you listened to the broadcasts of sporting events, or have you been to the events themselves? Have you not seen people, under the excitement, shouting until they lose their voices, standing up and waving anything that comes to hand? They hit people, they do not know what they are doing. Now it is not regarded as strange, nor unusual when it happens in sport, but because it should happen in a revival people say, 'Ah, this is all psychological.' Have you not seen people weeping in theatres and in cinemas beside themselves under the influence of music? Of course. You see, man is body, soul, and spirit, and you cannot divide these. And anything which comes powerfully to any part of man is liable to affect the other parts of men. We all know what it is for our bodies to affect our minds. If you are not feeling well, if you are bilious, or ill, your mind does not function so well. On the other hand, if something happens to your mind, it affects your body. If, suddenly, you are stimulated, your whole body seems fit and strong and powerful. Let us be very careful that we do not do violence to man's very nature and constitution. Man reacts as a whole. And it is just folly to expect that he can react in the realm of the spiritual without anything at all happening to the rest of him, to the soul, and to the body.

And so we must expect this kind of reaction in a period of revival, and we must expect different people to react in different ways. We have a perfect proof of that, of course, in the Scriptures themselves. The same Holy Spirit inspired Paul and Peter and John, and yet I think that if you read out a few verses to me, I could tell you every time which of the three had written them. The same Holy Spirit inspired the three. Yes, but the message comes to us through the men that have been used, through their brains, through their temperament, through their mentality. That is not done away with. You can see the different style, the different representation. The same Spirit, but the manifestations differ. So it is in revival. And thus, you see, you would expect children in a time of revival to react more violently than adults. You would expect certain types of persons to react more violently

145

than others. And so it proves to be the case. All, therefore, that can be proved is that these phenomena are indicative of the fact that some very powerful stimulus is in operation. Something is happening which is so powerful that the very physical frame is involved.

I would say further that we must remember that the phenomena are not of importance in and of themselves. The phenomena should not be sought, they should not be encouraged, they should not be boasted. The phenomena, if I may use a modern term, are 'epiphenomena', incidental, occasional concomitants, and not of vital essential import. That explains why the phenomena tend to disappear as the revival goes on. Also I would not hesitate to add that sometimes there are phenomena in connection with revivals which seem to me to be due to nothing but a sheer breakdown of the physical. You do get some people who become hysterical, actually hysterical, in revival. There are people who manifest other psychic phenomena. There is no doubt about this, but I do not think there is any difficulty in explaining that. The body is weak, some bodies are weaker than others. And so when this mighty spiritual power comes there are certain bodies that break down, and these should be helped, they should be dealt with in a semi-medical manner, and they should be prayed for, they should be pacified. That is how the great leaders of revival have always dealt with them.

But let us also remember that whenever the Spirit of God is working in mighty power, the Devil always seeks his opportunity. If he can discredit the work he will. And he has always tried to do so. He has tried to bring in his counterfeits, he has tried to drive people to excesses, and he has often suceeded with particular individuals. That is why there is so much in the Bible about testing the spirits, and proving the spirits. We must not be misled. There are tests which are given, and it is our business always to employ them.

So, I would conclude that the phenomena are not essential to revival, they are not vital to revival, they are not religious in and of themselves. I believe that in their origin they are essentially of the Spirit of God, but we must always allow for the fact that because of the very frailty of human nature, and of our physical frames, you will have the tendency to an admixture, partly along the physical, partly along the psychic, and partly as the result of the Devil's activity. But there is nothing more foolish or more ridiculous than to dismiss the whole because of a very, very small part. If you begin to do that you will have to dismiss the whole of the New Testament, because here we are told that the other forces are ever trying to interfere, and we must realise the existence of the true and the false, and understand it, and withstand the false. The New Testament teaches us to expect this, and to be on guard against the false and the spurious.

So, then, we end by saying that these phenomena may appear in a revival, which, as the Apostle Peter says, is the result of an outpouring of the Spirit of God. But we must not seek phenomena and strange experiences. What we must seek is the manifestation of God's glory and his power and his might. What we must seek is revival. And when that comes it will be so amazing that strange and unusual things may happen, but we shall always know that God is moving amongst us, and we shall be ready to identify and restrain the false, the spurious, and indeed all which belongs to the evil spirit. Anybody who tries to work up phenomena is a tool of the Devil, and is putting himself into the position of the psychic, and the psychological. No, we must not concentrate upon these things. We must leave it to God, in his sovereign wisdom, to decide whether to grant these occasional concomitants or not. There should be no difficulty in distinguishing between the work of the Spirit, and the work of fanatical men, the work of these unseen forces and powers, or the work of the Devil himself.

Let us, therefore, be careful lest we quench the Spirit, and let us keep our eyes fixed upon the glory of God, and the outpouring of his Holy Spirit upon us.

Chapter 12

Exodus 33.4

And when the people heard these evil tidings, they mourned: and no man did put on him his ornaments (Exod. 33.4).

Now this particular chapter is one of the great chapters of the Old Testament. Judged from any standpoint whatsoever it is a great and a glorious chapter. It certainly is one of the crucial episodes in the long, and chequered history of the Children of Israel, and, as the New Testament tells us, these things were written 'for our ensamples'. There is no doubt at all that it was for that very reason that the Holy Spirit led the early Church, even when it had become mainly Gentile, to incorporate the Old Testament Scriptures with their new Scriptures. The Old Testament is full of teaching and of illustrations which are of great and profound value to all of us who are in the Christian life, and the Christian faith. That is why it is always the height of folly to ignore the Old Testament and to fail to see the gospel, and the principles of gospel teaching, in the Old Testament as well as in the New. You will find the New Testament writers constantly referring back to what happened to the Children of Israel, those people who were the Church under the old dispensation.

But now, I am drawing our attention to this, in particular, because it throws very great light indeed upon this whole question, which we are studying, of revival, and of spiritual awakening in the Church. This story, again, in many respects, is one of these perfect Old Testament illustrations of what happens to the Church when she is in a period of aridity and dryness, and then comes into a period of re-awakening and of revival. What we shall be considering here is something that has been repeated many, many, times in the long history of the Christian Church. Now, the peculiar feature of this particular account is that it enables us, perhaps more clearly than everything else that we have considered hitherto, to realise how revival comes, the kind of process, the mechanism, which is to be seen so clearly in the coming of revival into and upon the Church. But we make this quite plain and clear. While I am thus, mainly, dealing with the Church in general and with the need for revival in the Church, obviously at the same time it is a perfect message for the individual. What a revival really means is, of course, something happening at one and the same time to a number of individuals. But there is no need for us to wait until revival comes to have individual experiences. So, all that we shall be considering has an immediate and direct application to any individual who may be in the condition that I am about to describe.

Now, what we are shown here in a particularly instructive manner is that there are, generally speaking, stages, and steps, in the coming of revival. You will hardly ever find, in all the histories of revival, that the Church suddenly, in one move, as it were, or in one step, passes from her condition of lifelessness and an almost moribund state into a condition of mighty power and revival and influence. No, there are generally particular steps and stages. And the glory of this incident in Exodus is that it helps to bring out very plainly, and clearly, in an anecdotal manner, these steps and stages, so that all I have to do is to put the story before you. Indeed it almost preaches itself. Nothing could be simpler than the exposition of this particular story in the life of the Children of Israel.

Let us start, then, with the position and the condition of the people. Chapter 33 verse 1–11 gives us the background. Here was one of the most serious declensions that ever took place in the story of the Israelites. You remember how, almost from the very moment that they were delivered from the captivity of Egypt, they began to grumble and complain and in various ways to backslide. But this is certainly the most serious thing that they ever did. Moses had been called up on to the Mount by God in order to receive the Law. And there he had remained a number of days leaving the people behind, with Aaron, as it were, in charge of them. But, as the record tells us, the people became impatient. 'Where is this Moses?' they said. This man who persuaded us to come out of Egypt, and who has landed us here in this wilderness? What has happened to him? Does he not care about us? Where is this God of whom he spoke, who was going to give us such blessings, and who was going to lead us into a land flowing with milk and honey? What has happened to this fellow Moses? They became utterly impatient, and they turned to Aaron, and said, 'Look here, we are tired·of this. We are not going to wait any longer for him, nor the God whom he claims to represent. Make another god. So Aaron, you remember, told them to pull off their earrings and he took them and threw them into a fire, and when they were all molten, he fashioned the gold into the form of a golden calf. Then they proceeded to worship the golden calf and they said, 'these be thy gods, O Israel, which brought thee up out of the land of Egypt' (Exod. 32.4). And not only did they worship the golden calf, but they proceeded to open sin, and vice, and evil. They danced before it, and behaved themselves in an utterly and thoroughly disgraceful manner. Now, that is the essence of the background. It is a story of disobedience and of rebellion, a story of their making their own god, and proceeding to worship it. And there you have false worship. Man arrogating unto himself the power to decide who is to be his god, and in turn, of course, it leads to sin, to open immorality, and to shameful behaviour.

We shall not go into the application of these things in detail. But surely anyone who has any spiritual sensitivity, and any knowledge of the Scriptures and of the history of the last hundred years in the Church, will know that this, alas, is far too true a portrayal and representation of the state of the Christian Church at this present moment. The Church has been re-enacting this very thing, chiefly, of course, in the matter of setting up its own god. And if anyone should ask how I can demonstrate that, I would simply point to what has been happening for the last hundred years in the so-called new critical attitude to the Scriptures. It has been just a repetition of that sin of the Israelites. Man has no longer been receiving the revelation and submitting to it. He has been setting himself up as a judge of the revelation, and has been determining what it ought to be. His sin has been the making of a golden calf. It has been the setting up of a new god. The Church, and I am speaking of the Church particularly, has set herself over the Book and above the Book. Philosophy has taken the place of revelation. And men have not hesitated, to express their opinions of the God of the Old Testament – they are still doing so. A prominent Church leader in another country has referred to the God of the Old Testament as a bully in whom he did not believe. There are men calling themselves Christian preachers in this country who say they do not believe in 'that God of the Old Testament sitting upon Mount Sinai and blowing out His threatenings'. They say they believe in the God of the New Testament, the God of the Lord Jesus Christ – just as if Jesus himself did not believe in the God of the Old Testament!

There is no need to dwell on these things. But, you see, it has all been a repetition of this Exodus story. Men have been fashioning their own god. They have done the same with the Lord Jesus Christ. They do not believe in miracles, therefore, they say miracles did not happen and that these accounts are but myths, not having real actuality, or fact, but representing spiritual truths. They deny the virgin birth, the miracles, the literal, physical, resurrection, and so on. Now, all this, of course, is just like the behaviour of the children of Israel. There they did it in a very crude way. They actually fashioned and made a calf out of gold, from their golden earrings, and set up some objective god. But, in principle, there is no difference whatsoever. It is man making his own god, deciding and determining what he is like, who is to be believed, and what is to be believed. And then they proceed to offer some kind of worship to their own creation. And, of course, as invariably happens, once man begins to do that, you inevitably get a moral declension. These people did not stop at making a golden calf, and worshipping it, they began to dance and to drink and to sin. They became guilty of gross immoralities. And, of course, we have witnessed the same thing. These clever people who set out to make a new god, because the old evangelical religion was not ethical, and was not moral and social, these people who did that, in those terms, have produced the moral conditions that we have today. You cannot have morality without godliness. The most moral periods in the history of this country have been the periods that have followed revivals, and spiritual awakening. What happens with the new god is a decline in ethics, and a collapse of morality. So, we have had the self-same thing in the Church and in the world. False worship, false religion, false gods, and an appalling state of evil, sin and vice.

And then what happens? Well, you remember what happened to the Israelites? God punished them, and he always punishes sin. I repeat again what I have often said, that I regard the two World Wars which we have experienced in this century as God's punishment of the apostasy of the last century. I see no other adequate explanation. God punished the Israelites in a terrible manner, Moses came down from the Mount and saw the appalling condition of the people and he sent out his great challenge. He stood in the gate of the camp and said, 'Who is on the Lord's side? Let him come unto me' (32.26) And all the sons of Levi gathered themselves together unto him. That invariably happens after such a state of affairs. A clarion call is issued, and there is a kind of separation. And thank God we know something even about this. There is a separation in the Church today, let us be perfectly clear about it. There are those, thank God, who have

151

always protested against a new attitude to the Scriptures. There have been those who have kept the flame alive, who have realised that this is the truth, and none other. And there is a call today to separation. It is the only distinction in the Church which I recognise at all. Those who submit to the word of God, and its revelation, and its teaching, and those who do not. I have no interest in denominations. My one interest is in this separation between those who are 'on the Lord's side' and those who worship their own god, and their own ideas, and their own thoughts. That is the first thing that we are told.

But then, and this brings us to our immediate matter, Moses interceded. It is one of the most glorious statements found in the whole of Scripture, and on the lips of a man. 'And Moses returned unto the Lord, and said, 'Oh this people have sinned a great sin, and have made them gods of gold. Yet now, if thou wilt forgive their sins – ;' And he paused. He did not go on immediately. And then he resumed after a while, 'And if not, blot me, I pray thee, out of thy book which thou hast written' (32. 31–32). Moses becomes an intercessor. He becomes a kind of type of the Lord Jesus Christ. He becomes a mediator. He stands between the people and the wrath of God and says, 'Punish me.' He could not have borne it, of course, it was too much. And yet the noble spirit of Moses shines out so clearly in this great incident. But the thing I am anxious to call attention to is God's reply to Moses' intercession. And that is what we have in the first three verses of chapter 33.

And the Lord said unto Moses, Depart, and go up hence, thou and the people which thou hast brought up out of the land of Egypt, unto the land which I swore unto Abraham, to Isaac, and to Jacob, saying, Unto thy seed will I give it: and I will send an angel before thee; and I will drive out the Canaanite, the Amorite, and the Hittite, and the Perizzite, and Hivite, and the Jebusite: unto a land flowing with milk and honey: for I will not go up in the midst of thee; for thou art a stiffnecked people: lest I consume thee in the way.

Now, this is the significant thing. God's reply to Moses was to this effect: 'I have given this promise to these people, that they shall go to that land of promise, that land of Canaan, which is flowing with milk and honey. And, therefore, I tell you now, *you* lead them up. *you* take them to the land of promise. In view of what they have done, I am no longer coming up with you. I have been in the midst of you . . .' – he had represented his presence, you remember, by the cloud by day and the pillar of fire by night – 'but I am not coming up any longer amongst you. In a sense,' says God, 'I dare not come lest I may consume you. I am going to send an angel to lead you and to remove your enemies from before you. And so,' he says to Moses, 'Go on. I appointed you as leader, take these people up, and enter into the land of possession, of Canaan, the land flowing with milk and honey. I am not coming with you, but I am sending an angel who will help you. Go ahead.'

That then, is the position. And what is of such great interest to us, is the reaction of Moses and the Church to this. This is always the first stage in revival. You see the position they were in – their sin, God's pronouncement, God's judgment upon it. And the first stage, the first step in revival is, as we see here, a realisation of the position. These people who had rebelled and turned their backs on God, who had blasphemed his name and had criticised his servant Moses, who had caused Aaron to make the calf and had worshipped it, and who had sinned, suddenly they were arrested. They realised something, at any rate, of the situation they were in. Now, obviously this is a matter of final importance. There is no hope of revival apart from this. It is an awakening to the situation. It is a consciousness of the seriousness of the situation. It is an awareness of the implications of what God has said; that he is going to withdraw his presence from us and that he has done so. The cloud disappears. The pillar of fire is no longer in evidence. God said he would withdraw, and God has withdrawn. The visible signs and symbols of his presence have gone. And furthermore there is a consciousness and a realisation of his displeasure.

Now, I defy you to read the history of any revival, any record that has ever been written of any great spiritual movement in the history of the Church, but that you will find at once that without a single exception this always happens. Do you remember, in the case of Martin Luther, the dawning consciousness of the abuses in the mediaeval church, the sale of indulgence, and other abuses? That was the first thing with which he really began to deal. Before he was clear about his doctrine of justification by faith, he became aware of the appalling state of the Church, the sin of the Church and its disgraceful condition, and all the idolatry that had come in and was concealing the worship of the true God, and of his Son, the Lord Jesus Christ. Luther awakened to that exactly as these people did. And this is, of necessity, the first stage. I would

153

be very much happier if I could say with confidence that there was evidence of this in the Church today, speaking generally. I would thank God if I could say that there was some indication that men and women had been halted and were pausing, and beginning to face the facts, and to see the true condition of the Christian Church. Is there any evidence of that? There is no hope of true revival until there is, to some extent at any rate. This is the first step.

Dare I say that I do not see much of this even in the evangelical section of the Church? Our peculiar danger, of course, is to segregate ourselves in mind and thought, and then to busy ourselves with our meetings as they come round every year, our anniversaries, and the reports of what we have been doing, our summer campaigns, and winter campaigns, and all . . . and it is all so marvellous and so wonderful. And we do not seem to realise that anything is wrong. But the way to test the condition of the Church is not to compare and to contrast her with what is evidently and obviously wrong. The way to test the condition of the Church is to examine her in the light of the New Testament picture of the Church; or to examine the Church in the light of what she has been like in every great period of reformation, and of revival, times with the presence of God in the midst, with great spiritual manifestations of his presence and of his glory. And I wonder what even the evangelical section of the Church looks like when she compares herself with that, when she estimates herself in terms of spirituality, in terms of her knowledge of God. Not a knowledge *about* him, but a knowledge *of* him, direct experiences, with him, and of his presence, the thing that we shall consider as we continue with these studies.

Are you satisfied with the condition of the Church? Are you satisfied with your own condition? You, who believe the truth, you who are evangelical, you who are not a liberal in your theology. That is good, but is that enough? What is our spiritual state and condition in reality? How do we feel when we read the experiences of these apostles, the Apostle Paul and others? Can we say honestly, with him, that we are in a kind of state of tension, saying, 'That I may know him, and the power of his resurrection, and the fellowship of his sufferings. . . . Not as though I had already attained. . . . forgetting those things which are behind. . . . I press toward. . . ' (Phil. 3. 10–14)? Do you feel the tension, the concern, the stretching, the pressing on? How much do we know of that? Can we honestly say that we rejoice in the Lord Jesus Christ with 'a joy unspeakable and full of glory'? Can

154

we say with Paul that to us 'to live is Christ, and to die is gain'? That we might 'be with Christ; which is far better'. How do you feel when you contemplate death? How do you feel when you are taken ill and laid aside, and begin to have to think about your possible death? Now, these are the ways in which we are to test ourselves. There is no hope for true prayer and intercession for revival unless we realise that there is a need. Is all well with us? Can we be satisfied? Can we sit back and fold our arms and say, 'Things are going marvellously, look at the reports.' Are we like the Israelites at this point, or are we like the Laodiceans saying that we are rich, that we have abundance, that all is well with us, and failing to realise that we are poor and wretched and blind?

May God give us grace to examine ourselves, and be honest with ourselves. Do we realise the difference between the Church, as she is depicted in the New Testament, and ourselves? Do we realise that God's displeasure is upon the Church? Why has there been such a long interval since last God came down amongst his people in revival? Why this appalling long period? Why are things as they are? Why is the Church counting for so little? Why is she so ineffective? Why is it that men and women are living in sin, as they are, and things are going from bad to worse? My dear friends, the first step is that you and I have to realise these things. We have to be pulled up by them, to begin to think about them, to become concerned about them and have a deep awareness of the position as it is.

But, of course, it does not stop there. That is of no value in and of itself. We must go on to the second stage, which is mentioned in verse 4 of chapter 33. 'And when the people heard these evil tidings, they mourned: and no man did put on him his ornaments.' Here is the next thing – repentance. You cannot, of course, repent unless you face the facts. But having faced them, the question is – do you go on to repentance? There is a cursory superficial facing of the facts that is of no value at all. Is that not the difference, really, between remorse and repentance. The man who suffers remorse is a man who, in a sense, looks at the facts but does not spend much time about it. 'Ah,' he says, 'I was a fool, I should not have done that, and I am suffering now because I did.' He forgets it and goes on. That is remorse, it is of no value. Repentance is a much, much deeper thing. The Apostle Paul has put it once and for ever in Corinthians chapter 7, where he makes the classic statement of what repentance means:

For though I made you sorry with a letter, I do not repent, though I did repent: for I perceive that the same epistle hath made you sorry, though it were but for a season. Now I rejoice, not that ye were made sorry, but that ye sorrowed to repentance: for ye were made sorry after a godly manner. that ye might receive damage by us in nothing. For godly sorrow worketh repentance to salvation not to be repented of: but the sorrow of the world worketh death. For behold this selfsame thing, that ye sorrowed after a godly sort, what carefulness it wrought in you, yea, what clearing of yourselves, yea, what indignation, yea, what fear, yea, what vehement desire, yea, what zeal, yea, what revenge! In all things ye have approved yourselves to be clear in this matter (2 Cor. 7.8–11).

That is a perfect definition of true repentance. But now look at it in the case of these Children of Israel, where it is illustrated so perfectly. Repentance does not just mean that you are pulled up, that you are aware that things are not as they ought to be, and that there is something wrong. No, you go on to a realisation of the seriousness of what is wrong, and its appalling character. The Children of Israel hated themselves for it. That is what Paul is saying about the Corinthians: 'You did not merely glance at it, you examined yourselves. You pummelled yourselves, you punished yourselves, you hated yourselves, you took revenge on yourselves. And that is an essential part of repentance. A man awakens to the seriousness of what he has done. These people said, 'We have turned our backs on God. We have made this god, this golden calf, and we have worshipped him, and we have sinned. We have disgraced ourselves. There, in our nakedness, we have been dancing before a mere idol, created by our own hands.' And it came home to them and they hated the thing, they abominated it, they condemned themselves root and branch. Ah, but still more important than that, they realised the seriousness of their sin in God's sight. They said, 'If it is as bad as this to us, now that we have come to ourselves, what must it be to God?'

The prodigal son knew that did he not? He thought he was wonderful until he found himself in that field with the swine. He came to himself. And the first thing that happened to him was that he saw himself and what a fool he had been. And he kicked himself, he hated himself, he condemned himself. Then he thought of his father: 'If I see it like this, what must it have been to father when, in my arrogance, I asked for my share of the goods and left home. I spurned all that he and home had represented to me. If it is this to me, what is it to him? How can I go back and face him? Oh, how he must have suffered!' Do we ever think of what our sin is like in the sight of God? I know that realisation of sin makes us feel uncomfortable, and we want to get over it quickly, so we ask his forgiveness. Do you go through the stage of realising what it must be to God? That we his creatures, his people for whom he has done everything, can turn our backs upon him, and in our folly and selfishness, make our own gods, and go our own way? Oh, go and read the history of revivals again. Watch the individuals at the beginning. This is invariably the first thing that happens to them. They begin to see what a terrible, appalling thing sin is in the sight of God. They temporarily even forget the state of the Church, and forget their own anguish. It is the thought of sin in the sight of God. How terrible it must be. Never has there been a revival but that some of the people, especially at the beginning, have had such visions of the holiness of God, and the sinfulness of sin, that they have scarcely known what to do with themselves. Some of them have felt it so acutely, as we have seen, that they have even collapsed physically. That does not matter. The thing that matters is the realisation of sin in the presence of God.

Then, even further than this, what these people suddenly came to realise was that because of their sin, and because of God's view of sin, God was withholding his presence from them, and was telling them to go up to the land of Canaan without him. He would send an angel, but he was not going himself. The God who had entered among them, as it were, in Egypt, the God whose power they had felt as they were travelling in the direction of the Red Sea, the God who was there among them, with the mountains of Pi-hahiroth, and Baal-zephon, one on each side, and the hosts of Pharaoh behind, and the Red Sea in front, the God who had come down and had divided the Sea; this mighty presence, this holy, glorious God – he was no longer going to be with them. That was the thing that filled them with dismay. That was the thing that alarmed these people and caused them to mourn. 'When the people heard these evil tidings . . .' – and that was the evil tidings. 'I will not go up in the midst of thee; for thou art a stiff-necked people: lest I consume thee in the way.' What troubled them was not the threat of being consumed but that God had said, 'I am not coming with you. You must go up alone. I am sending an angel, but I am not coming.'

Oh, this is a tremendous thing, this is the heart of the whole matter. Men and women, when they are truly awakened, begin to realise that there is nothing so serious as to be without the

157

presence of God. Do you get its full force? God was sending them to the promised land. God was saying, 'Go up. I promised you the land of Canaan, I am going to give it to you. You shall go to the land flowing with milk and honey. I will send my angel before you to destroy these enemies, the Amorites, the Hittites and the others. Go on, go up to your promised land. I have brought you out of the captivity of Egypt, and I am sending you on. Go ahead. Lead them, Moses. I will send an angel with you.'

And the people said, 'No. If you are not coming with us, we do not want to go.'

Now that is the essence of spiritual understanding. And that is the position that you and I must come to. Here were the people who, suddenly awakened, came to this tremendous, profound realisation, that to be given every other blessing is of no value if God is not with you. What is the value of Canaan? What is the value of milk and honey? What is the value of having possessions, if God was not with them? They saw that the realisation of the presence of God, having his fellowship and company, was infinitely more important than everything else.

Need I apply this to the Church today? We can have successes over our enemies without this great realisation of God in the midst. Oh yes, there are angels who can do that for us, who can destroy certain of our enemies and take us to the land. We are in Canaan, we have got the milk and honey, everything seems to be all right. There is an appalling verse in Psalm 106 where we are told of the Children of Israel, 'God gave them their request; but sent leanness into their soul.' You can have an outward prosperity and affluence, the Church may seem to be doing remarkably well, good finances, good figures, successes, conversions, the enemy is defeated, everything going well, and the Christian newspapers report it. It all seems to be marvellous. But the appalling question I ask is this – is God in the midst? Is he really amongst us? Are we aware, as we should be, of his glorious presence? That is the thing that got these people. And what they said, in effect, was 'Canaan is no use to us, milk and honey are of no value, we are not interested in these enemies. We want you.'

'Oh,' says the Psalmist, 'It is for thee I cry out. As the hart panteth after the water brooks, so panteth my soul after thee, O God' (Ps. 42. 1). He is not after blessings, he is after God, the living God.

Yes, says Paul, I have been a successful evangelist. I have done so much, but oh I am not satisfied – 'That I may know him, and the power of his resurrection, and the fellowship of his sufferings.'

'No,' said the people of Israel, 'we can't go on without you. The presence of God is essential.' They came to the realisation that no outward prosperity, and no type of success, can compensate for the absence of God. 'What shall it profit a man, if he shall gain the whole world, and lose his own soul?'

Christian people, I am not asking you whether you are living a good life. I am not asking you whether you are happy. I am not asking you whether you read your Bible, or whether you pray. I am not asking whether you are active in Church work, or some other form of Christian activity. What I am asking you is this – do you know God? Is he with you? Is he in your life? Is he in the camp? Or are you travelling on, with God, as it were, somewhere in the distance, giving strength and power by his angel, and by his leader? But the question is – what of you in your personal relationship, and your personal dealings with God? These people repented. And the end of repentance, and the ultimate aim of repentance is just that, to realise that nothing matters except my relationship to God. 'Let nothing please nor pain me apart, Oh Lord, from thee.' They not only faced this situation, they repented.

But, furthermore – and how perfect the Scripture is – they gave absolute proof that they had repented. And again this is one of the differences between remorse and repentance, because repentance is not just a passing, temporary feeling, repentance is something that is so profound that it affects a man's will. As the Apostle again puts it in 2 Corinthians 7 it leads to action. 'You put things right,' says Paul, 'you did something about it.' And a man has never repented until he has done in practice what he feels he ought to do. And these people did it, for we read,

And when the people heard these evil tidings, they mourned: and no man did put on him his ornaments. For the Lord had said unto Moses, Say unto the children of Israel, Ye are a stiffnecked people: I will come up into the midst of thee in a moment, and consume thee: therefore now put off thy ornaments from thee, that I may know what to do unto thee.' And the children of Israel stripped themselves of their ornaments by the mount Horeb.

And we have not repented truly, until we have done that, in whatever shape or form it may be true of us. It means that having had this profound realisation of our sinfulness, especially in his sight, our one desire now is to do everything we can that is well pleasing in his sight. And that means forsaking sin, and doing his commandments: 'Pluck off your ornaments' – and the Children of Israel stripped themselves of their ornaments. Yes, it was these ornaments that had led to their downfall. These were like the things out of which the golden calf had been made. And they hated the very thought of the whole thing. And God says, 'Strip yourselves of them.' And they stripped themselves.

Now you have only to read Christian biographies and the story of revivals, to see exactly what I mean. There is always this stripping. Men and women are aware that they have been doing things that they should not do. Not very harmful things, perhaps, in and of themselves, but they stand between them and God, so they must go. Ornaments – vanish. They strip themselves. And they give themselves to God, in a new consecration, and in a new dedication. This, I say again, is of the very essence of repentance. But we realise that we must act. We have got to take some steps. It is not for me to tell you what they are, because if I do, I shall be speaking to some and not to others. But every one of us has got to be stripped of something. Every single one of us, without exception. It is no use just pointing at smoking or drinking, or this and that, there is something in everybody's life – some ornament – and it must go. When a man realises his sinfulness, and sees that the state of the Church is due to the fact that he and others like him are so sinful, and what it means in the sight of God, a true repentance will lead each one to such an examination. And one will see certain things, and one will deal with them gladly and readily. 'They stripped themselves of their ornaments.'

That is obviously not all. These are but the first steps, the first beginnings, the dawning realisation, that there is something wrong, and profoundly wrong, and that the call is a call to a godly sorrow, a profound and a deep work of repentance. Are you happy about yourself? Are you happy about the state of the Church? Is all well? Can we go jogging along? Meetings, services, activities – wonderful! Is it? Where is the knowledge of God? Is he in the midst? Is he in the life? What is our relationship to him? Face that question, and it will lead to this true godly sorrow and repentance, which will manifest itself in a practical manner. May God have mercy upon us, open our eyes to the situation, and give us honest minds, and truth in our inward parts.

Chapter 13

Exodus 33.7–11

And Moses took the tabernacle, and pitched it without the camp, afar off from the camp, and called it the Tabernacle of the congregation. And it came to pass, that every one which sought the Lord went out unto the tabernacle of the congregation, which was without the camp. And it came to pass, when Moses went out unto the tabernacle, that all the people rose up, and stood every man at his tent door, and looked after Moses, until he was gone into the tabernacle. And it came to pass, as Moses entered into the tabernacle, the cloudy pillar descended, and stood at the door of the tabernacle, and the Lord talked with Moses. And all the people saw the cloudy pillar stand at the tabernacle door: and all the people rose up and worshipped, every man in his tent door. And the Lord spake unto Moses face to face, as a man speaketh unto his friend. And he turned again into the camp: but his servant Joshua, the son of Nun, a young man, departed not out of the tabernacle (Exod. 33. 7–11).

The last chapter ended by bringing us to see the Children of Israel showing true repentance for their sinfulness and a longing for God to come again into their midst. We go on from there, for that is but the preliminary, as it were. And it enables us now to come to the next section of this matter which we are looking at together. And here we are reminded of something that is very important in connection with this whole subject. There are definite steps and stages in this process of revival. You will never find, whatever histories you may read, that the Church suddenly passes from gross sin or failure into mighty revival. No, there are intermediate steps, and it is important that we should know about them, in order that we should recognise them when they come, if it be God's gracious will to have pity on us and to revive us again.

So then, the next step we come to is this step of prayer and of intercession. But I am particularly anxious to emphasise that in many ways the lesson of this chapter is that there are steps and stages even in that. The first stage runs from verse 7 to verse 11 in chapter 33. But then there is a second stage, which runs from verse 12 to verse 17. And then there is a third stage, the highest stage of all, which we read from verse 18 to the end of the chapter in verse 23.

Now, I do commend to you the careful study of these sections and particular stages, because here, I think, we really are brought to the very nerve and centre of this whole question of revival. And the confusion which is in the minds of so many people is often because they have never realised the possibility of these three stages. They have excluded revival altogether from their thinking and from their doctrine of the Holy Spirit. They have left no room at all for an outpouring of the Spirit. Their misunderstanding of the doctrine of the baptism of the Spirit is such that they leave no room for revival, or for the exceptional, which is, of course, the great characteristic of revival.

Now the people of Israel have been arrested. They have been apprehended. They have this dawning realisation of their sinfulness, and they have repented. But that is not enough, something happens beyond this. So then, let us look at this first stage of prayer. And we begin in the seventh verse, where we are told, . . . 'And Moses took the tabernacle, and pitched it without the camp, afar off from the camp, and called it the Tabernacle of the congregation. And it came to pass, that every one which sought the Lord went out unto the tabernacle of the congregation, which was without the camp' (Exod. 33.7). Here is profound teaching. Let us be clear about this tabernacle which is mentioned. This was not the tabernacle which was ultimately made and constructed according to the specifications given by God to Moses on the mount, the precursor of the Temple, about which we read so much in the Old Testament books. That comes later. This was a kind of tent, which Moses had already made and set up in the middle of the congregation, in the middle of the camp of Israel, where he and others would pray, a 'tent of meeting', where people might go together to meet with God. The tent of meeting – I pause for just a second over that, because it is such a significant and such a wonderful term. The Nonconformist fathers generally referred to their places of worship as meeting houses, and it is a good old term. You see, it is a place, not so much where people meet with one another, though that is included, but the essential meaning is this – the place where they meet with God. God grant that in our minds and in our thinking our churches may become more and more meeting houses, that, as we gather there, Sunday by Sunday, we shall say to ourselves, 'We are going to meet with God.' The meeting house, the place of meeting.

It is important that we should understand that Moses was clearly led to take this peculiar action. He took this tabernacle out of the centre of the camp and put it outside, far off from the camp. Now at this point there are many things which must detain us. The first is, of course, that this was an action taken by Moses, Moses himself. And I must pause with that, because you will always find as you read the history of these movements of the Spirit in the long story of the Christian Church, that generally the very first thing that happens, and which eventually leads to a great revival, is that one man, or a group of men, suddenly begin to feel this burden, and they feel the burden so much that they are led to do something about it. Look at the great history. Look at the Protestant Reformation, that mighty movement, where did it come from? How did it originate? I know that there were precursors even of that – Wycliffe, John Huss and others – but you see the real thing happened when just one man, Martin Luther, a very ordinary kind of monk, suddenly became aware of this burden. And it so burdened him that he was led to do something about it. Just one man, and through that one man, God sent that mighty movement into the Church.

The same thing could be abundantly illustrated from the stories of other revivals. Read again the story of the revival in Northern Ireland, a hundred years ago, that great movement, which led not only to so many conversions, but which quickened the whole life of the Presbyterian Church and the other churches in Northern Ireland, and transformed the whole situation. It did the same in Wales also, and in the United States of America at the same time. Now, you will find that in all these instances, the movement began with just one man. Take the man who began the prayer meetings in Fulton Street in New York City in 1857, a most ordinary man, but he felt this burden, and did something about it. The revival in Northern Ireland, started with just that one man, James McQuilken. And the same was true in Wales, with one man only, called Humphrey Jones, who, feeling the power of revival in America, felt a burden for his own country and crossed the Atlantic back to Wales, and began to tell people about it. Now, I emphasise this for one reason only, that this is what I like to call the 'romantic' element in the Christian life and in the history of the Church. That is to me what is so glorious about it. I dare not pass lightly over a point like this because somebody reading this book, whom I do not know, may be the person that God is

163

going to use. And that sort of thing can only happen in the Christian Church, it does not happen in the world. The world looks to the leaders and the great people, but God, as the Apostle Paul says in 1 Corinthians is constantly confounding the wise by taking hold of the foolish. He 'brings to nought the things that are', by using the things that are not. It may be anybody. There are no rules about this matter. It is not of necessity a great leader, as it happened to be Moses on this occasion. You will find that the insignificant prophets were taken up now and again and used by God. And so it has continued in the long history of the Christian Church. Whoever would expect a saviour to come out of Nazareth? Can any good thing, said the proverb, ever come out of Nazareth? That is the world's way of thinking. But it was out of Nazareth that the Saviour of the world came. And so let us realise this, let us get out of this deplorable modern habit which seems to have possessed the Christian Church, and which makes the ordinary church member think that he or she can do nothing at all, that they must sit back in crowds in large meetings, and that some two or three people are going to do everything. No, the teaching of the Bible is the exact opposite, it may be *you* that God is going to use. You are an unknown church member. It does not matter. In the hands of God, you may be the channel.

So then, one man or a group of men may begin to feel the burden. And, therefore, I am entitled to ask whether you have felt the burden? And if you have not, what is the reason? Are you concerned about the situation? Have you got a zeal for the glory of God? Does it grieve you to see his Church as she is? If not, why not? If this is a burden that can come to anybody, why has it not come to you? Let us leave it at that, but remember that it may be the action of just one man. And now let us observe this act of Moses because it is very significant.

Moses took this tabernacle, which had been, formerly, in the midst of the camp, and he pitched it 'without the camp', far off from the camp. Here, also, is something which we must underline because it is again one of those points which you find invariably in the history of revivals. It is a point that can be misunderstood, as most Christian truth can be misunderstood, but the fact that certain foolish people can misunderstand it, does not mean that it is not true, and that it should not be emphasised. What then is it? Well, here Moses takes this action of setting up a place of prayer and of intercession. He was glad that the people had repented, but, oh, that was not enough. The presence of God had gone. The cloudy pillar had disappeared, and God had made this statement that he was not going to accompany them. Of course, we must repent, but as we have seen we do not stop at repentance. Moses was anxious that the presence of God should return. So he set up this place of prayer.

Now notice the way in which it was done. It did not seem to be an elaborate organisation. He did not make any statement, he made no speech about it, he did not address the people. Feeling the burden, he felt that he could not intercede as he was there, in the midst of the camp, so he put it outside the camp, and it was open to anybody who might feel the burden to go out also. You notice how that is emphasised: 'It came to pass, that every one which sought the Lord went out unto the tabernacle of the congregation, which was without the camp.' An apparently unobtrusive action. It was done quite quietly, no fanfare of trumpets, no great declaration, but just taking this action; feeling the need of intercession; feeling the need for some unusual action. He wanted to do this himself, and he left it open for anybody who felt the same thing to join him in that action. That is all we are told about it.

And in exactly the same way you find this in the history of all these revivals. That man James McQuilken began to talk to two others and they saw the whole situation, and these three men alone met together in a little schoolroom on just a narrow lane. I had the privilege of visiting it when I was in Northern Ireland. I went out of my way to do so, because I like to look at a place like that. They did not meet even in their village of Connor or of Kells, they went to this lonely little schoolroom outside the village, where in peace and quietness they could pray to God and intercede on behalf of the people who lived with them in the villages, and the people who lived in the surrounding area. They felt this call to prayer.

Now that is what is emphasised at this point. I rather like the way it is put: 'It came to pass, that everyone which sought the Lord. . . .' They did not all go, but there were individuals in the camp who began to feel the very thing that Moses had been feeling, and they said, 'Moses is going out there to pray on his own, well, let us go out too. We will go, and we will join him.' And thus they came, one by one. No, it was not a great organised thing, no big announcements were made that this was going to happen at a certain time, and in a certain way. Revival has never happened like that, and this is what almost alarms me about the state of the Christian Church at the present time. We must start with our organisation. Our first move is to set up a committee, and then our judicious advertising, all done in a big and organised manner. It is the exact opposite of what we find in the Scriptures. And it has always been the exact opposite of the accounts of revivals in the long history of the Christian Church. Believe me, my friends, when the next revival comes, it will come as a surprise to everybody, and especially to those who have been trying to organise it. It will have happened in this unobtrusive manner. Men and women just slipping away quietly, as it were, to pray because they are burdened, because they can not help themselves, because they can not go on living without it. And they want to join with the others who are feeling the same thing, and are crying out unto God. They set up the tabernacle.

Then the next point is that Moses set the tabernacle up outside the camp – afar off from the camp. Now here is the point at which I am most liable to be misunderstood, but it is here, and it is part of the teaching. There is invariably, in the history of every revival, this drawing aside. Let us not forget that the camp of Israel was the, then, Church of God. In the Old Testament the nation of Israel was the church in the wilderness. This is the Church we are talking about and yet you see what Moses did? He took his tabernacle from the midst of the Church as it were, and put it up outside, afar off from the camp. No revival that has ever been experienced in the long history of the Church has ever been an official movement in the Church. That is a strong statement, is it not? But I repeat it. No revival that the Church has ever known has ever been an official movement. You read of the great precursors of the Protestant Reformation, the people I have referred to already, Wycliffe, John Huss, and others. It was always unofficial, and the officials did not like it. It was the same with Martin Luther. Nothing happened in Rome. No, it happened just to this monk in his cell. And so it has continued to happen.

Even after the reformation of the Church of England in this country, there were men who began to feel dissatisfied, and they began to follow this pattern and do this self-same thing. That is the origin of Puritanism. Then you are all probably familiar, with the story of Methodism in its various branches. How did that begin two hundred years ago? It began in exactly the same way, with the two Wesley brothers, and Whitefield, and others, who were members of the Church of England. They did not begin to do something in the Church of England, but formed what they called their Holy Club, outside the camp. They met privately on their own, just a handful of people. For some time nobody knew that it was happening, but they just met together because they were drawn together by the same thing. It was unofficial, it was outside, as it were. That is the beginning of Methodism, both Calvinistic and Arminian. And the same thing precisely is true in the early story of the Plymouth Brethren, as they came to be called. But in the first stages it was just this getting together of like-minded people, concerned about the Church.

Now this, therefore, is something which we must surely note carefully. 'Are you proposing,' says someone, 'to set up a new denomination?' That is the very last thing that this teaching suggests. That makes it official, that makes it a movement, that means you have brought in your organisation, and that is the very thing I am not saying. But what I am saying is that when God begins to move in his Church, and when he is preparing the way for revival, this is how he always seems to do it. He puts this burden upon certain people, who are called apart, as it were, and who meet together, quietly, unknown, and unobtrusively, because they are conscious of this burden.

Here again is somethng that seems to me to be very grievous at the present time, because the great word of today is sponsorship. Even evangelical Christians, spiritually minded people, when they feel led of God to do something, want a big sponsorship and they do not care very much who is the sponsor. They want the sponsorship of the official Church, the sponsorship of men who are not evangelical at all and they want to go to the great cathedrals for their sponsors. There was no sponsorship here in this story and in times of true spiritual awakening and revival the men most used of God, are not concerned about sponsorship. Their eye is upon the living God. Of course, if you want to do things in a worldly way you have to advertise, and you want to use great names, so that if you propose to hold a meeting in a town, you want the presence of the Lord Mayor of that town, though he may not be a Christian, a professing Christian, at all. Or again, it does not matter whether the governor of a state is a Christian or not, you must have your meeting sponsored by him, and then the people will be attracted and it will become a great thing. All that is the exact opposite of this action of Moses and others like him. Because, you see, when you are calling upon the living God and his inimitable power, you do not need the sponsorship of men. The sponsorship you are interested in is the sponsorship of the Holy Spirit. The Apostle Paul goes into Corinth, and what does he do? He does not send in his preliminary agents to prepare and get everybody ready, and to organise a great public meeting. No, ' . . . weakness, and in fear, and in much trembling. And my speech and my preaching was not with enticing words of man's wisdom. . . .' (1 Cor. 2. 3–4). What is he concerned about? Oh, the 'demonstration of the Spirit and of power'. He dare not go without the Spirit. He must have the Spirit, but having the Spirit, who are men, and what do they count? Sponsorship? There is no such sponsorship in the Bible, nor in the history of the Church in her mightiest periods, in all reformation and revival. No, individuals just went out and gathered together because they knew the pressure of the same burden.

And then there is another element in this that I must emphasise. It is clear that in putting the tabernacle outside the camp, Moses had another motive and a very important one. It is this whole idea of consecration. Moses felt that this could not be done in the midst of the camp. The camp had become unclean, and he deliberately took the tabernacle out, afar off from the camp. It was a very deliberate action. By doing it, he said in effect, 'We must do this thing in God's way, we must get right out of the impurity, and this sinful atmosphere. We must get together here instead.' Yes, that is consecration. That is, if you like, the call to holiness. And again, I am suggesting to you that the history of every revival brings out this same factor in exactly the same way. What is it that has happened to these men whom God has used? Take any one of them and you will find almost invariably that their first concern has not even been the state of the Church, it has been the state of their own souls. It has been the holiness of God. I have already referred to that little movement which began in Oxford two hundred years ago – and you notice the name they gave it? They called it the Holy Club. What happened to them? What happened to the Wesleys and Whitefield and the others who met with them? It was just this – they said, 'Yes, the Christian Church is still the Christian Church, but she is very unworthy and sinful. People are riding very loose to the commandments of God and to the whole of the Christian life as depicted in the New Testament. This is wrong, we must give ourselves to holiness, we must purify ourselves.' They probably went too far and became a little bit legalistic, but they drew up rules and regulations as to how they should live. Hence they were called Methodists. They said, 'We must meet to study the Scriptures together, we must pray together and we must live methodically in everything.' Methodists! Yes, but what they were searching for was holiness. And that has always been God's way. One man or a number of men suddenly become awakened to their distance from God, to the fact that they are in the far country. And their first concern

168

is to be holy as God is holy, and to come into his presence, and to know his glory.

So, inevitably there is a kind of separation. 'Ah,' says someone, 'are you going to divide up the Christian Church?' I am not dividing it. What I am saying is that when the Holy Spirit of God begins to deal with any one of us, there will be this separation. It will not be paraded, it will not be the Pharisees' 'I am holier than thou' attitude. No, once a man begins to be burdened for the glory of God and the state of the Church, he immediately feels this call to consecration, he 'goes out' as it were. We must not overemphasise the physical aspect. It had to be physical there, but it is the principle that matters. Oh, what I am trying to say is this. In a day of grievous immorality, ungodliness and irreligion, such as this, in a day when vice is not only shouting at us, but is arrogant and is boasting, when it is being thrown at the people everywhere – all I am asking is whether we know anything about the call to a separation from that kind of thing? We are living in days when, as Christians, we are called to go the second mile. Ordinary Christianity is not enough, more is demanded. Are we not beginning to feel that nothing can deal with this situation but a manifestation of true life and living, holy living, as it is under God? That is what these men felt.

So Moses put his tabernacle outside the camp and a long way from it. 'It must be separate,' he said. 'It has got to be holy.' And another emphasis I would draw from his action is that he is showing clearly the need of some unusual action, and of some extra effort. Now there are two things that always happen in this early stage of revival. The people who are concerned about revival, in a true sense, are not just out for a little bit of excitement, or interest, or some happiness, or phenomena, or coming with an attitude of 'something marvellous is going to happen and we are going to have a great good time' That is not how they think about it at all. And if you, my dear friends, are simply thinking about meetings, and excitement, and something wonderful, you have not begun to understand this matter.

The first indication of a true and a genuine concern is that we are aware of our unworthiness and uncleaness. We have got to separate ourselves. We have got to set up this tabernacle somehow somewhere outside the ordinary. It has got to be exceptional; it has got to be unusual. We have got to go out of our way. Now, this is the question that I want to impress upon your minds and to leave with you. In these days of exceptional evil, are you doing something exceptional? Or are you just content with coming to the services in the house of God, and doing some routine things? Of course, in the time when the Church was being blessed and all was well, people came to the house of God, they worked in the mission societies, they taught in the Sunday schools, and did all that as part of the ordinary work of the Church. I am not talking about that. What I am asking is this: have you felt that, because of the times through which we are passing, you are called to do something exceptional, to go out, as it were, to take some deliberate action, that in a way separates you? That is the great lesson here.

And then, that I may complete this review here, I am rather interested in what we are told about the remainder of the people. They saw that Moses and one or two individuals used to go out of the camp to the tabernacle to pray. In verse 8 we read,

And it came to pass, when Moses went out unto the tabernacle, that all the people rose up, and stood every man at his tent door, and looked after Moses, until he was gone into the tabernacle.

There is something very wonderful about this. All they did was to look on with interest. They were aware that something was happening, but they did not know what it was and they did not understand it. They did not go out of the camp with Moses into the tent of meeting with God, and pray, and intercede. All they knew was that Moses had taken the tent outside the camp and that he and certain others periodically visited it. So they just stood at their tent doors, watching Moses as he went and talking about him, wondering what he was doing and what exactly was happening. Now the appalling thing is that the right place for the tent was in the midst of the camp. But it was not there.

As you read the history of the Church, you will find this repeated. At first just a few people feel the call, and separate themselves, and then the others begin to say, 'What is happening to so and so? Have you heard about this man or that woman?' They stand at their tent doors and they look on. They have a feeling that something is happening. But they do nothing at all. Oh, if we wait until the whole Church moves, it will never happen. It will never move. Do not worry about that. God's way is to take hold of individuals and to use them and then eventually the majority will be affected. But at this stage, they simply have this vague general awareness that something is happening, and they begin to look on wistfully at the action of Moses and his few companions. I should be very happy to think that that is the position in the Christian Church today. I believe it is. I believe, and I thank God I can say this, I believe that we have turned a corner. I am not talking about the local church only, this is included, but I am speaking generally. I believe that at long last there are just a certain few individuals here and there who are beginning to see that nothing but the intervention of the living God can suffice, and who are, metaphorically, going to this tabernacle that is set up outside, afar off from the camp, and are waiting upon God. And I believe I discern some dawning, vague interest in the body of the Church as it looks on.

What, then, is the result of this action? We will find the answer in verses 9 to 11. I just summarise them for you. God recognises this action, and he begins to add encouragement to it. He gives tokens of the fact that he is well pleased with it: 'And it came to pass, as Moses entered into the tabernacle, the cloudy pillar descended, and stood at the door of the tabernacle.' It had not been doing that because God had taken it back. The visible sign of his presence had been withdrawn. But as a result of what Moses had done, back came the cloudy pillar, as before. God gave a manifestation of his presence. And if someone is wondering what this means to us, it means that the first indication of revival is always that something begins to happen to the life of the Church. There seems to be a new quickening. The worship of the Church becomes warmer, something comes back which had gone, a warmth and a tenderness. There is an encouragement. There is a new wistfulness, a new sense of expectation, a new freedom given in the prayers of the people. That is the return of the cloudy pillar. We must be on the alert to discern this. We must be looking for tokens of encouragement from God. Less of the hardness and the glibness, and a new tenderness, a new concern, a new note of agony. Some old people I remember used to say that the thing they were looking for in the prayer meetings in the church was the element of 'Oh', the longing, the groaning, the waiting, the 'Oh'. And when that comes it is a sign that the cloudy pillar has come back.

Then, God, you remember, gave Moses some very definite indications that he was well pleased with him. He looked upon him and he spoke unto him face to face as a man speaks to his friend. In other words, the man who felt the burden first of all, is given an intimation by God that God has heard him and that he is going to answer. Now, that is once more, the invariable. In all the histories of revival these men go through a period of agony, then they come to a point when they feel that it is all right, God

171

has heard, something is going to happen. God did that with Moses. God gave him an assurance that his prayers were heard and that he was going to be answered. And then, you notice a significant thing in these people who were simply standing by their tent doors, and watching Moses and the others as they went. They saw the cloudy pillar, and they began to worship God even at their tent doors. Now, you see, the whole Church is beginning to be affected and involved. This may take a long time, but that is the next thing, and it will happen.

Lastly we come to verse 11 and, indeed, it is very marvellous. 'And the Lord spake unto Moses face to face as a man speaketh unto his friend.' There is all the encouragement. Then notice this, 'And he [Moses] turned again into the camp: but his servant Joshua, the son of Nun, a young man, departed not out of the tabernacle.' That is the wonderful thing. You see what it all means is this. Moses, having had this intimation from God that he was heard, and that God was going to answer, went back to the camp to report to the people, to tell them what had happened, to say that the meaning of the descent of the cloudy pillar was that God was favourably disposed once more, was turning his face towards them, instead of away from them, and that he had spoken to him face to face. He went back to encourage them. But you notice what a spiritually minded man Moses was, and how well versed he was in the ways of God. He went back to report to the camp, but he left his servant Joshua in the tabernacle until he got back again. Why? Ah, Moses was expecting more to come, he did not want any of it to be missed. So while he himself went back to report to the camp, he left Joshua in the tent of meeting. What if God would do something further? They were expecting more. This was only the beginning, the early stage. Indeed, I would not hesitate to say that as far as we have gone up to this point we really have not begun to see revival. This is the preliminary, the preparation. But you notice the spirit of expectation. Joshua left behind in the tent, lest, while Moses is reporting to the people, God might grant a further revelation. He knows that there was more to come. Moses was taking no risks. He was holding on. He remained in the presence of God through his deputy, his servant. And when the day comes that you and I are on the tiptoe of expectation, we can be sure that God is moving, and that something unusual is about to take place.

And so, as we finish our study of stage one, we must ask ourselves, whether we have arrived at that stage. Do we know anything about that tabernacle and this call to separation and to urgent intercession? Those are the two things – holiness and intercession on behalf of the mass of the people, and waiting in the presence of God, expecting more and more.

Chapter 14

Exodus 33.12–17

And Moses said unto the Lord, See, thou sayest unto me, Bring up this people: and thou hast not let me know whom thou wilt send with me. Yet thou hast said, I know thee by name, and thou hast also found grace in my sight. Now therefore, I pray thee, if I have found grace in thy sight, shew me now thy way, that I may know thee, that I may find grace in thy sight: and consider that this nation is thy people. And he said, My presence shall go with thee, and I will give thee rest. And he said unto him, If thy presence go not with me, carry us not up hence. For wherein shall it be known here that I and thy people have found grace in thy sight? is it not in that thou goest with us? so shall we be separated, I and thy people, from all the people that are upon the face of the earth. And the Lord said unto Moses, I will do this thing also that thou hast spoken: for thou hast found grace in my sight, and I know thee by name (Exod. 33. 12–17).

We have seen how God had withdrawn his presence from the Children of Israel because of their sin, how they repented, how Moses interceded on their behalf and then how God heard his prayer and the cloudy pillar returned to the door of the tabernacle.

And there is a sense in which it can be said quite truly that it is here, at this point, that the prayer for revival, as such, really begins. All that had happened hitherto was a prayer that God may return amongst them. That he may not withold his face altogether, as he had been doing, as a part of their punishment.

But now we go beyond that and come to the point that I am so anxious to emphasise here. Moses, obviously, was very grateful for all that had happened. The coming back of the cloudy pillar was a remarkable thing, even the people could see that, because we read that all the people saw the cloudy pillar stand at the tabernacle door, and all the people rose up and worshipped, every man in his tent door. Moses could understand it much more clearly, and, of course, he was grateful for it, profoundly grateful.

174

God had returned, as it were, and God was listening to him, and speaking to him. Now you would have thought that he might have stopped at that point. You might have felt that surely there was nothing necessary beyond that, and yet the whole purpose of this section that we are considering is to show that Moses was not satisfied. He desired more, so he went back again into the tabernacle, and he continued to pray. All that he had been given, he said, was not enough. He longed for more and he began pleading for more, for something extra. And it is just there that we really come to the vital point in this whole matter of revival. Revival is something extra. It is something additional. It is something which is quite unusual. I emphasise this, because it seems very clear to me that there are large numbers of good Christian people today who have never grasped the point that revival, by definition, is something quite out of the ordinary, something special, unusual, exceptional.

In other words, by revival we do not mean the Church being blessed by God, and conscious of his presence, and enabled to do his work. Moses, in a sense, was already conscious of all that. God had come back. God had promised to bless. God had given him that personal assurance, as it were, when he spoke to him face to face. From that Moses might have argued, 'Well now then, we are back to where we were. All is right again. God's presence has come back to us and we can go forward.' But Moses was not satisfied. And revival, I repeat, is not the Church being blessed and being conscious of God's presence, and being enabled to do her work. Revival goes beyond all that. And we can see this clearly, here in this particular case. Moses felt that the circumstances were such that something quite special and out of the ordinary was needed. And so he proceeded to pray for it.

Now this, it seems to me, is the crucial point in the whole understanding of revival and of what it means. There are many today, and, alas, there are many evangelical people among them, who have completely failed to see this. They argue like this, 'Surely there is nothing necessary except that we should be orthodox, that God should bless, that we should be aware of his presence amongst us, and that we should carry on with our regular ministry, with conversions taking place, and with greater efforts being made? What,' they ask, 'do you require beyond that? What do you require beyond the fact that men and women should be converted, and should know the fullness of the Spirit? Is that not the most desirable thing? Is that not the ideal state of the Church? That men and women know whom they have believed and be orthodox in their beliefs, and thus go on being filled with the Spirit according to the exhortation of the apostle in Ephesians 5. 18?'

That argument displays a complete ignorance of what is meant by revival. Revival is something beyond all that, something additional to all that, something exceptional, something which is, in a sense, startling in its amazing character.

Now it is obvious that if we are not clear about this, we shall not be concerned about revival, and we shall not pray for revival, and that has been the attitude of the vast majority of people. They say that things are going well. Look at us, look at the societies, look at the reports in the religious weeklies, everything is going well, it is all marvellous. And so they do not think about revival, and they do not feel it is necessary, and they do not pray for it. 'All we have to do,' they say, 'is to keep on as we are. God is blessing us. Everything is all right.' And that is because they have this crucial failure to understand the meaning of revival in its essence, that they find themselves in that position. So, here we are looking at what I would call the most crucial aspect of this whole question of revival. And here it is depicted so plainly in this second section of this chapter. Moses, who had had so much, went back because he wanted more. And he began to plead for this 'more', and for this extra.

The first question before us, therefore, is, what did he pray for? What did he feel was this additional need. You will find that as we look at the answers to that question, as they are indicated here, we shall be looking at something that has at all times characterised the prayers of men and women who have felt a burden for revival. There is a sameness about this which is really almost incredible. But of course, the moment we realise the principles governing these matters, we should not be surprised at it. Here are the things that the intercessors, who have done their work before the revival comes, have always concentrated upon. Therefore, if we are concerned about the situation today, these are the things which should concern us. What did Moses pray for? First and foremost, he prayed for a sense of personal assurance. That is the message of verse 13. 'Now, therefore,' he says, 'I pray thee, if I have found grace in thy sight. . . .' He knew that he had, he was using it as an argument. You can read it in the following way: 'Because I have found grace in thy sight, show me now thy way, that I may know thee, that I may find grace in thy sight, and consider that this nation is thy people.' This almost sounds contradictory, does it not? He said, 'If I have found grace in thy sight, do this in order that I may find grace in thy sight.' God had already told him that he knows him and speaks to him as a man does unto his friend, and yet Moses' prayer was, 'that I may know thee'.

So what does this mean? Well here we have one of these differentiating points. Moses was not content with a mere knowledge of the fact that he was accepted by God, and that he was in God's care. He knew that, but he was not content with it, he wanted more. 'That I may know thee,' said Moses. Oh, he knew about God, he had had manifestation of God's living interest in him and of God's kindness to him. But he was not satisfied. He wanted more. He wanted a personal knowledge of God. He wanted a direct knowledge of God. He wanted to know beyond a doubt and a peradventure that God really loved him. He knew it of course, but he wanted a manifestation of it. He wanted an absolute certainty with respect to it.

And, here is something that you will find in the lives of all the great saints of God in the Church throughout the ages, and particularly in men on whom God lays his hand in this matter of revival and of intercession. The first thing that happens to them is that they themselves feel this desire for a deeper knowledge of God. Of course, they are good men, they are orthodox men. They believe in God, they know they are saved, they have assurance of salvation – they may have had it for years, – but now they begin to feel a hunger and a thirst for something bigger and something deeper. They read their Bibles, and they feel that here there is some deeper and some fuller knowledge of God, and God's love, and that is what they want. They are no longer content with what I may call the ordinary condition of the Church. They want something extraordinary, something unusual. Let me give you some lines from a hymn which seem to me to put it very well indeed. Here is a man, you see, writing

> Speak, I pray thee, gentle Jesus;
> Oh, how passing sweet, thy words,
> Breathing o'er my troubled spirit,
> Peace, which never earth affords.

and then he goes on to say:

> Tell me thou art mine, O Saviour;
> Grant me an assurance clear. . . .
> *William Williams*

177

That is the thing. He knows that the Saviour loves him. But, you see what he wants:

Tell me thou art mine, O Saviour;

It is only the man who knows the Saviour's love who asks him for that. Here is a man asking for something special, something unusual, something additional. I need not belabour this point, surely. On the human level we all know something about this. It is a great thing to be told that you are loved. You may know that you are loved, but it is not enough. You like to be told it. It is extra. It is additional. There is nothing like it.

Tell me thou art mine, O Saviour;

That is what Moses was praying. He wanted God to tell him. You see, he was not content with the general, the average, the ordinary. 'No,' he said. 'I am in such a position, that I want something beyond that, something additional, oh, some special sealing of all this to my spirit and to my heart.' That is what he was crying out for.

Now this is something that happens in the experiences of individuals who begin to long for this blessing of God which we call revival. It is, in other words, a desire to have a very living and real consciousness of the presence of the Holy Spirit in the Church. Oh, we know the Holy Spirit is in the Church. The Holy Spirit has been in the Church since the day of Pentecost, yes, but what this man is asking for, and what men who plead for revival are always asking for, is not simply that we may know or be aware of the fact that the Spirit is in the Church, but that this may be demonstrated and manifested to us in such a way that every doubt or hesitation has gone. It is for a clear manifestation, an unusual manifestation, some additional manifestation of love. That is what Moses was praying for. And that is what we should pray for if we are concerned about revival. Because with all our orthodoxy, and all our consciousness of the fact that the Holy Spirit is in the Church, and that God does bless us, are we not aware that there is much more that we know so little about? When we compare ourselves with the people in the book of the Acts of the Apostles, for instance, there is more that we have not touched, that we know nothing about. We are like children paddling in the sea. There is the mighty ocean and its depths, what do we know about that? Now here is the cry from a man's heart for this additional

178

something, these depths of the ocean of God's love, these unusual manifestations: 'That I may know thee.'

And then, of course, Moses said, 'Show me now thy way.' Here he was referring to God's purposes and God's plans. He was asking for this absolute certainty that God was going to go with them as they marched up in the direction of Canaan and entered into the promised land. God had told them, you remember, that he himself was not going with them, that he was going to send an angel. 'Now,' said Moses, 'you must come with us. And I want to see your way, I want you to give me some glimpse into your great plan and purpose.' That was his prayer. Not content with knowledge, by faith, that God was going to bless, and that he was going to honour, Moses was here beginning to be daring. He said, 'I would like to have a glimpse into the plan. I would like you to share the secret with me. I would like you to take me into your confidence. I would like you to give me now an absolute assurance, before we go any further, that you really are going to come with us.'

Now there is all the difference in the world between that, and *assuming* that God is going to be with us. We tend to do that, do we not? We tend to assume it. How do we go to a church service? Do we offer any special prayer that God might be with us and look upon us, or do we come assuming it? Is that not the trouble with us, that we assume the presence of God? There is a sense in which that is perfectly right, and we walk by faith and not by sight. Yes, but here, in this story, is the cry for something more. Here is the Church, represented as it were by Moses and the people and they have a great task in front of them, with many difficulties and great enemies. 'Now,' said Moses, 'can I venture, can I dare to come into your presence in the light of what you have already said to me, and in the light of what you have already done for me? Can I come in and ask? Oh, just tell us what you are going to do. Give us some certainty. Let us know that you are going to be with us.'

That is the prayer for revival – not being content to go on from week to week, and month to month, year to year. Certainly enjoying God's blessings, do not misunderstand me. I am not despising the day of small things – I just want us to realise that we *are* in the day of small things. But there are big things, and I am talking about the longing for these bigger things. And that is what Moses was praying for. He was asking God, 'Will you just tell me that you are going to do great things?' Now this is the filial spirit. It is only a child who does a thing like that. The child ventures to ask the father things that the servant would never dream of asking. The father has given some indication of something that is going to happen, the child is a bit impatient, and he says, 'Do tell me what you are going to do. Let me have a peep into it. Let me see.' He cannot wait, he is so anxious. Is that wrong? Of course it is not. That is the childlike spirit, going to the Father and saying, 'Just let me know so that I can enjoy peace, and be happy.'

And that was God's answer to him. He said to him, I will go with thee: 'My presence shall go with thee, and I will give thee rest.' I will take your anxiety away from you. I will let you know what I am going to do, so that you need have no concern and no apprehension. God answered his prayer.

That, then, was the petition – a desire for personal assurance, that the Church may know this love of God, and may be let into the secret of his plans, and his purposes, his proposals, and his ideas. Have you felt anything of this desire? Have you felt this longing to be allowed into the secret? Would you not like to know even at this moment whether God is going to do something for us or not? That is the prayer of Moses.

So, there is the first thing that Moses prayed for, but let us now consider the second. It follows, of course, of necessity; it is an accompaniment. It is the prayer for power. God had said to Moses, 'My presence shall go with thee, and I will give thee rest.' And Moses said to God, 'If thy presence go not with me, carry us not up hence.' This prayer for power is always in evidence in the history of the Church prior to revival. This is the need of which the intercessors always become most conscious, and there are many reasons for this. The first, of course was their awareness of the magnitude of the problem confronting them, the strength of the enemy that they were going to meet, the powerful nations in the land of promise – the Amalekites and others – and the tremendous task of occupying a land. Here they were, just a kind of nomadic people travelling along like this, and they were going to settle a land, and conquer it, and make their homes there. And suddenly they became aware of the immensity of the problem. I have to emphasise this once more, because to me there is nothing so tragic about our position today, as the obvious failure of so many people to realise the magnitude of the problem that confronts us. If we only realised the magnitude of the problem, there would be no need to urge prayer for revival. But our eyes seem to be shut. 'Everything is going well,' we say, 'look at the reports. Marvellous. Look at the activities. Is all not well?'

But wait a minute. You must always analyse figures. You have got to be careful that you are not carried away by certain enthusiasts, without going any further. But there are other figures too. Keep your eye on the papers, and on the statistics of the various denominations. Look at these figures. Look at the decline in the membership of the church, attendance at Sunday Schools, attendance in church services. It is going down in all the denominations, and at an alarming rate. You would think by looking at some Christian newspapers that everybody is being converted in some countries. But it is not so. The statistics of the churches prove that such is not the case. The churches are going down, steadily, year after year. And as to the increase in vice, and sin, and godlessness and profanity, we can surely see it? Can we not see it in this country and other countries? Can we not see this modern intellectualism that will not even consider the Gospel? Can we not see how men in a state of prosperity are not concerned about their souls and about God? This is true not only of this country, but of every other country as well.

How can we be at ease when only some ten per cent of the people in this country claim to be religious, and only half those ever think of attending a place of worship? Is that a position about which we can be complacent? Is everything all right? The position, I say, is going from bad to worse, it is becoming increasingly alarming. And I see plainly that all our efforts are not touching the main situation. That is not to disparage individual conversions, of course it is not. The whole point I am making is this, Moses and his people were already in that position, but they were pleading for the extra, they were pleading for the unusual, they were pleading for the exceptional. And that is my plea. That is not to criticise what is happening, but it is to show that it is not enough.

And the tragedy, as I see it, is that men are saying, 'This is enough. It is happening.' But it is not. The main position is worse than ever. And that is where the cry and the plea for power and for an unusual manifestation begins to come in. Moses and the people realised the nature of the problem, but they not only realised the nature of the problem, they realised their own weakness. Moses said to God, 'If thy presence go not with me, carry us not up hence.' Moses, we are told, was the meekest of men, and that was his glory. He realised his weakness, his own inability. I will not go another step, he said to God, unless you promise to be with me. Who am I to meet this situation? Even with the wisdom that you have given me, it is not enough. I want this absolute certainty. I want this strength, and I want this power.

Moses, you see, was afraid to go on without God. He would not go on without this absolute certainty of the presence and the power of God. There again is the thing that you will always find in the Church before a time of revival, and that is what makes me sometimes think that we have a long way to go. We are still so confident in what we are doing. We are still so proud of it. We are still so convinced that we are doing marvellous things. We are not aware of our impotence, we are not aware of our weakness, and of our need of power. As long as we think we can organise these matters, there is no hope for us. The beginning of revival is to realise that without this manifestation of God's power we can do nothing. We have got to get back to that position, in which the Apostle Paul so constantly found himself. I am never tired of quoting it. It is the text, more than any other, that needs to be held before every section of the Church today.

And I was with you in weakness, and in fear, and in much trembling. And my speech and my preaching was not with enticing words of man's wisdom, but in demonstration of the Spirit and of power: that your faith should not stand in the wisdom of men, but in the power of God (1 Cor. 2. 3–5).

I never tire of quoting the cases of certain ministers used of God in the past who would not dare to go into the pulpit to preach until they had an absolute assurance that the Holy Spirit was going to accompany them there, and was going to empower them. That is what Moses had come to. He realised his need of this exceptional power, so he prayed to God for it.

So we have considered Moses' prayer for God's presence, for God's personal assurance and power, and then thirdly he prayed also for a special authentication of the Church and her mission. That is the message of verse 16. You can hear him argue, 'Wherein,' he said – 'For wherein shall it be known here that I and thy people have found grace in thy sight? is it not in that thou goest with us? so shall we be separated, I and thy people, from all the people that are upon the face of the earth.' In other words, this is a prayer that the Church should be as she is meant to be. The Church is meant to be separate. The Church is meant to be unique. 'Now,' said Moses to God, 'I am asking for this something extra, because I am concerned. Here are we thy people. How are all the other nations to know that we really are your people? They are looking on at us, they are laughing at us, mocking us and jeering at us, they are ready to overwhelm us. Now, I am asking for something,' said Moses, 'that will make it absolutely clear that we are not just one of the nations of the world, but that we are thy people, that we are separate, unique, altogether apart.'

The prayer for revival, then, is the prayer that the Church may again become like that. And my argument is that nothing but some unusual outpouring of the Spirit of God can do that. What is needed, as we have seen, is something that cannot be explained in human terms. What is needed is something that is so striking and so signal that it will arrest the attention of the whole world. That is revival. Revival always does that. Now we of ourselves can never do anything like that. We can do a great deal, and we should do all we can. We can preach the truth, we can defend it, we can indulge in our apologetics, we can organise our campaigns, we can try to present a great front to the world, but, you know, it does not impress the world. It leaves the world where it was. The need is for something which will be so overwhelming, so divine, so unusual that it will arrest the attention of the world, and prove that we are indeed what we claim to be, the unique and separate people of God. That is the essence of the third petition in this prayer.

Now, if I understand the times in which we are living at all, this is our most urgent need today. What is the matter with us? Well, what has disappeared is the uniqueness of the Church. The Church seems to be so much like other agencies and other bodies, or just like any other institution. How difficult it is to see any difference between the church and some good societies and organisations that belong to the world. Have a look at a church assembly, that of any denomination, and then have a look at a political society, or a cultural society. I wonder whether you could tell any difference between them – that is, if you did not notice the particular dress that is affected by certain dignatories and officials. If you just went in and they all happened to dress like everybody else, I wonder whether you would realise that there is something unique about the Church of God, because she is God's Church, and God's people? My dear friends, we have lost our uniqueness. We are nice people, we are respectable people, we are well dressed people, yes, we are religious people. Oh, but there are many other agencies of which you can say that, and yet they are not Christian.

'But,' you may say, 'we can do big things. We can organise great campaigns, and we can get many adherents to come to the Church.' But Buddhism is doing exactly the same thing at the present time. There is a great revival of Buddhism going on.

Thousands of people are turning to Buddhism, in India, and in other lands, even in this land. The cults, too, are thriving. They can do all this, they can stage big efforts, and they will get large numbers of adherents. They can do it all. False religions can do it, and the world, in general, is not influenced nor affected, it is not even impressed. There is nothing unique about all that. What is needed is some supernatural manifestation which will make it perfectly clear and plain that it is not of men, but that it is of God. The demonstration of the Spirit and of power, says the Apostle Paul. What is needed is what happened on the day of Pentecost. Read Acts 2 – that is what is needed. 'Are you asking,' says someone, 'for a sound of a mighty rushing wind?' No, I am not, of necessity, asking for that, neither am I asking, of necessity, for speaking with tongues, but I am asking for such a descent of the Spirit, that everybody knows that something has happened. That is what I am asking for.

Again, I am asking for something like that which happened in that incident which is recorded in Acts 4. There was that little church faced with a great difficulty. There was a ban on the preaching, with the threat of imprisonment and death, and what did they do? They went back and they prayed. They asked God to have mercy, they said, 'Do something special. Enable us to preach with power, and send signs following.' The building shook. That is what they were asking for, and God gave it them. And 'with great power gave the apostles witness of the resurrection'. Yes, it was another outpouring of the Spirit of God. It was a repetition of Pentecost. It was another baptism. Again, he poured the Spirit upon them, and they were filled once more, the men who had already been filled on the day of Pentecost. What I am asking for is what happened in Acts 10, when Peter was there preaching to Cornelius and his household. We are told that as he was preaching, the Holy Ghost fell upon them, and even convinced a narrow minded man, a narrow minded Jew, like Peter that these people, these Gentiles, really were converted. You remember how he says, 'Who was I that I could refuse when I saw that God had done to them what he did to us at the beginning?' That is what I am asking for. Some manifestation of the power of God, that will make it plain and clear that this is not man acting, but that it is God. That is what makes the difference.

Let me give you some other illustrations. Do you remember what we are told in Hebrews, 2. 3–4? It is a striking illustration of this very thing. 'How shall we escape,' says this man, 'if we neglect so great salvation; which at the first began to be spoken by the Lord, and was confirmed unto us by them that heard him, God also bearing them witness, both with signs and wonders, and with divers miracles, and gifts of the Holy Ghost, according to his own will?' God bearing them witness. God confirming it, that is the thing that established the early Church: God giving this unusual, exceptional attestation and confirmation of the fact that these men were his, and that they were preaching his gospel. And the Apostle Peter says exactly the same thing. You will find it in his first epistle in the first chapter, in verses 11 and 12: 'Searching what, or what manner of time the Spirit of Christ which was in them did signify, when it testified beforehand the sufferings of Christ, and the glory that should follow. Unto whom it was revealed, that not unto themselves, but unto us they did minister the things, which are now reported unto you by them that have preached the gospel unto you with the Holy Ghost sent down from heaven. . . .'

That is the thing – this unusual attestation, this indication by God that the Church is his, that it is his power that is within her, that she is unique, that this is not of men. Men can preach, alas, how well I know it. A man can preach without the Holy Spirit, I can expound this word with intelligence, but that is not enough. We need the demonstration of the Spirit and of power. Men can conduct services. Men can get converts. Men can give additions to the Church. What a man can never do is what God does. The Holy Ghost sent down from heaven, the descent of power, this uniqueness, this special manifestation of the presence and of the power of God. That is what Moses prayed for. And that is always the third, and in many senses, the most urgent petition in the mouths and on the lips of those who see the position as it is, and who see the need of revival – 'Authenticate thy word. Lord God, let it be known, let it be known beyond a doubt or a peradventure, that we are thy people. Shake us!' I do not ask him to shake the building, but I ask him to shake us. I ask him to do something that is so amazing, so astounding, so divine, that the whole world shall be compelled to look on and say, 'What is this?' as they said on the day of Pentecost; as they said at the Protestant Reformation; as they said two hundred years ago when the Spirit was poured upon Whitefield and the Wesleys and others; as they said a hundred years ago in the revival in America, Northern Ireland, Wales and Scotland, and in other places. 'What is this? What is it?' And it is clear that it is nothing that man can produce or organise, it is plain that it is an act of God. God authenticating his people, their work, and their message, and saying 'Yes, these

185

are my people. And I am doing something in their midst that I have never done among you, and that I never will do among any but my own people.' Are we clear that the prayer for revival is not the prayer for regular blessing on the work – we must always go on doing that – it is the prayer for the unusual on top of it, in addition to it, something special, something that authenticates God and his work amongst his people.

Chapter 15

Exodus 33.12–17

And Moses said unto the Lord, See, thou sayest unto me, Bring
up this people: and thou hast not let me know whom thou wilt
send with me. Yet thou hast said, I know thee by name, and
thou hast also found grace in my sight. Now therefore, I pray
thee, if I have found grace in thy sight, shew me now the way,
that I may know thee, that I may find grace in thy sight: and
consider that this nation is thy people. And he said, My presence
shall go with thee, and I will give thee rest. And he said unto
him, If thy presence go not with me, carry us not up hence. For
wherein shall it be known here that I and thy people have found
grace in thy sight? is it not in that thou goest with us? so shall
we be separated, I and thy people, from all the people that are
upon the face of the earth. And the Lord said unto Moses, I will
do this thing also that thou hast spoken: for thou hast found
grace in my sight, and I know thee by name (Exod. 33.12–17.)

Before we continue with our study of this great chapter from
Exodus, let me remind you of what we have learned from it up
to this point. Moses has prayed for a personal assurance as far as
he himself is concerned; he has asked for power, power for himself
and for the people and, thirdly, he has asked for some exceptional
authentication of the Church and his message. And now we must
go on to consider *why* he prayed for these things. What were his
motives? Surely this is all-important for us, because, if I understand the situation at all, it is in this realm of purpose and of
motives that we so constantly go wrong. We start at the wrong
end. And, therefore, shall derive great benefit and instruction as
we watch Moses praying here. And, of course, you will find
everywhere in the Scriptures that what is true of him at this point
is true of God's intercessors, God's saints, as they plead with
God, wherever you find them in the Scriptures. Moreover, I would
remind you that if you read the history of the great revivals of
the past, you will find that, as you read of the men whom God

has used most signally, as you study them in the period before the revival came, when they were pleading and interceding, you will find invariably that they were animated by exactly the same motives as we find here in the case of Moses.

So we must be perfectly clear with regard to this matter of our motives. I am calling you to pray for revival. Yes, but why should you pray for revival? Why should anybody pray for revival? And the answer that is first given here is this: a concern for the glory of God. You will find it at the end of verse 13: 'Now therefore, I pray thee, if I have found grace in thy sight, shew me now thy way, that I may know thee, that I may find grace in thy sight; *and consider that this nation is thy people.*' That is the motive. That is the reason. Moses was concerned primarily about the glory of God. Now, you will find that he constantly used this particular argument with God. There is an illustration of this in the previous chapter, chapter 32 verses 11 and 12. God was angry with the Children of Israel because they had made the golden calf and had rebelled against him, and God said to Moses,

I have seen this people, and, behold, it is a stiffnecked people: now therefore let me alone, that my wrath may wax hot against them, and that I may consume them: and I will make of thee a great nation. And Moses besought the Lord his God, and said, Lord, why doth thy wrath wax hot against thy people, which thou hast brought forth out of the land of Egypt with great power, and with a mighty hand? Wherefore should the Egyptians speak, and say, For mischief did he bring them out, to slay them in the mountains, and to consume them from the face of the earth? (Exod. 32. 9–12).

You see Moses' concern? He is concerned about the name, and, as it were, the reputation and the glory of God. And that is the point he is making here again. 'This nation,' he says, 'is thy people.' He is saying, in effect, that God's honour, and God's glory is involved in this situation. They are, after all, his people, they have claimed that, he has given indications of that, he has brought them out of Egypt in a marvellous and a miraculous manner. He has brought them through the Red Sea, is he going to leave them here in the wilderness? What will the Egyptians say? What will the other nations say? Has he failed? He promised them great things. Can he not execute them? Can he not bring them to fulfilment? Moses is suggesting to God that his own glory, his own honour, is involved in this whole situation. Now you will

188

find this plea endlessly in the Psalms. You will find it constantly in the Prophets. Their prayer to God is, 'for thine own name's sake', as if to say, 'We have no right to speak, and we are not really asking it for ourselves, but for thine own name's sake, for thy glory's sake, for the sake of thine eternal honour.' Moses, thus, had a concern for and was jealous about, the name and the glory of God. And here he is asking God, for his own sake, to do this extra, this special, thing.

Now, we cannot go into all these points in detail, but this is the thing that matters is it not? The Church, after all, is the Church of God. 'She is His new creation, by water and word.' We are a people for God's own peculiar possession. And why has he called us out of darkness into his own marvellous light? Surely it is that we may show forth his praises, his excellences, his virtues. And, therefore, we should be concerned about this matter primarily because of the name, and the glory, the honour of God himself. Whether we like it or not, it is a fact that the world judges God himself, and the Lord Jesus Christ, and the whole of the Christian faith, by what it sees in us. We are his representatives, we are the people who take his name upon us, we are the people who talk about him, and the man outside the Church regards the Church as the representative of God. And, therefore, I argue that we must emulate the example of Moses, as we find it here. Our first concern should be about the glory of God.

But am I being unfair when I suggest that this is scarcely ever mentioned? There is great concern about the Church today, of course, but what is the concern about? Today's concern is about statistics, and figures. People are talking about churches being empty, and they talk about means and methods of trying to fill them and of getting the people in again. They are interested in the figures, in membership, in finance, and in organisation. How often do you hear annual conferences and assemblies expressing a concern about the glory of God, and the honour of the name of God? No, our attitude seems rather to be that the Church is a human organisation, and of course we are concerned about what is happening to it, as a man is concerned if his business is not going well. We are businessmen, and we are concerned about the institution, and the organisation. But this was not Moses' primary concern. His first and chief concern was about the glory of God. Are you grieved at the state of the Church? If so, why are you grieved about it? Is it because you are old enough to remember the end of the Victorian era, or the Edwardian period, when it was the custom for people to crowd into churches? Is it just a sort of nostalgia for the great days of the Church? Or do we know something of a concern for the name of God? Are we pained? Are we hurt? Are we grieved? Does it weigh heavily upon our hearts, and minds, and spirits, when we see the godlessness that surrounds us, and the name of God taken in vain? Do we know something of this zeal, this holy zeal?

Have you noticed the concern of the Psalmist in Psalm 79, when he says, 'Wherefore should the heathen say, Where is their God?'. That is what they are saying. They are laughing as they say 'They talked about some great God, who was the God above every other god. They said that the God of Israel was *the* God, they gloried in him, they said he was wonderful. Where is he? Look at them! How can these people claim that they are in the hands of such a God? They would never be in such a condition if that were really true.' You see, what is involved, primarily, is the glory and the honour and the name of God. It is not our institutions, it is not our success or failure, that matters, the primary thing is the glory of God. Of course, the Psalmist sees it. Take the second Psalm, how well he puts it. 'The kings of the earth set themselves', he says, 'and the rulers take counsel together, against the Lord, and against his anointed, saying. . . .' Of course, they were attacking David, they were attacking the Children of Israel, but David has the insight of a spiritually minded man. He says, 'It is not against me, it is against God. It is against the Lord and his anointed that these people are setting themselves,'.

Indeed, this is the great theme that you will find running everywhere through the Psalms. Let me give you just one other instance of it, in Psalm 83. 'For, lo,' says the Psalmist, 'thine enemies make a tumult: and they that hate thee have lifted up the head. They have taken crafty counsel against thy people, and consulted against the hidden ones.' Yes, but it is all against God. And there is that marvellous, and almost lyrical example to be found Acts 4.

After they had tried Peter and John and forbidden them to preach the gospel, the authorities were determined to exterminate the Church and put an end to all her preaching, so they made serious threats to the Apostles. Peter and John went back and they began to pray with all the assembled company of believers. And this is what they said – notice how they were quoting the second Psalm – 'The kings of the earth stood up, and the rulers were gathered together against the Lord, and against his Christ.' Then their own words, 'For of a truth against thy holy child Jesus, whom thou hast anointed, both Herod, and Pontius Pilate, with

190

the Gentiles, and the people of Israel, were gathered together, for to do whatsoever thy hand and thy counsel, determined before to be done. And now, Lord, behold their threatenings . . .' (4.26–28). You see, they had a clear insight. You would have thought that they would have prayed entirely about themselves, but they did not do that primarily. They recognised that all that was happening was really against God. And here is the thing, surely, that we must needs recapture. We are so subjective in our approach, always thinking about ourselves. And that is not the way to pray for revival. We must, in the first place, be concerned about God, his glory, his honour, his name.

This, to me, is the essence of the whole matter. Go through the great prayers of the Old Testament and you will find it always there. These men had a passion for God, they were in trouble, they were unhappy, because this great God was not being worshipped as he should be. And they prayed God for his own sake, for his glory's sake, to vindicate his own name and to arise and to scatter his enemies. That is the first thing.

Then the second thing – and it must always come in the second place, never in the first – is a concern about the honour of the Church herself. Incidentally, in this particular passage, there is nothing more wonderful than the way in which Moses shows his concern for the Church, which was then the nation of Israel. God had been giving Moses some wonderful intimations of his loving interest in him, but Moses is not content with that. Moses does not merely seek personal blessings. He wants to make sure that the Children of Israel, as a whole, are going to be involved in this blessing. He is given again a wonderful example of that in Exodus 32, one of the most glorious passages in the Old Testament. 'It came to pass on the morrow, that Moses said unto the people, Ye have sinned a great sin: and now I will go up unto the Lord; peradventure I shall make an atonement for your sin. And Moses returned unto the Lord, and said, Oh, this people have sinned a great sin, and have made them gods of gold. Yet ' pause. It is as if he broke down and could not speak any longer. He is in a great agony of soul – 'Yet now, if thou wilt forgive their sin – . . .' and then he is able to speak – 'and if not, blot me, I pray thee, out of thy book which thou hast written' (32. 30–32). I do not want to go on living, he says, if you are not going to include them in the blessing.

God had said, 'I am going to blot out this people, I am going to make a nation out of you.'

'No,' says Moses, 'blot me out as well. I do not want to go on without them.'

Oh, this is true intercession. The man is concerned about the state of the whole Church, and his personal life and welfare and well-being are nothing to him, unless the Church is to be blessed. And here he is in this chapter repeating all that. 'Thy people, this nation.'

We could linger over this, but we must move on. I would simply leave it like this. It seems to me that there is no hope for revival until you and I, and all of us, have reached the stage in which we begin to forget ourselves a little, and to be concerned for the Church, for God's body, his people here on earth. So many of our prayers are subjective and self-centred. We have our problems and difficulties, and by the time that we have finished with them, we are tired and exhausted and we do not pray for the Church. My blessing, my need, my this, my that. Now, I am not being hard and unkind, God has promised to deal with our problems. But where does the Church come into our prayers and inter-cessions? Do we go beyond ourselves and our families? We stand before the world and we say the only hope for the world is Christianity. We say the Church, and the Church alone, has the message that is needed. We see the problems of society, they are shouting at us and they are increasing week by week. And we know that this is the only answer. Very well, then, if we know that and if we believe that, let me ask you in the name of God, how often do you pray that the Church may have power to preach this, in such a manner that all these citadels that are raising themselves against God shall be razed to the ground and shall be flattened in his holy presence? How much time do you give to praying that the preachers of the gospel may be endued with the power of the Holy Ghost? Are you interceding about this? Are you concerned about it? Moses, I say was more concerned about this than about himself. He would not go up alone to the promised land. He did not want to be made the great man alone. 'No, it is the Church,' he said, 'I am not going on unless they are all coming with me, and with you in the midst.'

We must learn to think again about the Christian Church. Our whole approach has become subjective. It is subjective in evan-gelism, it is subjective in the teaching of sanctification, it is subjec-tive from beginning to end. We start with ourselves, and our own needs and problems, and God is an agency to supply an answer, to give us what we need, but it is all wrong. Evangelism, and everything else, must start with God and his glory. The God who is over all and to whom all things belong. It is because men are not glorifying him that they need to be saved, not to have some little personal problem solved. And if the motive for evangelism is to fill the Churches, it is doomed to failure. Of course, you may fill your Churches, and it will not help you, it will not avail you, it will not make any difference to the main problems. It is this conception of the Church as the people of God, who bear his name and who have been brought into being by him, it is this that matters. We must cease to think of the Church as a gathering of institutions and organisations, and we must get back this notion that we are the people of God. And that it is for his name's sake, and because his name is upon us, we must plead for the Church. Yes, and for her glory and her honour, because she is his.

And then, of course, the third reason is that Moses is concerned about the heathen that are outside. He wants them to know: 'For wherein shall it be known here [in the wilderness, where we are], that I and thy people have found grace in thy sight? is it not in that thou goest with us? so shall we be separated, I and thy people, from all the people that are upon the face of the earth.'

These are the motives in praying for revival. For the name, and honour, and glory of God and for the sake of the Church which is his. Yes, and then for the sake of those people that are outside, that are scoffing, and mocking, jeering, and laughing, and ridiculing. 'Oh, God,' say his people, one after another, 'arise and silence them. Do something so that we may be able to say to them, "Be still, keep silent, give up." '

'Be still, and know that I am God' (Ps. 46. 10). That is the prayer of the people of God. They have got their eye on those that are outside. And you find illustrations of this right through the Bible. And this has been true also of all men who have felt the burden of the condition of the Church, and whose hearts are breaking because they have seen the name of God blasphemed. Oh, you will find it in very strong language here in the Bible, sometimes so strong that certain little people are troubled by the imprecatory Psalms. But the imprecatory Psalms are just an expression of the zeal these men have for the glory of God. 'Let the sinners be consumed out of the earth,' says the man in Psalm 104. There they are, he says, spoiling your great creation. I see the mountains, and the valleys, and the streams. I see the cedars of God which are full of sap. . . . He thinks of the birds and all creation conspiring together to show the wonder, and the glory of God. But here is the sinner, who, in spite of all God's goodness to him, still reviles, and rebels and blasphemes. And the Psalmist, in his righteous indignation and zeal, says, 'Let the sinners be consumed out of the earth.'

And that, I would say, is the real explanation of these people. It was not a desire for personal vengeance. It was that these men were consumed by a passion for God and his glory and his great name. And there is something wrong with us if we do not feel this desire within us that God should arise and do something that would shut the mouths, and stop the tongues of these arrogant blasphemers of today, who speak with their mincing words upon radio and television – these supposed philosophers, these godless arrogant men. Do we not feel, sometimes, this desire within us that they might know that God is God, and that he is the eternal God? Ah, yes, there is a desire that they may be answered, that they may be silenced, but it does not stop at that, of course. Following that comes a desire that they may be convicted, that they may be convinced, that they may really see the truth. A desire that God should do something so strange, so wonderful, that they would be arrested and apprehended, and say, 'What is this? Are these people right after all? Do our arguments not seem to be falling astray? We thought that God had failed, that he had left them there in the wilderness. Everything was going against them.' Then if God should suddenly break in and do something miraculous, and lead them through, the heathen will have to think again and say, 'Ah, perhaps they were right after all.' And that is the first step in the direction of conviction and conversion. Their interest has been aroused, and whenever you get a revival that always happens. People who have always scoffed at the name of God, have gone to look on in sheer curiosity, and that has often led to their conversion. Now Moses is praying for that, that these people may be arrested and apprehended, and may develop an interest in which God is leading them, and is directing them.

This should make us ask, therefore, whether we are concerned at all about these people who are outside. It is a terrible state for the Church to be in, when she merely consists of a collection of very nice and respectable people who have no concern for the world, people who pass it by, drawing in their skirts in their horror at the bestiality, and the foulness, and the ugliness of it all. We not only want the scoffers to be silenced, we should desire that these men and women, who are like sheep without a shepherd, might have their eyes opened, might begin to see the cause of their troubles and be delivered from the chains of iniquity, and the shackles of infamy, and vice, and foulness. Are we truly concerned about such people and are we praying to God that he would do something, that they may be influenced and affected?

There, as I understand it, are the three main motives which animated Moses as he offered up these petitions to God. There is something else for us to notice and that is the way in which he prayed. We have seen what he prayed for, we have seen why he prayed for it, now let us watch his method of prayer. And if ever we needed instruction, it is just here.

There are certain elements that always come out in all the great biblical prayers, and the first characteristic of Moses' prayer is its boldness, its confidence. There is no hesitation here. There is a quiet confidence. Oh, let me use the term, there is a holy boldness. This is *the* great characteristic of all prayers that have ever prevailed. It is, of course, inevitable. You cannot pray truly, still less can you intercede, if you have not an assurance of your acceptance, and if you do not know the way into the holiest of all. If, when you get down on your knees, you are reminded of your sins, and are wondering what you can do about them, if you have to spend all your time praying for forgiveness and pardon, wondering whether God is listening or not, how can you pray? How can you intercede, as Moses did here? No, Moses was face to face with God, he was assured, he was bold with a holy boldness. As we have seen, God had granted him intimations of his nearness and so he was able to speak with this confidence and assurance.

Now this is absolutely vital to prayer. Do you know the way into the holiest of all? There is only one way – Hebrews 4.14 puts it so perfectly – 'Seeing then that we have a great high priest, that is passed into the heavens, Jesus the Son of God. . . .' Then the writer goes on to describe him as a high Priest who can be touched with a feeling of our infirmities, tempted in all points like as we are, yet without sin. Then, he comes to the prayer, 'Let us therefore,' he says, 'come boldly unto the throne of grace, that we may obtain mercy, and find grace to help in time of need.' You notice his 'therefore'? 'Therefore, let us come boldly.' What does it refer to? Oh, it refers to the truth about the great High Priest, Jesus, the Son of God, who has passed through the heavens, and to all the truth about him. That is the only way to be bold in the presence of God. If I look at myself I cannot be bold, I become speechless. With Job, I put my hand upon my mouth: 'I have heard of thee by the hearing of the ear: but now mine eye seeth thee. Wherefore I abhor myself and repent in dust and ashes' (Job 42. 5–6). I cannot speak. But I must speak if I am to intercede. How can I do so with confidence and assurance? There is only one answer – it is to know that my great High Priest is Jesus, the Son of God, and that by his blood I have a right of entry into the holiest of all, and can go there with boldness. Notice the confidence and the assurance with which Moses prayed. And, if you read some of the prayers of the saints of the centuries, you will find this self-same thing.

But, there is a second point, which is most valuable and interesting, and that is the element of reasoning, and of arguing that comes in. It is very daring, but it is very true. Let me remind you of it. 'Moses said unto the Lord, See . . .' – which really means that he is arguing with God – 'See, thou sayest unto me, Bring up this people: and thou hast not let me know whom thou wilt send with me. Yet thou hast said. . . .' You see, he is reminding God of what he had said. He is having an argument with God: 'And yet thou hast said, I know thee by name, and thou hast also found grace in my sight. Now therefore,' says Moses, as if he were saying to God, 'Be logical, be consistent, carry out your own argument. You cannot say this to me and then not do anything.' 'Now therefore, I pray thee, if . . .' – still arguing – 'if I have found grace in thy sight, shew me now thy way, that I may know thee, that I may find grace in thy sight: and consider that this nation is thy people.' And then in verse 16, 'For, wherein' – if you do not do this – 'wherein shall it be known here that I and thy people have found grace in thy sight? Is it not in that thou goest with us? so shall we be separated. . . .' He reasoned with God. He argued with God. He reminded God of his own promises and he pleaded with God in the light of them. He said, 'Oh, God, can you not see that having said this you must . . . ?'

Is it right, someone may ask, to speak to God like that? Is this not presumption? No, these things go together. The author of the epistle to the Hebrews, who talked so much about our going boldly to the throne of grace, at the same time reminds us that we do so always with reverence and with godly fear. This is all right. What is happening here is this: we are not seeing a man under the Law speaking to the Law-giver. No, it is a child here speaking to his Father. And the little child can take liberties with his father that a grown-up man, who is not his child, would not dare to take. Oh, yes, this is a child speaking, and he knows it. God has spoken to him, as it were, face to face, and Moses knows that. And he comes with his love, and his reverence, and his godly fear, and he ventures to argue. He says, 'You have said this, therefore. . . .'

196

Again I commend to you the reading of biographies of men who have been used by God in the Church throughout the centuries, especially in revival. And you will find this same holy boldness, this argumentation, this reasoning, this putting the case to God, pleading his own promises. Oh, that is the whole secret of prayer, I sometimes think. Thomas Goodwin in his exposition* of the sealing of the Spirit in Ephesians 1.13 uses a wonderful term. He says, 'Sue him for it, sue him for it.' Do not leave him alone. Pester him, as it were, with his own promise. Tell him that what he has said he is going to do. Quote the Scripture to him. And, you know, God delights to hear us doing it, as a father likes to see this element in his own child who has obviously been listening to what his father has been saying. It pleases him. The child may be slightly impertinent, it does not matter, the father likes it in spite of that. And God is our Father, and he loves us, and he likes to hear us pleading his own promises, quoting his own words to him, and saying 'in the light of this, can you refrain?' It delights the heart of God. Sue him!

Another thing we should notice about prayer is its orderliness, its directness. The specific petition. Notice that Moses here does not offer up some vague, indefinite general prayer. No, he is concentrating on the one great need. Of course he worshipped God, of course there was the reverence and the godly fear, yes, but at this point he concentrates on this one thing, this presence of God. He will not get away from it. He says, 'I will not move unless you come. You must come with us.' And he gives his reasons and plies him with all these arguments about it. And if I may speak for myself, I shall not feel happy and encouraged until I feel that the Church is concentrating on this one thing – prayer for revival. But we have not come to it, we are still in the state of deciding in committees to do this, that and the other, and asking God to bless what we have done. No, there is no hope along that line. It must be that one thing. We must feel this burden, we must see this as the only hope, and we must concentrate on this, and we must keep on with it – the orderliness, the arrangement, the concentration, the argument, and always the urgency. Moses here is like Jacob was in Genesis 32. This element always comes into true intercession. 'I will not let thee go,' said Jacob. I am going on. The morning was breaking, he had been struggling through the night.

*An exposition of the first Chapter of the Epistle to the Ephesians, Thomas Goodwin.

197

'Let me go.'

'No, I will not let thee go, except thou bless me.'

There is the urgency. Read the great biblical prayers; it is always in them. In Acts 4 we read of the Christians asking God to act '*Now*.' Oh God, they said, in the light of this, in our situation – now – do this. Give us some indication, give us some signs, enable us to witness with this holy boldness, and to bear witness to the resurrection that they are prohibiting us to speak about. See the urgency of the prayer. Moses keeps on coming back to it, repeating it, putting it in different forms and from different angles. But there was just this one thing: 'If thy presence go not with me, carry us not up hence.' Insisting urgently, 'I will not let thee go.'

There, it seems to me, are some of the lessons from this passage. We say our prayers, but have we ever prayed? Do we know anything about this encounter, this meeting? Have we the assurance of sins forgiven? Are we free from ourselves and self-concern, that we may intercede? Have we a real burden for the glory of God, and the name of the Church? Have we this concern for those who are outside? And are we pleading with God for his own name's sake, because of his own promises, to hear us and to answer us? Oh, my God make of us intercessors such as Moses. It is no use anybody saying, 'Ah, but he was an exceptionally great man.' God, as we have seen in the past history of revivals, has made use of men who are mere nobodies in exactly the same way as he used Moses here. A hundred years ago, the unknown James McQuilken was the man whom God burdened in this way. He was the Moses in Northern Ireland. It can be any one of us. May God make of us intercessors such as Moses was.

Chapter 16

Exodus 33.17

And the Lord said unto Moses, I will do this thing also that thou hast spoken: for thou hast found grace in my sight, and I know thee by name (Exod. 33.17).

So far in this particular study we have considered what Moses prayed for, and why he prayed for it, and how he prayed for it. We come now to the point where God heard Moses, and gave him an answer, promising him that he would do the very thing for him and for the Children of Israel, which Moses had requested. So, our subject is, God having pity and mercy upon the Church, and sending his blessing. For, revival, after all, is nothing but God hearing the people and answering them by giving this manifestation of his glory, and his strength, and his power. And it is important, therefore, for us to understand, and to know something of what we should be anticipating and what we should be seeking in our prayers. And, of course, the way to discover that is to go back to the second chapter of Acts. It is a truism to say that every revival of religion that the Church has ever known has been, in a sense, a kind of repetition of what happened on the day of Pentecost, that it has been a return to that origin, to that beginning, that it has been a reviving. Today there is a great deal of very loose and dangerous talk and writing about what happened on the day of Pentecost. People go accepting uncritically the explanation that what happened on the day of Pentecost was once and for all and never to be repeated.

Now, it is important that we should examine that because, if that is really true, it is very wrong to pray for revival. But, of course, it is just not true. There is only one sense in which what happened on the day of Pentecost cannot be repeated and that is simply that it did happen to be the first of a series. And, of course, you cannot repeat the first. But the fact that you cannot repeat the first does not mean for a moment that what happened on the first occasion cannot happen again. And every revival of religion,

I say, is really a repetition of what happened on the day of Pentecost. It is really almost incredible that people should go on saying that what happened at Pentecost was once and for all. Because if you go to Acts 11, and look there at Peter making his defence to the other Apostles for having baptised the Gentile Cornelius and his household, you will see that what he said was,

And the spirit bade me go with them, nothing doubting. Moreover these six brethren accompanied me, and we entered into the man's house: and he shewed us how he had seen an angel in his house, which stood and said unto him, Send men to Joppa, and call for Simon, whose surname is Peter: who shall tell thee words, whereby thou and all thy house shall be saved. And as I began to speak, the Holy Ghost fell on them, as on us at the beginning. (Acts 11.12–15).

You notice what he says. He says that the Holy Ghost fell on Cornelius, and his household, '*as on us at the beginning*'. He said, 'The same thing happened to them, as happened to us on the day of Pentecost.' In other words, the baptism of the Holy Ghost took place on the day of Pentecost, but it also took place later upon Cornelius, and his household. That is exactly Peter's argument: 'Then I remembered the word of the Lord, how that he said, John indeed baptized with water; but ye shall be baptized with the Holy Ghost. Forasmuch then as God gave them the like gift' – the same gift, you see – 'as he did unto us, who believed on the Lord Jesus Christ; what was I, that I could withstand God?' And he repeats the same argument again in Acts 15.

So, then, I do trust we are clear about this, and see that we really must cease to say that what happened on the day of Pentecost happened once and for all. It did not, it was simply the first of a series. I am ready to admit that you cannot repeat 'the first'. But that is nothing; what matters is the thing that happened. And the thing that happened at Pentecost happened later in exactly the same way, while Peter was preaching to Cornelius and his household. The Holy Ghost fell upon them, as he had fallen upon these people in the upper room, there in Jerusalem. And, of course, that is exactly what happens in every revival.

There is indeed even further evidence which I can adduce for you. You will find in Acts 4 that the same thing happened even a few days after the day of Pentecost, to the apostles and to others. There, after they had been prohibited to preach any longer in the name of Jesus Christ, they went back to the gathered

Christians and they all prayed together. Then we are told in verse 31, 'And when they had prayed, the place was shaken where they were assembled together; and they were all filled with the Holy Ghost.' That is exactly the term used in the second chapter. The term baptism is not used in the second chapter, but it means the baptism. Our Lord had said, 'Tarry ye in the city of Jerusalem' (Luke 24.49), and had commanded them that 'they should not depart from Jerusalem, but wait for the promise of the Father, which, saith he, ye have heard of me. For John truly baptized with water; but ye shall be baptized with the Holy Ghost not many days hence' (Acts 1.4–5). So what happened on the day of Pentecost was the baptism of the Holy Ghost. It is described in these words, 'They were all filled with the Holy Ghost.' but here, in Acts 4, they were filled again with the Holy Ghost. It was not anything that they did, it was that which happened to them. All they did was to pray, then God poured out his Spirit upon them again, and filled them until they were overflowing: 'They were all filled with the Holy Ghost, and they spake the word of God with boldness', (Acts 4.31).

Now, that is precisely what happens in revival. It is God pouring forth his Spirit, filling his people again. It is not that which is talked of in Ephesians 5.18, which is the command to us, 'Go on being filled with the Spirit.' That is something you and I do, but this is something that is done to us. It is the Spirit falling upon us, being poured out upon us. These are the terms: 'I will pour forth my Spirit.' God alone can do that. But it is you and I who are responsible for going on being filled with the Spirit. We must not grieve the Spirit, we must not quench the Spirit, we must give obedience to the Spirit. And as long as we do that, we shall go on being filled with the Spirit. But this is different, this is the Spirit being poured out upon us until we are filled to overflowing, the Spirit being shed forth – these things are the terms. But so much of the modern teaching never uses these scriptural terms at all. You never find them talking or writing about the Spirit being poured forth, or shed forth, these terms are never mentioned. No, and that is because of the theory, that what happened on the day of Pentecost happened once and for all. There is not a word in Scripture to say that. Indeed, as I have shown you, the Scripture shows quite clearly and explicitly the exact opposite: 'The Spirit fell on them even as on us at the beginning.' Let us be careful that we do not quench the Spirit in the interest of some theory or in a fear of certain freak religious bodies.

Having cleared that point, let us go on to consider what happens when this takes place. 'What is revival?' says somebody. 'Why are you concerned about this? Why do you go on urging us to pray for it?' The answer is that this, above everything else, is what is needed today. When will the Christian Church come to realise that? The feast of Pentecost, our Whitsuntide, is in particular the festival of the Church. Oh, is there any tragedy comparable to the failure of the Church to realise that this is her need, and that this is her only hope? But the Church does not realise it. It is tragic to see different branches of the Church getting together in conferences and assemblies to investigate the situation and to discover the problem of the Church. They are investigating the situation, the problem confronting the Church. 'Here are the facts,' they say, 'now then, what are we to do?'

And what do they suggest? Has there been a great call to prayer and fasting and humiliation? A crying out to God to have mercy, and to baptize us afresh with the Holy Ghost? Is that what is done? No, I think what you will find is that they will appoint special commissions. One group has appointed eight special commissions to enquire into the situation: if it were not so tragic, it would indeed be almost laughable. Of course, that is what the politicians do, and that is what a businessman does, and in those realms it is absolutely right. It is the obvious commonsense thing to do. But in the name of God, I ask, is it not tragic that the Christian Church should be doing that? With the world as it is today – commissions to investigate, commissions of enquiry! And, indeed, in one case there is a commission even to report on what the Christian faith really is, and how it is to be expressed. With the world on fire, with hell let loose, the Christian Church is trying to discover what her message is. She is seeking for some way of meeting the situation.

It is true of all sections of the Christian Church. They are all in exactly the same condition. Not a word about the need for the power. Not a call to prayer and humiliation and to agony in the presence of God. The Church does everything except that which the Lord himself commanded the early Church to do. 'Ah,' but the Church says, 'you know, the conditions are different now. This is the twentieth century.' I would insult you by giving you an answer to that. The twentieth century has nothing to do with the situation at all. Man in sin does not change. But, my friends, we are talking about the power of God. And when we are talking about the power of God, to talk about superficial changes in men is not only an irrelevance, it is non-sensical. The world, I say, has always been the same. Look at the position in the book of Acts.

202

Can you imagine any more hopeless position than that? There we find just a handful of people, and they are very ordinary men. They are described later as illiterate and ignorant men. The Lord of glory goes back to heaven, and he leaves his cause and his interest in the hands of these men. The Jews are all against them, as they had been against him. The Gentiles are all pagans. That is the position. A handful of people in an entirely hostile and gainsaying world. Nothing could have been worse than that. Nothing could have been more difficult. But you remember what happened when the Holy Ghost came down upon them. They were like lions, mighty in power. Very soon they began turning the world upside down, and within three centuries, this little sect became the official religion of the great Roman Empire. How did it happen? Did they hold commissions of enquiry and investigation? Nonsense. They just went on praying, waiting for the promise, the gift of the outpouring of the Holy Spirit.

And so it has been through the ages. Again I could take you over the history. Was it not like that at the Protestant Reformation? What hope had that one man, Martin Luther, just an unknown monk? Who was he to stand up against all the Church, and fifteen centuries almost, or at least a good twelve to thirteen centuries, of tradition in the opposite direction? It seems a sheer impertinence for this one man to get up and say, 'I alone am right, and you are all wrong.' That is what would be said about him today. And yet, you see, he was a man with whom the Spirit of God had been dealing. And though he was only one man, he stood, and stood alone, and the Holy Ghost honoured him. The Protestant Reformation came in, and has continued, and it has always been the same.

The question, therefore, for us to ask is this: What happens, then, when God does hear the cry, and the plea, and sends forth his blessing? Here is the pattern. The details may differ. While all revivals, in a sense, are identical, there are always minor differences, although the main character is always the same. There are individual differences and variations which do not matter. It is the central big things that matter. What happens to the Church, first of all, when God hears the cry and begins to answer? The first thing really is that the Church becomes conscious of a presence and a power in her midst.

When the day of Pentecost was fully come, they were all with one accord in one place. And suddenly there came a sound from heaven as of a rushing mighty wind, and it filled all the house where they were sitting. And there appeared unto them cloven tongues like as of fire, and it sat upon each of them. And they were all filled with the Holy Ghost, and began to speak with other tongues, as the Spirit gave them utterance (Acts 2.1–4).

Consciousness of a power, and of a presence. Sometimes it may be physical, as it was here, in the 'sound of a mighty rushing wind'. It is not always physical, but it has often been so in revivals – you can read it in the stories and the accounts. It does not matter who writes them, they will all testify to these things. But what they are all conscious of always is the sudden awareness of a glorious presence in the midst, such as they have never known before – a sense of power, and a sense of glory. And so, I say, it always happens.

It may be accompanied by phenomena, as it was here ' . . . cloven tongues like as of fire . . .', speaking with tongues. These things are not always repeated. Sometimes this sense of power and glory is so great that people are prostrated to the ground by reason of it. As you hear of people literally fainting when they suddenly get a piece of good news, which they have not expected, so, when men and women experience this glorious presence, sometimes, it is too much for the physical frame. We must not stay with these things, but they do emphasise this great thing, this sense of God, the presence and the presidency of the Holy Ghost. If you read the book by Sprague* on revivals, you will find this same thing. Men give their testimonies at the end. Great men of the Church give an account of how they have passed through periods of revival of the Church, and you will always find that what they have experienced is not that they no longer merely have a belief in God, God has become a reality to them, God has come down, as it were, into their midst. The meeting is taken out of the hands of whoever may have been in charge, and the Holy Ghost begins to preside, and to take charge, and everybody is aware of his presence, and of his glory, and of his power. That is what happened on the day of Pentecost. That is what happens, in some measure, and to some extent, in every revival that the Church has ever known.

But there is more. The Church is given, as the result of this, great assurance concerning the truth. She does not have to investigate the truth, or set up a commission to look into it, she is given an absolute certainty about it. That is the thing that comes out so

*William Sprague: *Lectures on Revival*

204

clearly, in the story in Acts. Take these men, these apostles, You remember how a few weeks before, after the crucifixion, they were very shaken and most uncertain? They had come to a belief in the Lord Jesus Christ, and they had come to see that he was the Messiah, but then he had been crucified and they were shattered, and confused in their minds.

You will find, in the last chapter of John's Gospel, that they were just talking to one another, when Peter suddenly said: 'I go a fishing.' I must do something to relieve this, it is too miserable, it is impossible.

And the others said, 'We also go with thee.'

You cannot imagine a more dejected picture. They were shaken and uncertain about everything. And then the Lord appeared to them, and he taught them, Ah, yes, this certainly put them in a better condition. But, it was only after what happened to them on the day of Pentecost that they were filled with an assurance, and with an understanding, and immediately began to speak to the people about the wonderful works of God. Never again was there any doubt, *never* again was there any difficulty about understanding.

Take Peter himself, look at the sermon which he preached on that occasion. You see him expounding the Old Testament, showing the meaning of Joel's prophecy. He has an understanding which he had never had before. Our Lord had taken them through the Scriptures, but they had not seen it clearly. But at last he has understood. And here he is with his mind illuminated, his heart moved, and he is speaking and expounding, and explaining, in this extraordinary sermon. Well, this again is something that is invariable in revival. People have no doubt about these great things at such times, they *know*, and that is what they testify to. In effect, this is what they say, 'I believed on the Lord Jesus Christ for years, and yet I was assailed by doubts. But from that moment I knew. He told me that he loved me, and that he had given himself for me.' Their testimony is that they are more certain of him, and of God, and of the spiritual realm, than they are of anything else. There is an immediacy. There is a directness. It is no longer indirectly, as it were, by faith; these things are brought in a most real way before them. And they are absolutely certain and assured, and that is something again that is a universal experience in times of revival.

The next thing I notice is that the Church is filled with great joy and a sense of praise. Read again the terms used towards the end of the chapter. 'And they, continuing daily with one accord in the temple, and breaking bread from house to house, did eat their meat with gladness and singleness of heart. Praising God, and having favour with all the people.' Now that is how the Christian Church is meant to be. Great joy, great praise to the Lord Jesus Christ, and to God, glorying in this great salvation, in the new life they have received, and in this sense of heaven. It is but the simple pattern of what has been repeated so frequently when God has poured out his Spirit upon the Church. I never tire of quoting something I remember reading in the journals of George Whitefield. He was preaching on one occasion in Cheltenham, and he said, 'Suddenly the Lord came down amongst us.' Do we know anything about that? Do we believe in that sort of thing or that it is possible? Now, George Whitefield, even at his worst, was probably the greatest preacher that this country has ever known. But there were variations, even in his ministry. On this occasion he was surprised himself. There he was, preaching, and having a very good service, when suddenly he knew that the Lord had come down amongst them. That is the wonderful thing, and it resulted in great joy, praise and thanksgiving. When the Church is in a state of revival you do not have to exhort people to praise, you cannot stop them, they are so filled with God. Their very faces show it. They are transfigured. There is a heavenly look that comes upon their faces, which is expressive of this joy, this praise. Can we not see that this is the need of the Church today? The people are outside because they find Christians so miserable. We can give the impression that they who are outside are much happier than we are. But when the Holy Ghost has fallen, people are filled with this joy. It is not a superficial, carnal, put-on thing, it is a thing that comes from within; the power of the Spirit irradiating the whole personality, and giving a joy which is 'unspeakable, and full of glory'.

And then the other factor that I must emphasise is this element of worship, and of thanksgiving, together with a great freedom. We read that 'they continued stedfastly in the apostles' doctrine and fellowship, and in breaking of bread, and in prayers. . . . And all that believed were together. . . . And they continuing daily with one accord in the temple, and breaking bread from house to house, did eat their meat with gladness and singleness of heart, praising God, and having favour with all the people' (Acts 2.42–46). Worship! Thanksgiving! Again you will find that when God sends revival you do not have to exhort people to come together to worship, and to praise, and to consider the word, they insist upon it. They come night after night, and they may stay for hours, even until the early hours of the morning. This will go on night after night for months exactly as happened here at the beginning. They met daily. They could not keep away from one another. Of course not, this marvellous thing had happend, this joy of the Lord, and they wanted to thank him together, and to pray together, to ask him to spread it and to extend it to others. If this happens to the Church, the world outside will be astonished as it always has been, in every period of revival and re-awakening. This is what is needed, not resorting to doubtful, worldly methods, to try and gather crowds and to bring people together. No, what we need is this inward urge, this constraint of the Spirit, this coming together of people who are sharing in the same glorious experience.

And then, the next thing that we should notice about the Church in revival is the power and the boldness that is given in the proclamation of the truth. Take Peter again. It is but a few weeks since he was so fearful, and so much the victim of a craven spirit that in order to save his life he even denied the Lord Jesus Christ to a servant maid. Here he is now, preaching in Jerusalem. He knows the authorities are watching him and listening to him, and he tells them quite plainly and in no uncertain terms what they have done in the crucifixion of the Lord Jesus Christ. He says, 'Him, being delivered by the determinate counsel and foreknowledge of God, ye have taken, and by wicked hands have crucified and slain' (Acts 2.23). He repeats that again in the next chapter. Here he is speaking again to the same people and he says,

The God of Abraham, and of Isaac, and of Jacob, the God of our fathers, hath glorified his Son Jesus; whom ye delivered up, and denied him in the presence of Pilate, when he was determined to let him go. But ye denied the Holy One and the Just, and desired a murderer to be granted unto you; and killed the Prince of life, whom God hath raised from the dead (Acts 3.13–15).

He attacks them, and their rulers and governors. He is not afraid of them any longer, nor of the whole world. Let hell be let loose, he is filled with a holy boldness, as he bears witness to the resurrection, and proclaims the truth of God without fear and without fail. And again, that is invariable in the history of revival. That is what happens to the whole Church, that is what happens to individuals. D. L. Moody, after his experience of thus having the Holy Ghost shed forth upon him, this baptism with the Spirit, said: 'I went on preaching the same old sermons as I had been preaching before. But,' he added, 'they were absolutely different.' And they were. And they were different in their results. The same sermons, and yet they were not the same sermons. There was this demonstration of the Spirit and of power. It is the same with many others.

These, then, are the things that happen to the Church at such a time. But what happens to the world that is outside? The Church experiencing this great visitation is now concerned about the world outside. So, it prays and preaches to the world. The Church is concerned about it. The first thing that happens, we are told, is that the world outside becomes attracted by curiosity. 'And there were dwelling at Jerusalem Jews, devout men, out of every nation under heaven. Now when this was noised abroad, the multitude came together, and were confounded . . .' – a great crowd gathered and they said, 'What meaneth this?' (Acts 2.5–6, 12). The problem confronting the Church today is what to do about these masses that are outside the Church. As we have seen, their way of solving it, is often to set up commissions to investigate – 'We will have a commission to investigate *what* we are to preach to them. And then we will have another commission to investigate *how* we are to preach to them.' The problem of communication, they call it: 'How can we get people to listen?' As if there had never been a problem of communication until this generation! But it has always been there. It was there at the beginning. What are we to do about these masses? How can we get them together? What can we do? Can we put on some sort of show to attract them? Can we put on something bright and gay, and can we start in the way I once heard in a conference. They began with comic songs, and then they became a little bit more serious until eventually they came to hymns. Is that the method? Oh, if you want to get a crowd into your churches, pray for revival! Because the moment a revival breaks out, the crowd will come, and, I assure you, it will not cost you a penny. I am speaking to the Church, that is spending thousands of pounds on advertising to try and attract the outsider. The moment you get revival the newspapers will report it. Their motive, of course, will be quite wrong. They will do it because they do not like it, because they think it is ridiculous, because they think that people have gone mad, or that they are drunk. It does not matter. They will give it a free advertisement. And the crowds will come to see what is happening, as they did on the day of Pentecost in Jerusalem. What fools we are! It is our 'cleverness' that is our undoing. We think we can fill the churches. When will we wake up to realise we cannot, but that the Holy Ghost can? He even does that part of it for us.

And then we read in Acts that the people came along sceptical and contemptuous: 'These men are full of new wine,' they said mockingly. 'That is what is the matter with them.'

But Peter stood up and said, 'These are not drunken, as you suppose, seeing it is but the third hour of the day.' 'Use your commonsense,' he says. 'Apart from anything else, how can they be drunk at this hour of the day? But,' he says in effect, 'that is a negative. The positive thing is that this is that which was spoken by the prophet Joel.' And he began to preach. 'Men and brethren,' he said when he came to his application. 'let me freely speak unto you of the patriarch David. . . .' And he continued, 'Therefore, let all the house of Israel know assuredly, that God hath made that same Jesus, whom ye have crucified, both Lord and Christ' (2.36). Then notice this. 'Now when they heard this, they were pricked in their heart, and said unto Peter and to the rest of the apostles, Men and brethren, what shall we do?' Peter had not yet arrived at the end of the sermon, but before he could finish they cried out. He did not finish his sermon, and then have a hymn, and say to himself, 'Now we come to the appeal,' and try to persuade them to come forward. No, not at all. Before he had finished preaching they were crying out, and saying, 'What shall we do?' There was no need to test the meeting. The Holy Ghost had done it. People were so deeply convicted of sin, so humbled and broken and alarmed and terrified, that they interrupted the sermon and cried out saying, 'Men and brethren, what shall we do?' They are in an agony of soul, suffering this profound conviction of sin.

That is the story of every revival. There is always that kind of interruption, almost a disorder, what somebody called a divine disorder. And then, that in turn leads to repentance. 'Oh,' says Peter, 'repent and be baptized every one of you in the name of Jesus Christ for the remission of sins.' And they did. It is not a mere question of decision when you have revival, it is deep repentance, it is reformation. People receive a new life and they leave the old life. When revival comes the whole neighbourhood is changed and moral conditions are revolutionised. Read the stories; these are facts. This is not my idea, this is not theory, but factual matter. The statistics are there. The whole moral condition is changed, when you get revival, when the Holy Spirit is doing his own work. Not only do individuals give up drink and so on, but public houses are shut and their businesses are ruined. There was actually a case in Northern Ireland, a hundred years ago, of a publican who himself was converted. He went to the meeting because all his customers had left him. There was nobody to serve in his public house, so he went to the meeting, saying, 'What is this nonsense?' And there he was converted himself, and he became a preacher of the gospel. That is revival. A true heart repentance, a forsaking of sin, a newness of life, manifesting itself in an entirely new deportment.

And the converts joined the Church. It was not a case of temporary decisions: they joined the Church, they were added to the Church. The churches were built up: 'and they continued stedfastly in the apostles' doctrine and fellowship, and in breaking of bread and in prayers.' It is a fact that, as the result of the revival of a hundred years ago, the number of chapels that had to be built was quite phenomenal, not because those who were already in the Church were given some new fillip, and were attending more regularly. No, it was that the people who were outside came in, converted and changed and added to the Church. And there is the very thing we are told the Church needs today. Membership is going down, Sunday School numbers are going down, everything is going down. Chapels are being shut and members try to group them together – hence the commissions to do this and that, but to no avail. If we want to get the people in, here is the answer. Here is the infallible, the certain, way – the falling of the Holy Ghost upon the Church, the shedding forth of the Spirit of God again, and the Church being given a new baptism of power, and of authority, and ability to witness and to preach.

Can more be said? Do you not see it all here? That is how God started the Church, that is how God has continued to keep the Church alive. When, in the hands of men, she has, so often, almost died, God has again done this self-same thing. He has repeated his original action. And the moribund Church has risen to a new period of life, and activity, and power. Is this not the supreme need of this hour? Well, if you believe that, pray to God without ceasing. Go on with all your activities, if you wish to do so. Go on with your work. I am not saying that you should stop all your efforts and just wait. No, go on, if you like, doing all that you are doing, but I do say this – make certain that you leave time to pray for revival, and to see that that has more time than anything else. Because when the Holy Ghost comes in power, more will happen in an hour than will happen in fifty or even a hundred years as a result of your exertions and mine. The power of the Holy Ghost – that is the meaning of the day of Pentecost;

210

that is the meaning of Whitsun, the power of God coming down, and in such a manner that the apostles were amazed, even as Peter was, as he taught in the household of Cornelius. There he was, again, halfway through his sermon, when the Holy Ghost came down among them, and Peter could scarcely believe it. He had not believed that Gentiles could come in to the Church. He had argued when he had been given the vision on the house top, you remember. He needed the vision to be convinced. But when he saw that God had done to the Gentiles what he had done to the Jews in Jerusalem at the beginning he said, 'Can any man forbid water, that these should not be baptized, which have received the Holy Ghost as well as we?' (Acts 10.47).

Pray God to have pity, and to have mercy, and to shed forth again his blessed Holy Spirit upon us.

Chapter 17

Exodus 33.18–23

And he said, I beseech thee, shew my thy glory. And he said, I will make all my goodness pass before thee, and I will proclaim the name of the Lord before thee; and will be gracious to whom I will be gracious, and will shew mercy on whom I will shew mercy. And he said, Thou canst not see my face: for there shall no man see me, and live. And the Lord said, Behold, there is a place by me, and thou shalt stand upon a rock: and it shall come to pass, while my glory passeth by, that I will put thee in a clift of the rock, and will cover thee with my hand while I pass by: and I will take away mine hand, and thou shalt see my back parts: but my face shall not be seen (Exod. 33.18–23).

Moses, you remember, had asked God to have pity and compassion and to return to his people. And then we saw how Moses asked God for something further. He asked him for a personal assurance. He reasoned – even argued – with God, and pleaded with him to give an unusual manifestation of himself so that the people round and about them might know that he and the Children of Israel had found grace in the sight of God. Then God's answer to him was, 'I will do this thing also that thou hast spoken: for thou hast found grace in my sight, and I know thee by name.' And we considered in the last chapter, in terms of the message of Pentecost, how it is that God answers that particular prayer.

So, then, that brings us to the third and final section of this great chapter which is surely one of the most extraordinary accounts that is to be found anywhere in the whole compass of holy writ. It is one of those paragraphs which one can only approach with considerable hesitancy and uncertainty. We are treading on very holy ground, and we should face statements such as this with awe. I feel that the word comes to us, that came to Moses himself on that occasion at the burning bush: 'Put off thy shoes from off thy feet, for the place whereon thou standest is holy ground'. (Exod.

3.5). It is a most extraordinary and amazing episode, and yet, we must follow it, because I think we shall see, as we do so, that it will take us yet a further stage in our understanding of what happens when God graciously visits his Church, and people, with revival and re-awakening. That is still our fundamental theme. All these considerations of different portions of Scripture are designed to that end, that we may have a deeper, and a clearer, conception of what exactly does happen when God gives and sends a special visitation of his Holy Spirit.

I want to make one thing plain at this point. Although we are here dealing with the subject in general, and as it affects a number of people at the same time, yet we must never forget that all this is possible at any time to the individual. There are people who do not seem to be quite clear about this, and that is why I am giving this word of explanation. It is possible for an individual, on his, or her own, to have any one of these experiences that we are describing, and illustrating from the Scripture. A revival is just that state and condition in which these things happen to a number of people at the same time. So, as we consider these principles, let us hold on to that fact. There is no need, in other words, for us, of necessity, to wait until revival comes in order to experience some of these things. We can seek them individually. But God from time to time is pleased to grant them to large numbers gathered together, to a whole church, to a district, to a country perhaps, or to many countries in the world, as he did a hundred years ago in 1859.

Bearing that in mind, let us proceed to consider what we are told here. We can divide our matter like this. The first thing, obviously, is Moses' request: 'And he said, I beseech thee, shew me thy glory.' Now, this is the thing, that really almost staggers one. Moses is still not satisfied. He is not satisfied in spite of all that God has promised, and in spite of all that he has just been receiving. Consider this man Moses who has been up on the mount forty days and forty nights, there in communion with God. He has already had that experience, he has already had the experiences that are recorded in this chapter, where God, we are told, 'spake unto Moses face to face, as a man speaketh unto his friend' – a most unusual thing. And then, in answer to his request for assurance and satisfaction, God says, 'I will even grant you that,' and gives him some degree of that immediately. And yet Moses goes further. He is not satisfied. He does not stop, he goes on and he says, 'Shew me thy glory.' This is what we may very well describe as the daring quality that always comes into great faith.

You will find other illustrations of this in other places in the Scriptures. But here is, perhaps, one of the most remarkable of all – the daring of Moses who, having received such answers already, ventures to go on and to ask for something still further. He seems to rise from step to step. As God says, 'Yes, I will grant you even this', 'Give me more,' says Moses. And here he makes what is, in many ways, the final and the ultimate request, namely, that he may see and know the glory of God.

This is what must concern us particularly at this point. Let us ask ourselves some questions before we go any further. Do we know anything about these advancing steps and stages? As we look back across our Christian experience, do we know what it is to rise, like this, from step to step, and from platform to platform? Do we know this increasing boldness in the presence of God, this increasing assurance, and the desire for yet more and more? While we thank God, as Moses did for all that we have received, do we have this longing for yet something above and beyond this striving, this rising, this scaling the heights, as it were? Now this is a principle which is taught in the Bible: 'For unto everyone that hath shall be given, and he shall have abundance' (Matt. 25.29). I am asking whether we know anything about this, simply because I have a most uncomfortable feeling that it is true to say of so many of us, yes, even those of us who are evangelical people, that our main characteristic is self-satisfaction. We have the feeling that we have arrived, because we are converted, and may even have had some further experience. We may be feeling that all we have got to do is to maintain the position, and we may even be feeling superior to those who have not yet come as far as we have. How much evidence is there of a striving, of a seeking, of rising on the wings of faith, following in the footsteps of Moses, and saying, 'Oh, I thank you for what you have promised, but show me now your glory'? Let me put it then more directly. To what extent are we aware of a desire for God himself and for a knowledge of the glory of God? I imagine that this is the highest peak of faith. Moses, you see, is no longer asking God for particular blessings. He has done that, but he does not stop at that, he has gone beyond blessings, he has gone beyond the gifts, he is now seeking God for himself. He is now filled with a passion for a personal knowledge, confrontation, meeting, with God himself. He does not despise the gifts, it is rather that, because of the gifts, and because of the glimpses he has received of the glory of God in the matter of the gifts, now forgetting himself, and all

214

gifts and blessings, he just has this longing for God himself and for the glory of God.

That is the question that I think should come to all of us. Do we know anything of such a longing? We may have been Christians for many years, but have we ever really longed for some personal, direct knowledge and experience of God? Oh, I know, we pray for causes, we pray for the Church, we pray for missionaries, we pray for our own efforts that we organise, yes, but that is not what I am concerned about. We all ask for personal blessings, but how much do we know of this desire for God himself? That is what Moses asked for: 'Show me thy glory. Take me yet a step nearer.' It is the same thing, of course, as the Psalmist voices in Psalm 42: 'As the hart panteth after the water brooks, so panteth my soul after thee, O God. My soul thirsteth for God, for the living God.' That is what he wants. He wants the living God himself, and that is why he pants and thirsts. You find the same thoughts in Psalm 17 verse 15: 'As for me,' says the Psalmist, looking forward to what is coming, 'As for me, I will behold thy face in righteousness: I shall be satisfied, when I awake, with thy likeness.'

I draw your attention to this because here, we must remember, were the desires of men under the Old Testament dispensation. Moses, and the Psalmist, were men who simply looked at the promises of the gospel afar off. They had not seen them, but they had their eye upon them, and they believed that they were coming. Yes, but they had not yet come, they had not yet happened. 'Your father Abraham rejoiced to see my day,' says Christ, 'and he saw it and was glad' (John 8.56). He believed it. He saw it by faith. So did all these men, said the author of the Hebrews in chapter 11. They had not yet received the promises, they believed them, they saw them afar off, and, you see, here are these men in such a situation, longing to see and to know the glory of God. But you and I are living in the new dispensation. We are not looking forward to the coming of the Messiah, we are not looking forward to Calvary, we are looking back. We have these records in the New Testament, explicit statements, the whole thing unfolded: the Holy Spirit has been given. And yet, I wonder how we compare with the Psalmist, and with Moses? What is the matter with us, my friends? We who like to boast about our superiority over the Old Testament saints, some of us even to the extent of being so foolish as to believe that they were not saints at all. How do we compare with them in actual experience? Of course, these people were the Children of God, but they were living in the dim

215

light of the old dispensation, whereas you and I are in the new. Yet here they cry, 'Show me thy glory.' And notice, too, the intimate knowledge which the Psalmist also has of God.

This, then, is the ultimate, the end of the true seeking for revival. The prayer for revival is, ultimately, a prayer based upon a concern for the manifestation of the glory of God, and remember that this can happen individually as well as collectively. Now Moses knew of the glory of God. He had not seen it, but he believed God. He had accepted the revelation and he had had odd manifestations here and there. And on the strength of this, he said, 'Now, let me see they glory, let it be manifested.' And that should be our position. Here we are in this difficult world, we see the Church languishing, we see the sin and the evil that are rampant round and about us. We know that God is there in all his glory, and the necessity is that we should be moved, as Moses was, to desire the manifestation of this glory. It is almost inconceivable, is it not, that there should be any Christian who does not offer this prayer of Moses? Is it not difficult to understand how anybody can be satisfied with things as they are now? But there are many such people. They say, 'What is all this talk about revival, and praying for it? Are things not going well? Is the Church, the evangelical Church, not doing well? What is all this?' Oh, my dear friend, if you speak like that you are just displaying the fact that you really know very little about God himself. You are interested in things happening, in results, in activities, in blessings, do you not know anything about a longing to see manifestation of the glory of God? Do you not know anything about some thirst for God himself? Is it, I wonder, that some of us are so busy that we do not have time even to think about God. God is not a force. God is personal. God is three persons, Father, Son, Holy Spirit. Have we forgotten this personal element, I wonder? And are we tending, in our great hurry and busyness, to think of God loosely, as only some agency that blesses? There is no doubt that, as we advance in faith, and in knowledge, and in experience, we shall more and more desire God himself, and not only, and not merely, the things that are given to us by God.

The Apostle Paul puts this so perfectly in his own case. He had received so much and had had such unusual blessings, yet what he says in Philippians 3:10 is, 'That I may know him. . . .' You would have said that if ever a man did know Christ, it was the Apostle Paul but he was not satisfied: 'That I may know him, and the power of his resurrection, and the fellowship of his sufferings, being made conformable unto his death; if by any means I might

216

attain unto the resurrection of the dead. Not as though I had already attained. . . .' says this man who has apprehended so much – this man who has had such unusual experiences. No, the point is that he has had such tastes of the knowledge that he wants more, he wants to know for himself. He forgets the things that are behind and presses forward toward 'the mark'. And all this emphasises the fact that it is no use our talking about these things if we do not desire them, if we do not know something about them. Let us ask ourselves once more – to what extent do we know of a longing for God himself, for the living God, and cry in our hearts, 'Show me thy glory'?

That then, brings us to God's answer. And this is a matter that we, of necessity, must divide up under various headings. The first thing that we see quite clearly in this account is that God answers Moses by telling him, 'Yes, I am going to answer your prayer, your petition, but I am going to do so in my own way.' And we must stay with this because it must strike us at once that this is a partial answer. We shall also go on to consider, secondly, the means, or the method, in which God gives the partial answer. And then, thirdly, the nature of the answer, because it is all here.

So, let us start with the first thing – the partial character or nature of God's answer. In verse 20 God said to Moses, 'Thou canst not see my face: for there shall no man see me, and live.' And in verse 23, 'And I will take away mine hand, and thou shalt see my back parts: but my face shall not be seen.' Here we are, face to face, with the final mystery. The answer is going to be given, yes, but in this partial manner. Now, this must be the case, and there should surely be no difficulty about this. 'There shall no man see me, and live.' In other words, no man is capable of standing the full vision of God's glory. He could not bear it, it would kill him, because of the inconceivable nature of the glory. There is no doubt but that 99.9 per cent of our troubles as Christians is that we are ignorant of God. We spend so much time in feeling our own pulse, taking our own spiritual temperature, considering our moods, and states and fears. Oh, if we but had some conception of him, of the inconceivable glory of God.

> Immortal, invisible, God only wise;
> In light inaccessible, hid from our eyes.

Moses does not quite realise what he is asking, so God corrects him, and teaches him. He does it gently, with tenderness, showing him exactly what is possible and what is not.

This is not peculiar to Moses. Isaiah once had a glimpse of him. It is recorded in chapter 6 of his prophecy. When he was given just a glimpse of that ineffable glory, he cried out saying, 'Woe is me! for I am undone; because I am a man of unclean lips. . . .' He heard the voices of the seraphim, 'Holy, holy, holy, is the Lord of hosts.' And the house was filled with smoke and the posts of the door moved. Just a glimpse of the glory, and – 'Woe is me,' says Isaiah, 'I am unfit for this. I am unworthy.' He is staggered.

John, the apostle, tells us that when he, too, was given just a glimpse of the glory, 'I fell at his feet as dead' (Rev. 1.17). These were men, let me remind you, living in the world, in the flesh, as you and I do. They have had such experiences of God, why have we not had them? Why do we know so little about these things? These are the things that are to be a part of the life of the Christian. Christianity is to know God: 'This is life eternal, that they might know thee, the only true God, and Jesus Christ whom thou hast sent' (John 17.3). Not only to know about God, but to know God.

Then again, the Apostle Paul himself, as Saul of Tarsus, travelling on the road to Damascus, suddenly saw that light above the brightest shining of the sun. You remember what happened to him? He fell to the ground, blinded. The glory did that to him, the sight of the glory was such. We ought to be able to have some increasing understanding of all this today. We read about the explosions of these atomic bombs, and how people have to be very careful to shade their eyes, because of the brightness of the flash. We need to multiply that by infinity to know something about the glory of God. You remember that when the apostles, the disciples, were with our Lord on the Mount of Transfiguration, and saw this transfiguration, a deep sleep came over them. Why? It was to protect them, because the glory is so transcendent, it is blinding, it is inconceivable.

Then you remember how Paul tells us in 2 Corinthians 12 that he had an experience, some fourteen years earlier, of being taken up to heaven, and he says, 'whether in the body, or out of the body, I cannot tell.' 'It was so marvellous,' he says, 'I do not really know.' He was in a state and in a condition which he really cannot describe with accuracy.

'Ah, but,' says someone, 'that has only happened to men in the Scriptures.'

No, that is not so. This is something that has gone on happening to God's people who have realised the possibilities, and who, throughout the running centuries, have sought God himself. Have you ever read of Jonathan Edwards describing his experience of it in a forest while he was there kneeling in prayer for about an hour? Have you read of David Brainerd, the great apostle to the American Indians, experiencing the glory of God, and literally sweating, though it was cold, and though it was freezing round and about him? What was causing the sweating? Oh, it was the glory, the character and the transcendence of the glory. And to give you a man who is much nearer to ourselves, D. L. Moody, a very strong man physically, a very sturdy man. And yet when God gave him a glimpse of his glory, he had to ask him to desist and to hold back his hand, because he felt it was killing him. He is not the only one who has felt that. I could quote you others who have said exactly the same thing. The man felt that his physical frame was cracking and was breaking under the glory, and he had to ask God to hold back his hand. 'Thou canst not see my face: for there shall no man see me, and live' – I will give you just some indication of the glory. I will give you a fleeting glimpse of it, but you cannot see me as I am. No, 'my back parts' only.

As you come again to the question of revival, you will find a great deal of this. You will find it when God manifests himself by an outpouring of the Spirit, whose special work and commission it is to manifest the Lord Jesus and his glory, and, through him, God himself. You will find that you will often read of things like this; that men and women in the presence of this glory, and of this presence, have literally fallen to the ground, have fainted. 'Ah,' says somebody, 'these phenomena!' We must not be interested in, nor frightened of phenomena. I am pointing out to you that God himself has said that the glory is so glorious that men's physical frame is inadequate. So do not be surprised when you read the reports of people fainting, or going off into a kind of dead swoon, it is a measure of the glory of God. It is beyond us, and it is not surprising, therefore, that it should sometimes lead to such consequences.

That, then, is the partial nature of God's answer. But though the answer is partial, it is nevertheless very definite. 'You shall not see my face,' says God to Moses, 'but you shall see something.' He will see God passing by.

And the Lord said, Behold, there is a place by me, and thou shalt stand upon a rock: And it shall come to pass, while my glory passeth by, that I will put thee in a clift of the rock, and

will cover thee with my hand while I pass by: And I will take
away mine hand, and thou shalt see my back parts. . . .

He is passing by. Do you know what a revival is? Well, that is a
perfect description of it. It is just this glimpse of God, of the glory
of God, passing by. That is precisely what it is. Just this glimpse
of God. The God who is there in the glory, as it were, comes
down and pours out his Spirit and ascends again, and we look on,
and feel, and know that the glory of God is in the midst, and is
passing by. It is only a touching of the hem of the garment, as it
were, it is but a vision of the back.

Let me give you a comparison which may help. What is thunder
and lightning? According to the Psalmist, and according to the
Bible everywhere, thunder and lightning are but a kind of indication of God's power, the God who said at the beginning, 'Let
there be light,' and there was light. He gives you just an indication
of what his power is, in the flash of the lightning, the roar of the
thunder. These are but the glimpses of God's might, God's power,
God's ability. In the same way, a revival is just a touch of his
glory, a fleeting glimpse of what he is, in and of himself. And I
want to emphasise this because you and I must come to realise
that these things are possible, and that these things are meant for
us. We were never meant to be content with a little. Let me,
therefore, give you some scriptural indications of the possibilities.
I have already reminded you of what happened to Saul of Tarsus,
there on the road to Damascus when suddenly there shone a light
from heaven. And then, think again of that description which he
gives in 2 Corinthians 12. 1–4:

It is not expedient for me doubtless to glory. I will come to
visions and revelations of the Lord. I knew a man in Christ
above fourteen years ago, (whether in the body, I cannot tell; or
whether out of the body, I cannot tell: God knoweth;) such an
one caught up to the third heaven. And I knew such a man,
(whether in the body, or out of the body, I cannot tell: God
knoweth;) how that he was caught up into paradise, and heard
unspeakable words, which it is not lawful for a man to utter.

That was an experience received by the Apostle Paul himself, a
man of like passions with ourselves, a man still in the body, still
in this world, still in the flesh. He had this experience of the
glory itself, in this veiled and partial manner. But he had other
experiences. When he was in Corinth, he found everybody against

him, and he went to bed one night very troubled. But this is what we read. 'Then spake the Lord to Paul in the night by a vision' (Acts 18.9). Visions, and experiences of the glory of God! And the result of this is that he is able to say that he knows the Lord Jesus Christ so well that, 'For to me to live is Christ, and to die is gain.' And again, ' . . . and to be with Christ; which is far better'. (Phil. 1. 21,23). Can we say that? Can we say, 'To me to live is Christ'? If we cannot say it, why is this? Why should we not say it? It is meant for all. The Apostle nowhere teaches that this was only meant for himself, or merely for the apostles. He is telling the Philippians this, that they might have the same experience. John writes, 'That which we have seen and heard declare we unto you, that ye also may have fellowship with us: and truly our fellowship is with the Father, and with his Son Jesus Christ' (John 1. 3). And again, 'These things write we unto you, that your joy may be full' (v. 4) and if our fellowship is truly 'with the Father, and with his Son Jesus Christ', we are all meant to be enjoying these experiences, 'I can do all things through Christ which strengtheneth me' (PPhil. 4. 13).

But then, again, Paul puts it like this – this is the counterpart to what we have in Exodus 33 – 'For now,' says the Apostle, 'we see through a glass, darkly; but then face to face' (1 Cor. 13. 12). The hand is covering us now, and we are only seeing through a glass darkly. Yes, but we *do see* through a glass darkly, and that is what I am emphasising. Even here in this world we see through a glass darkly, in an enigma or a riddle, if you like. Yes, but we *can see*. And my question is, are we seeing it? One day I know it will be face to face. 'But we all, with open face beholding as in a glass . . .' – it is still only partial, you see. It is beholding as in a kind of reflection from a mirror, yes, but it *is* that. ' . . . beholding as in a glass . . .' – what? ' . . . the glory of the Lord. . . .'

Is that true of us? Can we say honestly with the Apostle Paul, 'God, who commanded the light to shine out of darkness, *hath shined* in our hearts, to give the light of the knowledge of the glory of God in the face of Jesus Christ'?

Can we appropriate the words of 1 Peter 1.8 and say, 'Whom having not seen, we love; in whom, though now we see him not, yet believing, we rejoice with joy unspeakable and full of glory' – can we say that? 'Ah,' you may say, 'but I believe in the Lord Jesus Christ, I have rejoiced in my salvation for. . . .' I am not asking you that. What Peter says is that the Christian is a man who so knows him and loves him, that he rejoices in him with a joy that is unspeakable, that baffles description, and is full of glory. In revival, men and women in large numbers are able to say that. The glory of God has come near, has passed by, they have seen his back parts, and they have been able to use those words with absolute honesty.

All this, you see, is a kind of foretaste of heaven, and we are to enjoy foretastes of heaven here in this world: 'Blessed are the pure in heart: for they shall see God.' Our Lord's prayer for his own is, 'Father, I will that they also whom thou hast given me, be with me where I am; that they may behold my glory, which thou hast given me: for thou lovedst me before the foundation of the world' (John 17.24). 'Then,' says John in 1 John 3.2, 'We shall be like him; for we shall see him as he is.' 'Then,' as the well-known hymn puts it, 'His glory full disclosed shall open to our sight.' Yes, but before we come to that, we should have these partial views, here in this world, not the full disclosure, that is to come, but the partial disclosure. And the question is, do we know anything of these things?

Well now, for our encouragement, let us look at a few passages. Take Jonathan Edwards first:

Sometimes only mentioning a single word, causes my heart to burn within me. Or, only seeing the name of Christ, or the name of some attribute of God, and God has appeared glorious to me. On account of the Trinity, it has made me have exalting thoughts of God that he subsists in three persons, Father, Son, and Holy Ghost. The sweetest joys and delights I have experienced, have not been those that have arisen from a hope of my own good estate, but in a direct view of the glorious things of the Gospel. When I enjoy this sweetness, it seems to carry me above the thoughts of my own estate. It seems at such times a loss, that I cannot bear, to take my eye off from the glorious pleasant object I behold without me, to turn my eye in upon myself and upon my own good estate.*

Then again from Jonathan Edwards:

Once as I rode out into the woods for my health in 1737, having alighted from my horse, in a retired place, as my manner commonly has been, to walk for divine contemplation and prayer, I had a view, that for me was extraordinary, of the glory

*Jonathan Edwards: *Works*, London 1840, Vol I p. xlvii

of the Son of God as mediator between God and man, and His wonderful, great full, pure, sweet grace and love, and meek and gentle condescension. This grace, that appeared so calm and sweet, appeared also great above the heavens. The person of Christ appeared ineffably excellent, with an excellency great enough to swallow up all thought and conception, which continued as near as I can judge about an hour, which kept me, the greater part of the time, in a flood of tears and weeping aloud. I felt an ardency of soul to be, what I know not otherwise to express, emptied and annihilated, to lie in the dust and to be filled with Christ alone, to love Him with a holy and a pure love. To trust in Him, to look upon Him, to serve, and to follow Him, and to be perfectly sanctified and made pure with a divine and heavenly purity. I have several other times had views very much of the same nature, and which have had the same effect.*

'What should I do about all this?' someone may ask. Let Spurgeon answer the question. You will find it in one of his revival year sermons.

Let me say now before I turn from this point, that it is possible for a man to know whether God has called him, or not. And he may know it too beyond a doubt. He may know it as surely as if he read it with his own eyes. Nay, he may know it more surely than that. For if I read a thing with my eyes, even my eyes may deceive me. The testimony of sense may be false, but the testimony of the Spirit must be true. We have the witness of the Spirit within, bearing witness with our spirits that we are born of God. There is such a thing on earth as an infallible assurance of our election. Let a man once get that, and it will anoint his head with fresh oil, it will clothe him with a white garment of praise and put the song of the angels in his mouth. Happy, happy man who is fully assured of his interest in the covenant of grace, in the blood of atonement, and in the glories of heaven. What would some of you give if you could arrive at this assurance. Mark, if you anxiously desire to know, you may know. If your heart pants to read its title clear, it shall do so ere long. No man ever desired Christ in his heart with a living and longing desire, who did not find Him sooner or later. If thou hast a desire, God has given it thee. If thou pantest, and criest, and groanest after Christ,

*Ibid. p. xlvii.

even this is His gift, bless Him for it. Thank Him for a little grace, and ask Him for great grace.

You see, these are the steps of Moses.

Thank Him for a little grace, and ask Him for great grace. He has given thee hope, ask for faith. And when He gives thee faith, ask for assurance. And when thou gettest assurance, ask for full assurance. And when thou hast obtained full assurance, ask for enjoyment. And when thous hast enjoyment, ask for glory itself and He shall surely give it thee in His own appointed season.

Are you on these steps? Having thanked God for what you have, have you got this longing for more? Hope, faith, assurance, full assurance, enjoyment, glory. Ask him for it. Climb the steps. Follow the example of Moses. Enter boldly in faith, and say to God, 'Show me thy glory.' And you have the assurance, not only of Spurgeon, that if you do so from your heart, and sincerely, in his own good season he will answer you. You have the infinitely higher and greater assurance of this word of God itself, of the promise of the living God: 'Draw nigh to God, and he will draw nigh to you,' (Jos. 4.8). Seek glory. For yourself, seek it. For the Church, pray for revival, for the passing by of the glory of God.

Chapter 18

Exodus 33.18–23

And he said, I beseech thee, shew me thy glory. And he said, I will make all my goodness pass before thee, and I will proclaim the name of the Lord before thee; and will be gracious to whom I will be gracious, and will shew mercy on whom I will shew mercy. And he said, Thou canst not see my face; for there shall no man see me, and live. And the Lord said, Behold, there is a place by me, and thou shalt stand upon a rock: and it shall come to pass, while my glory passeth by, that I will put thee in a clift of the rock, and will cover thee with my hand while I pass by: and I will take away mine hand, and thou shalt see my back parts: but my face shall not be seen (Exod. 33.18–23).

We have described revival as being a passing by of God's glory, a manifestation of it. The answer that God gave to Moses' prayer does therefore, include some sensible realisation of the presence of the glory of God. By sensible, I mean something that one feels, something that one is conscious of experimentally. Not only something that one deduces from the word, and receives from the word, which we should always do, but something over and above that, some sensible realisation of the glory and the power, the presence of God. That is a testimony which is quite universal in the Church at all times, and in all places, when God graciously visits in revival. But the record tells us that God did not stop at that. He did give Moses this view, this glimpse, this sensible realisation, but in particular he went on to do certain other things. And we must consider them now because the answer that was actually given to Moses was, 'I will make all my goodness pass before thee, and I will proclaim the name of the Lord before thee; and will be gracious to whom I will be gracious, and will shew mercy on whom I will shew mercy.'

Now this is the subject that we must analyse. It is not merely this sensible realisation of the nearness, and the presence, of God that is given to Moses, but this particular, special, manifestation of what God calls his goodness: 'I will make all my goodness pass before thee. . . .' What that really means, obviously, is that God's glory is mainly, and chiefly, manifested to us in and through his goodness. And that, in turn, means that we are given a manifestation and an understanding of the character of God. For God's goodness is something that is a manifestation of his character, his person, his attributes, and, in particular, certain of his attributes, as we shall see. And, therefore, the teaching here is that our supreme need is a knowledge of the character of God. It is an astonishing thing to have to say, but it is nevertheless the truth, that all our troubles in this Christian life ultimately arise from our ignorance of the character of God. If only we knew God as he is, we then, of course, would be like the Lord Jesus Christ himself, who lived in this world as we do, and was subject to the same difficulties and trials, indeed subject to all the same temptations as we are. And yet how different was his life. And that was because he knew God, he knew the character of God, and he knew the goodness of God.

There can be no question at all but that God emphasises this to Moses, at this point, for a very good, and a special reason. It seems to me that there can be no doubt but that Moses here was tending to be a little bit too interested in what we may call the spectacular. It is very natural; we are all aware of it. God had given him some very wonderful answers. He had already given him some extraordinary revelations of himself. Moses had been up on the mountain with him forty days and forty nights, and he had heard things, and he had seen things, yet Moses, encouraged by God's gracious dealings with him, and God's kindness to him in answering his prayers, ventures here to step further, and says, ' . . . shew me now thy glory.' And I am sure that here there was included some desire for some spectacle, something visible to the naked eye. Now, this desire is innate in our characters. And I have no doubt that it is essentially a result of the fall and of sin in us. We are always asking for the spectacular. We all, I am certain, have a feeling within us that if only the heavens could open and we could see God, how wonderful it would be. We want some visible demonstration.

That, I would suggest, is the result of sin, and I am fortified in saying that by the way in which the Devil tempted our Lord in the three recorded temptations. Each time he called for something spectacular, something striking. It is always the tendency of man in sin to demand something in that realm. People are always seeking visions. They talk about them, and they tend to rest their faith upon them – something unusual, some spectacle, some vision, some dream, some peculiar ecstasy. And I feel that Moses here was animated by some such idea, and so God deals with him very tenderly. He says, 'All right, I will grant you something along the lines that you are asking. You shall not see my face, that is impossible, for no man shall see my face and live. But I will stoop to your weakness. I will let you see something. But, much more important than that, I will cause all my goodness to pass before you. I will give you a deeper insight and understanding into myself, into my character, into what I am. That is what you really need to know.

And this is still our greatest need. Over and above all that we might see of the miraculous power of God in demonstration is the character of God himself. Miracles and things of that kind God uses when he feels the time is appropriate, but men and women are always demanding them. There are those in the Church today who are so interested in faith healing for this reason. They say, 'If only we could do that, then the people would be interested.' But, you see, God does not grant it. No, we must not be interested in God's activities at the expense of God himself. Our ultimate need is to know God himself and this is possible to us, in, and through, his goodness. And so he tells Moses here, 'I will make all my goodness pass before thee.' Now there is an emphasis, I believe, upon that word 'all', and I think that again the reason for that is perfectly clear. God had already revealed to Moses a great deal of his goodness, but now he is promising him, 'I am going to give you a deeper view of it, a deeper insight into it. I am going to display it before you in a manner that you have never experienced before.' As if God were saying to Moses. 'You seem to be uncertain about me. I have promised that I am going to come with you. I have promised you various things that you have asked of me, but you still seem to be uncertain. You ask, 'Show me now thy glory.' What you need, Moses, is really to know me. So I am going to cause all my goodness to pass before you.' So I suggest to you that the supreme blessing that comes to the Church in a time of revival is this deeper knowledge of God in his goodness toward us.

How then, does God make this known to us? The answer is that he does it in the proclamation of his name. He says, 'I will make all my goodness pass before thee; and I will proclaim the name of the Lord before thee. . . .' All who are familiar with the Old Testament will know that God manifested himself to the Children of Israel through his various names. The name conveys the character. And as God was stooping to man's weakness, and granting revelations of himself, he did so by saying, 'I am' this, or, 'I am' that, and gave many descriptions through his name. The power of the personality is in the name. Even we, today, use this expression, in a sense. For instance, talking about a man, a professional man, perhaps a doctor, or a solicitor, or a barrister, we may say, 'He's got a great name.' What we mean by that is that he is a very successful man, he is very good at his work and people are talking about him. In other words, the character of the man and his work is conveyed to us by this name. And it is exactly the same with regard to God. And so he told Moses here, 'Now I am going to let you know the real truth about myself. I am going to proclaim my goodness. And I am going to do so by proclaiming ny name before you.' So he proceeded to do so and Exodus 34.6–7 tells us how he told Moses,

> *And the Lord passed by before him, and proclaimed, The Lord, The Lord God, merciful and gracious, longsuffering, and abundant in goodness and truth. Keeping mercy for thousands, forgiving iniquity and transgression and sin, and that will by no means clear the guilty; visiting the iniquity of the fathers upon the children, and upon the children's children, unto the third and to the fourth generation.'*

That is the proclamation of the name, and we read that Moses made haste and bowed his head toward the earth, and worshipped. God was revealing his goodness to him through the medium of these words and telling Moses the truth about himself.

What, then, does this mean? What is this knowledge of God that we stand in need of? It is a question for Christian people. Do you feel burdened and weary and tired? Are you unhappy and perplexed? Do you sometimes find yourself full of doubts and uncertainties? Do you find the Christian life a hard one, and a grievous one? If you do, it is because you do not know God. You have never really understood what he has revealed concerning himself in his name. Let us listen to what he has said himself about himself. 'The Lord, the Lord God', 'Jehovah, Elohim' is a compound name. Let me tell you some of the things that it teaches us so clearly.

This term, God, is the term that is used of God as all-powerful, of God as the Creator. When God said, 'Let *us* create man' that was the term that he used. It is a plural term, immediately suggesting the Trinity, the Father, the Son, and the Holy Spirit, and particularly conveying to us this idea of power. It is the God who said, 'Let there be light', and there was light. There is no limit to his power, it is eternal. He is omnipotent. That is the first thing.

But then, you see, this other term is added to it: 'The Lord, the Lord God' 'Jehovah'. Here is the name on which we must concentrate, because it is in this name that God has always chosen to reveal the most precious truths concerning himself. You notice its repetition: 'The Lord, the Lord God. . . .' If we only realized something of the meaning of that, the whole situation would be transformed. Our personal lives would be transformed, the whole condition of the Church would be transformed. It is because the Church does not know him as Jehovah that she is fearful, and anxious, and apprehensive, and so busily trying to save herself and the whole situation. If we but realised who he is – Jehovah.

What then, does it mean? Well, in this name, God is revealing his own essential character because what the term means is 'the self-existent one'. It means, 'I am'. Indeed it means more. You remember in Exodus 4 that God called Moses as he was watching over his sheep. He said, 'Moses, I want you to lead my people out of Egypt and to take them to Canaan.'

'Ah,' said Moses, 'who am I to do a thing like that? When I go to them and tell them that they are going to be led out from the captivity and taken to Canaan, they will say, "Who sent you? How do we know?" '

'Tell them,' said God to Moses, 'that *I am* hath sent you – *I am that I am*.' What a statement. That is the essential character of God. He is. And God alone is. No beginning, no end, this term suggests to us the eternity of God, the everlasting character of God, from eternity to eternity, self-existent, in and of himself.

The name also suggests his unchangeableness. It is very difficult for us to grasp these notions, is it not? We belong to time, and are so subject to time that it is very difficult for us to grasp this blessed truth that the God whom we worship, and to whom we belong, is unchangeable, 'the Father of lights, with whom is no variableness, neither shadow of turning'. He is not under the sun, he is above it. Everything is under him and he is, he always was, he always will be. 'I am that I am', eternal, unchangeable, omnipotent, omniscient, omnipresent. He is, and he is everwhere. Now, this great term, Jehovah, conveys all that meaning to us, and there is nothing more glorious than that. 'Show me now thy glory,' says Moses.

'Very well,' says God, 'that is my glory, that I am that I am.'

229

Have you realised it? He is not like the gods of the nations made by men. There was a time when they were not, then they were made, and they were set up, then they disappeared, and others came. No he is altogether different, alone.

But, also in this term there is another wonderful suggestion. This is the term that God always uses about himself when he is revealing himself. He is the self-existent One, but he deigns to make himself known. He reveals himself. He did it to the Children of Israel. And that is what you will find in the third and sixth chapters of this book. In Exodus 6.2–3 we read, 'And God spake unto Moses, and said unto him, I am the Lord: and I appeared unto Abraham, unto Isaac, and unto Jacob, by the name of God Almighty, but by my name Jehovah was I not known to them.' Now that means that whereas he had already used that name to them, he had never given it this special connotation and significance. It is at this point, when he is giving this unusual revelation of himself, that he defines the term, shows its content and gives its full meaning. So, we must remember that this self-existent, and eternal, and omniscient God has chosen to reveal himself to us, and has come down to our level. 'That is what I am going to show you,' said God to Moses. 'That is my goodness.' It is God revealing himself to man whom he has created.

But it goes even further than that. This is always the name that God uses with regard to himself when he makes a covenant with man. A covenant, as you know, is an agreement. And this is the full glory of the gospel, that God, this self-existent God, who could be independent of man, has humbled himself, as it were, and has made an agreement with man: he has made a covenant. He made a covenant, you remember, with Abraham. We are reminded of it there in Exodus 6.3. He pledged himself. He took an oath. That is an agreement, a covenant. Then God was making a special covenant here with the Children of Israel and the covenant was that he would be their God, and they should be his people. And that is the position of every Christian – he has come into God's covenant. You remember how Paul puts it in Ephesians 2, where he says, in effect, 'You know you were once strangers from the covenant of Israel, and aliens, and enemies, outside the commonwealth. But you have been brought in.' And he says that the wonderful thing that has been revealed in Christ is this: that the Gentiles are going to be made fellow heirs and members of the household of God. They have been brought into the covenant. And God was here reminding Moses of this covenant relationship. God has pledged himself to save his own people.

So, that brings us to the last great truth contained in this term, which is that God is the Redeemer. He is not only the Creator and the Sustainer of everything that is – the term *Elohim*, God, suggests all that. No, *Jehovah* goes further. He is God the Redeemer. Do you remember what he said to Moses at the burning bush? 'I have surely seen the affliction of my people. . . . and I am come down. . . .' And there is the whole of the Christian gospel: God coming down, God descending, God the Redeemer, God saving his own people. This is the term that God elaborated as he spoke to Moses on this great occasion. What is it that is true of God as our Redeemer? What are the things that he emphasises? The first is his own holiness. He says he will by no means clear the guilty, 'visiting the iniquity of the fathers upon the children, and upon the children's children, unto the third and to the fourth generation.' So as God was revealing his goodness to Moses, the first thing Moses was aware of, in addition to the power, and the might, and the glory, was the holiness of God, and we read that he bowed himself to the earth and worshipped.

Now, as you read your Bible, you will find that many people have been given these glimpses of God's glory. And you will notice that they all react in the same way. If you read Isaiah you will find that the moment he was given this glimpse of the glory of God, he said 'Woe is me! for I am undone; because I am a man of unclean lips' (Is. 6.5). It was the holiness of God that made him feel that. And there has never yet been a revival of religion, but that the moment that God's people have this experience, though they may have been Christians for years and years, they feel utterly unworthy, they see themselves as sinners as they have never done before. Some of them have even doubted whether they have ever been Christians. They are wrong, of course, but the sight of the holiness of God, the realisation of it, has made them see nothing but their own sinfulness and their own unworthiness. It is invariable. It is our blessed Lord himself who always prayed, saying, 'Holy Father. . . .' He knew him. He was the only begotten Son. He was the Son in this unique sense, but he prayed, 'Holy Father'. The holiness of God, my friends, is the first thing that we understand when we are confronting God the Redeemer.

And then the next thing is his hatred of sin and his judgment upon us. Let there be no mistake about this. God said to Moses, 'I am going to show you my goodness.' Yet he says he will by no means clear the guilty. He will visit the iniquity of the fathers upon the children, and upon the children's children, unto the third and fourth generation. He is righteous, he hates sin, and he will punish sin. Do you not have a feeling that this is the one thing that this modern world of ours needs to know? This world that feels that it can dismiss God, and laugh at him, and break all his laws with impunity. My friends, is not this the thing we need to preach to the world, that God is holy, that God is righteous, that he hates sin with an eternal hatred, and will punish sin. That is his own revelation of himself.

But, thank God, that having revealed that, he goes on to reveal something else, and that is his love for his own, and his purpose to redeem them. Hear the terms: 'The Lord, the Lord God, merciful and gracious, longsuffering, and abundant in goodness and truth. Keeping mercy for thousands, forgiving iniquity and transgression and sin.'

'That is who I am,' said God, in effect, to Moses. 'You do not need some spectacle, you just need to know my heart of love. You just need to know that it is my purpose to redeem. This is my character.' But you notice that he qualifies that immediately, lest we might misunderstand it. Having reminded him of his mercy for thousands, forgiving iniquity and transgression and sin, he adds, ' . . . and that will by no means clear the guilty. . . .' Now, this is of tremendous significance. It is here that you see the cross of Christ in the revelation of the names of God, as given to Moses. God will never clear the guilty. God only shows his love, and his forgiveness, his mercy and his compassion to those who are no longer guilty.

Now the tragedy is that we have been separating these things in the character of God. I have often asserted, and I repeat it again, that the condition of the Church today is due to one major factor. And that is that during the last century, from about the thirties of the last century, a new attitude towards the Scripture came in in which men decided that they knew much more about the character of God than what was revealed in this book. And what they did was to say that God is love and nothing else. So they have put out the wrath, they have put out the justice and the righteousness, and all that God has revealed about himself, and they have said that God will clear the guilty. 'God,' they say, 'is love. It does not matter what you do. Go and tell him you are sorry. Ask for forgiveness, all is well.' But it is a lie. And the lawlessness that we are witnessing in the world, and the lawlessness in the Church, arises from that and from nothing else. God will by no means clear the guilty. He is a God of compassion, and of mercy, and of kindness, and of all that he says here. Yes, but he is still a holy God, remember. He is still the righteous God. And when he forgives, he forgives in a righteous manner. He has made a way of taking away our guilt and that is the central glory of his revelation. What he is really saying here to Moses, in embryo, is, 'I am going to send my only Son into the world. I am going to put the guilt upon him. I am going to punish him. And then the guilt will have been removed and I will be compassionate, and merciful, and gracious to them, and I will forgive all their sins. But only in that way.'

That is the revelation of God, and that is the thing that always stands out in every period of revival – this amazing combination of all the glorious attributes of God. You must never divide them. They are all there and they are all there together, and at the same time. God is not at one time loving, and at another time righteous. No, he is always the same. He is loving and righteous at the same time. He is holy and loving at the same time. You can not divide these things. God is one, and all his glorious attributes are revealed together, and they are all here. That is his goodness towards man, and there is no more wonderful discovery that a human being can ever make than that that self-existent God, who is all-powerful in his glory and majesty, who is light, and in whom is no darkness at all, who is a consuming fire, has so loved you that in his holy righteousness he has put your sins upon his own beloved Son, and given to him to bear the anguish and the suffering, and the shame, and the punishment of them all, that you and I might be forgiven and delivered, and might become the sons of God.

Yes, God reveals himself in all these terms, but there is yet one other term I must add. Did you notice it there in this 33rd chapter, in verse 19?

And he said, I will make all my goodness pass before thee, and I will proclaim the name of the Lord before thee; and will be gracious to whom I will be gracious, and will shew mercy on whom I will shew mercy.

What is this? Oh, this is the sovereignty of God. Here is the self-existent, and the eternal, the righteous, the holy God, and yet the merciful and the compassionate. And he is going to forgive sins. Whose sins is he going to forgive? Here is his own answer: 'I will be gracious to whom I will be gracious, and will shew mercy on whom I will shew mercy.' And this is an essential part of the revelation. This is as much a part of God as everything else and you must not leave it out. It means that our salvation is entirely, and altogether, by the grace of God. It is not in any sense dependent on anything in us. It is, indeed, in spite of us. It is entirely of God's own will. He is not under an obligation to anybody. He has never consulted anybody. 'I will be gracious to whom I will be gracious, and have compassion on whom I will have compassion, I will show mercy to whom I will show mercy.' It is the free, and the sovereign grace of God. He himself revealed it.

This is a great mystery, and man in sin does not like it, and pits his puny mind against it. But God has said this, 'Jacob have I loved, and Esau have I hated' before they were born when they were yet in the womb.

'But how can that be?' says someone. And there is only one answer, the answer given by Paul: 'Nay but, O man, who art thou that repliest against God?' (Rom. 9.20).

You say, 'I do not understand this.' Of course you do not understand it. Did you ever imagine that your little mind or mine was sufficient to understand this eternal God, this, 'I am that I am'? You do not understand. Of course you do not! You mind is not only small, but it is sinful, it is twisted, it is perverted, it is selfish and self-centred. Are you trying to understand? Be careful what you are doing, my friend. You are entirely in God's hands. You know nothing about him apart from that which he has graciously been pleased to reveal. And this is what he has revealed. What man would ever dare say a thing like this? I would not. No man in his senses would. I do not understand it, but here is the revelation: 'I will be gracious to whom I will be gracious, and will shew mercy on whom I will shew mercy.' He is the potter, I am the clay. Salvation is entirely and altogether in God's own sovereign will. He chose Israel for his own possession and not any of the other nations. Why? Do not ask me, he knows. 'I will be gracious to whom I will be gracious.' And if you do not feel that you are what you are by the grace of God alone, and in spite of yourself, all I can say is I do not understand you. I know if I had what I deserved it would be hell. No, we have not chosen him, he has chosen us. Why, I do not know. It is just this great principle of his sovereignty. Why did he ever look upon me? I am the last man to know why. It baffles me increasingly. But I am what I am by the grace of God. That is his revelation.

And, there is no one feature, I sometimes think, that comes out so prominently in times of revival as just this question of the sovereignty of God. I sometimes think also, that revival is the supreme manifestation of the sovereignty of God. He shows it like this. Take the timing of revival. A revival happens in God's own time, and never at any other time. That, as I have shown, was the tragic blunder of Finney in his lectures on revival. He taught that you can have a revival whenever you like if you only do certain things, and fulfil certain conditions. It is a complete denial of the sovereignty of God. Not only that, it is proved by history to be wrong. I, in my own lifetime, have known numbers of ministers who have taken Finney's lectures on revival and have honestly put them into practice in their preaching and in their churches, and have persuaded their people to do them. But they have not had a revival. Thank God for that. You will never organise a revival. It is God who gives it. And, he does it in his own time. He does it when you least expect it; when you think it is coming, it generally does not come. He keeps it in his own hands: 'I will be gracious to whom I will be gracious, and will shew mercy on whom I will shew mercy.'

Then, as we have seen, he does it in strange places. You never know where a revival is going to break out. That is glorious, that is marvellous to me. We have considered how the next revival will probably not break out in a big congregation, but in some little village church where there are only two or three people. Thank God that it is his choosing. He chooses the place as well as the time, and you never know where it is going to be, you can not find any rules.

People have been trying to do this, to work out rules. They read the history of revivals in the past, and then they say, 'I notice that before that revival, a number of people had been praying right through the night.' So they decide to pray right through the night. Then they notice something else, and try that. But the revival does not come. Of course not, if it did they would say it was the all night of prayer that did it, and so the glory would be taken from God.

No, it is the sovereignty of God with regard to time and to place, and with regard to how he does it. Have you noticed the persons whom he chooses? Have you noticed the variations in the methods that he employs? You will never be able to draw up rules with respect to revival. There is something new every time, and it is always a change, something different, lest man should say, 'Now then, I am going to do it.' No, it is God in his sovereignty, and, perhaps, you see it supremely in the way the revival comes to an end. It may have been going for a number of months, and the people are rejoicing. It is wonderful, and they really think that they can keep it going. Suddenly God stops it. And the foolish people try to keep it going, but they cannot. They try to work themselves up, they try to pray as they did before, they try to sing, but suddenly it is gone, the Spirit that was given is taken back. That is the sovereignty of God. You can not stop a revival, any more than you can start it. It is altogether in the hands of God. It is the sovereignty of God who says, 'My glory I will not give to another,' (Is. 42.8). 'I will be gracious to whom I will be gracious, and will shew mercy on whom I will shew mercy.'

What have we got to say to these things? There is only one thing to say. We must repeat with the Apostle Paul.

'Oh the depth of the riches both of the wisdom and knowledge of God! how unsearchable are his judgments, and his ways past finding out! For who hath known the mind of the Lord? or who hath been his counsellor? or who hath first given to him, and it shall be recompensed unto him again? For of him, and through him, and to him, are all things; to whom be glory for ever. Amen' (Rom. 34–36).

Who hath known the mind of the Lord? Who has been his counsellor? Who has ever suggested anything to him? Man in his folly has done it frequently, but the suggestion has never been accepted. Of him, through him and to him, are all things. There is no greater madness than to attempt to pit our puny, sinful minds against this Lord, Lord God, Jehovah, great 'I am', under whom, and by whom are all things, and who in his own eternal wisdom has deigned to look upon us, and to be gracious unto us, and to be merciful unto us. Oh, the wonder of his grace.

Chapter 19

Exodus 33.18–23

*And he said, I beseech thee, shew me thy glory. And he said, I
will make all my goodness pass before thee, and I will proclaim
the name of the Lord before thee; and will be gracious to whom
I will be gracious, and will shew mercy on whom I will shew
mercy. And he said, Thou canst not see my face: for there shall
no man see me, and live. And the Lord said, Behold, there is a
place by me, and thou shalt stand upon a rock: and it shall come
to pass, while my glory passeth by, that I will put thee in a clift
of the rock, and will cover thee with my hand while I pass by:
and I will take away mine hand, and thou shalt see my back
parts: but my face shall not be seen (Exod. 33.18–23).*

We come back to a final consideration of this notable and most
extraordinary incident in the life of Moses, the servant of God.
We are looking at this, as we have been looking at the whole
chapter, because of the instruction and the enlightenment that it
gives us with regard to the whole general subject of revival, and
of God's manifesting himself at special times, and in special
circumstances to his people. Now, we have seen, let me remind
you of this, that the ultimate motive for desiring revival, and for
praying for it, is the glory of God. I emphasise that because the
first reason for desiring revival is not that a large number of people
may be converted. That is *a* motive, but it is not the first, nor the
greatest motive. The chief motive in evangelism is the glory of
God, and the desire to see God's glory manifested. It can all be
summed up, therefore, in this one petition of Moses: 'Shew me
thy glory.' And, if this is not the deepest desire of our hearts
there is something seriously and sadly defective in our whole
position. Our chief desire at this moment should be, with the
world as it is, and the Church as she is, that the glory of God
might be manifested amongst us, and before our wondering gaze.
 Now we have seen that what happens in revival is that God
gives us a glimpse of his glory, and we have also seen that the

great lesson, which is always learned in every time of revival and of reawakening, is the great truth concerning the goodness of God. The great character of God is made evident and his great attributes are displayed: his mercy, his longsuffering, his graciousness, his kindness, his compassion, yes, and his righteousness, and above all, his sovereignty, his sovereign majesty; the God who visits us, and sends revival, and then causes it to cease. It is all in his hands and we bow to the earth before him, as Moses did, at the realisation of his majesty, his glory, and his sovereignty.

Those, then, are the general lessons which are conveyed by a time of revival. A special visitation of God's Spirit, God, as it were, coming near to his people and giving them this glimpse of his everlasting glory. There remains, however, just one thing for us to consider because it is here, and it is emphasised in the text. And that is the precise way in which this happens. So we concentrate now, in particular, on verses 21, 22 and 23 of Exodus 34.

We are told in these verses exactly how this vision of the glory of God, the sight of the glory of God, was given to Moses. Note the details: 'You cannot see my face,' said God. 'No man can see my face and live. But now I am going to give you this glimpse in this way. Here is this rock by me. You are to stand on that rock. Then I am going to take you and put you in a cleft of the rock, protected, as it were, by the two sides, and then I will put my hand over you, as I pass by. Then after I have passed by I will take away my hand and you will see my back parts.'

Now, you notice the way in which we are given these extraordinary details. But, obviously, our concern must be with the principles, and I suggest that the principles that are taught here in these details are the principles that always govern every manifestation of God, and his glory, to his people. You go right through your Bible from beginning to end, and you will always find that at every moment of revelation this same teaching is given. The same principles are very clearly enunciated, and we must therefore discover the principles that are taught in this particular action. And, surely, they are perfectly simple.

There are just two main principles, and the first is that there is a combination here of revealing and concealing. God is revealing, yes, but at the same time he is concealing. He puts his hand upon Moses. He puts him in the cleft of the rock. He is showing him something of his glory, yet he is hiding something of his glory at the same time.

The second principle is that at one and the same time, he is blessing, but also protecting. There is obviously this great element of blessing here, yes, but at the same time God is protecting Moses by putting him in the cleft of the rock, and by putting his hand upon him, and covering him. He is protecting him, as we see, from the account, from his own glory: 'No man shall see me and live.' So he is protecting him against death, which would be the immediate result of seeing God with the naked eye, God as he is. It is a great blessing, but it is also conveying this element of protection. The expression, of course, that is used in the schools about this is that this is a paradox. And it is, of course, the great paradox of the Bible. These four things are happening at the same time, whenever God draws near to his people – revealing and concealing, blessing and protecting, all happening together at one and the same time. You cannot separate these things. And we must never attempt to dissect them from one another or to divide them from one another in some false dichotomy.

There, then, is the great principle of revelation, and that is what actually happened on that occasion so long ago to Moses, the servant of God. This is history. This literally, and actually, happened. This was not just a picture. Moses is recording sheer historical fact. Yes, it is history, but, you know, it is more than that. It is a kind of prophecy, and we must consider how it is a perfect prophecy of what has happened since, and happened perfectly in the person of our Lord and Saviour, Jesus Christ. In other words, what we have here, in this dramatic and pictorial form, is nothing but a kind of perfect summary of the great message of the New Testament. This is Christianity. Paul has put it once and for ever in 2 Corinthians 4.6: 'For God, who commanded the light to shine out of darkness, hath shined in our hearts, to give the light of the knowledge of the glory of God in the face of Jesus Christ.' That is Christianity. That is the whole meaning of everything that is recorded in the New Testament. That is the whole meaning of the incarnation, and everything that has followed it. It is God revealing his glory in the face of Jesus Christ. In other words, it is a great fulfilment, a perfect fulfilment, in a yet more glorious manner, of what God did here so long ago to his servant, Moses.

Now, before we come to work out the details, therefore, let me emphasise this central principle. It is the realisation of this, and the experience of this, that really makes us Christian. What is a Christian? This is an important question is it not? There are so many false notions current today as to what a Christian is. Some may say that a Christian is a good man. Yes, but there are many good men who are not Christians. Others say that a Christian is a man who has had a marvellous experience. Ah yes, but there are cults that can give people experiences, and they are very wonderful. A Christian, says another, is a man whose life has been entirely changed. I know, but the psycho-therapists can do that and the cults can do that. Then again, a Christian, according to some people, is a man who has taken a decision. Yes, but you can take many sorts of decisions to be better and to live better, and to join a church, and to do a thousand and one other things, yet clearly there are many people who have done all that and still are not Christians. Well, others maintain, a Christian is one who has had some sort of a vision, who has seen a ball of light or something like that. No, there are many people who have had that kind of experience but who clearly cannot be admitted as Christians. They do not believe the very elements of the Christian faith. They have had the oddest and most strange and eerie experiences and have been conscious of some strange power coming into them, and upon them. Ah yes, but if you read books on spiritism and spiritualist phenomena written by spiritists, you will find that they can duplicate all that, and most astounding things can and do happen. And it would be folly to deny the testimony to such things which has been given by eminent scientists like Sir William Crooks, and Sir Oliver Lodge and various other people. So, I am not prepared to accept any of these statements as being determinative of whether we are Christians or not.

What is it, then, that makes a man a Christian? Well, surely it is the realisation of the fact that God has given a revelation of his own glory in the face of Jesus Christ: 'God who commanded the light to shine out of darkness, hath shined in our hearts . . .' – what for? – 'to give the light of the knowledge of the glory of God in the face of Jesus Christ.' A Christian is a man who believes that. A Christian is a man who has experienced that in a measure, or to a certain extent. This is the thing that constitutes the Christian. Not a change of life, or habits or of behaviour. Not merely being religious, not merely attempting to worship God. No, it is the realisation that God has done this, has given this manifestation of his glory in the face of Jesus Christ. So, having thus isolated and identified our principle, let us now see how the New Testament is but a fulfilment of what we read here. We can see it point by point.

The first is this. Here is a definite statement: 'There shall no man see me, and live.' It is repeated again. 'My face shall not be seen.' Now the New Testament is equally clear about that. We read in John 1.18, 'No man hath seen God at any time.' The New Testament starts from that postulate. There it is in John's prelude where he is introducing the message of his gospel. 'No man hath seen God at any time.' That is why the Son has come. Or see how Paul puts it in 1 Timothy 6.16: 'Who only hath immortality, dwelling in the light which no man can approach unto; whom no man hath seen, nor can see: to whom be honour and power everlasting.' That is, one might say, the preamble to the gospel. It is the essential, first, pre-supposition that no man by searching can find out God, that no man can see God. He dwells in that light which is unapproachable. 'God is light, and in him is no darkness at all' (1 John 1.5).

Then, the second principle is that God reveals himself in his own way. He determined everything here on this occasion with Moses. 'Shew me thy glory,' says Moses.

'Yes,' says God in effect, 'I am going to give you a glimpse, but it has got to happen in this way.' And so he determines it, he decides it, he causes it to happen. And this is still the truth. God is to be known only in his own way. There is no other way. There are people who say that they can find God in their own way, but according to the Bible, that is a sheer impossibility. You can arrive at what you imagine to be God. You can have some spurious experience. Many things can happen to you. The power of psychology is endless, and there is all this other spiritist power that I have referred to. But, according to the Bible and its message from beginning to end, God is to be known only in his own way. It is the way that he has determined and planned. We see in Exodus how Moses is placed in the cleft of the rock, and God's hand is put on top of it. Then the hand is removed, and Moses has his glimpse.

What does the New Testament say about that? Look again at John 1.18: 'No man hath seen God at any time; the only begotten Son, which is in the bosom of the Father, he hath declared him.' He has led him out; he has manifested him. No man can see God, so, are we hopeless then? No, the only begotten Son, he who was in the bosom of the Father, he has declared him, he has come to manifest him. That is the gospel. That is the whole of the gospel. That is the meaning of everything that he did. This is God's way of revealing his glory. So, you see, the Apostle John can also say this, 'And we beheld his glory, the glory as of the only begotten of the Father, full of grace and truth' (John 1.14).

Then there is a still more explicit statement of this in the four-teenth chapter of John's Gospel, the most important verses in this connection. Thomas, you remember, was in trouble, because our Lord had said that he was going to leave them, and he said,

> Lord, we know not whither thou goest; and how can we know the way? Jesus saith unto him, I am the way, the truth, and the life: no man cometh unto the Father, but by me. If ye had known me, ye should have known my Father also: and from henceforth ye know him, and have seen him.

And Philip blurted out, 'Lord, shew us the Father, and it sufficeth us.' 'That is all I want,' says Philip. 'Show us the Father. You are saying "whosoever hath seen me hath seen the Father." '
And Jesus answered,

> Have I been so long time with you, and yet hast thou not known me, Philip? He that hath seen me hath seen the Father; and how sayest thou then, Shew us the Father?

'Why are you so slow,' he says, 'to understand these things? You say, "Shew us the Father, and it sufficeth us." But you have seen, you have seen me, you have seen the Father.'

Again, our Lord, in his high priestly prayer, turns to his Father, and says, 'I have glorified thee, in the earth' (John 17.4). There it is quite plainly and explicitly. He has come to reveal the glory of the Father, and he is able to say at the end, 'I have done it. I have glorified thee in the earth.' And so when the apostles now look back upon all this, and announce their gospel and describe it, that is how they put it. Consider once more 2 Corinthians 4.6. 'For God, who commanded the light to shine out of darkness, hath shined in our hearts, to give the light of the knowledge of the glory of God in the face of Jesus Christ.' And so Paul has been able to say earlier, in 2 Corinthians 3.18, 'But we all, with open face beholding as in a glass the glory of the Lord, are changed into the same image from glory to glory, even as by the Spirit of the Lord.'

Then again, in writing his first epistle to Timothy, Paul says, 'According to the glorious gospel of the blessed God . . .' (1.11). That should be translated, 'According to the gospel of the glory of the blessed God. . . .' That is what the gospel is. It is the gospel of the glory of the blessed God. 'It is a faithful saying, and worthy of all acceptation, that Christ Jesus came into the world to save sinners; of whom I am the chief' (1 Tim. 1.15). That is the gospel, yes, but it is the gospel of the glory of the blessed God, and the saving of sinners is but one of the manifestations of the glory of this blessed God.

Or take it as it is summarised by the author of the epistle to the Hebrews – I am anxious that we should see that this is the great message of the New Testament – 'God, who at sundry times, and in diverse manners, spake in time past unto the fathers by the prophets, hath in these last days spoken unto us by his Son' (1.1). Who is this? He is 'the brightness of his glory, and the express image of his person' (Heb. 1.3). Jesus Christ is the effulgence, the brightness, of the glory of God.

'Show me thy glory,' cries humanity.

And God says, 'I will show you my glory, but in my own way. And this is the way – in the face of Jesus Christ', in this person who is the brightness of his glory and the express image of his person.

And then we read what the aged Apostle Peter writes in a letter of farewell to various Christian people. He knows that he is about to be put to death, and he says to them that as long as he is in this tabernacle, he is going to go on reminding them of these things. 'For,' he says, 'we have not followed cunningly devised fables, when we made known unto you the power and the coming of our Lord Jesus Christ' (2 Pet.1.15). We are not writers of fiction. We are not drawing on our imagination. We have not had dreams, we have not seen things, we have not reported to you cunningly devised fables when we declared unto you the power and the coming of the Lord Jesus. No, 'We were eye-witnesses of his majesty.' Peter says, in effect, 'We were with him on the mount in the excellent glory. And a voice came from the excellent glory, saying, and we heard it, "This is my beloved Son, hear him." Now, after I have gone, and after the rest of the apostles have gone, false teachers will come in, and they will say this and that. Do not believe them. Here is the record. This is the thing on which you bank and base your whole faith and all your position.' Not cunningly devised fables – 'We were eye-witnesses of his majesty.' We saw him transfigured, there upon the holy mount, and we heard the voice from heaven. There, then, you see, is the New Testament fulfilment of all this. The New Testament counterpart of the story in Exodus.

And yet, you must notice, and I must emphasise, that the same paradoxical features characterised this fuller revelation in the New Testament, as characterised the former incomplete revelation that was given to Moses. Let me just remind you of these things – and is there anything more glorious or wonderful that Christian people can do than just remind one another of these extraordinary facts?

The first thing, as we have seen, is the concealing. 'I am going to take you,' said God to Moses, 'and I am going to put you in the cleft of the rock, and I will put my hand upon you.' Have you ever noticed that concealing in the New Testament? Have you ever dwelt upon it? It is all stated so perfectly in Philippians 2 5–8: 'Let this mind be in you, which was also in Christ Jesus: Who being in the form of God, thought it not robbery to be equal with God.' There he was in eternity. He was in the form of God. He was God. He is the second person in the blessed Holy Trinity. And his form was the form of God, the glory of God. He thought it not robbery to be equal, which means that he did not hold on to that. But 'made himself of no reputation, and took upon him the form of a servant, and was made in the likeness of men: And being found in fashion as a man he humbled himself, and became obedient unto death, even the death of the cross.'

There is the cleft in the rock, and the hand of God covering Moses. The Lord did not come in the form of God, though he is God, but came in the form of a servant, and was made in the likeness of men. He came, says Paul, in the likeness of sinful flesh. That is the concealing. But he was still God, remember, in all his fullness. He had not left any of the Godhead behind him. That kenotic theory is a complete lie, and a contradiction of what is being said. He did not empty himself. What he did was to make himself of no reputation, which is a very different thing. He cannot empty himself of Godhead, that is a sheer impossibility. God cannot cease to be God. No, what he did was this: though he was still God, in all his fullness, he made himself of no reputation. He came in the form of a man, though he was still perfect and absolute God. He was concealing the Godhead. He came incognito, still the monarch, but travelling as a private individual. That is how he did it; the concealing, the hiding.

The prophet Isaiah was given to see beforehand that he was to come in this way. He says he will come 'As a root out of a dry ground: he hath no form, nor comeliness; and when we shall see him, there is no beauty that we should desire him' (Is. 53.2). His visage is marred. That is how he came. That is how the light of the knowledge of the glory of God is revealed and manifested in the face of Jesus Christ. The Son of God comes down to earth. How does he come? With blazing glory? No, born in a stable as a babe in Bethlehem. There is the concealing of the glory. The babe, the boy, the carpenter, the man who appeared to be just an ordinary man like everybody else, who was so tired on one occasion that when the disciples went to a town to buy provender he sat by the side of a well, and began talking to the woman of Samaria. A man, you say, and a very tired man. Yes, but that is the concealing of the glory of God. It is the cleft of the rock, and the hand of God. Tired and hungry.

Do you see him praying? Praying all night, rising up a great while before dawn and praying. Why does he need to pray? He is the Son of God, co-equal with God? Yes, but the glory is being concealed. He is come in the likeness of man. He has made himself of no reputation. He is come in the form of a servant. And, again we read of him that one day, 'Jesus wept.' God weeping? Oh yes, God, in the likeness of man, the Word made flesh, the concealing of the glory.

Then you remember that extraordinary incident that happened on the Mount of Transfiguration? He went up on to the mount taking Peter, and James, and John with him, and he was transfigured before them. His raiment became exceeding white beyond the brightest shining of the sun, or beyond the brightest shining that the fuller can ever produce. He was transfigured, his whole visage, everything. 'Ah,' you say, 'now at last they are seeing it in its fullness.' No they did not. We read in Luke 9 in the account of that transfiguration that a deep sleep came upon these disciples, and that a cloud overshadowed them. It is the hand of God again, you see, concealing, and protecting. They suddenly began to feel sleepy and heavy, and a cloud overshadowed them. Of course, the thing is still true. They could not see the absolute glory and live. So they were covered by the sleep, and by the cloud.

And finally, look at him dying upon the cross. What is this? This, again, is a veiling of the glory, the concealing of this absolute glory and power. Charles Wesley says it all for us in the hymn which is only sung at Christmas time, but which should be sung much more frequently: 'Veiled in flesh, the Godhead see . . .' Yes, you can see it, but veiled in flesh. 'Hail incarnate deity!' What happened at Bethlehem? It was this – 'Mild, he lays his glory by . . .' Charles Wesley does not mean that he laid the glory itself by, but that he laid the signs of the glory by, the accompaniments of the glory. That is what it means by 'making himself of no reputation'.

> Mild, he lays his glory by;
> Born that man no more may die.

There is the concealing.

The next element in Exodus is the protecting. It is not merely a concealing, but also a protecting. 'No man shall see me and live.' said God to Moses. 'So, while I give you this glimpse of my glory, I have got to protect you against my own glory lest it kill you.' So, he put him in a cleft of the rock, and put his hand over him. He was protecting him, I say, against his own holiness, his own majesty, his own glory, his own wrath against sin, his own eternal justice and righteousness. Moses had to be protected while he was given a glimpse of God's glory and God's goodness, because God is one, and all these various elements are in his character. You cannot, as we have seen, divide the attributes of God. When we are at the communion service, we eat the bread and drink the wine. We remember the Lord's death upon the cross. What was happening on that cross on Calvary's hill? I can tell you. It was our being protected against the glory and the holiness, and the righteousness, and the justice, and the wrath of God against sin. That is the meaning of the cross, and the death upon the cross.

We can summarise it in the famous words of Augustus Toplady. He had seen this thing so clearly, so he sang like this:

> Rock of Ages, cleft for me,
> Let me hide myself in Thee!
> Let the water and the blood,
> From Thy riven side which flowed,
> Be of sin the double cure –
> Cleanse me from its guilt and power.
>
> While I draw this fleeting breath,
> When mine eyes shall close in death,
> When I soar through tracts unknown,
> See thee on thy judgement-throne –
> Rock of Ages, cleft for me,
> Let me hide myself in Thee!

His only hope, his only protection against the majesty, and the judgment, and the glory, and the wrath of God, is that Christ is the Rock of Ages, and that he is covered by what Christ did upon the cross. The hand of God is upon him, and he is safe. That is the meaning of the death upon the cross. It is this protection without which we would be undone. And so that is the meaning, too positively, of our being clothed with the righteousness of the

Lord Jesus Christ. That is the hand that comes upon us. And, Toplady again, puts it like this:

> The terrors of law and of God,
> With me can have nothing to do.

Why?
'Oh,' he says,

> My Saviour's obedience and blood
> *Hide* all my transgressions from view.

It is the hand of God upon us, hiding us, hiding our transgressions from view. And the result is that we need have no fear of the terrors of law or of God. We are in the cleft of the rock, which is in Christ Jesus. And his righteousness, his hand of righteousness is upon us. There is the protection, the concealing, the protecting.

But we must also look at the revealing. For it was not only concealing and protecting that took place on that occasion with Moses. The object of it all was the revelation. And look at it in the case of our blessed Lord. We have seen that he came, and was born as a babe, yes, but you remember how it happened? This was not an ordinary birth. The archangel Gabriel is sent to a virgin. She is not married, she has never known a man, but she is to produce a child. Ah, an ordinary babe, you say. No, there is a miracle here, there is a marvel, there is a glory about it all. It needs an archangel to announce it. Though he is a helpless babe, born in a stable, both the concealing and the revealing are there. Look at him in his infancy. He seems, again, to be just an ordinary infant, but he is not. Certain wise men living in the east have heard something, and they have seen a star which announces this child and which leads to him. And they come and they worship him, and they offer their gifts. Not an ordinary infant this. There is something unusual here. Wise men come and fall on their knees, and they adore him, and they worship him. The concealing, yes, but the revealing also.

Then, listen to his own words. He is now thirty years of age, and he has started teaching and preaching. We could look at the whole of his life and illustrate this. I am simply picking out the most salient features. He speaks for the first time in the synagogue of his home town of Nazareth, and this is what we are told about him: 'They wondered at the gracious words which proceeded out

247

of his mouth' (Luke 4.22). They said, 'This is Jesus. This is the son of Mary and of Joseph. This is the boy we have known, the carpenter. How did he speak like this? He is only a man.' No, there is something more. They wondered at the gracious words that proceeded out of his mouth, and have you noticed that his miracles always led to the same result? When the multitude saw it, they marvelled, and glorified God who had given such power unto men. We read that when he healed the paralytic man, they were all amazed and glorified God, saying, 'We never saw it on this fashion' (Mark 2.12). We read in Luke 5.26, 'They were all amazed, and they glorified God, and were filled with fear, saying, We have seen strange things today'. This man, and yet not a man. Who is he? What is this? We must remember also what happened on the Mount of Transfiguration.

Then, look at him dying upon the cross. That, you might have argued, was the final proof that he is only a man after all. And yet you remember that the Roman centurion looking at him and seeing him already dead, stood back and said, 'Truly, this man was the Son of God' (Mark 15.39). He is marvellous even in his death; there is something unusual; there is a glory even in his cross. Isaac Watts has seen it, and so he sings, 'When I survey the wondrous cross, on which the Prince of glory died. . . .' There is a paradox. The Prince of glory – died. 'The Prince of life,' says Peter preaching later. The Prince of life you have put to death. It is a paradox, of course; revealing and concealing at one and the same time, in everything, and especially there upon the cross.

You see the combination of these opposites. The justice of God, but the love of God; the righteousness of God and the mercy of God; the wrath of God, and his everlasting compassion. All have met together, righteousness and peace have met together in this one person who conceals and reveals the glory of God. Think of the resurrection. Think of the ascension. Think of the appearances, his appearance to Stephen: 'He [Stephen] being full of the Holy Ghost, looked up stedfastly into heaven, and saw the glory of God, and Jesus standing on the right hand of God' (Acts 7.55). And the appearance to Saul of Tarsus, who had hated and reviled this Jesus, but then he saw him, and said, 'Who art thou, Lord?' (Acts 9.5). The revelation of the glory of God in the face of Jesus Christ: he is the King of glory. There, then, is the New Testament way of describing what we have in Exodus 33.

What is revival? Revival is a period in the history of the Church when the things of which I have just been reminding you become the greatest reality in the world to God's people. We believe them

248

now, yes, but do we feel their power? Do we thrill at them? Are we moved by them? Do we glory and exult in them? Revival is a time when these things are made so clear by the Holy Spirit that the whole Church is filled with this glimpse of his glory; the light of the knowledge of the glory of God in the face of Jesus Christ. Jesus said that when the Holy Spirit came he would glorify him. And so when he comes in exceptional power, the glory of Christ is made unusually plain and clear. It is the Holy Spirit's special work. And so you will find that in every period of revival the hymns of the Church, the prayers of the Church, are filled with thanksgiving and with praise, for the glory of the Lord, and especially for his death upon the cross. The glory of the cross. The wonder of the blood. These things are the theme of the Church. The Spirit coming in unusual power has given an exceptional glimpse of the glory of God in the face of Jesus Christ. Do you not long for it? Do you not long to see it and to feel it? Do you not long to know what it is to be almost overwhelmed by a sense of his glory, his majesty and all the fullness of his goodness? Seek it, my friend. Seek it personally. Seek it for the Church in general, not only in this country, but everywhere throughout the world. The need of the hour, individually and collectively, is the knowledge of the glory of God in the face of Jesus Christ.

Chapter 20

Isaiah 62.6–7

I have set watchmen upon thy walls, O Jerusalem, which shall never hold their peace day nor night: ye that make mention of the Lord, keep not silence, and give him no rest, till he establish, and till he make Jerusalem a praise in the earth (Isa. 62.6–7).

If anything shows our need of revival at the present time, it is what we see as we look around and about us. The Church seems to have been overcome by such a spirit of lethargy, and of defeatism, thereby giving the impression to those who are outside that she is filled with a sense of despair. We need, very badly, what Isaiah has to tell us in the 62nd chapter of his great prophecy. Here is a man facing the condition of the Church. He has been given a foreview, and he therefore prophesies the coming of the enemy, that is the Chaldean army, against Jerusalem. And he can see that they are going to conquer the Israelite army, that they are going to capture the city, destroy it, raze its great buildings to the ground, and carry its people away captive into Babylon. But he was not only given that to say, he was also shown the coming restoration. And thus his prophecy is divided largely between these two things. Here we find him looking at the situation when it was at its worst, and, in the light of the gracious promises of God, showing how he reacted to such a situation, and what he called upon the people to do.

Now there is no doubt that the primary reference of this chapter is to that event, to the captivity in Babylon and the return of the remnant to Jerusalem, that has been the traditional interpretation in the Church throughout the centuries. Here also, undoubtedly, is a foreview of a great ingathering which is going to take place amongst the Jews. But it does not stop at that, there is still something else here and that is a picture of the Christian Church. Our Lord himself quoted several times from this particular section of Isaiah's prophecy, showing quite clearly, that it does refer to the Church and to gospel times – you remember how in that first address of his, in the synagogue at Nazareth, he quoted from Isaiah 61. All this is a part of the same picture. And so it has been customary in the Church throughout the running centuries for God's people to see in such a statement as this the call to the Church in a time of declension, in a time when she is beset round and about by enemies, and problems, and when in a large measure she has suffered defeat at the hands of her foes. So we can take this picture today and apply it to ourselves, and see how we should react to our present position.

I call attention to this in a particular manner, because it is a very practical chapter, and it reminds us, therefore, that in our consideration of the need of revival, we are not to be content with a mere theoretical examination of the position. Indeed, that can be quite fatal. The whole object of theoretical consideration is to lead to action. It is to lead to something in practice. When the prophets delineate the condition of Israel, they never merely stop at that. They do that in order to rouse the people, to bestir themselves, and to do something to meet this tragic situation in which they find themselves. And here, as we shall see, the whole emphasis is upon the response, the action, the determination to do something. And there is really no purpose in looking at the present situation, and considering the great movements of the Spirit in the past, unless it leads to a determination on our part to act and to do something in the light of the position in which we find ourselves.

So, all I have to do at this point is just to pick out the things which are stated here so clearly, and what we find in the first place is the prophet's concern. The prophet is deeply moved: 'For Zion's sake,' he says, at the beginning of chapter 62, 'will I not hold my peace, and for Jerusalem's sake I will not rest. . . .' Zion, Jerusalem, these were not mere names to the prophet, they were names which conveyed so much to him, and of which he was so proud. Zion, he knows, is the city of God. Not merely the city of David but the city of God. And Jerusalem? Well, she is the city of the great King. and so the prophet is concerned because he knows the real meaning of these names. They do not just mean an ordinary city to him, just a city among cities, but *the* city of God. God had made this place and established it for himself, and had given this people, his own people, the great privilege of living in such a city, Jerusalem or Zion. And, therefore, realising, as he did, the greatness and the glory of this city of God, the prophet is grieved and deeply concerned as he sees her present condition.

So this is the starting point – 'For Zion's sake . . . for Jerusalem's sake. . . .' He starts with that and we must start with it, because the first thing that is necessary for us is a concern about the state of the Church. You read the prophets and you will find they do not spend their time in being concerned about the state of the other nations, and those who are outside. No, the burden of these men is the state and the condition of the Church. That is what they keep on writing about: that the Church of the Living God, that Zion, should be reduced to this. They think of a former glory, they think of all their associations, and now they see her in this condition. And that is the thing, that moves them and is their chief concern.

The question therefore, that comes to us is whether we can say that we know something about the same concern. What is our burden? To what extent can we say that the condition of the Church is on our hearts and minds and is deeply concerning us? Do we realise what the Church is? Do we remember that she is the city of God? Do we remember that she is his new creation by water and the word? The city of God. That is what the Church is. This is Zion; this is God's dwelling place. God has made her for himself; he has brought her into being even at the cost of the blood and the death of his own Son. So are we concerned about the state of the Church? Surely we must admit, many of us, that we are so occupied with ourselves and our own personal problems, and difficulties, all that we talk so much about, that we never stop for a moment to look at the Church objectively, and see her, and begin to mourn because of her condition.

As you read these prophets, and as you read the Psalms, you will find that this is the thing that is always uppermost in the minds of these men; they had such a conception of the nation to which they belonged as the people of God. All God's purposes were in her, and were involved in her well-being. Seeing her as she was, they could not think of anything else, in a sense. And what is sad about the present time is that this aspect of the matter seems to be almost absent. Men and women can not see any need to be concerned. And if we are not concerned, there is only one explanation. It is because we have not the right conception of the Church of God. This is because we do not see her as the prophet saw the nation, and Zion, and Jerusalem. If only we had a true conception of the Christian Church! If we only really saw her as she is in the New Testament, if we had but some dim and vague notion of what she was in the early years, and indeed in the early centuries, if we but really understood what she was like in every period of revival and re-awakening, then we would be heartbroken at the present condition. We would be grieved and filled with a sense of sorrow. Are we all troubled when we see something that once was great and famous going down or ceasing to be? The decline and fall of an Empire is a sad spectacle. It is a sad thing to see a great business going down. It is sad to see a great professional man losing his grip. It is sad to see a man who is great at sport suddenly, because of age, beginning to fail. It is something that always fills us with a sense of sorrow and of sadness. Well, multiply all that by infinity, and then try to conceive of the Church of God as she is in the mind of God, and as she was formed and founded, and contrast that with what she is today. 'Oh,' says this man, 'for Zion's sake, for Jerusalem's sake, I will not hold my peace, I will take no rest.'

There, then, is the starting point for the prophet, and this is so because he sees her as she was at that present time. Look at his terms. She is forsaken, she is desolate – he says that in verse 4. When the reformation comes, he says, 'Thou shalt be no more termed Forsaken.' But she is forsaken now. 'Neither shall thy land any more be termed Desolate.' But it *is* desolate. God seems to have left her, the people have been carried away, and the sight of Jerusalem presented by Isaiah is that of desolation. Not only that, in verse 8 he gives us another picture: 'Surely I will no more give thy corn to be meat for thine enemies.' but at the moment that was what was happening. 'And the sons of the stranger shall not drink thy wine, for the which thou hast laboured.' There she was forsaken, desolate. The people were working, yes, but, the results of their work were taken, the corn was taken, the wine was taken, the enemy, their conquerers, were eating the corn and were drinking their wine. And all their activity, and effort, and labour, finally, as it were, came to nothing. That was his picture of the Church in his own day and generation, and as he looks at it, and contrasts it with what she was and was meant to be he is burdened, he is concerned, his heart is almost broken. Christian people, are we really satisfied with the state of the Christian Church today? Do we ever stop to think about it? There are towns and villages in this land which were once filled with a praying, and praising, and glorying people, towns and villages which stand out in the annals of Christianity in this country once filled with a sense of the glory of God. But today they are desolate, they are deserted, they are forsaken.

Now, the whole call of the prophet is that we must face these things and we must begin to realise them. We must not be misled by the reports which we read in the religious press, which would give the impression that everything is going remarkably well and that there is no need to trouble ourselves. We have got to think of the Christian Church as she is to be found in the towns, and villages, and hamlets, and country districts of this land. The vast majority of people are outside the Church, only ten per cent claiming any allegiance at all, and only half those visiting a place of worship with any regularity. That is the position; the Church has become a remnant, weak and small. And those who are still faithful, for various reasons, are discouraged. They are dispirited, and the others look upon them almost with pity because they are still holding on to something that is so obviously outmoded and exploded.

There, then, is the position that confronts us. And the question I ask is, to what extent are we conscious of the feeling that animated the prophet? It is our business, as members of the Christian Church, every one of us, to be concerned about these things. We must be concerned not only about our personal problems, we have them, I know, but we must deal with them and go beyond them. We must become intercessors, as the prophet was calling upon his fellow countrymen to become intercessors.

Isaiah, then, has this concern, because he sees Zion as she is, and because of what he desires her to be. There she is, down and out, as it were, and he says he is not going to keep silent, nor give himself any rest, 'until the righteousness thereof go forth as brightness, and the salvation thereof as a lamp that burneth.' That is his vision for Jerusalem. That is his vision for the Church. That is what he wants her to be like. With his prophetic vision, he can see her in faith, and he can see her becoming again what she is meant to be. This is a tremendous statement. This is what has happened to every man whom God has ever used to stir the Church, and to lead in the matter of revival. It was a thing like this in the heart of Martin Luther that suddenly set him aflame. He saw the Church in which he had been brought up and to which he belonged. He saw what a travesty she had become. he said, 'This is desolation. This is tragedy.' Then he saw in the New Testament the Church of God as she is meant to be, a lamp of burnished gold, holding the light before the nations, and he began to be stirred and to be moved. That is how it happened.

And you and I must catch this vision of what the Church can be. No, there is no excuse for us. You see it in the Bible itself. We see that handful of people in the book of Acts of the Apostles burning with power like a lamp that burns, 'the righteousness going forth thereof as brightness'. Can you not see the flame and the power? Read the accounts, I urge you, of all the great revivals in the history of the Church. Go back to the glorious period of the Reformation. Go back to two hundred years ago. Acquaint yourselves with the days when Whitefield and the Wesleys and others were preaching here in London, with the unction of the Holy Ghost upon them and mighty things happening. The trouble is that we have no conception of the Church, we have never seen her like that, have we? No, we have seen a kind of outward prosperity, but that is not the prosperity of the Church. We have not seen, we know nothing about the Church going forth with brightness, and as a lamp that is burning. But she is meant to be like that, she can be like that, and we must realise that. That is the way in which the prophet speaks.

Then Isaiah adds another description. He says of her 'Thou shalt also be a crown of glory in the hand of the Lord, and a royal diadem in the hand of thy God.' What tremendous faith this is. He was looking at a Church desolate and forsaken, 'all is well,' he says, 'I can see what you are going to be, what you are meant to be, as a crown of glory in the hand of the Lord, the royal diadem in the hand of thy God.' And then, you remember these other terms which he uses: 'You are no longer going to be Forsaken,' he says, I can see a day coming when the Church shall no more be Forsaken. 'Thou shalt be called Hephzibah' – which means 'His delight is in her'. 'Neither shall thy land any more be termed Desolate . . . but thou shalt be called . . . Beulah' – which means 'Married'. Now, we must be clear about these terms. What the prophet is saying is that God's delight does not seem to be in his people. God is like a husband who has gone away from home and who seems to have forgotten his wife. That is what he is saying. And that was certainly true of the condition of Israel at that time. There she was, at the mercy of her enemies – she who had conquered everybody, she who had been so great under King David, and under King Solomon after him. Now here she is, a remnant, weak and small. The majority of her people have been carried away to Babylon, working as slaves under the hand of that cruel Chaldean power. And he looks at all this, and he says, 'What does it mean? Well, God has forsaken us. God has turned away from us.' But he is not going to give himself rest or peace until God looks back, and returns to them, and says, 'My delight is in thee. I am coming back': 'Thou shalt be called Hephzibah ['my delight is in thee'] and thy land Beulah ['married'] for the Lord delighteth in thee, and thy land shall be married.'

Then, in addition to that, Isaiah makes this statement, 'And give him no rest, till he establish, and till he make Jerusalem a praise in the earth', – until everybody looks on, and praises. And, indeed, he adds, in verses 8 and 9, that she is going to be prosperous again: 'They that have gathered it [the corn] shall eat it, and praise the Lord; and they that have brought it together shall drink it in the courts of my holiness.' This, you see, is the thinking that leads to what follows. The prophet sees the Church as she is and he says 'God seems to have left us. God has forsaken us.' Is that true of us today? I do not hesitate to say that it is. The terms, of course, are relative. We must not despise the day of small things, but, believe me, we are living in the day of very, very small things. When you contrast the condition of the Church today with what she has been, you cannot but come to the conclusion that for various reasons God is not looking upon us and smiling upon us. There is a sense in which we are forsaken. There is a sense in which we are desolate. Speaking generally the Church today, throughout the whole world, is an abandoned Church. She is in a desolate condition, and I maintain that that is the thing that we must realise.

Furthermore, we must see the possibilities. Jerusalem was not meant for this. She was meant to be something completely different. Then Isaiah has got one other thing which animates him and which moves him. He is anxious that the Gentiles shall really see her as she is meant to be. That is the second verse: 'And the Gentiles shall see thy righteousness, and all kings thy glory: and thou shalt be called by a new name, which the mouth of the Lord shall name.' This was a constant note. Nothing worried these men of God more than that the heathen, the Gentiles, should be scoffing. Israel had made a great claim for herself, she had said. 'We are the people of God. Zion is the city of the living God. Look at the Temple,' they said, 'God dwells in that Temple. You Gentiles, you are in the outer court, you have never been into the Holiest place of all. You have never seen the Shekinah glory, but God is there between the cherubim'. That is what they had claimed. They were God's own people. And here they were defeated and desolate, and knowing that the enemy was laughing and scoffing and full of derision and of sarcasm. And the kings, the great potentates, who defied God and his armies and his people were mocking. 'Oh,' said the prophet. 'I am not going to be quiet until the Gentiles shall see thy righteousness, and kings, thy glory.'

Are we moved by such thoughts? Does it grieve us and trouble us as we hear the jokes, and the laughter about the Christian Church? Are we not moved as we hear these modern 'kings', people like philosophers, and scientists, and others, dismissing and deriding, not us, but God of the City of God, the Christian Church, the Church which Christ purchased with his blood? They are laughing at her. They are spitting upon her. And are you and I unmoved? Is there not a deep and a burning desire within us that these Gentiles, these 'kings', shall see the Church in her glory, in her brightness, with the light of God upon her face, and the power and the flame of the Holy Spirit within her? That is the thing that animates the mind, and the heart, and the spirit of this prophet Isaiah. He looks forward to a day when the Gentiles and kings shall call them God's people, the holy people, the Redeemed of the Lord, sought out, a city not forsaken. He says, 'I am not going to keep quiet until Zion is once again a city which men shall seek. They shall come from the ends of the earth to seek Zion, the city of God, exalted above all the nations and all the cities of the world.'

There, then, is the thought that provides the background to what the prophet proceeds to exhort, and this leads me to the second matter. What was it that the prophet decided to do in the light of all this? And what did he exhort all others to do? The answer is given in verses 6 and 7. Indeed, as we have seen, he starts off at the very beginning by saying, 'I will not hold my peace, I will not rest.' He says, 'I am going to speak. I am going to talk about this. I am going to preach to people. I am going to talk about this without ceasing. I will not rest while things are as they are, not until they become what I see they can be, and are going to be.' In other words, he is a man consumed by this one idea. It has gripped him and moved him. He is whole-hearted. He does not merely do it now and again. So often, when people see something particularly bad, they begin to think, but then they forget all about it, and they go back to the dull routine. They pray for a while, then they forget. But there is nothing spasmodic about this man. There is nothing fitful about him. The condition of Zion has become his one concern, the passion of his life, the one thing about which he always speaks. It has become a burden upon his spirit.

And that is how revivals have always begun. God has put a burden in this way upon somebody, upon one man, perhaps, or upon a number of men – the number does not matter. You might say that a man develops a kind of 'one-track mind', it is all he talks about: 'I will take no rest, I will not hold my peace.' He is speaking about it, telling people about it, exhorting people to consider it. Thus, I say, God begins to move. That was the truth about the prophet Isaiah. Of course, there were many people who thought he had gone mad, and they thought the same about Jeremiah. They said, 'What is the matter with these men who seem to be harping on the same point always? Why can't they go back and let us get on with the happy routine of Church life? Why always this one thing? Isn't it beating a dead horse?' That is how such people speak. There has never been a man yet who has had a true vision of what the Church of God should be and can be, and who has contrasted that with our present position, but that he has begun to speak about it, and become obsessed by it, and people have thought he is mad, and they have criticised him. 'Why all this bother?' they say. 'Isn't everything all right?' That is what the false prophets were saying in Israel. And they are saying it today. There are people who are actually opposed to the whole notion of revival. You can read their books on the Holy Spirit, you can read their articles in the periodicals, on the Holy Spirit, and you will find that they do not mention revival at all. They do not believe in an outpouring of the Spirit of God, in spite of the history of the Church. They do not seem to want it. God have mercy upon them. At ease in Zion, with Zion as she is, and the world as it is.

That, then, is the first thing that Isaiah tells us, but then he goes on to a practical measure. 'I have set watchmen,' he says in verse 6, 'upon thy walls' – this is the practical step – 'which shall never hold their peace day nor night.' What is the purpose of these watchmen? They are there to guard, of course. That was the custom with an ancient city. There was a surrounding city wall and they set watchmen on the wall to keep a look-out day and night. They were guarding the city. They were keeping a look-out for the coming of a possible enemy. If they saw a sudden movement in the trees, or suspicious activity in some distant field, they would report it at once. These were the men who were guarding the life and the safety of the city. And the watchmen are as necessary today as they have ever been. There are certain enemies always waiting to attack, unseen and always mustering their forces. Who are they? They are the enemies that will attack the truth, the doctrine, and not only the doctrine, but the life of the Church, her holiness, her deportment and her behaviour. 'I have set watchmen,' says the prophet. 'These men must keep their eyes open, and they will do that day and night. They will never hold their peace, they will always be on the lookout.' And if

258

ever this were necessary, it is today. There are ideas insinuating themselves increasingly, even into evangelical circles. For example, people say that what you believe finally does not matter very much, but if a man is a good man and if he calls himself a Christian, you can co-operate with him. You will get men coming together and speaking in the same meeting, who are diametrically opposed to one another in their ultimate doctrine, 'But,' they say, 'that does not matter.' There is terrible confusion; there is a slipping and a sliding in terms of expediency and unity and things like that, but it is not a good thing, my dear friends. Zion is the city of God, she is a holy people, she is a holy place, it is where *God* dwells and you cannot afford to play fast and loose with doctrine, or with the life, either.

But the business of the watchmen is not merely to look for enemies – when a city was hard pressed and besieged the watchmen had to keep their eyes upon the horizon, to see if perchance some relieving force were on the way, to see if some friend were gathering his forces and coming to attack the enemy in their rear. Keeping a look out. Is there a hope of deliverance? Is there someone coming with relief? Watchmen upon the walls, waiting for the good news, waiting to see the messengers of peace – as Isaiah has already put it in chapter 40 – coming across the tops of the mountains, proclaiming the day of salvation. A watchman, like Habakkuk, having prayed, goes into his watch-tower and waits for God's answer. (Hab. 2. 1) This is a very essential part of the procedure. We should be waiting, and looking, and watching, and if we hear of any stirring of the Spirit of God, we should with eagerness pray that it may continue, that it may increase, and that it may go on. If we hear of something that is just smouldering flax, we must pray that it may burst forth into a flame.

So the prophet has set his watchmen upon the walls. But there is one last thing that we must consider: 'Ye that make mention of the Lord, keep not silence, and give him no rest till he establish, and till he make Jerusalem a praise in the earth.' This is a wonderful statement. 'Ye that make mention of the Lord . . .' – yes, but in the margin you will find an alternative translation, which is undoubtedly the right one: 'Ye that are the Lord's remembrancers. . . .' That is how the Revised Version puts it: 'You that are the Lord's remembrancers. . . .' Or, as the Revised Standard Version puts it, 'You who put the Lord in remembrance. . . .' 'You who are the Lord's remembrancers, keep not silent, and give him no rest until he has done this.' Here, then, is the call to prayer, the call to intercession. And what does it mean? Well, I think we can interpret it like this, according to the translations. He is addressing people who still remember the Lord. He is addressing people who do not look to men so much as to God: 'You who remember the Lord,' he says, 'I am addressing you, and I am telling you keep no peace, keep on praying. Do not keep silent, take no rest.'

But this injunction has another meaning also. These are not only people who remember the Lord themselves, they remind others of the Lord. And they exhort others also to pray to him. And this where I would appeal to everyone of you. If you have begun to see something of the burden of the age in which we live, and you are yourself praying God to visit us, and to revive his work, stir up others also, remind them also. Say to them, 'Remember that God is still there. Why do you not pray to him? Why do you not turn to him?' Stir them up, you remembrancers of the Lord. You who remember him, remind others of him.

But these words have a still higher and more wonderful, and indeed a very daring meaning, which is this: 'You that are the Lord's remembrancers. . . .' – you who are to remind God himself of his own promises. It is a daring meaning, but it is here, and all are agreed about this. We are to remind God of his own promises. When we pray we are to go to God with words, and we are to remind him of what he said about Zion and about Jerusalem, of what he has said about the Church. And we are to remind him that he never changes his word, that he never breaks a promise and that he cannot change himself. We are to go with him, we are to go to him with the promises, his own promises, and say, 'Lord, this is what thou hast said, look upon us.' You who are the Lord's remembrancers, keep not silence. . . .' Remind him. Speak to him. Tell him about these things. You will find that the Psalmists were always doing that, that is what their prayers were. Read them. You will find that the people in the New Testament did exactly the same thing. They would quote the Psalms, they would remind God, and then they would bring their petitions. You and I are to become the Lord's remembrancers.

And, lastly, we are to go on doing this. Did you notice this element of importunity? 'For Zion's sake,' says this man, 'will I not hold my peace, and for Jerusalem's sake I will not rest, *until*. . . .' He is going on with it *'until'*. He says about these watchmen that he has set them upon the wall and they shall never hold their peace day nor night. He has got to go on doing it, and they are to go on doing it. Notice this other wonderful phrase here: 'Ye that are the Lord's remembrancers, keep not silence,' says the Authorised Version. But the Revised Version and others are better here. They translate it, 'take no rest'. It comes to the same thing. If you are not keeping silence you cannot be taking rest; if you are taking rest you are silent. They mean the same thing ultimately.

But notice this too, 'You that are the Lord's remembrancers, take no rest. . . .' The times are desperate, they are urgent. When we are in the midst of a great war, trade union rules and regulations are relaxed, every kind of regulation is relaxed. People say, 'We cannot afford to live leisurely as if we were in a state of peace, we are fighting for our lives.' Were we not told that in the Second World War? The leaders said, 'Look here, give in, give up every unnecessary thing. What is the point of having all these things if you lose your life? If you lose your country? Relax your rules. Take no rest. Let us be "all out" the whole time.' That was the appeal. Here is the same appeal in Isaiah. 'Take no rest, be not silent.' And then this daring statement: ' . . . and give him no rest. . . .'Give God no rest until he establish, until he make Jerusalem a praise in the earth. What a bold statement. And yet, of course, Isaiah was perfectly right. We are to take no rest ourselves, we are to give God no rest, until he has heard us, until he has answered us, until Jerusalem is clothed in her beautiful robes again, and is like a burning shining light. Give him no rest, give yourself no rest. Keep on. Bombard God. Bombard heaven until the answers come.

We have the authority of our Lord for this, have we not? In Genesis 32 we read that Jacob did something like that: 'I will not let thee go,' he said.

The man wrestled with him and said, 'It is the dawn, it is the breaking of day, let me go.'

'But I will not let thee go,' said Jacob. 'I'm not letting go until you give me my request' – wrestling Jacob. I have reminded you of how Moses did exactly the same thing. We have been considering it in Exodus 33. Moses made a request, God said, 'Yes.'

'More,' said Moses.

'Right,' said God.

'More,' said Moses.

Here is Isaiah doing the same thing. And our Lord has taught us to pray like this. It is one of the most glorious, and wonderful statements even he ever made about God and God's relationship to us. He said, 'You know, you must not just pray fitfully, you

261

must become importunate. You must be like that man who suddenly is visited by a friend late at night. He has no food to give him, so he says, 'Oh, my friend up the street, will have some loaves.' So he goes and hammers at the door.

But the friend shouts and says, 'I cannot come down, I am in bed and my children are with me.'

'No,' says the man, 'you must give me something. I know you have got bread and I've got a stranger here, I can't let him go without a meal.' He goes on hammering.

'I can't,' says the man, 'I'm in bed.'

But the suppliant goes on and on, until at last the man gets up and gives him the bread.

The man in the bed, in our Lord's illustration, is none other than God himself. Because of his neighbour's importunity he arose and gave him the bread. And if we, who are earthly, sinful, evil fathers, know how to give good gifts to our children, how much more shall our Father which is in heaven give the Holy Spirit to them that ask him? (Luke 11. 5–13). He will not mock us.

But, like a father, he seems to keep us waiting. He seems to say 'no' at first, that we may go on asking, and we must become importunate. Again in Luke 18 you find the same thing. Our Lord there teaches about the unjust judge. It is called the parable of the unjust judge, though I think it should be called the parable of the importunate widow. She went before the judge and he seemed to be dismissing the case. Back she came and he dismissed it again. Back she came again, and at last the judge said, 'This woman is worrying us, she is hitting us black and blue, as it were. She is going on, she is importunate.' And at last he said, 'Very well then, let's consider her case.' And he granted her request. Our Lord spoke that parable under this heading: that men should always pray and not faint. 'Take no rest,' says Isaiah. 'Give him no rest.'

My dear friends, have we got a vision of what the Church is meant to be? Do we see the contrast between our present state and what she can be, and will be? Well, if we have, let us set watchmen upon the wall. Let us become the Lord's remembrancers in every sense of the term. And let us take no rest, and let us give him no rest, until Jerusalem shall again become a praise and a glory, and her brightness, and her righteousness shall shine. And the Gentiles and the kings shall all see her, and shall come seeking her, that they, through her, may seek her Lord and the salvation, which he alone can give. May God open our eyes to the urgency of the time, and to his own way of dealing with us.

Chapter 21

Isaiah 63.1–6

Who is this that cometh from Edom, with dyed garments from Bozrah? this that is glorious in his apparel, travelling in the greatness of his strength? I that speak in righteousness, mighty to save. Wherefore art thou red in thine apparel, and thy garments like him that treadeth in the winefat? I have trodden the winepress alone; and of the people there was none with me: for I will tread them in mine anger, and trample them in my fury; and their blood shall be sprinkled upon my garments, and I will stain all my raiment. For the day of vengeance is in mine heart, and the year of my redeemed is come. And I looked, and there was none to help; and I wondered that there was none to uphold; therefore mine own arm brought salvation unto me; and my fury, it upheld me. And I will tread down the people in mine anger, and make them drunk in my fury, and I will bring down their strength to the earth (Isa. 63.1–6).

In our consideration of Isaiah 62, we saw how the prophet grieves at the desperate condition of Jerusalem, the Church of God. And we saw his reaction to this, and how he decides to watch and pray. He is going to set watchmen upon the walls, and he is going to urge the people to pray without ceasing, not to give God rest, not to take any rest themselves, until Zion shall be restored once more and Jerusalem shall be a praise in the earth. It was a call to action, to face the urgency of the situation. And there we left the prophet, exhorting his people, and pledging himself, thus to give themselves to waiting upon God, that he might send relief and restore unto them again their ancient position of privilege and of power.

And now in this paragraph we come suddenly to this extraordinary picture that we find in these six verses. At first glance one might very well be tempted to feel that this is something that has been interpolated. It does not seem to have any direct connection with what has gone before. The prophet's prayer goes on in the seventh verse which continues, more or less, what we left off at the end of chapter 62. But here is this paragraph which comes suddenly into the midst of his prayer, and his great act of intercession. Of course, there have been those who have said that this is something quite extraneous that has just been thrown in here. That is the view of those who do not believe in the unity of this book of the prophet Isaiah, but regard it as a collection of odd prophecies given at various times, which were then patched and pieced together by some general editor. They, of course, are ready to say, and do indeed say, that this paragraph should not be here at all, at this point, but that it belongs somewhere else. They say that it was a vision given to the prophet on some other occasion, but that unfortunately it was put in here and it interrupts the prayer.

Well, that, of course, is just to display a complete lack of spiritual insight, an appalling ignorance of the ways of God with his people. That is how such rationalistically-minded men, always miss the brightest glories of the Christian experience and the Christian life.

No, this is not an interpolation. This is one of the most characteristic actions of God with respect to his people. Here is the prophet in this desperate situation, exhorting and urging his people to join him in watching, and in prayer, for the position is indeed desperate. And God looks down upon them, and realises their weakness, and their desperate plight, and he grants them an encouragement. He just does something which enables them to continue in prayer and watching, and that is what we have in these six verses. This is a vision that was given to the prophet, a glimpse of the ultimate, in order that he might not faint nor falter, but that he might continue and enable his fellow-countrymen to continue to wage this great fight in the spiritual realm. In other words, it was given to encourage him, and to strengthen him. And this is one of the most typical actions of God with respect to his people. We have need of encouragement in the fight in which we are engaged. Indeed, we would not be able to continue at all were it not that God gives us these encouragements from time to time. Our hymnbooks are full of it.

> Sometimes a light surprises
> The Christian while he sings;
> It is the Lord who rises
> With healing in his wings:
> *W. Cowper*

He does it periodically. Suddenly there is a break in the clouds, and a flash, and a streak of sunlight. It is given by God in his graciousness, in order to encourage us, in order to help us to go forward. We are called upon to face the situation. It is dismal, it is dreary, it is trying, it is weary. And our tendency is to fail and to faint. In fact, we would all faint were it not that God sometimes does the very thing to us that he did at this point to the prophet Isaiah and to the Children of Israel.

What we have to realise, then is that there are certain things of which we must constantly remind ourselves. The Scriptures have been given, as we are told by the Apostle Paul, not only for an example, but also for our encouragement. He talks also about the consolation of the Scriptures. That is why the New Testament Church in her wisdom was led by the Holy Spirit to incorporate these Old Testament Scriptures with the New. It is the same God acting, and what he did then, he still does for us. This is how God still deals with his faithful people. And, therefore, I want to suggest that what we are going to look at now is the greatest possible encouragement to prayer and to intercession. And it is only as we grasp the meaning of this great picture, this vision that was given to the prophet, that we shall be able to continue in a way that is likely to lead to the blessing of a mighty visitation of the Spirit of God. This is God's way. First we have the problem, then the exhortation to prayer, and then, as we begin, just an encouragement, lest we become discouraged even before we have started.

So then as we look at this passage we see that it is a vision. The prophet was suddenly given a vision of someone coming up from Edom, and from Bozrah, which was the capital of Edom. He comes up, and he is marvellous to behold. But the thing that at once attracts the attention of the prophet is that his garments are stained with blood. Here comes someone who has obviously been engaged in a great fight, a great skirmish. And yet at once it is obvious to the prophet that he is a conqueror. He has been through a most bloody battle, and yet he has triumphed, and here he is bespattered with blood, coming in the power of his might. What does this mean? What is the message that is here for God's people?

There is really very little difficulty about this. You notice that Revelation 19 is a most amazing commentary upon all this, and there are other places, too, in the Scriptures that refer to the same thing. Edom is always used in the Bible to signify and to represent the powers that are opposed to God and his people. Edom comes originally from Esau. So, if you like, you can see this as a picture of the contrast between Jacob and Esau. Esau is the profane man, the man who does not get the birthright, the man who values a mess of pottage, other things, more than a birthright – the worldly outlook, everything that is opposed to God and to the things of the Spirit. Now as you read your Scriptures keep your eye on this word Edom, and the references to the Edomites, and you will always find that they stand in the scriptural typology for the enemies of God, the ultimate enemies of God, those who are set against God, and his glory, and his kingdom.

And so, as you read about them in the Scriptures, you will find that they stand for those who literally and actually oppose the Children of Israel. They did so as the Children of Israel were going to enter into the promised land of Canaan and they did so on many subsequent occasions after they had entered in. These people of Edom are the traditional enemy of God's Israel in the Old Testament. But, of course, it does not stop at that. The Edomites also represent the powers that were opposed to the Lord Jesus Christ. It does not matter who they belong to, or what nation they come from, symbolically this is Edom. All the forces and powers that were arrayed against the Son of God, that is spiritual Edom. And, in the same way, it represents the opposition and the enmity that was displayed against the early Church. The Church had not long come into being before persecution arose, and attempts were made, as you remember, to exterminate her. There is a great illustration of that in Acts chapter 12. But there are many others, many powers that gathered together to try to stifle and to kill the early Church.

And Edom also represents the power that has been opposing the Christian Church throughout the centuries. If we have seen nothing else during these past studies on this question of revival, I do trust that it has given us a sense of history. The Church is fighting for her life today but this is not the first time that she has done so. This has happened many a time before. Edom remains, Edom is always watching, ready to pounce upon us, ready to destroy. Edom, spiritual Edom, has been there, and oftentimes she has been highly successful, very triumphant, and the Church seems to have been moribund and almost dead. It is still the same today, and all the powers and the forces that are arrayed against us are typified by Edom: the kingdom of darkness, the kingdom of hell, the kingdom of the Devil, the kingdoms of this world. That is Edom. And I need not remind you of the whole situation in which we find ourselves. We are back, as we saw earlier, in

266

the same condition as obtained in this period in Isaiah's history, forsaken and desolate.

But finally, we must bear in mind that Edom also represents the forces that will gather together for the last, and the final, attempt to defeat God and his Christ, and the Christian, in a mighty battle, an Armageddon. That is Edom; all this power that hates God and would bring him down, mustering its unseen arrays for the final conflict. Edom!

So now you see the picture which has been painted here by the prophet in his vision. And in ages past, indeed throughout the centuries, when she has been fighting for her life, and has been faced with the fear of extinction, it has been the custom of the Church to refer to this passage, and it has often put new life into God's people. They had, perhaps, been praying for years, but nothing happened. The enemy seemed to be waxing stronger, and the Church's powers seemed to be waning, and men were beginning to wonder whether it was worthwhile going on any longer. Everything was going against them. Suddenly they come back to this, and they have seen the vision coming anew and afresh, and they have taken fresh heart, and they have gone on praying. May God grant that that will be the effect upon us of looking at this vision again. Are you faint and weak? Are you feeling discouraged? Are you feeling a sense of hopelessness with regard to the whole future of the Christian Church, and of God's cause? We know something about these hostile powers. We are constantly being told about them, in this country and in other countries. What can avail us? Is there any hope for us at all? When we begin to feel like that, there is nothing more important than that we should keep our eyes open, that we should be watchmen upon the walls, keeping our eye upon the horizon, and on the distant hills. Is there any hope? There is none here, so let us look into the distance. Here we are in our desperate position. We have organised our forces, we are praying, we are watching, and yet, we wonder how anything can save us, when suddenly somebody cries out, 'Who is this? Who is this, that cometh from Edom, with dyed garments from Bozrah?' And immediately there is a new hope. Into the midst of the darkness and the despair, and the hopelessness, this person suddenly appears. 'Who is this?' And so the story proceeds.

And that is what we have to do at this point. We simply have to remind ourselves of this blessed person, the only hope, the last hope, yes, but the certain hope. 'Who is this . . . ?' Let us look at him together. Let us stop looking at the world around us, and let us look at him. This is what the Church needs to do – to lift up her head to look at him. 'Who is this . . . ?' Let us stop looking at Communism. Let us stop looking at materialism, and science, and all the things about which we hear so much, and about which we talk so much. Let us turn away from them. 'Who is this . . . ?' Here is the hope for the Church. Here is the way to be encouraged in prayer, and in intercession. You know, my friends, our trouble is due to the fact that we are looking so much at these other things, that we have forgotten the truth about him. And hence our excitement, and our feverishness, and our sense of despair and of hopelessness. Our business, I repeat, is to look at him. And what do we see?

The first thing that strikes the prophet is the glory of his person. 'This that is glorious in his apparel, travelling in the greatness of his strength?' Here is the point at which we must ever start. The word translated 'travelling' really means 'stately': 'glorious in his apparel, stately in the greatness of his strength?' What a personage? Look closely at him. Who is this? 'Come,' cries the prophet, 'you despondent, discouraged people. Come and have a look at this person. Who is this?' And they stand back in amazement at the sight of his glory, his stateliness, his dignity, his majesty, his power. Here is a deliverer coming up out of Edom. There has been a great fight and he has conquered. Who is he? Here is the only hope for the Church – to behold him.

But who is this so weak and lowly? Who is this who works as a carpenter? Who is this who lies asleep in the stern of a ship, who is hungry and is thirsty? Who is this who is arrested, and tried, and condemned, and put to death in apparent weakness, who expires upon a cross, and is buried in a grave? Who is this? Thank God we know the answer – the King of glory, the Son of God! My dear friends, that is the whole of Christianity. In every situation this is the thing that we must hold on to and ever look to. Our Saviour is the Son of God, none other.

Of course, that is the great theme of this prophet. When he turns to this aspect of his prophecy in chapter 40, he introduces it immediately by putting it in these words.

The voice of him that crieth in the wilderness, 'Prepare ye the way of the Lord, make straight in the desert a highway. . . .'
For whom? . . . for our God. Every valley shall be exalted, and every mountain and hill shall be made low: and the crooked shall be made straight, and the rough places plain: and the glory

*of the Lord shall be revealed, and all flesh shall see it together:
for the mouth of the Lord hath spoken it.*

It is this mighty, glorious, person, none other than the eternal, everlasting, Son of God.

The prophets, and the Psalmists in their prophetic moments, all saw this. In the depths of Israel's despair, and hopelessness, a Psalmist cries out, 'He has laid help on one that is mighty' (Ps. 89.19). 'What are you looking at?' they say. 'Why do you only look at your enemies? Look at him, he hath laid help upon one that is mighty.' What is our hope today? It is this: 'Great is the mystery of godliness: God was manifest in the flesh' (1 Tim. 3. 16). We look out upon the world. We remember that the Psalmist, in the 8th Psalm, talks about the heavens and the moon, and the sun, and the stars, and says, 'What is man? . . . thou hast put all things under his feet.'

But we look around and we say, 'We do not see them put under man.'

'You say the Christian Church is the Church of God, but look at her position,' says somebody. Attacked by the Edomites, defeated by her enemies, struggling to keep going, resorting to this and that. We feel that everything is against us, that we are desolate and forsaken. We do not see all things subdued unto us.

'No,' replies the author of the epistle to the Hebrews, 'But we see Jesus . . . crowned with glory and honour' (Heb. 2. 9). That is the answer. And because we see that, he says, 'We see everything.' Let them despoil us of our goods, let them put us to death, let them massacre us, let them do what they will. We see Jesus, and because he is there, we are going to be there. He is the anchor within the veil. We see Jesus crowned with glory and honour. And it is only the Christian people, who can see him crowned with glory and honour, who are confident and assured and who can go on with their prayers and with their intercessions. 'Who is this . . . ?' It is the King of glory; it is the almighty Son of God. We are not left to ourselves, he is on our side, he is amongst us, he is in the camp.

We must now go on to consider the other things that we are told about him, but there is the point at which we must always start. If I believed, as some do, that Jesus of Nazareth was only a man, and not the everlasting Son of God, and that our only hope was that we had got his teaching, and that we must strive to put it into practice, I would, of all men, be the most hopeless, and the most pessimistic. I would say, 'Let us shut down the

Church. We are done for. It is the end.' But he is the everlasting Son of God. He is the King, the eternal, immortal, invisible, God, in the glory of his apparel, in the dignity and the stateliness and the greatness of his strength.

Then we go on to read about his righteousness. He answers himself. The prophet says, 'Who is this . . . ?' He replies, 'I that speak in righteousness.' Here is his great characteristic. He is the King of righteousness. The world is full of lies and deceit, and vanity, and sham. But God is just and holy, and God made a perfect and righteous world. Then sin and unrighteousness came in. And the Lord is concerned about righteousness. It is the passion of his life. He came into this world because of righteousness. He is described as the branch of righteousness, the righteous branch (Jer. 33. 15). That is why he came. Sin is disorder and unrighteousness, sin is lawlessness, and rebellion. And God is righteous, and the whole object of this Person coming to this world is to bring righteousness back. That is why he taught as he did, that is why he died as he did: 'Whom God hath set forth to be a propitiation . . . that he might be just' – righteous – 'and the justifier of him which believeth in Jesus' (Rom. 3. 25–26). The whole object of salvation is the restoration of righteousness, righteousness in earth, as well as the righteousness that is in heaven. His object is to produce a state in which peace shall be like a river, and righteousness as the waves of the sea. 'I speak in righteousness, this is my dealing, this is my conversation, this is my way of thinking, everything is concerned with righteousness.'

He is the truth; he is the life. Yes, it means that, but I think it means something else too, which is very comforting. And it is this. He speaks righteousness, which means that there is no equivocation in his speech, there is no uncertainty. He has given a promise, he has outlined his proposal, He has indicated his plan, and he says to his trembling, frightened people, 'I speak in righteousness.' What he has promised, he will most surely perform. 'For His mercies aye endure, ever faithful ever sure.' One of the designations applied to him, you remember, in the book of Revelation, is 'faithful'. He is not only righteous, he is faithful. And, discouraged people, remember that. Whatever may be happening round and about you, he has promised, he has said, and he will most surely perform: 'I speak in righteousness.'

But there is more. I am trying to give a composite picture here. We could spend our time on any one of these descriptions of him, but I want to mention another thing which he repeats. You notice that there is a repetition of anger and of fury. The prophet asks,

'Wherefore art thou red in thine apparel, and thy garments like him that treadeth in the winefat?'

The answer is, 'I have trodden the winepress alone; and of the people there was none with me: for I will tread them in mine anger, and trample them in my fury; and their blood shall be sprinkled upon my garments, and I will stain all my raiment. For the day of vengeance is in mine heart, and the year of my redeemed is come' (vv. 3–4). And again, 'I will tread down the people in mine anger, and make them drunk in my fury, and I will bring down their strength to the earth' (v.6). There is nothing more comforting than that. Do we realise what it means? It means, and this is our comfort and our hope today, that his anger, and his fury, are against the Edomites. He said, 'There was none to help . . . therefore mine own arm brought salvation unto me; and my fury, it upheld me.' There he was, left alone to fight this terrible power, and he says, 'my fury, it upheld me.' Thank God for the fury. 'What does it mean?' asks someone. Let me put it in ordinary terms, like this: Righteousness and the glory of God are his passion. You know that is why he came from heaven. He came from heaven primarily to vindicate God's glory and God's honour, and not just to save us. Do not misunderstand me, but the great motive was the glory of God, which had been violated by the Devil and by sin. And Christ has come to re-establish, as it were, the glory and the honour of God. He is furious against evil. His anger is roused against the enemies of his holy and righteous Father. He was consumed by a zeal for God's house. Did he not say so? 'The zeal of thine house hath eaten me up' (John 2. 17).

I know of nothing more comforting than that. We see something of the might and the fury of the enemies of God, of modern Edom. What can be done about it? Can you and I organise a way of quelling it and controlling it? We are patently failing. Things are going from bad to worse in spite of all our efforts. Is evil to triumph over all, can nothing be done with the forces of hell? Here is my only comfort. See the blessed Son of God, he hates it all with a divine and a holy hatred. His wrath is upon it. His fury is against it. And he is determined to crush it and to quell it and to destroy it, that God's name and glory may reign over all, and his people may be redeemed.

Then the next thing he emphasises is his conquest. Though stained with blood, and bespattered in this way, as if he had been treading down vines in a winefat, in a winepress, he has triumphed, he has slaughtered them, he has destroyed them and

271

he has crushed them. And another emphasis is upon the fact that he has done it alone: 'I have trodden the winepress alone; and of the people there was none with me. . . . And I looked, and there was none to help; and I wondered that there was none to uphold.' He trod the winepress alone. And we must emphasise this for a moment, because it is the great, central fact about Christian salvation. It is the great theme of the Bible from beginning to end, that the work of salvation is entirely, and only, and exclusively, the work of the Lord Jesus Christ. Nobody had a share in it. There was nobody with him. All that has been done, He has done it alone. The first prophecy in the Bible tells us that the seed of the woman shall bruise the serpent's head (Gen. 3. 15). And it is this one person. The Apostle Paul, in Galatians 3. 16, goes out of his way to emphasise this point. He says, 'Now to Abraham and his seed were the promises made. He saith not, And to seeds, as of many; but as of one, And to thy seed, which is Christ.' Yes, there came a point at which the people of God came down to one person and it was this blessed person, who has taken unto him the seed of Abraham, and not the nature of angels. He and he alone became our representative in the fight. And how often he referred to that. How often he was lonely. 'And every man went unto his own house,' I read at the end of John chapter 7, and the next sentence is, 'Jesus went unto the Mount of Olives.' Why? Well, he had no house. The lonely Jesus, alone.

You remember him, towards the end, saying to these disciples of his who were protesting their loyalty: 'The time is coming when every man shall leave me, and forsake me, and I shall be left alone' (see John 16. 32). And again, in that terrible moment of agony in the garden of Gethesamene, he selects Peter, and James, and John out of the twelve, takes them apart, and leaves them and goes on alone. There they were; he asks them to remember him, and to pray, he wants them to watch with him. They sleep. He goes on, and he is alone in his agony. Alone, facing this ultimate question, the drinking of the cup. 'If it be possible, let it pass by from me, nevertheless not as I will, but as thou wilt' (Matt. 26. 39). Alone, with no one to help, he takes the cup. Alone, for we read, 'Then all the disciples forsook him, and fled.' Peter denied him. The bold, impulsive, self-confident, Peter, who protested that he would go with him through hell. They all forsook him, and fled. He trod the winepress alone. He died alone. He took upon himself, upon his own shoulders, the sins of the world, alone.

And it even continues afterwards, for we read this in Revelation

5. John is given his vision of a scroll with the seals of history, the scroll of history.

And I saw a strong angel proclaiming with a loud voice, 'Who is worthy to open the book, and to loose the seals thereof?' And no man in heaven, nor in earth, neither under the earth, was able to open the book. Neither to look thereon. And I wept much, because no man was found worthy to open and to read the book, neither to look thereon. [No man.] And one of the elders saith unto me, Weep not: behold, the Lion of the tribe of Juda, the Root of David, hath prevailed to open the book. . . .'

When no one else in heaven or earth can do it, One can. 'I have trodden the winepress alone.' And he alone is the Lord of history, and can open the book, and clear away the seals. Salvation is altogether, and entirely, and exclusively in the Lord Jesus Christ. Do not bring a scrap, or a shred, of your righteousness which is as filthy rags anywhere near him. He that glorieth, let him glory in the Lord. Do not talk about your goodness, and your efforts, it is all in him. Thank God it is. 'I have trodden the winepress alone' He can do it alone, he has done it alone. What has he done? In the Old Testament he conquered the enemies of Israel. He was the angel that was with the Church, says Stephen in his great sermon. He was the one who appeared to Moses in the burning bush. He was the captain of the Lord's hosts that appeared to Joshua, outside Jericho at that moment of crisis. He, the Lord of hosts, the captain of the armies of Israel, the same person.

And so we could go on in the Old Testament looking at him and considering what he has done. But let us now come to the Cross. What was happening there? A great fight was going on, a great battle. All the powers of hell were out against him. 'But this is what happened,' Paul tells us, in Colossians 2:15: 'And having spoiled principalities and powers, he made a shew of them openly, triumphing over them in it.' In his death. They thought they had finished him. They mustered their last reserves, the fight was on. The Edomites brought out their last reserves, but he conquered them, he smashed them, he put them to an open shame, triumphing over them, he did it alone. No one helped him. No one was able to assist him. He, through his lone and solitary death, destroyed him that had the power of death, that is the Devil.

Then finally, let us look at him, there, dying on the Cross. He

273

expires, they take down his body, and they put it in a grave. They roll a stone over the entrance to it, they seal it, and the soldiers are set to watch and to guard. There he lies, he is finished. But wait a moment. What is this, I see? Who is this that I see suddenly standing there upon the shore in the morning after Peter and the others had been fishing all night and had caught nothing? There is somebody on the beach. Who is this?

The grave is empty. The believers have met together in a closed room, because of their fear of the Jews. Suddenly someone stands amongst them. Who is this? It is the same person. He has even triumphed over death, and the grave. He has brought life and immortality to light. He can look at death, and the grave, and so can we, and say, 'Oh death, where is thy sting? Oh grave, where is thy victory?' (1 Cor. 15. 55).

> Look, ye saints: the sight is glorious:
> See the man of Sorrows now,
> From the fight returned victorious:
> Every knee to Him shall bow.
>
> *T. Kelly*

Have you seen him? Look, you saints, lift up your heads, look at him. Who is this? It is the King of glory. 'Lift up your heads, O ye gates, and be ye lift up, ye everlasting doors; and the King of glory shall come in' (Ps. 24. 7). Oh, the glorious, royal, eternal, reception of heaven. That is what he has done.

And throughout the story of the Church, throughout the centuries, he has been doing the same thing. The Church has been dying, she has seemed to be finished. Suddenly, he appears, and his enemies are scattered and the Church is revived. That is what is meant by revival: times of refreshing from the presence of the Lord. That is what revival means: that the Church has another glimpse of the vision. The Church sees him, and, seeing him, can smile, and laugh, at all her enemies. Revival is always his work. He always treads the winepress alone. Of course, he uses men, but you must not give the praise to men. No matter who they are, whether they be Calvin, Luther, Wesley, Whitefield, or anybody else. He treads the winepress alone. It is when he arises with healing in His wings, that the enemy is defeated, and the Church is revived. It is always he, and he alone. And revival is to see him in his glory, to turn to him, and to pray to him.

That is revival, but wait a minute. There is a great and a mighty day coming. A day that surpasses in glory, and in amazement, anything that we can even imagine. There is a day coming when there will be a sight of One coming on the clouds of heaven, riding upon them, surrounded by his holy angels. And the peoples will cry, 'Who is this that is coming?' And the answer is the same. This majestic person, that is glorious in his apparel, travelling in the greatness of his strength, is the King of kings, the Lord or lords, coming for the final battle, the ultimate defeat of all that belongs to hell. It is all there in Revelation 19. 'And he was clothed with a vesture dipped in blood: and his name is called The Word of God. . . . He shall rule them with a rod of iron; and he treadeth the winepress of the fierceness and wrath, of Almighty God,' (vv. 13, 15). He is the King of kings, and Lord of lords. And he is come to destroy for ever, every enemy, and everything that is opposed to Him: 'And I saw the beast, and the kings of the earth, and their armies,' yes, all the empires of this world. All the 'isms' – Communism, materialism, scientificism, and all the rest. The Apostle John saw them all:

And their armies gathered together to make war against him that sat on the horse, and against his army. And the beast was taken, and with him the false prophet that wrought miracles before him, with which he deceived them that had received the mark of the beast, and them that worshipped his image. These both were cast alive into a lake of fire burning with brimstone. And the remnant were slain with the sword of him that sat upon the horse, which sword proceeded out of his mouth: and all the fowls were filled with their flesh.

Do you believe that that is to come? It is coming. We live in the hope of that.

This is the essence of Christianity. He is coming. Are you frightened by these present enemies and foes? He will destroy them by the word of his mouth, and by the brightness, and the glory of his coming. The horror that seems to be let loose upon the earth today is itself going to be destroyed completely, until there shall not be even a vestige left behind. He will come to do it. The Christ who came as a babe at Bethlehem, the carpenter, the son of Mary, will come in his glory and his full majesty. And the whole world, every eye, shall see him, yea, even those that smote him and pierced him. And the kings and all the great ones of the world will be humbled and defeated. 'The crowning day is coming by and by.' Christian people, have you seen him? Have you been amazed by him? Have you cried in astonishment, 'Who is this? Who is this that has saved me? Who is this that guarantees my eternity? Who is the Lord of the Church?' And do you know the answer? There is nothing more wonderful than this, to be a citizen in such a kingdom, to belong to such a Saviour.

> Glorious things of thee are spoken,
> Zion city of our God;
> He Whose Word can not be broken,
> Formed thee for His own abode.'
> On the Rock of Ages founded,
> What can shake thy sure repose?
> With Salvation's walls surrounded,
> Thou mayest smile at all thy foes.
>
> *J. Newton*

Look at them again and look at them with contempt. Smile upon them, laugh at them. Even the Devil, resist him in the name of Christ, and he will flee from you. What a privilege to belong to such a king. What a joy and comfort and encouragement to know that his victory is assured, that his triumph will be complete.

So, as we find ourselves today, let us look to him, let us plead with him, let us ask him to give us a visitation, just a sample of what he is going to do, an encouragement in the meantime. Let us ask him to arise and to blow upon these enemies and to lift us up again, and make us mighty in his strength and power. What a privilege to be able to do so. Is there anything, on the other hand, more terrible, or more appalling than *not* to belong to him? Oh, the tragedy of men and women who belong to the world, and not to Christ and his kingdom. Is this true of you – you who live for the world, and whose hearts are ravished by it, and who delight in it, and who apologise for your Christianity; you whose heart is with the world, and not with this Christ? Do you know that if you die like that, a day will come when you will be trampled under his feet, as grapes in the winepress, and destroyed from the glory of his presence, and the enjoyment of his blessed company?

Christian people, that is going to be the fate of all unbelievers. Does that not press upon your heart, and mind, and spirit? Does it not alarm you? Do you not pray for them? Do you not ask for God to empower his servants? Do you not pray for revival? They are going to hell, they are going to be crushed beneath his feet. Do you not think it is about time we began to feel the burden of their souls upon our spirits? Do you not think we should be praying without ceasing, asking him to give power unto his gospel, to visit us, and to revive us, and to give us this might, and this irresistible authority, that they might be saved from the wrath to come – yes, from the wrath of the Lamb, the 'Lamb of God, that taketh away the sins of the world'?

There is the encouragement that was given to the prophet. Thank God, it is given to us still. Have you seen him? Have you asked, do you now ask, 'Who is this?' My Lord. My God. My Saviour. My Redeemer. My all in all.

Chapter 22

Isaiah 63.7

I will mention the lovingkindnesses of the Lord, and the praises of the Lord, according to all that the Lord hath bestowed on us, and the great goodness toward the house of Israel, which he hath bestowed on them according to his mercies, and according to the multitude of his lovingkindnesses (Isa. 63.7).

In our consideration of the first six verses of this chapter, we saw how Isaiah was greatly encouraged by God through a vision. He then proceeds to offer up his prayer, and it is this prayer that is to be the subject of our study now.

It begins at the seventh verse of the 63rd chapter, and it really goes on to the very end of chapter 64 and though obviously we cannot take it as a whole, we can take certain big sections. My concern is to hold the prophet's prayer before you, and merely to comment upon it, and to underline what I would call its leading principles. And I do this because I feel that it is necessary that we all should be instructed on how we pray. It is a very easy thing to say, 'Let us pray.' But the Bible, in the accounts which it gives of various prayers, and of the whole method of prayer, makes it perfectly clear that we need instruction, lest we indulge in mere vain repetitions, and lest we fail to pray with the understanding, as well as with the heart. You will always find in these prayers recorded in the Bible, that there is always a scheme and a system. The prayers do not just ramble on from point to point without any sequence or any connection. There is a definite arrangement and order, and as these prayers prove to be so effectual and efficacious, surely there is nothing better for us than to study them, and to follow them, and to emulate their example?

Here, before us, we have a great, and a typical prayer offered by the Church in a period of declension. Indeed, we might say that it is a great prayer for revival, a prayer to God to look down from heaven and to visit his people once more. And, as we follow the method of the prophet, we observe that the first thing he does is to remind himself of the character of God. And not only that, he also reminds God of that. That is the great burden of the verse 7.

'I will mention,' he says, 'the lovingkindnesses of the Lord, and the praises of the Lord, according to all that the Lord hath bestowed on us, and the great goodness toward the house of Israel, which he hath bestowed on them according to his mercies, and according to the multitude of his lovingkindnesses.' That is a great and a comprehensive statement. He is starting with the character of God. And that is ultimately the secret of all true prayer. Prayer must always begin with a realisation of God and of his character, otherwise it can be a mere attempt at discovering some kind of psychological relief or ease. Prayer can just be the offering up of pious hopes and aspirations, the mere expression of our fears. If prayer is to be real, surely the first thing we have to do is to realise the One to whom we are speaking. That, surely, is obvious in every walk, and in every department, of life. To have an intelligent conversation, you must know something about the one to whom you are speaking. You must know something about his background, about his knowledge and the things he is interested in, and it is exactly the same in prayer. Prayer is personal communion with the living God. And there is nothing more important than that we should remind ourselves of God's glorious character – and the prophet does that.

We must notice, too, of course, the way in which he does not put these things in the singular, but in the plural: 'lovingkindnesses', 'praises', he says, 'great goodness . . . mercies . . . multitude of his lovingkindnesses.' He repeats the lovingkindnesses, you notice, and in doing that he reminds himself of the abundance of these characteristics in God. God is one who is full of lovingkindness, full of compassion, full of goodness, full of mercy – 'the multitude of his lovingkindnesses'. How good is God. That is what he is reminding himself of, you can see the value of doing this, especially in the circumstances in which the prophet was praying. The need was desperate, the people of God seemed to have been abandoned. Many of them were given to grumbling and to complaining. So, the prophet realises that the first thing he must do is to be perfectly certain about God, as if to say, 'Whatever the explanation is of our present state and condition, it is not God. God,' he says, 'I know to be full of these lovingkindnesses, and goodness, and mercies, and compassions, and praises.'

And you and I must ever learn to pray in this way, whether it is an individual prayer or whether it is a prayer on behalf of the

Church. If we go into the presence of God with any doubt in our minds as to his goodness, there is very little point or purpose in our praying. When the Devil comes and suggests that God is against us and that God does not care and so on, then the first thing to do is to clear our minds and to get rid of any doubt or uncertainity about the being, and the character of God. You remember how the Apostle Paul puts it. He says, 'Be careful for nothing.' Well, how are you to avoid this anxious care, and burdened anxiety? He says, 'Be careful for nothing, but in every thing by prayer and supplication with thanksgiving . . .' – thanksgiving! – ' . . . let your requests be made known unto God' (Phil. 4. 6). We may find ourselves in very trying circumstances, everything may seem to be against us. We are beginning to wonder and to doubt, perhaps, whether God is really concerned about us, and we are beginning to query and to question his promises. The first thing we must do is to get our thinking clear, and straight. If there is any such lingering doubt in our mind and heart about the character of God, our prayer is already useless. Start like the prophet, 'I will mention the lovingkindnesses of the Lord.' 'The Lord is good to all: and his tender mercies are over all his works' (Ps. 145. 9). There is no doubt about that. That is God's character, and it is eternal, and it is unchangeable. He is everlastingly a God of lovingkindnesses, of mercies, of goodness, and compassion. And as the prophet starts with the lovingkindnesses, he repeats it at the end of the statement: ' . . . according to the multitude of his lovingkindnesses.' Whatever may be the explanation of our individual condition, or of the state of the Church in general at the present hour, it is not to be found in any lack of lovingkindness, or mercy, or compassion in God, our heavenly Father.

That then is the point at which the prophet starts. And if we are not clear about this, there is no point in proceeding. If we have any criticism of God in our mind or heart, we must stop praying. It is an insult. If we feel that God is against us and unfair to us, I repeat, we must stop praying. There is no purpose in our going on another sentence. We start by worshipping God, by adoring him, by praising him, by ascribing unto him not only all might and majesty and dominion and power, but all the excellences of his holy nature, that he has been so graciously pleased to reveal to us. That must ever be our starting point.

Then you notice that having done that, the prophet proceeds to do something else. He elaborates this, and, therefore, this is something which we must consider in detail. Having reminded himself of the character of God, he makes a review of the history of the Children of Israel, and he does that at great length from verse 8 to verse 14. Now, here is something that I am most anxious to emphasise in connection with his method, because it is such a common method in the Scriptures. You see it in all the prophets, and you see it likewise in the book of Psalms. The Psalmist finds himself in difficulties, or he may find the Church as she then was, the nation of Israel, in trouble, surrounded by enemies, perhaps defeated. And in this situation they invariably look back to the past, as if to say to themselves, 'Well now then, why are we in this position? How have we come to this? Has this ever happened before?' And obviously to do that is the very essence of wisdom.

Let me put it like this: what we are dealing with here is not something theoretical, it is essentially historical. When we talk about praying to God, and the benefits of prayer, we are not in the realm of mere academic knowledge. We are remembering the dealings of God with his people. God's dealings with us today, yes, but we are reminded that we are not the first people to be in this world, we are not the only people to find ourselves in difficulties. Fortunately, we have this long record, the history of God's dealings with his people in past ages and centuries, going right away back to the beginning and origin of the human race. And there is nothing, surely, that is of more priceless value to us and to the Church in general than to be familiar with this very history. God does not merely give us teaching, he gives us history. He tells us what he is going to do with his people and for them, but he has not only done that, he has also given us a record of what he has done. And this is invaluable for the Church.

The prophet, therefore, begins to look back, and he says, 'Now, what is the relationship of Israel to God? Let me go back to the very origins to the beginning of this story.' And we must learn to do exactly the same thing. Take the way in which the Apostle Paul puts this. Referring to the history of the Children of Israel, in 1 Corinthians 10, he says, 'All these things happened unto them for ensamples: and they are written for our admonition, upon whom the ends of the world are come.' 'Why,' he asks in effect, 'have we got the history of the Children of Israel in the wilderness, and what happened to them, and all the rest of it? The purpose', he says, 'is that all this has been written for our example, for our help, for our aid. That is how God dealt with them, let us learn the lesson. God is still the same, and the principles of his dealings with mankind never vary. These things are written for our example. And we are studying this paragraph in Isaiah for precisely that reason.

But we can supplement that. We can not only go back to the Bible and look at the principles there enunciated of God's dealings with his people, we can also go back and look at the whole history of the Christian Church. And that brings the position much more nearly to our contemporary position. This is surely one of the first lessons that the Church needs to learn at this present time. The trouble is, of course, that we are so obsessed with ourselves, and with the twentieth century, that we fail to learn the lessons of history. And yet they are there for us, in great abundance and profusion. It is an odd thing to say, perhaps, but to me it is a great comfort that the Church of God in the past has often been in the same sort of condition that she is in today. And it is the people who forget that, who are most depressed at the present time. I mean the people who are always talking about our difficulties, about the radio and the television and about Communism. 'Ah,' they say, 'here' is the trouble.' As if nobody had ever had a problem before. Now the antidote to all that is to go back into the history of the Church. There is nothing new about the present position. The only thing that appears to be new is the particular forms in which the difficulty presents itself. But many and many a time the Church has been down in the depths, at the bottom of the trough, with Christian people beginning to think that the end was at hand. So let us go back and study the history. Let us follow the prophet as he does so.

This is how he begins: 'For he said, Surely they are my people, children that will not lie: so he was their Saviour.' He is reviewing the history of God's dealings with his own people, the Children of Israel, and what he sees above everything else is God's goodness to the people. He sees it in that it was God who called them, in that God said, 'Surely they are my people. . . .' How did they ever become his people? It was all God's doing. The nation of Israel came into being through God calling a man whose name was Abram, and changing his name into Abraham. It was God's action. It was God who called him out of Ur of the Chaldees. It was God who took him to the promised land. It was the action of God, the calling of the children of Abraham: 'They are my people.'

'Now that is the fundamental thing,' says the prophet, 'which we must grasp. We are not like the other nations of the world. We are in a special and in a peculiar relationship to God. We are his people.' And therefore, because he has called them, and he has started this work in them, he is their Saviour. That is the pronouncement. This word 'so' should not be here. 'He said,

Surely they are my people, children that will not lie: . . . he was their Saviour.' Not because they did not lie – because they did – but because he has called them, he is going to save them. They are his people, he has separated them unto himself, and they belong to him in this peculiar and extraordinary manner.

So this is the first thing which we must realise about the Church. The Church of God is not a human institution. She is not one among a number of institutions and societies, any more than Israel was just one among a number of nations in the ancient world. No, 'She is his new creation, by water and the word.' The Church is the people of God. The whole of the origin of the Church is the result of God's purpose. It is God who has made her and created her. It is he who calls us out of darkness into his most marvellous light. We have no being, we have no existence apart from our relationship to God.

Then he goes on to remind himself and the people, of God's dealings with them. 'In all their affliction he was afflicted, and the angel of his presence saved them: in his love and in his pity he redeemed them; and he bare them, and carried them all the days of old.' You see what he is doing? He says, 'Here are we, the Children of Israel, the Chaldeans have come and have conquered our city, and ruined it, and carried us away captive. Well, who are we? We are the people of God, to whom God gave these extraordinary, and marvellous, and wonderful things. Then he goes on to say that he will remind himself of the origin and of the beginning, of the times in the past when 'the angel of his presence saved them'. And we too should read again the story of the angel of the covenant who came and visited them and helped them, that is 'the angel of God's presence', undoubtedly a prefiguring of the Lord Jesus Christ, if indeed, it was not the Lord Jesus Christ himself actually appearing in that particular form.

Then there is this most tender statement: ' . . . and he bare them, and carried them all the days of old.' That was literally true. So you see the value of reminding ourselves of these things? 'We are like this now,' says the prophet, 'but, Oh, I think of the times, I go back to the times, when God was carrying his people.' As an eagle carries her young on her wings, so God carried his people, he carried them through the wilderness and in the desert, through the Sea and across the river. This is how God dealt with the people in times past. The goodness of God to his people!

And as the Christian Church looks back to her origin, she sees exactly the same thing. Read again the Acts of the Apostles and look at that handful of people with nothing to recommend them.

Why are they there at all? Why do we call them the Church? Well, it was the Lord who chose them. He called them, he set them in this position, he left his word with them. But look at them. Just a little handful of people with the whole world against them. The Jews against them, the leaders, the authorities, the Gentiles against them. The whole world was against them, yet look how God blessed them. See how God carried them. Look at his tender dealings with them. Look at the angel of his presence, the power of the Holy Spirit, and see that little Church, that helpless, defenceless band of people, see them triumphing, prevailing, conquering, going forward, with God in his love and in his pity leading them on, and giving them mighty victory.

Follow, too, the history of the Christian Church throughout the centuries, and you will find exactly the same thing. Does not the early history of the Protestant Reformation seem almost impossible? What can one man like Martin Luther do with all that was against him? What can these little bands of people conceivably achieve with such mighty opponents standing over and against them? But God carried them along. And that is what happens in all the great periods of revival that the Church has ever known. God carried them 'all the days of old'. There is nothing so thrilling as to go back to these stories, and to see the Church as she is being carried along by God, thrilled with the power and the might of his great authority, and his great goodness. There is the origin of God's people. There is the beginning. But what happened to them? Was the history of Israel always a history of blessing, and of being carried along by God's goodness? No, says the prophet. This is what happened. 'They rebelled, and vexed his holy Spirit: therefore he was turned to be their enemy, and he fought against them.'

Now, here again, is something that you find recurring as an almost endless theme in the writings of the Old Testament. This furious alternation in the history of the Children of Israel. They started well, but then you find them utterly downcast and almost destroyed. What was the matter? It was always the same story. It was because these Children of Israel who had been so called and so greatly blessed rebelled against God, and vexed, and grieved his holy Spirit. There they were, the special people of God, who were in this unique relationship to him. Though they had experienced these abundant blessings, we find that they began to feel envious of the other nations and their gods. They began to feel that the religion of the God of Israel was too narrow. 'These ten commandments,' they said, 'we are not allowed to eat what we like. We cannot marry whom we like. We cannot live seven days a week as we like.' They rebelled against God, and said, 'This religion is intolerable. This yoke is something we cannot bear.' So they turned to other gods, and they sinned against the God of Israel. Though he had revealed himself to them, and had given them his holy law in detail, so that there was no doubt about it, they rejected it all, turned their backs upon him, plunged into sin, imitated the other nations, took up their gods and their idols, and bowed before them, and worshipped them. That was their story. In spite of all that God had been to them, and had done for them, they thus deliberately rebelled against him, and grieved, and vexed his Holy Spirit.

And their story has been recorded for our example. The Children of Israel would have continued in a state of blessing if they had not rebelled, if they had not vexed and grieved the Holy Spirit of God. And when you see them down, that is always the explanation. They rebelled against God in belief and in practice. And here we come to the very nerve of our present position. Why is the Christian Church as she is today? Why is it that only ten per cent of the people of this country claim even a nominal relationship to Christianity, and only half of those do so with any regularity, and any constancy? Why are the places of worship in this land as they are today, in contrast with what they were, say, a hundred years ago? Think of a hundred years ago. Think of the size of the new churches built then. They had to replace the earlier buildings because they were not big enough. And at the same time Mr Spurgeon was attracting thousands south of the Thames to the Tabernacle. All places of worship in London were crammed full, and it was the same throughout the country. God was blessing. There was that great revival in 1859 affecting parts of the country. But before that, and in addition to that, God had been blessing the people. The great blessings of the revival of the eighteenth century were still continuing. Religion was flourishing, and the Church was in a dominant position. Even the statesmen had to pay attention to her. They talked about the Non-Conformist conscience, and the Non-Conformist vote, and they had to pay attention to what the Church said. The Church was flourishing, rejoicing in the blessings of God.

Why are things so different today? That is exactly the question confronting us. Why are we down? Why are we being carried away to Babylon? What has gone wrong? How has it come to pass that these people who were so great and so blessed have come down to this? It is the same question in principle as that

285

confronting that prophet. And, alas, the answer is still the same. When Israel, when the Church, is in trouble, and is desolate, and forsaken, it is always because of her own rebellion, her own grieving of the Holy Spirit of God. That is the only explanation. 'But they rebelled, and vexed his Holy Spirit'. And as the Children of Israel did that, so the Church of God has done that in the last hundred years. This is the only explanation. You notice that the prophet does not say that the trouble with Israel was that enemies had come and attacked them. 'No,' he says, 'that is not the explanation.' That had happened, of course, but that was not the reason. Read the writings of this prophet. Go through all the other prophets, and the Psalms, and you will find that they always say this and this alone. Whenever Israel is down and defeated, it is never because of the strength and the power of the enemy. No, because if they are right with God, it does not matter what the enemy is, however powerful, God will always make them victorious. That is never the explanation. Whenever Israel is defeated and is down, it is invariably, because of her own rebellion, her own folly, her own vexing, and grieving of the Holy Spirit of God.

And alas, my friends, that is the diagnosis today. Whether we like it or not, that is the real explanation. It is not because of these new enemies that have arisen against the Church. They are always there. It is not Communism, it is not the two World Wars, it is not the competition of the radio and the television, and the cinema. No, there has always been opposition to the people of God. These things are not variable, they are constants. What has happened is that the Church herself, in her unutterable folly, has rebelled against God, and grieved, and vexed his Holy Spirit, in exactly the same way as Israel did, in belief and in practice. The Children of Israel turned from God and his revelation. They turned to other gods and to their own notions and ideas. They deliberately set God on one side and made their own god. And that is precisely what the Church has done in the last hundred years. The only true explanation of the state of Christendom and the state of the Church today is that in the last century the Church herself deliberately rejected God's revelation, and put philosophy in its place.

It was the Church that did it, not the common people. The Church and her own leaders began to criticise this book, to set themselves up as authorities, to deny certain aspects of the teaching. They deny the God of the Old Testament, they do not believe in him, they say. They made a mere man out of the Lord of glory, they denied his virgin birth, they denied his miracles, they denied his atonement, they denied the person of the Holy Spirit, and they reduced this Bible to a book of ethics, and of morals. That is why the Church is as she is. The Church rebelled in her doctrine and in her belief. She set up the wisdom of men in the place of the wisdom of God. She became proud of her learning, and of her knowledge, and what she asked about her preachers and her servants was not any longer, 'Is he filled with the Spirit? Has he a living experience of God?' but, 'Is he cultivated? Is he cultured? What are his degrees?' Now, I am not romancing, am I? This is literal history. Man substituted his own notions and ideas for God's revelation, and God's teaching. It is an exact repetition of what the Children of Israel did.

Furthermore, of course, it was not only done in belief, and in teaching, it was done also in practice and in conduct, and in behaviour. People began to feel that the old evangelical way of living was too narrow. That was the word: 'narrowness'. They wanted a broader kind of outlook and a broader kind of life, so in belief, and in practice, they turned their backs upon God, and lived according to their own devices. And, of course, the enemy came in. The Church as a mere organisation can never compete with the world. She is beaten at the very beginning. It was pathetic to see how the Church tried to do it, how she tried to bring in things from the world. She introduced dramatics, and this and that and the other, but it has not worked. Of course not. The Church cannot do things like that, it is the world that can do things like that and do them so much better. The Church has only one source of strength, and that is the power of God, the power of his Holy Spirit. And when she turns against that, and rebels against it, she invariably finds herself beaten and defeated. And this is what happens, of course. Because she did that, God punished her. They rebelled and vexed His Holy Spirit, therefore he was turned to be their enemy, and fought against them.

Now we must be perfectly clear about that. This is literally true. I said at the beginning that God's character is unchangeable, yes, but absolutely true. And this is unchangeable, and also absolutely true. God warned the Children of Israel before he took them into the promised land. He said, 'If you will obey me, I will bless you' – on Mount Gerizim, the mount of blessing. 'On the other hand, if you disobey me, cursing, I will curse you' – on Mount Ebal, the mount of cursing. (See Deut. 11. 26–28.) He told them He would do it and he did it. He said, 'If you do not obey my laws, if you do not walk in unison with me, I will curse you.' And he cursed them, though they were his own people. In other words, having rebelled against him, these people began to discover that they were fighting against God. And that God not only did not bless them but he fought against them. There are endless examples of that in the Old Testament history. Who was it that raised up the Chaldean army to destroy Jerusalem? The Bible says it was God who did it. He raised up an enemy. Why? To chastise his own people. He temporarily, metaphorically, became their enemy in order to reduce them, and in order to subdue them. He did it repeatedly in this long Old Testament story.

And I have no hesitation in asserting that he has done the same thing many and many a time in the long history of the Christian Church. If the Church, in her cleverness, rebels against him, and vexes his Spirit, and turns her back on him, she must not assume that she is just going to be left to herself. No, God will raise enemies, and he will attack her, he will become an enemy to her, he will scourge her, he will humble her.

And I have no hesitation in asserting that we are witnessing that very thing today. The Church is still not humble, she still does not realise that she is the cause of her own troubles. She does not realise that it is her rebellion that has led to God's action. Is there any evidence of repentance for the devastating, higher critical movement of a century ago? Have they gone back on that? Have they admitted their error? No, they are still holding on to their results, though they see that it does not work, even by trying to add other things to it. There is no repentance. And so God raises enemies against the Church. He has always done it, and he will continue to do it. But, thank God, that is not the end of the story. What happened here? 'Then . . .' says the prophet, 'Then he [the nation of Israel] remembered the days of old, Moses, and his people, saying, 'Where is he that brought them up out of the sea with the shepherd of his flock? where is he that put his holy Spirit within him? that led them by the right hand of Moses with his glorious arm. . . .' This means that when God had chastised his people, had thus raised up enemies against them, to humble them, and to subdue them, in their utter defeat and hopelessness and despair, they suddenly came to themselves, and remembered Moses and the days of old, and the origin of their being.

There is a perfect counterpart to that in the New Testament which gives us the whole picture. It is the story of the prodigal son. He walked away from home, despising his father, with his pockets full of money. He knew what he was going to do so much better than his father, and away he went. Yes, and he went on in his wilful way until he found himself sitting in a field with the husks and the swine. There he suddenly came to himself, and said, 'What am I doing here? I am my father's son.' He thought of home, he thought of his father. Yes, but it took all that misery to make him think of his father. He had to be in rags, dishevelled, empty pockets, stomach empty, starving, dying, before he came to himself. But then, he remembered and he got up, and he went back to his father, and he went home.

My dear friends, that is what has always happened to the Church before she begins to experience revival. She has to come to herself, and remind herself of who she is and what she is, that she is the people of the living God, brought into being in this miraculous manner, and that she belongs to God. She comes to herself. And then she repents and begins to speak and to pray. And oh what a wonderful prayer this is! 'Then he remembered the days of old, Moses, and his people, saying, Where is he that brought them up out of the sea with the shepherd of his flock? Where is he that put his Holy Spirit within him?' That is the phrase: 'Where is he?' Where is the God that called Moses that afternoon when he was a shepherd, on the back side of the mountain. Where is he? Where is the God of Moses? Where is the God of Elijah? The God who does such marvellous things, where is he, that we should be like this? That was their prayer. They turned back, confessing their sins, and they saw God. They said, 'He is still the same God. We know he is there, but why are we like this?'

Let me repeat to you the particular petitions that they offered.

Where is he that brought them up out of the sea with the shepherd of his flock? where is he that put his holy Spirit within him? that led them by the right hand of Moses with his glorious arm, dividing the water before them, to make himself an everlasting name? that led them through the deep, as an horse in the wilderness, that they should not stumble? As a beast goeth down into the valley, the Spirit of the Lord caused him to rest: so didst thou lead thy people, to make thyself a glorious name.

'Oh,' they said, 'where is this God of power? Where is this God of deliverance? Where is this God with such teaching? Where is the God who leads, and guides? Where is the God who gives us rest? Where is the God of glory?' That is his nature, that is what he did. Where is he? We know that his power is still the same, we know that he can still give rest and glory to the Church. We

289

know that he can divide the sea, and divide the river, that he can give manna in the wilderness, that there is nothing impossible with him. There he is, and here we are, desolate, and forsaken. Where is he, the God who, when he arises, can scatter all the modern enemies, as he scattered the ancient enemies, and dismiss them with the breath of his mouth? Where is he?

Beloved people, that is the prayer of the Church, that is the only way of salvation. We look at our enemies, and in our folly we say, 'What can we do? What fresh organisation can we set up?'

'No,' says this man, 'when these people of old came to themselves, I find that this is what they did. They said, "Oh, if only we could find him. He is there, he is somewhere with all his inimitable power. But the question is, where is He?" So they set themselves to seek the Lord, and to seek his face.'

'Now,' says the prophet, 'that is what we must do.' And so he begins to do it in verse 15 by praying, 'Look down from heaven. . . .' This God, he is there. Let us seek him. Let us drop everything else. Let us concentrate on finding him and seeking his face. Let us be urgent. Where is he, the God of Moses, the God that filled them with his Spirit, that led them, that conquered their enemies, divided the sea, and led them into the promised land? Nothing matters but that we should find him.

'Yes,' said the prodigal, 'I will arise and go to my father, and I will say unto him, Father, I have sinned against heaven, and before thee, and am no more worthy to be called thy son: make me as one of thy hired servants.' That is the prayer. In utter humility, seeing our rebellion and our folly, our foolish pride and our shame, let us arise and go to our Father. And the moment we find him, we shall find that he is still full of lovingkindnesses and mercies, and compassion, and love, and mercy, and all we need. His power is undiminished. When he looks upon us, and blesses us again, we shall become his people, and our enemies shall be scattered, and Zion shall again be filled with the glory of the Lord. Where is he? Is that the cry of your heart? I see no hope for the Church until her people are filled with this cry. Nothing matters but to know him, and be in the right relationship to him.

Chapter 23

Isaiah 63.15–19

Look down from heaven, and behold from the habitation of thy holiness and of thy glory: where is thy zeal and thy strength, the sounding of thy bowels and of thy mercies toward me? are they restrained? Doubtless thou art our father, though Abraham be ignorant of us, and Israel acknowledge us not: thou, O Lord, art our father, our redeemer; thy name is from everlasting. O Lord, why hast thou made us to err from thy ways, and hardened our heart from thy fear? Return for thy servants' sake, the tribes of thine inheritance. The people of thy holiness have possessed it but a little while: our adversaries have trodden down thy sanctuary. We are thine: thou never barest rule over them; they were not called by thy name (Isa. 63. 15–19).

We now come to a particularly interesting point in our consideration of this great prayer of the prophet Isaiah, which is recorded in this chapter, and in chapter 64.

Fortified with all the knowledge of the history of the children of Israel, which we were considering in the last study, the prophet now proceeds with his prayer. He realises, obviously, that the only thing to do is to repeat what had always been done by the Children of Israel at such times. And what we have to consider now, is the beginning of this prayer of the prophet, and of the nation. Realizing, first of all, that they are where they are because of their own folly and rebellion, they turned back to God in penitence and in contrition, and the prayer really begins here, at verse 15, and goes on, right to the end of chapter 64. So, we must now consider the first section, which is to be found here in these verses at the end of chapter 63.

As we look at this prayer, we must realise that this is the only hope for us, too, at this present hour because our position today, our predicament, is almost exactly like that of the children of Israel when they had been carried captive to Babylon, and like that of the Church during her subsequent periods of disobedience.

As we realise that, we must see that our only hope lies in praying this kind of prayer.

Now before we come to look at the particular petitions, it is essential that we should be clear about the mode, or what I would describe as the general characteristics, of the prayer. And as we look at it, the first thing that strikes us is the urgency, the importunity. There is nothing half-hearted about this prayer, nothing slack or vague. No, the man's whole soul is moved to its very depths. And he is urgent, because he realises the position. Here are God's people with their cities sacked and ruined, and the sanctuary desecrated. The prophet gives his description of it, and then he pleads with God because the matter is urgent. We have already considered this, but we must never forget this note of urgency. And, of course, we can only remember it as we realise something of the serious condition in which we find ourselves. To me, it is astonishing that, as God's people, we can be so much at ease in Zion, when we see the state of the Church and the state of the world round and about us. I am not only thinking of armaments and bombs, I am thinking of industrial unrest and the selfishness that is so obvious in every walk of life, and in every rank of society. Lawlessness, self-seeking – there is only one cure for this kind of thing, and that is that men and women should begin to realise again who and what they are, and their subservience to God. We all need to be humbled before God, before a final disaster overtakes us. And it is only as we realise this that we shall begin to pray with the urgency and the importunity that characterises the prayer of the prophet.

Then, notice his strong emotion. You see this in the very way in which the man prays. There is a kind of form to his prayer, and yet there is a sense in which it has no form. There is an alternation here between confession and pleading. And that is always a sign of strong emotion. A man who is experiencing a strong emotion is not over-punctilious about form, and about diction, and about arrangement. No, he is so moved that he does not take time to think in an orderly way in a sense, he just utters the controlling feeling of the moment. And that is what we have in this prayer. The prophet does not, first of all, gather his petitions and pleas together, and then give his reasons and so on. No, the man's heart is too profoundly moved, for he is in the grip of a strong emotion, and so he prays from the depth of his heart. And whenever the Church is in a state of revival, you find the same thing. Whenever the Spirit of God comes down upon the Church, forms are forgotten, liturgies are put into abeyance, and the Spirit moves in men's hearts. And out of the hearts of praying people come their expressions of worship, their pleas, and their petitions – exactly what you have here, and in every other great prayer in the Bible.

And then the next element is that of pleading, the element of reasoning with God. Indeed, I can use a stronger term, the very element of wrestling with God. Have you noticed it here in the way in which he plies his arguments? He says, 'Thou, O Lord, art our father. . . . O Lord, why hast thou made us to err from thy ways . . . ?' And so on. And not only that, we can see here, too, an element of boldness. There is almost an element of daring here as we have seen in considering the prayer of Moses. You will always find this in every great prayer of intercession, the one praying pleads with God, he reasons with God. Hear this man doing it. He says, 'Why hast thou made us to err. . . . The people of thy holiness have possessed it [the land] but a little while: our adversaries have trodden down thy sanctuary. We are thine: thou never barest rule over them; they were not called by thy name.' He is arguing, he is reasoning, he is pleading and wrestling with God. This is a very wonderful element of all true intercession. There is a paradoxical element about it. The prophet is very conscious of his unworthiness and the unworthiness of the people, and yet, in spite of that, he is aware of something that makes him feel that he has a right to plead with God, to reason, and to argue, and, as it were, wrestle with God, and to say, 'I will not let thee go', O Lord, you can not refuse us.

Now that, it seems to me, is the real key to the understanding of this particular prayer, and I would put it therefore, in the form of a principle. There is an apparent problem for us here. Here is a man pleading for a nation that has rebelled, and has sinned against God, and which God has punished. He is deeply aware of this sinfulness and the shame of it all, and yet he prays with this holy boldness. And the explanation is that he is aware of a certain relationship to God, which in spite of all his unworthiness makes him feel that he has a right to go into the presence of God to reason, and to plead with passion. The principle involved, then, is that, in the last analysis, our only hope is our understanding of the doctrine, the truth of our relationship to God. Great prayer is always the outcome of great understanding. Deep knowledge is always based upon a grasp of the truth. You can get a very superficial and glib kind of praying which may at first sight seem wonderful, but when trials come, it seems to lose its way. The glib phrases seem rather empty, they die upon the lips. It is when a man is in the furnace of affliction, it is then, indeed, that he falls back upon certain fundamental truths of which he is absolutely sure and certain. The key to great praying is a deep knowledge and grasp of the doctrines of grace.

Now that is not simply my assertion, the Bible is full of it, and if you read the story of the Church throughout the centuries you will find it exemplified time and time again. The men who can stand in the furnace of affliction are the men who have got a rock beneath their feet, and the rock is the holy Scripture and its blessed doctrine.

Let us see all this working out in practice. We have considered the great characteristics of this man's prayer, so now we must look at his actual petitions. And the first great petition, of course, is in these pregnant words, 'Look down . . . behold.' There it is in verse 15: 'Look down from heaven, and behold from the habitation of thy holiness and of thy glory.' This, of course, is the first thing which we must realise – here is the first great need. Israel is defeated. The great bulk of the people are carried away, and are captives and slaves in Babylon. The Temple, the great city of David, lies in ruins. The great city of God lies a heap of rubble. How has this ever come to pass? What has gone wrong? I need not translate all that into modern language for you, but that is the picture of the modern Church. Let us make no mistake about that. The Church of God is down, she is, in a sense, a ruin. And the enemy is triumphant and laughing at us.

So what is the matter? What is the supreme need? According to this man, there is no doubt about the answer, and we find the same thing in the Psalms – it is the same everywhere in these great prayers in the Bible. The need is the presence of God, the face of God. He seems to have turned his back upon us, he is not looking upon us, he is turning away. I do not hesitate to use these terms. The term 'father' is used in verse 16, God is our Father, and God treats us, his children, as we treat our children. The little child has been doing something that he should not do, and then he comes to you, and what do you do? You do not look at him, you turn away from him. And he holds on to you, and he just wants you to look at him. The thing he can not bear is that you are not looking at him. And he pulls at you, and he pleads with you, he wants to see your face. And that is exactly what this prophet is doing here in his prayer. 'Look down,' he says. 'Look at us. Oh God, why do you turn your face away? Why do you avert your face? Why is your back turned towards us? Why are

you like a traveller, a stranger, going away from us? Look down.'
It is a cry, and a plea for the face of God, and the smile of God.

My dear friends, the test of your spirituality, and mine, is whether we know anything about that petition or not. You know, just to get down on your knees and recite the Lord's Prayer, and to ask his blessing upon yourself and your family, and the things you are going to do that day, that is not praying. Oh, let me not be too hard. Very well, I will grant that it is prayer of a kind, but it is a very small, a very primitive kind of praying. It is the prayer of a tyro. What really tests us is whether we long to see the smile of God, to know that God is looking upon us, and that we are living and moving under his eye. 'God of mercy, God of grace, show the brightness of thy face.' That was what was troubling the prophet, you see: God had averted his face. 'Oh Lord,' he says, 'Look down upon us.'

I maintain that this is still the position, and this is the supreme need, of the Church today. Are we sufficiently sensitive, I wonder, to the presence of God? Do we know the difference between God smiling upon us and God not smiling upon us? It is the test of a preacher. There is all the difference in the world between preaching merely from human understanding and energy, and preaching in the conscious smile of God. I can not describe the difference to you. There is an eternity of difference between the two things. To me there is nothing more terrible for a preacher, than to be in a pulpit alone, without the conscious smile of God. No wonder the prophet prayed, 'Look down.' Do you know his smile? And do you, therefore, know what it is to be bereft of it? and like the little child, to plead with him to turn round and just to look at you again? God seems to be turning away from the Church. He seems to have lost his interest in us. That is the beginning of the prayer.

But, let us go on and follow him and see how exactly, and in practice, he pleads with God to look down again and to smile upon them once more. Here are the steps. They are invariable, there is no other way. The first is that he starts by worshipping God and adoring God. Listen to him. 'Look down,' he says. But where from? ' . . . From heaven, and behold from the habitation of thy holiness and of thy glory.' We have got to start there. We do not start with ourselves. We must never start with ourselves, we must always start with God. And when we start with God there are certain things we have to realise about him, for if we do not, we might as well not get on our knees, we might as well not begin to pray. To whom are we going to pray? Whom are we

295

addressing? Well, we are addressing one who lives in heaven. 'Look down from heaven. . . .' We are so self-important, and so self-concerned, and we rush into the presence of God and pour out our needs our personal need, and the need of the Church, and we go on as if. . . .

Stop, my friend! I do not care what your predicament is, even if you feel as if hell is yawning beneath you, I do not care if all your enemies are gathered against you, I do not care what is true of you. If you are going to pray to God, you must realise who God is, and where he is. 'Look down from heaven. . . .' We know it all, but we do not realise it. We are so familiar with the Lord's Prayer that we do not really pray it. 'Our Father,' said our Lord, 'which art in heaven.' God is in heaven, and we are upon the earth. It is a good thing to remember that, if it were only for this reason – that we are surrounded by perplexities and are wondering what is going to happen, and we are so conscious of the strength of Communism, or any other 'ism', that we begin to quake, and fear. It is good then to remember that he is above all these things and looks down upon them. He is not in it. He is outside the flux of it all. And that will put us right at once. 'Look down from heaven, and behold . . .' – from where? – 'from the habitation of thy holiness.' 'Yes,' says our Lord, 'this is how you are to pray: "Our Father which art in heaven, Hallowed be thy name."' Hallowed, holy. It is the same thing, it is invariable.

Do we remember who God is when we pray? Do we tell him? Do we use this terminology? Do we think it out? Do we remember the holiness of God? How essential it is to remind ourselves of these things. Look at our Lord himself, when he was here in this world, he who, though he was on earth, was still in heaven, the only begotten beloved Son of the Father. When he was praying he said, 'Holy Father.' We do not pray truly unless we realise these things. We are like spoilt children, we want forgiveness, we want blessings, we want. . . . Wait a minute, we are approaching a holy Father. And then as we remember that, we remember our own sin, our own unworthiness. We will forget our rights, we will forget our demands, and we will just prostrate ourselves before him.

Then, ' . . . from the habitation of thy holiness and of thy glory.' The glory of God is something which no man can define. The glory of God is his essential and ultimate attribute. It means his greatness, his splendour, his majesty. The real trouble with all of us, I repeat once again, is that we do not know God. We think we do, but really we do not. The glory of God – have you ever thought of it? The Psalmist knew this much about it. He said, 'I had rather be a doorkeeper in the house of my God, than to dwell in the tents of wickedness [the ungodly]' (Ps. 84.10). He would sooner be a man in the vestibule, giving out the hymnbooks, even doing the most menial task, perhaps, than to be in power and in the innermost citadel, in the very midst of the ungodly. He tells us why this is: it is for grace and glory; to see the glory of God in the tabernacle; just to peep through the door now and again, and to see something of the Shekinah glory of God. ' . . . from the habitation of thy holiness and of thy glory.' In other words you see, it is still a prayer for a glimpse of the glory of God, of the face of God, to see God. 'Look down from heaven, and behold from the habitation of thy holiness and of thy glory.' The prophet starts with that.

Then he goes on to remind God, and himself, of the relationship that subsists between them. We start with God as he is in himself, and then we go on to the relationship between us and God. Here are the terms he uses. He puts it in the form of a question. He says 'Where is thy zeal . . . toward me?' What is he talking about? Well, he knows the past history of the Children of Israel, and of God's dealing with them. He knows what God has said about them, and he knows what God did for them. And what he finds is that God in the past has been zealous on behalf of his people. There were the Children of Israel long ago in the captivity of Egypt, and the taskmasters were flaying their backs with the whips, making them produce more bricks with less straw. They were in a terrible state. Then, God arose, in his zeal for them, and he said to Moses, 'Go back. I want you to lead those people out.'

And Moses said, 'What can I do with Pharoah?'

'Do not worry,' God said. 'I will be with you.'

Read the story and see how God intervened and acted and did mighty things and brought them out. The zeal of God for his people. 'Where is that zeal now?' says the prophet. 'That is how you used to be, but where is thy zeal?' We would not be defeated if you were still zealous for us and for our cause. Where is this energy that you once displayed on our behalf? You said we were the apple of your eye, and that you would allow nothing to harm us. 'Where is thy zeal?' That is his prayer. He is reminding God of his ancient relationship to the nation and to the people, and his zeal on their behalf.

Then he adds another term. Not only 'where is thy zeal?' but 'where is thy strength toward me?' This is very wonderful – God's almighty strength, and ability, and power. I rather like the way in which the prophet puts it here. He does not doubt the strength, he knows it is there. He is confronted by the power of Babylon, and the Chaldeans who have sacked the city of Jerusalem and carried away the people captive. And they might have come to the conclusion that, of course, this has happened to them because God had not the strength to prevent it, and was not strong enough to conquer the enemy. 'No,' says the prophet. 'It is not that. God has the same strength still. He is the 'Father of lights, with whom is no variableness, neither shadow of turning' (Jas. 1.17). Oh yes, he has the strength, but the question is, where is it? It is there but he is not exercising it toward us. And if we ourselves are not clear about this we must be feeling rather hopeless these days. You say, 'Why is the Church as she is? Why is God's cause going down? Why is the enemy rampant, and powerful, and triumphing? Is it because God can not stop them?' No, the strength is there, but let us ask him where it is. Why is he not showing it with respect to us? 'Where is thy strength?'

And then, there is this most extraordinary term. 'Where is . . . the sounding of thy bowels and of thy mercies?' That is, of course, a typical biblical, and especially Old Testament, expression – ' . . . the sounding of thy bowels . . .'. The ancients believed that the bowels were the seat of the emotions. Why? Because when a man is under a strong emotion he is aware of the movement of his bowels. He may even have a pain, a colic, an agony. Strong emotion gives a disturbance of the bowels. And that is what this man says, 'Where is . . . the sounding of thy bowels and of thy mercies towards us?' You remember Jeremiah crying out in his pain, 'My bowels, my bowels' (Jer. 4.19)? He was in agony because of the state of his people. And that is where he felt it; that is where he related it. And the prophet, you see, venturing, daring, applies it all to God. He says, 'Why are you not being moved towards us as of old? Why is not your emotion towards us as it once was? The movement, the disturbance, the sounding of thy bowels, and of thy mercies with respect to us. Where is this? Why are we not knowing it and experiencing it?' Well, that is the second thing that he pleads in his prayer.

Next we must consider the third aspect of this great prayer, which is the actual plea that he offers, and you notice that it is a threefold plea. The first, I have already been expounding, in a sense, in the words, 'Where is . . . ?' He is well aware that these mercies that he pleads for are still there, that God has not changed, because God cannot change. He knows that God is as he always has been, but he is concerned about the manifestation of this fact. In other words, he is acknowledging and confessing his sin, and that of the nation. 'How can a holy and a glorious God ever look upon us? How can he feel compassion, and pity, and mercy with respect to us, we have forfeited it all. How can such a holy God ever have any interest in us again? Oh, Lord,' he says, 'there is nothing to do. I plead, I just ask for mercy, and for compassion. Look down,' he says. 'Behold . . . .' And then in verse 17: 'Return for thy servants' sake.'

'Oh, God,' he says, 'come back to us. Why art thou like a stranger? Why art thou like a journeyman? Why not come back to us?'

> Return, O holy Dove, return
> Sweet Messenger of rest!
> *W. Cowper*

That is his second plea. Having acknowledged that they have no right to ask him, he pleads, and urges God to look again, and to exercise his compassions and his tender mercies, and his strength.

And then, thirdly, there is the most extraordinary petition of all, in verse 17: 'O Lord, why hast thou made us to err from thy ways, and hardened our heart from thy fear?' Have you pondered that? Do you realise exactly what this man is saying? We must be clear about this. We must not evade this difficulty: we must face it with open eyes. Some people have tried to avoid the problem by saying that it just means that God permits us to be hardened, that it is God, as it were, just allowing us to err from his ways. That is not what the prophet said. The prophet says that God has actually caused this. Caused them to err, caused their hearts to be hardened. He has already said it in chapter 6, in verses 9 and 10. God says to the prophet,

> *Go, and tell this people, Hear ye indeed, but understand not; and see ye indeed, but perceive not. Make the heart of this people fat, and make their ears heavy, and shut their eyes; lest they see with their eyes, and hear with their ears, and understand with their heart, and convert and be healed.*

God commands the prophet to do that. And, of course, in the New Testament, our Lord himself quotes these very words in John 12.37–41:

But though he had done so many miracles before them, yet they
believed not on him: that the saying of Esaias the prophet might
be fulfilled, which he spake, Lord, who hath believed our report?
and to whom hath the arm of the Lord been revealed? Therefore
they could not believe, because that Esaias said again, he hath
blinded their eyes, and hardened their heart; that they should not
see with their eyes, nor understand with their heart, and be
converted, and I should heal them. These things said Esaias,
when he saw his glory, and spake of him.

The same words are quoted in Acts 28. What do they mean?
The Apostle Paul tells us in Romans 9.18: 'Therefore hath he
mercy upon whom he will have mercy, and whom he will he
hardeneth.' 'What has all this to do with us?' asks someone.

The answer is that it is a terrible and a dangerous thing for
God's people to be disobedient. For sometimes God punishes our
disobedience not only by turning his face from us, by leaving us
to ourselves, but he even seems to drive us into sin, and into
error, and to harden our hearts. He sends afflictions, and afflictions harden us. That is one of God's ways of punishing us. And
what the prophet is praying is this: 'Oh God stop dealing with us
judicially. We deserve it. We have sinned against you, we have
rebelled against you. We said we could go on without you, and
you have let us go on without you. And you have even hardened
our hearts, you have made us obdurate. God have mercy.'

Be careful how you treat God, my friends. You may say to
yourself, 'I can sin against God, and then, of course, I can repent
and go back and find God whenever I want him.' You try it. And
you will sometimes find that not only can you not find God but
that you do not even want to. You will be aware of a terrible
hardness, a callosity in your heart. And you can do nothing about
it. And then you suddenly realise that it is God punishing you in
order to reveal your sinfulness, and your vileness to you. And
there is only one thing to do. You turn back to him, and you say,
'Oh God, do not go on dealing with me judicially. Though I
deserve it. Soften my heart. Melt me, I cannot do it myself.' You
cast yourself utterly upon his mercy and upon his compassion.
That is the third great plea.

So we have seen the prophet's method, his worship, his adoration. We have listened to his threefold plea, and now let us see
how he brings his arguments, the grounds on which he ventures
to make his plea. And, oh, how interesting they are. He does not
plead anything in the people themselves, no merit in themselves

300

at all. Of course not, there is none. We deserve nothing from God. If you think you do, you do not know him. You have not seen that glory. You know nothing about that holiness, and you have not known the plague of your own heart. No, there is nothing here for us to do, but just to say. 'Oh Lord!' Is there an 'Oh' in your praying? That is another very good test of prayer, that this 'Oh' comes in. 'Oh, Lord.' Or are you such good people, and doing such excellent work, as evangelicals, busy with this organisation and the other, that all you need do is to ask God to bless you and to keep on . . . ? Do you know what it is to say, 'Oh, Lord'? That is how the prophet prayed. That is how the men of God have always prayed: this, 'Oh.' Somebody once said that a sign, the best sign, of a coming revival is that the word, 'Oh' begins to enter into the prayers of the people. 'Oh, Lord!'

Then, the grounds of his pleas are there: he pleads first the covenant relationship. 'Doubtless,' he says, 'thou art our Father.' *Thou* art our Father.' This is most significant. The trouble with these Jews was that they were always talking about Abraham. 'Abraham is our father,' they said. 'These Gentiles, who are they? Abraham is our father.' They rested upon the fact that they were the children of Abraham. John the Baptist knew that very well, because, you remember, when he preached to them he said, 'Think not to say within yourselves, We have Abraham to our father: for I say unto you, that God is able of these stones to raise up children unto Abraham' (Matt. 3.9). And you and I must not go into the presence of God merely in the name of tradition, merely in the name of the fathers, merely in the name of those who have gone before us. I do not care who they were, whether they were the Methodist fathers, or the Puritans, or the Reformers. No, we do not plead their names, Abraham, Jacob, – not at all. 'Thou art our Father.' The Reformers cannot save us, the Puritans cannot save us, the Methodist fathers cannot save us. And there is a grave danger that we fall back upon the fathers. No, it is God. 'Thou art our Father', and nobody else.

And how right the prophet is. It is God who has made the covenant: it is God who owns us and we are his people. God is the founder of Israel. Through Abraham, through Jacob, yes, but they are not our fathers, God is our Father. Then he draws another contrast. ' . . . though Abraham be ignorant of us, and Israel acknowledge us not: thou, O Lord, art our Father, our redeemer; thy name is from everlasting.' Abraham, of course, was a great man. Thank God. Jacob, too, was marvellous. Yes, but Abraham is dead, and Jacob is dead. They cannot rise up and save us. God, *'thy* name is from everlasting.' And it is to ever-lasting. God is not the God of the dead, but of the living, and he is the living God. We do not fall back on the fathers, however august and great. We go back to God.

Not only that. ' . . . though Abraham be ignorant of us, and Israel acknowledge us not', by which I think he is saying something like this: 'Do you know, I believe if Abraham and Jacob could come back and see us, they would not recognise us, they would not acknowledge us. They would say, "Those people do not belong to me. They are not my offspring. I renounce them." Abraham was a holy man, so was Jacob, and they would not recognise us, they would disallow us and disinherit us.'

'Thank God,' says the prophet, 'that you are our Father. For you are a holy God in glory. You have got more love and compassion than Abraham or Jacob ever had, the two of them together, and multiplied by infinity. You are our Father. They would probably repudiate us.'

'But there is forgiveness with thee, that thou mayest be feared' (Ps. 130.4). Thank God we are in the hands of God after all, and not of men. ' . . . though Abraham be ignorant of us, and Israel acknowledge us not: thou, O Lord, art [still] our father, our redeemer; thy name is from everlasting.'

Then he goes on to say: 'The tribes of thine inheritance.' We are thine inheritance. This is the truth: that is who we are; we are thy people. The other nations are not thy people. 'We are thine: thou never barest rule over them, they were not called by thy name.' This is a tremendous statement. The Lord's portion is his people. Though we may be full of sin and unworthiness, as indeed we are, we are still the people of his holiness. Let us go to him, remembering that, and reminding him of it. Bad as we are, we are still his. Plead with God. Ask him to return. We are thine, the people of thy holiness.

Then his final argument is that God has no relationship to these other people – the Chaldeans, in the time of the prophet, the Egyptians, at an earlier period. Anybody looking on might have thought that the Egyptians and the Chaldeans were the people of God. They seemed to be blessed and were affluent and full of prosperity. And these others, the people of Israel, were slaves, and serfs. 'Oh, God,' says the prophet, 'can you go on doing this? Can you go on behaving in such a way as to give the impression that those big nations are thy people? But they are not thy people. The people of thy holiness have possessed the land but a little while. We were taken out of it, and the Chaldeans are possessing

302

it, but it is not theirs. Our adversaries have trodden down thy sanctuaries. We are thine, thou never barest rule over them. They were not called by thy name.' And that must be our prayer. The godless world stands out in its brightness, and its glory, and its fatness, and, as the Psalm 73 puts it, 'There are no bands in their death. . . . Their eyes stand out with fatness.' They seem to be having everything, while God's people are a little handful, suffering, and full of troubles and problems. And the world laughs and says, 'Where is their God?'

And we should turn that into a prayer, and with humility, and yet with confidence, and boldness, we should go to God and say, 'Oh, Lord, can you let this go on? They are not your people. These people whom you are allowing to have so much prosperity. They are blasphemers, they are your adversaries as well as ours. Oh, God, can you go on doing that? Though we are weak and feeble, though we are down, though we are rebellious, though we are sinful, though we have nothing to recommend us, even still, we are thy people. God have mercy upon us. You are our God. Look upon us, behold us, smile upon us, acknowledge us and turn back to us. Oh, do not keep turning away. Come back.

> Return, oh holy dove, return,
> Sweet Messenger of rest!

We are yours still. They are not. Return to us, arise for our deliverance. Have mercy upon us.

God grant us grace to pray as the prophet prayed.

Chapter 24

Isaiah 64.1

Oh that thou wouldest rend the heavens, that thou wouldest come down, that the mountains might flow down at thy presence (Isa. 64.1).

As we come to the end of our studies on this great subject, we turn to what I have described as the second great petition in the prayer that was offered by the prophet Isaiah at this particular juncture in the life and history of his people, when they were in a forsaken and desolate condition. The prophet, you remember, having seen the position, has decided to pray to God, giving him no rest nor peace, and giving himself no rest, until Jerusalem shall again be made a 'praise in the earth'. And we have been following his exact prayers.

This man knew how to pray and did not need instruction about prayer. Prayer is not easy; prayer, because we are what we are, is difficult and we need instruction. If we have never felt what our Lord's disciples felt when they turned to him one afternoon and said 'Lord, teach us how to pray', it is probably because we have never really prayed at all. So God in his kindness has provided well for us, with great patterns and examples and illustrations and we have seen that the prophet looks back at them. He sees how God has dealt with his people in the past, and then, having done that, he beseeches him to look down upon them now, to behold their condition, and to take again the interest that he once took in them. He has a desire to see the face of God again, to know that he is well disposed towards them and to feel that he is taking a loving interest in them.

But he does not stop at that, and true prayer through the ages has never stopped at that; it can never be satisfied with that alone. There is always this further petition which is contained in this sixty-fourth chapter. Here again we find that there is really only one prayer, but it has all the characteristics which true praying always has – you notice the first word 'Oh'. I would remind you again that true praying is always characterised by the use of that word, 'Oh' – 'Oh that thou wouldest rend the heavens.' There is no word that is more expressive of longing than that word. It expresses the thirst of deep desire, it is the cry of a man at the end of his resources and waiting and looking for, and longing for God.

That is one obvious characteristic, but we also find here, as we have already seen, the alternation of petition and confession, the claims that are made, and all the arguments and disputations with God. These are always the characteristics of true praying. In other words this man is really, as he puts it himself, laying hold upon God. He is lifting himself up to pray, and he is taking hold of God. It is an extraordinary expression and yet how true it is. That is true prayer – not a mere casual expression of our desire, not something perfunctory and half-hearted. Real prayer means taking hold of God and not letting go. You will find it all in the famous instance of Jacob, struggling with the 'man' who appeared to him on that critical night before he had to meet his brother Esau. Jacob struggled with him, he wrestled with him and when the day broke and the man said that he must go, Jacob said, 'I will not let thee go, except thou bless me' (Gen. 32.26). Taking hold of God, laying hold upon him, pleading with him, reasoning, and even beseeching, and I say that it is only when the Christian arrives at that position that he truly begins to pray.

So we have here his final great petition – 'Oh, that thou wouldest rend the heavens, that thou wouldest come down' – and I do not hesitate to assert that that is the ultimate prayer in connection with a revival. It is right, of course, always to pray to God to bless us, to look upon us and to be gracious unto us, that should be our constant prayer. But this goes beyond that, and it is here that we see the difference between what the Church should always be praying for, and the special, peculiar, urgent prayer for a visitation of God's Spirit in revival. There is no term that better expresses this ultimate petition than does that phrase in Cowper's hymn

> Oh rend the heavens, come quickly down,
> And make a thousand hearts thine own.

We do not often see a thousand hearts turning to God in Christ, do we? but that is what happens in revival. Cowper has got the right petition – 'rend the heavens' – and when God rends the heavens we may well see a thousand, or three thousand as on the day of Pentecost – 'Make a thousand hearts thine own'. This is a prayer for something unusual, something quite exceptional and it is at the same time a reminder to us of what revival really is, there is no better way of putting it than this. It is indeed God's coming down, God, as it were, no longer merely granting us the blessings. We have to use such terms, and yet, in a sense, they are very foolish. Everything that God does is marvellous and wonderful and transcends our highest imagination and yet we find these contrasts in the Scriptures between God doing what he normally does, and God doing the unusual, God coming down. I must quote again a statement found in the Journals of George Whitefield about an occasion when he was preaching at Cheltenham. He says that, suddenly, during his sermon, 'God, the Lord, came down amongst us'. That is what I am talking about. George Whitefield was a man who rarely preached without being aware of the unction and the power of the Holy Spirit, but there were variations even in his ministry, and there, in Cheltenham, something quite exceptional happened, so exceptional that he makes a note of it. God came down. Oh yes, they had been enjoying the presence and the blessing of God before, but not like this, something wonderful had happened, God was in the very midst, God came down. That is exactly what happens during a revival.

What does this mean? Well, we can describe it like this. It is a consciousness of the presence of God the Holy Spirit literally in the midst of the people. Probably most of us who are here have never known that, but that is exactly what is meant by a visitation of God's Spirit. It is all above and beyond the highest experiences in the normal life and working of the Church. Suddenly those present in the meeting become aware that someone has come amongst them, they are aware of a glory, they are aware of a presence. They can not define it, they can not describe it, they can not put it into words, they just know that they have never known anything like this before. Sometimes they describe it as 'days of heaven on earth'. They really feel that they are in heaven – they have forgotten time, they are beyond that, time has no longer any meaning for them, nor any real existence, they are in a spiritual realm. God has come down amongst them and has filled the place and the people with a sense of his glorious presence.

And, always, of course, accompanying this is the thing which the prophet in particular emphasises here: it is also a manifestation of the power of God, not only the glory and the radiance of God's presence, but especially his power – notice the terms which he uses – 'Oh,' he says, 'that thou wouldest *rend* the heavens'. There is a tearing process, God erupts into the midst. We are told that he has come down, 'that the mountains might flow down at thy presence', these great mountains that seem everlasting and eternal, that are always there whether the wind blows or not, whether the rain comes or is withheld, whether the sun shines or is clouded over. These are the everlasting hills and mountains, but when God comes down even the mountains begin to flow. Or, as he takes up another comparison, 'when the melting fire burneth', fire with its tremendous power. Look at that lump of metal, of ore, how solid it seems, but throw it into the furnace and it begins to melt and to flow, so great is the fire and its power. Or, as he says in another comparison, 'the fire causeth the waters to boil'. Have you not seen the movement and the motion in the water? What is it? It is the fire, it is the heat, it is the power in the flame, boiling and churning up the water. So the prophet uses these very graphic and dramatic images to convey some impression of the power of God.

There is very little doubt but that at this point the prophet was thinking of what God did at Mount Sinai in the giving of the Law. In Exodus 19 we read:

And it came to pass on the third day in the morning, that there were thunders and lightnings, and a thick cloud upon the mount, and the voice of the trumpet exceeding loud; so that all the people that was in the camp trembled. And Moses brought forth the people out of the camp to meet with God; and they stood at the nether part of the mount. And mount Sinai was altogether on a smoke, because the Lord descended upon it in fire: and the smoke thereof ascended as the smoke of a furnace, and the whole mount quaked greatly. And when the voice of the trumpet sounded long, and waxed louder and louder, Moses spake, and God answered him by a voice. And the Lord came down upon mount Sinai, on the top of the mount: and the Lord called Moses up to the top of the mount; and Moses went up.

Now that was something which happened early in the story of the Children of Israel, something they had never forgotten. God gave them that manifestation of himself and his glory and power, in order that when they went on their journeys they should never be afraid. They would have hostile nations to meet, enemies would gather against them, but what did it matter? Here is a God who can shake mountains and that is what he is praying for. He realises that he is praying to a God who is still the same and who can still do now what he did in ancient times.

This, then, is the power that we, too, should realise and should pray for. Indeed, half our troubles in our praying are due to the fact that we fail to realise the greatness and the power of God. We are troubled about the enemies of the church, we see the arrogance and the power of the world, but there is a prophecy which will be fulfilled one day. – 'But the day of the Lord will come as a thief in the night; in the which the heavens shall pass away with a great noise, and the elements shall melt with a fervent heat, the earth also and the works that are therein shall be burned up' (2 Pet. 3.10). That day is coming, let there be no mistake about this, that is the power of God. This solid universe, these everlasting hills, the elements, they are all going to melt away, all will be dissolved, and disrupted. The heavens themselves will pass away, heaven and earth will pass away. So we must remind ourselves to whom we pray. He is a God of great power. 'Oh, that thou wouldest rend the heavens, that thou wouldest come down, that the mountains might flow down at thy presence.' That is the power of God and we must never lose sight of that.

The Apostle Paul, too, puts it in his way. There were troubles in the church at Corinth and the Apostle writes to them, 'For the weapons of our warfare are not carnal, but mighty through God to the pulling down of strong holds; casting down imaginations, and every high thing that exalteth itself against the knowledge of God, and bringing into captivity every thought to the obedience of Christ'(2 Cor. 10.4–5). Are we clear about this power of God? Are we clear about its illimitable character? Do we modern Christians realise that 'the weapons of our warfare are not carnal, but mighty through God to the pulling down of strongholds'? Are you troubled still about all these philosophies and ideologies and politics, and everything that is opposed to God – the anti-God movements? Why all this talk about the enemy? Have we forgotten about the power of God? Our God is a God who can rend the very heavens, and cause the mountains to flow and the sea to boil, as if it were but water in a kettle. The everlasting God. The power of God – that is what the prophet prays for. He prays that the glory and the power of God may be made manifest. Are we praying that prayer? Is that our innermost desire? Are we at all concerned about the present situation? Why should Isaiah pray like this? And why should we not pray in the same way? Why should praying like this be confined to certain people now and again in the long history of the church? Why does every Christian not feel this?

Now that is the question, so let me put it positively, why should we pray like this? Let that now be our second consideration. The prophet answers that question. He has a reason, these men of God always have a reason for praying, and you and I must, too, have reasons or we shall never pray. The prophet is praying that God may come down as when the melting fire burns and causes the waters to boil (v. 2), and the reason for this prayer is – 'To make thy name known to thine adversaries'. That is the first reason, and you notice that in the Bible, it is always the first reason. These men prayed to God as they did, because they had a zeal for the name and the glory of God. Come down, he says, that these adversaries of thine may know thy name. You notice that he says that they are *God's* adversaries. Why does he not say that they are our adversaries? That would have been true, yes, but he has a deeper insight than that, and that is where we go wrong so frequently. We will persist in regarding the Church as a human institution, we are fighting for our lives, trying to keep the doors open, trying to keep the church going, so we put up our commissions and we multiply our organisations – our adversaries, that is what we are fighting. No, says the prophet, they are God's adversaries.

So if you and I do not see behind the visible and the seen we are the merest tyros in the spiritual world. We talk about the manifestations of evil; the Bible is concerned about the ultimate cause of evil. You see the fight is not merely a fight against radio and television, the car and all these things, no, that is not the fight at all. It is not even against men. The Apostle Paul sees it clearly and he says, 'we wrestle not against flesh and blood, (Eph. 3.12), that is not the problem. It is not with men and what they do. We wrestle not against flesh and blood – against what then? Against 'principalities and powers, against the rulers of the darkness of this world, against spiritual wickedness in high places'. These things that we see are the mere pawns, the dupes, only the instruments and channels; it is the devil, it is hell, hating God – 'thine adversaries'. So the first reason for praying that God should come down is that his name should be known and recognised among his adversaries. That is the trouble with the world, it does not know God. And the world will never be interested in the Christian message until it has some knowledge of God.

Oh, the church has been blind to this. She has been trying to attract people to herself for fifty years and more, putting on popular programmes, dramas, music, this that and the other, trying to entice the people, especially the young people, but they do not come. Of course not. They never will until they know the name of the Lord, and then they will come. The reason why men and women are outside the Church is that they do not know God, they do not know his name; 'to make thy name known to thine adversaries,' says Isaiah. And they will never know it until they see a manifestation of it, and, so, we pray, descend, come down, rend the heavens that these adversaries may know thy name. Nothing will make them listen but that. We have tried everything else, have we not? The church has never been so brilliant in her organisations as she is at the present time and as she has been during the whole of this century, she is using every means that the world can use and can give her, but the statistics go on repeating their miserable tale. One Church conference after another reports a serious decline in the membership of her body, and on it goes. What is the matter? These people do not know the name of the Lord, and there is only one thing that we can do, we must pray to him to rend the heavens and to make his name known, so that not only may they know it, but further, so that the nations may 'tremble at thy presence', that knowing the name of the Lord, they may begin to fear him, and to desist from sin.

This is a great theme in the Old Testament and in the New. In Psalm 99 the Psalmist says 'The Lord reigneth; let the people tremble: he sitteth between the cherubims; let the earth be moved.' The Lord reigneth. Let the people tremble, for he is the living God, the everlasting God, the God in whose hand all things are. Oh, the tragedy of a world that does not know him, oh, the arrogance and the pride of these nations and people and rulers who defy him. If they have but a glimpse of his glory, they tremble in his presence. He is going to shake them, he is going to shake their world, there will be nothing left. It is all going to be dissolved, everything will vanish.

In Revelation 6 we are told that at the manifestation of his glory kings and the great of the earth will cry out unto the rocks and unto the mountains, 'Fall on us, and hide us . . . from the wrath of the Lamb'. The Lord reigneth, let the nations tremble at thy presence. In Psalm 46 the Psalmist works it all out, and concludes with these great words 'Be still, and know that I am God' (v. 10). You foolish people who are arguing against God – 'He maketh wars to cease' (Ps. 46.9). Of course he does. He can do anything that he likes, there is nothing that he cannot do. He created everything out of nothing, he said, 'Let there be light', and there was light. He is the eternal God, the Creator, the controller of the ends of the earth. 'Be still, and know' – and admit – 'that I am God'. That is what this man is praying for. Oh God, he says, why do you not come down, that these adversaries of thine may know thy name, and tremble in thy presence? Christian people, I do not understand you if you are not offering this same prayer, as you see the arrogance of so-called learning and the impudence of all that claims to be cultural. As you see men and women, in their fineries, and in their rags, blaspheming the name of this Holy God, do you not feel like asking him to give just a part of his power to silence them and to cause them to tremble in his holy presence? That is what this man felt. That is what God's people have always felt when they have truly prayed for revival.

And then the last reason for his prayer is the one that Isaiah gives at the very end of the chapter – the state of God's realm. But he puts that last, you see. We start with it, of course, we are all so subjective and self-centred, we start with ourselves and we end with ourselves. Not this man, oh, this is the thing that is hurting him – those adversaries. Come down, he says, let them know thy name, let them be humbled before thee and finally,

Be not wroth very sore, O Lord, neither remember iniquity for ever: behold, see, we beseech thee, we are all thy people. Thy holy cities are a wilderness, Zion is a wilderness, Jerusalem a desolation. Our holy and our beautiful house, where our fathers praised thee, is burned up with fire: and all our pleasant things are laid waste. Wilt thou refrain thyself for these things, O Lord? wilt thou hold thy peace, and afflict us very sore?

Have mercy upon us, say those who pray for revival, and upon the state of thy Church. Behold what we are and remember what we once were, think of thine own heritage, thine own Church, make her again glorious. There, then, are the reasons for praying as the prophet did.

But let us now consider the encouragements that there are for us to pray like this. I shall just give you some headings, and you can work them out for yourselves. The first encouragement to such prayer is what God has done in the past. In verse 3 Isaiah says, 'When thou didst terrible things which we looked not for, thou camest down, the mountains flowed down at thy presence'. It is as if he were saying, 'I am not asking the impossible, I am simply asking you to do what you have already done before.' Let me repeat: the greatest tonic to a drooping spirit is to read the history of the Church. Read the history of the Church, my friends, it did not start when Moody first came to this country, it goes back through the running centuries; go back, read the story and consider what God has done in ages past. There is nothing so stimulating to prayer as that, and you notice the interesting way in which he puts it. 'When thou didst terrible things which we looked not for.' 'You know,' says this man, in effect, in his prayer, 'In the past, Oh God, you surprised your own people. You did things that they would never have imagined.' He did it of course in Egypt, where they were in an impossible situation; slaves in the hands of powerful Pharaoh and his hosts, and his chariots. They had not a sword, they had nothing. Taskmasters laid their lashes upon the backs of the poor people; what hope was there for them? But out they came – God led them out. 'Thou didst strange things, terrible things which we looked not for.' Pharaoh did not want to let them go, but God soon made him. He sent plagues upon Pharaoh – plagues of lice, plagues of frogs, blood in the river, everything to humble him, and God brought him to the dust, and God's people went out.

And then there they were, facing the Red Sea with the hosts of Pharaoh behind hem. Impossible? Not at all. God divided the sea. This is the God whom we are worshipping and to whom we are praying, when we see these things 'which we looked not for'. And again, in the desert, there they were, in a howling, barren wilderness, with nothing to eat; and God provided them with bread from heaven. Then there was no water, and it seemed they would die of thirst. At God's command Moses struck the rock and out came the gushing water; 'things that we looked not for'. That is our God, my friends.

Then Jordan at last – how could they cross it, how could they enter into the land of promise? Jordan in flood? What is Jordan to our God? He divided it. Then came the conquest of the land, and the many deliverances that he gave them. 'When Thou didst terrible things that we looked not for.' That is the encouragement to pray.

And you and I have even greater encouragements than those which this prophet Isaiah had. The greatest thing happened when the fullness of the times had come and God sent forth his Son, made of a woman, made under the Law. Shall God verily dwell with man? He has done. God rent the heavens and sent forth his Son, and the Son came out of the clouds of glory and entered the

Virgin's womb. Things that we thought not of, things that we had never looked for. God has done them. Ah yes, you say, but Jesus of Nazareth was defeated by his enemies, he was taken and condemned and killed. He died, they buried him in a grave, there is the end. No, he burst asunder, he rent asunder (the same word) the bands of death, and he rose triumphant o'er the grave. The resurrection is behind us. He is the God of the resurrection, death is conquered, the grave has lost its power. 'O death, where is thy sting? O grave, where is thy victory?'

But, you may say, that does not help us very much because he has gone back to heaven and left just these twelve ordinary, ignorant men, these disciples, these apostles so-called. What is the use of leaving twelve such men in a hostile world with Judaism against them, and the pagans and everybody against them, all hell against them? But you know what happened. As these twelve men and some companions of theirs, were meeting together in an upper room at the Feast of Pentecost, suddenly there was a sound from heaven as of a mighty rushing wind. What has happened? Oh, God has rent the heavens and has come down. It is the descent of the Holy Ghost. The sound of a mighty rushing wind filling the house. God rending the heavens. We can look back on that. Let us remind God of it, he is the same God. He sent the Holy Spirit, he has sent him since. Go back and read the story of the Protestant Reformation, read of the mighty revival of two hundred years ago affecting London and the provinces and other countries. Go back and read again the story of 1859. What are all these? Rent heavens! God rending the heavens and coming down, coming among his people, displaying his power and his glory. 'The sound of a rushing mighty wind.' 'When thou didst terrible things which we looked not for.' The encouragement of history is a great encouragement, is it not?

But there is another encouragement which the prophet gives here, when he reminds the people of the possibilities when they are praying to God. Have you noticed verse 4? 'For since the beginning of the world men have not heard, nor perceived by the ear, neither hath the eye seen, O God, beside thee, what he hath prepared for him that waiteth for him.' Oh, what an encouragement this is. 'What should I pray for?' asks somebody? My dear friend, there is no limit to what you should pray for, no limit at all. Paul says the same thing in his first Epistle to the Corinthians chapter 2: 'Eye hath not seen, nor ear heard, neither have entered into the heart of man, the things which God hath prepared for them that love him.' Have you realised the possibilities or are you putting your little pigmy limits on them? There is no end to them, man has no conception of it, says Paul, the highest imagination cannot get there.

It is beyond all that.

You notice also how he puts it in Ephesians 3? His prayer was that they might be able to comprehend with all saints what is the breadth, and length, and depth, and height; and to know the love of Christ, which passeth knowledge, that ye might be filled with all the fulness of God. He was praying that for Christian people like you and me, and that' is Christianity. It is not only being saved, knowing that your sins are forgiven and being a good, respectable church member now. It is 'that ye might be filled with all the fulness of God'. And then he goes on, in order that there might be no mistake about this, and he says: 'Now unto him that is able to do . . .' for us – what? ' . . . exceeding abundantly above all that we ask or think.' That is the measure of it.

It is not surprising that in the hymn which begins, 'Come, my soul, thy suit prepare; Jesus loves to answer prayer', John Newton says:

> Thou art coming to a King;
> Large petitions with thee bring;
> For His grace and power are such
> None can ever ask too much.

Shame on us for our puny prayers, for putting our limits to God's illimitable power!

'But,' people say, 'we are in the twentieth century, it is no use talking to us about 1859 and the eighteenth century and the Protestant Reformation and Pentecost. Look at our problems, look at the sophisticated world, what are you talking about? 'Eye hath not seen, nor ear heard. . . .'; ' . . . exceeding abundantly . . .' says Paul.

'The sky is the limit,' says the modern man,' but we are praying to one who is above the sky! Oh rend the heavens, come down, there is no limit, we are praying to the eternal and the illimitable God.

And then let me encourage you with the promises of God. What a glorious word we find in verse 5 'Thou meetest him that rejoiceth and worketh righteousness, those that remember thee in thy ways.' Thank God for this. How do I know that God is going to listen to me and to give me my petition? Here is the answer – he is ready to meet certain people – 'Thou meetest'. He has promised to do this. Who does he meet? He meets with those who work righteousness and who rejoice in doing so. He meets with all, as the end of verse 4 has told us, who wait for him. Have no doubt about that, my dear friends. Listen to James as he says, 'Draw nigh to God, and he will draw nigh to you' (Jas. 4.8). It is a fact, it is certain, he meets such people. 'If, with all your heart ye truly seek me, ye shall surely find me.' Have you sought him? Have you found him? He has promised it. Draw near unto God and he will draw near unto you. 'Thou meetest . . . those that remember thee in thy ways.' Of course he does. Blessed be his name.

And lastly we remember the gracious character of God. Have you been puzzled by this strange expression in verse 5? 'Behold, thou art wroth; for we have sinned: *in those is continuance*, and we shall be saved'? What does it mean? It means just this: 'Oh God,' says this man, 'you have averted your face from us because we have sinned; you are displeased with us. Your anger and your wroth are against us because of our sinfulness.' I know it, says the man, and then, in effect, he says this daring thing, 'But, you know, O God, that is not really you. You do not always stay like that. *In those is continuance*,' and in that expression Isaiah is referring to God's promise to meet with 'him that rejoiceth and worketh righteousness'. God's wrath is, as it were, temporary, his mercy endureth for ever. Thank God, says this man, I know that your mercy and your love and your compassion are deeper than your wrath and therefore I hold on to them.

Listen to the Psalmist saying the same thing: 'His anger endureth but a moment; in his favour is life: weeping may endure for a night, but joy cometh in the morning' (Ps. 30.5). Thank God it is not perpetual night. The God of the morning, the God of love, the God of compassion, will not always chide, says the Psalmist in Psalm 103 – 'He will not always chide: neither will he keep his anger for ever', but in these is continuance' – mercy, love, compassion and pity. Hold on to these, in these is continuance and we shall be saved.

> But thy compassions, Lord,
> To endless years endure,
> And children's children ever find
> Thy word of promise sure.
> *Isaac Watts*

Oh what blessed encouragements to pray. The character of God,

315

not only his might and his power and his glory, but his compassion, his loving kindness, his tender mercy, yes, grace abounding to the vilest of sinners. While we were yet dead in sins, while we were enemies, we were reconciled to God by the death of his Son. 'God commended his love towards us, in that, while we were yet sinners, Christ died for us' (Rom. 5.8).

God's displeasure is upon the church because of her sin, because of her apostasy and her rebellion, but if she truly repents and really seeks him, he will yet meet with her. 'Thou shalt find him, if thou seek him with all thy heart.' (Deut. 4.29).

Seek him, stir yourself up to call upon his name. Take hold upon him, plead with him as your Father, as your Maker, as your Potter, as your Guide, as your God. Plead his own promises. Cry unto him and say, 'Oh that thou wouldest rend the heavens, that thou wouldest come down.'

> Oh rend the heavens, come quickly down,
> And make a thousand hearts thine own.
>> *W. Cowper*

If you wish to receive *regular information* about *new books*, please send your name and address to:

London Bible Warehouse
PO Box 123
Basingstoke
Hants RG23 7NL

Name..

Address ....

....

....

....

I am especially interested in:
☐ Biographies
☐ Fiction
☐ Christian living
☐ Issue related books
☐ Academic books
☐ Bible study aids
☐ Children's books
☐ Music
☐ Other subjects

P.S. If you have ideas for new Christian Books or other products, please write to us too!